THE SEVEN DEADLY SINS

SEVEN DAYS

ORIGINAL STORY BY:
NAKABA SUZUKI
(WEEKLY SHONEN MAGAZINE –
THE SEVEN DEADLY SINS)

LIGHT NOVEL BY:
MAMORU IWASA
(KODANSHA KCDX LIGHT NOVEL –
THE SEVEN DEADLY SINS: SEVEN DAYS)

ART:
YOU KOKIKUJI

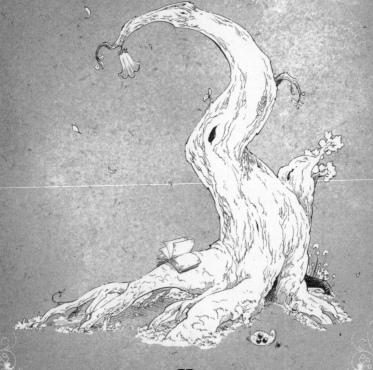

II

characters

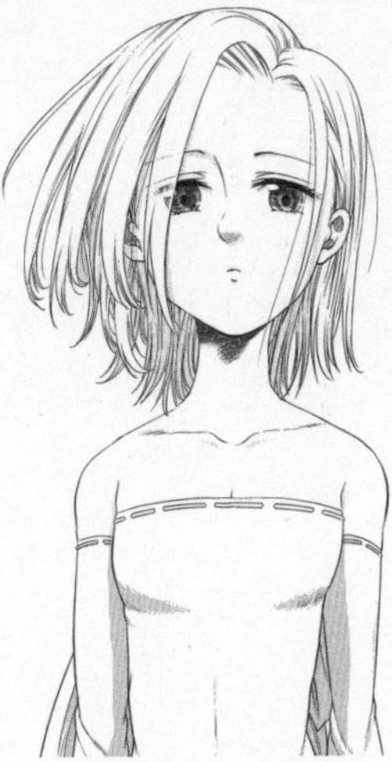

ELAINE

A Fairy whose elder brother Harlequin is the ruler of the Fairy King's Forest. When he disappeared, she was left alone as the forest's sole guardian for 700 years.

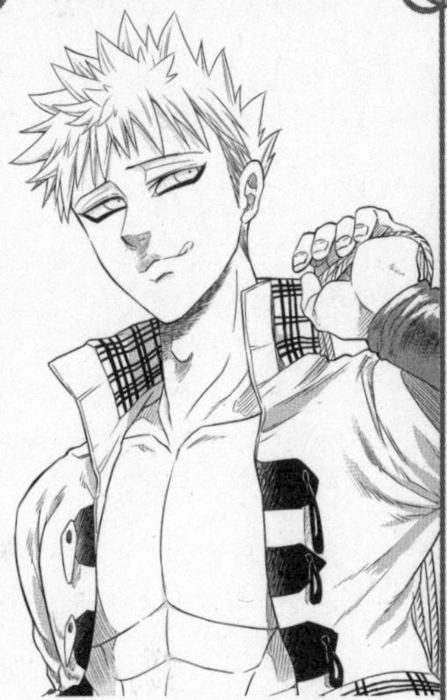

BAN

A bandit who snuck into the Fairy King's Forest alone, seeking the Fountain of Life.

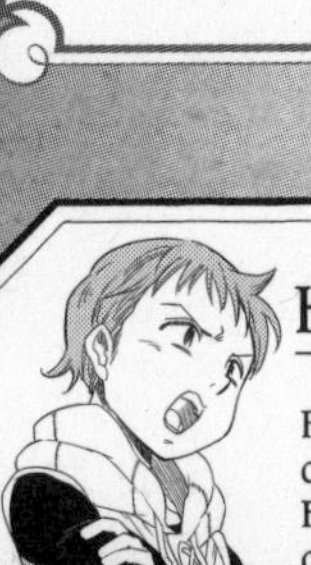

HARLEQUIN

Ruler and protector of the Fairy King's Forest, and Elaine's older brother.

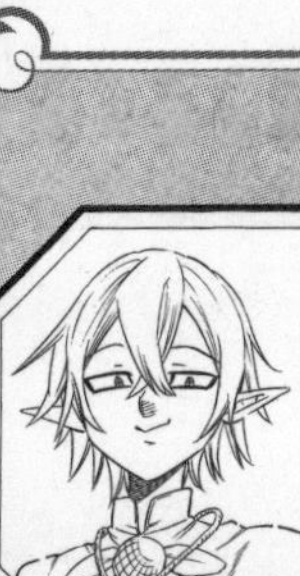

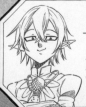

HELBRAM

A Fairy who actively mingled with Humans.

THE STORY SO FAR

The Fairy Elaine enjoyed a peaceful life, always heeding the words of her brother Harlequin, ruler and protector of the Fairy King's Forest: "Humans cannot be trusted." Then one day, Helbram, a Fairy who was fascinated by Humans, fell into a trap and was captured by them. To save his fellow Fairy, Harlequin took off in pursuit, entrusting Elaine with the protection of the Forest. He never returned. Thus, for 700 years, Elaine guarded the Forest alone.

At the continued intrusions of greedy Humans, seeking the eternal life-giving effects of the Fountain of Life, Elaine's heart sank into an ever darker, colder place.

Please, take care of the forest for a little while!
Elaine...
Broooooooother!!
This is the origin of the Fairy King's Forest, the Fountain of Life.
As His Majesty decreed, you will protect the Fountain.
BURBLE
BURBLE
BURBLE

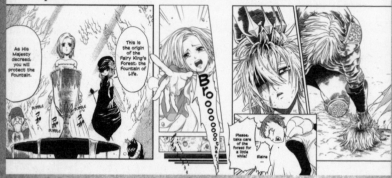

Then one day, a lone bandit called Ban came seeking the Fountain. Elaine used her powers to chase him off, and he relented. But she was startled to find he was without guile, and so Ban became the first Human to learn Elaine's name. On hearing how long she had been isolated, Ban spent time entertaining her with conversation and his collection of ale labels. And so, Elaine's days with Ban began to melt her cold heart.

What's your name?

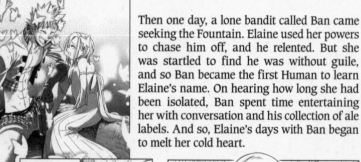

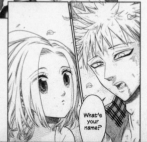

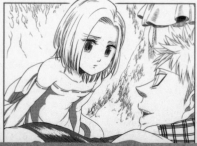

contents

You Kokikuji Presents
The Seven Deadly Sins: Seven Days

The Thief and the Saint

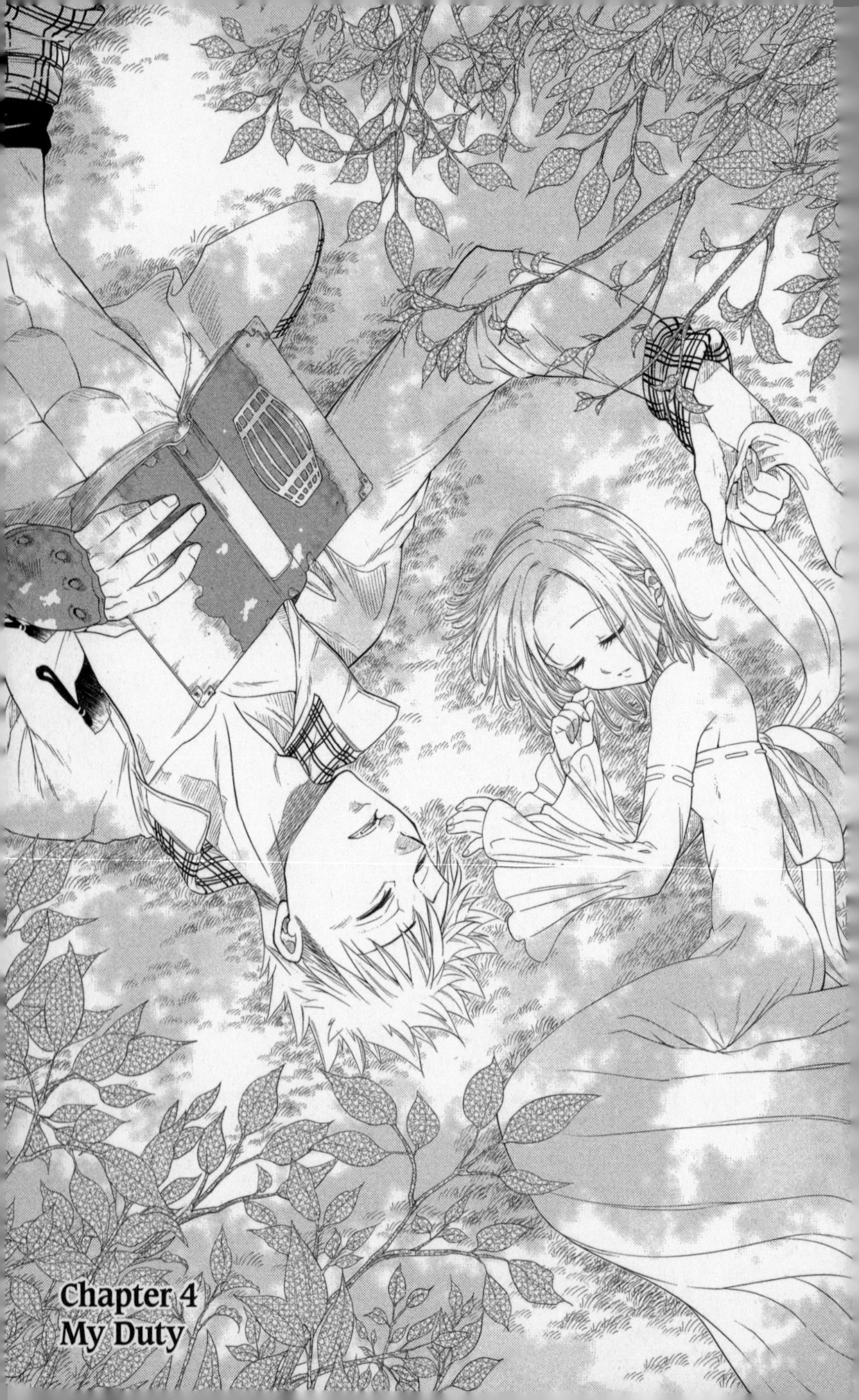
Chapter 4
My Duty

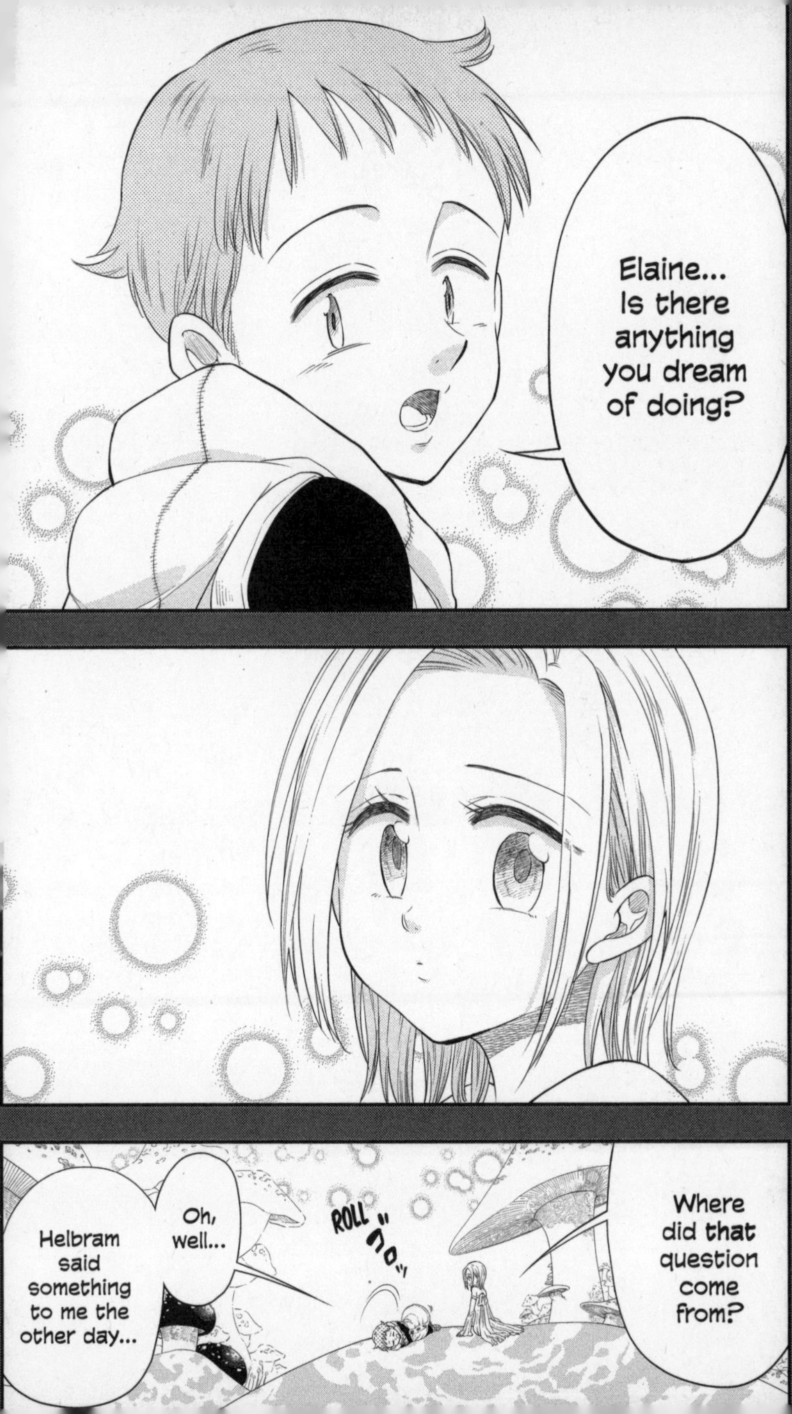
Elaine... Is there anything you dream of doing?
Where did that question come from?
ROLL
Oh, well...
Helbram said something to me the other day...

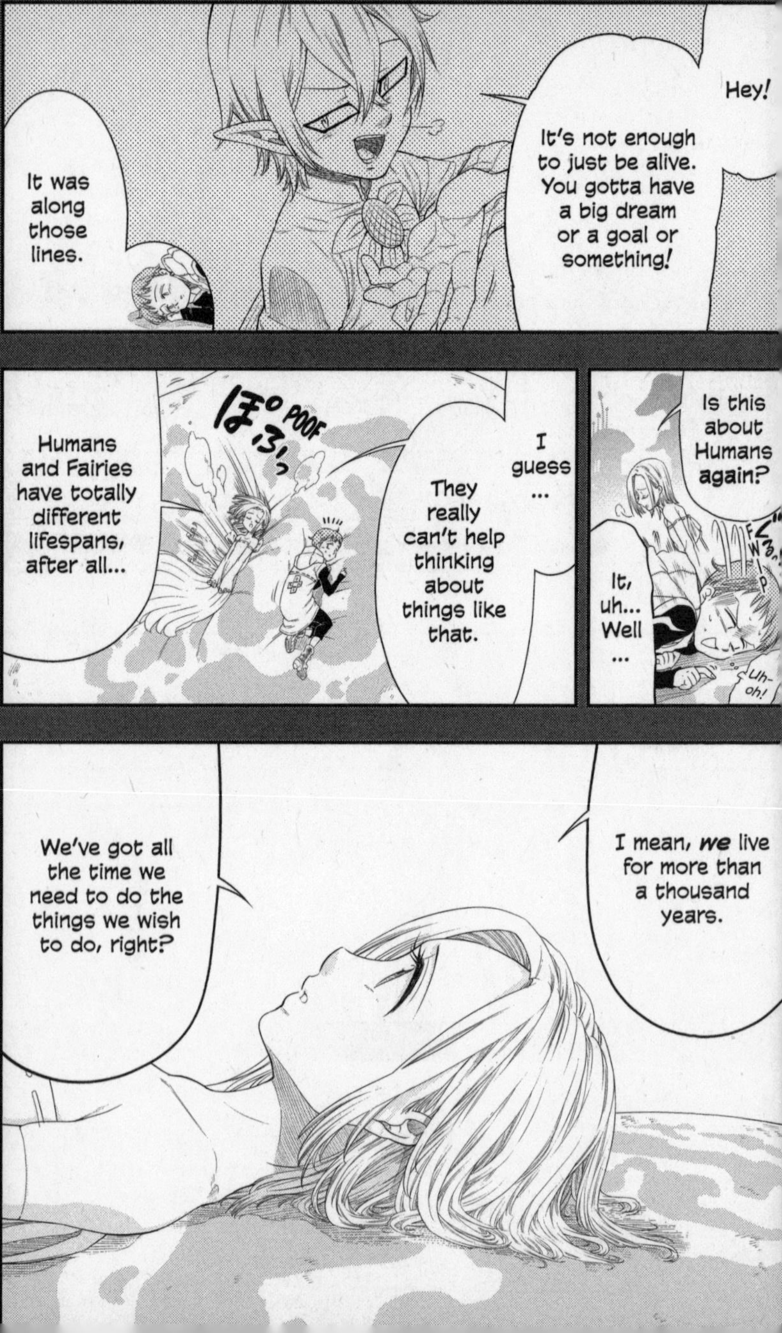
Hey!
It's not enough to just be alive. You gotta have a big dream or a goal or something!
It was along those lines.
Is this about Humans again?
FWIP
It, uh... Well...
Uh-oh!
I guess...
They really can't help thinking about things like that.
ぽふっ POOF
Humans and Fairies have totally different lifespans, after all...
I mean, *we* live for more than a thousand years.
We've got all the time we need to do the things we wish to do, right?

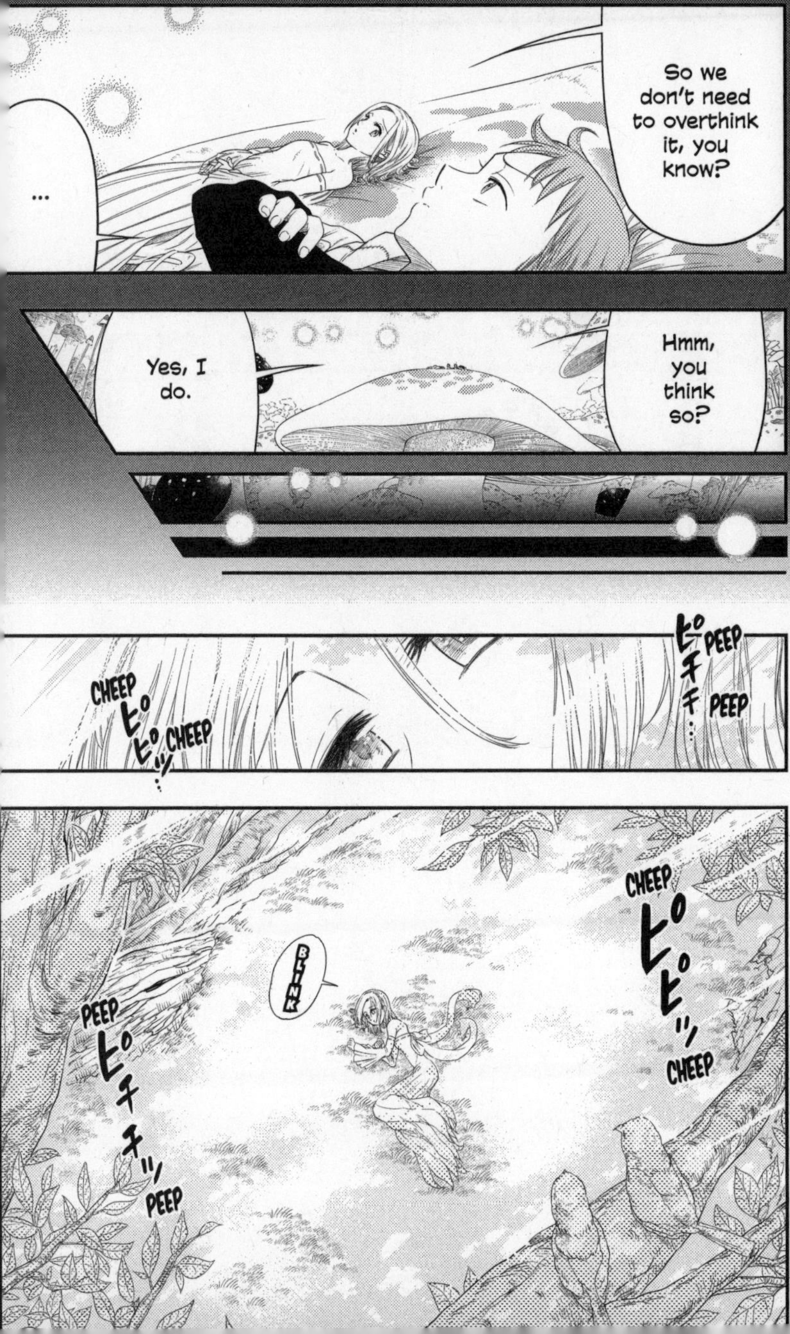
So we don't need to overthink it, you know?
...
Hmm, you think so?
Yes, I do.
ピチチ…
PEEP
PEEP
ピピッ…
CHEEP
CHEEP
ピピッ
CHEEP
CHEEP
BLINK
ピチチッ
PEEP
PEEP

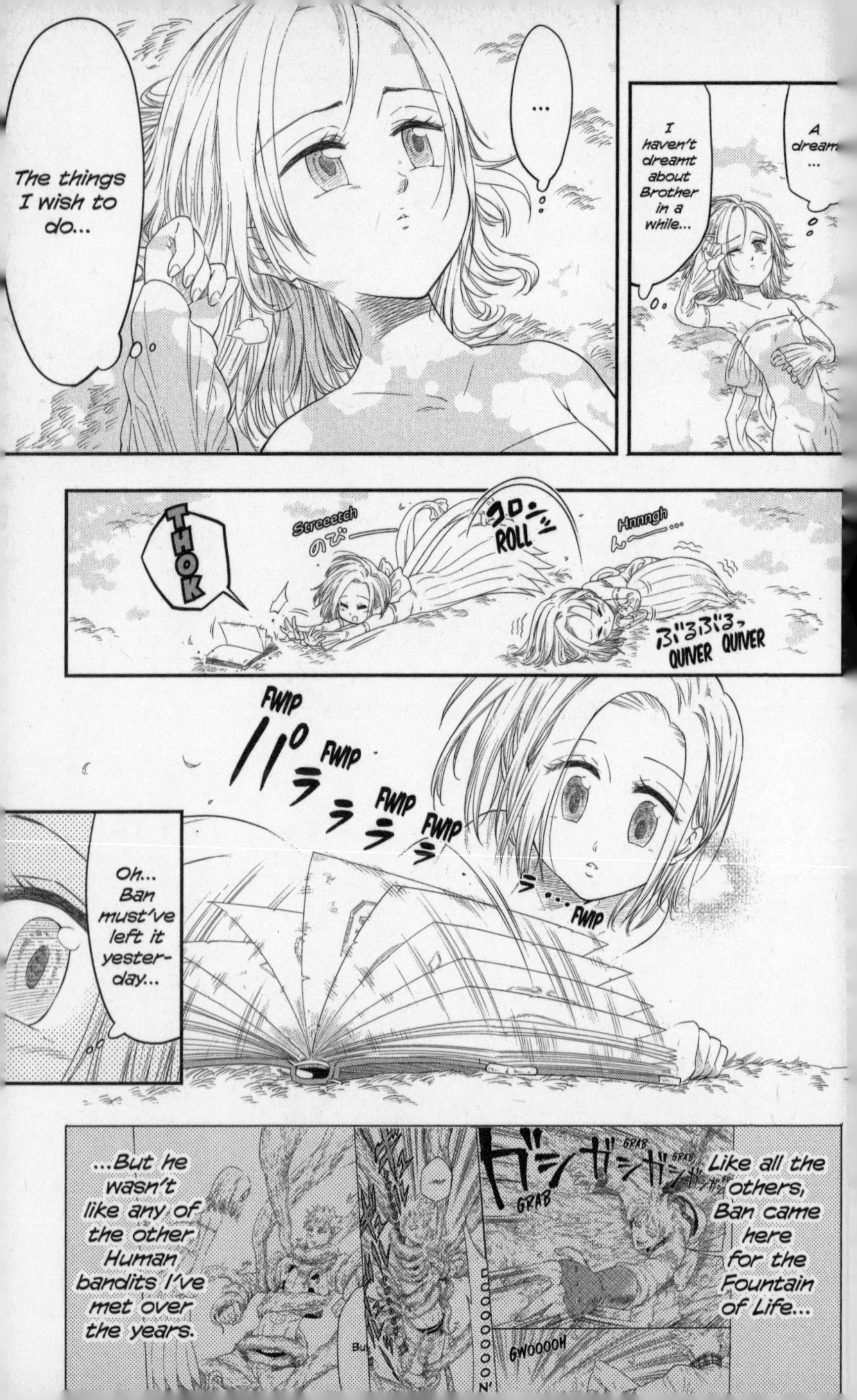
A dream...
I haven't dreamt about Brother in a while...
...
The things I wish to do...
ぶるぶるっ QUIVER QUIVER
ん〜… Hnnngh
ROLL
のび〜 Streeetch
THOK
FWIP
FWIP
FWIP
FWIP
FWIP
Oh... Ban must've left it yesterday...
Like all the others, Ban came here for the Fountain of Life...
GRAB GRAB GRAB
GWOOOOH
...But he wasn't like any of the other Human bandits I've met over the years.

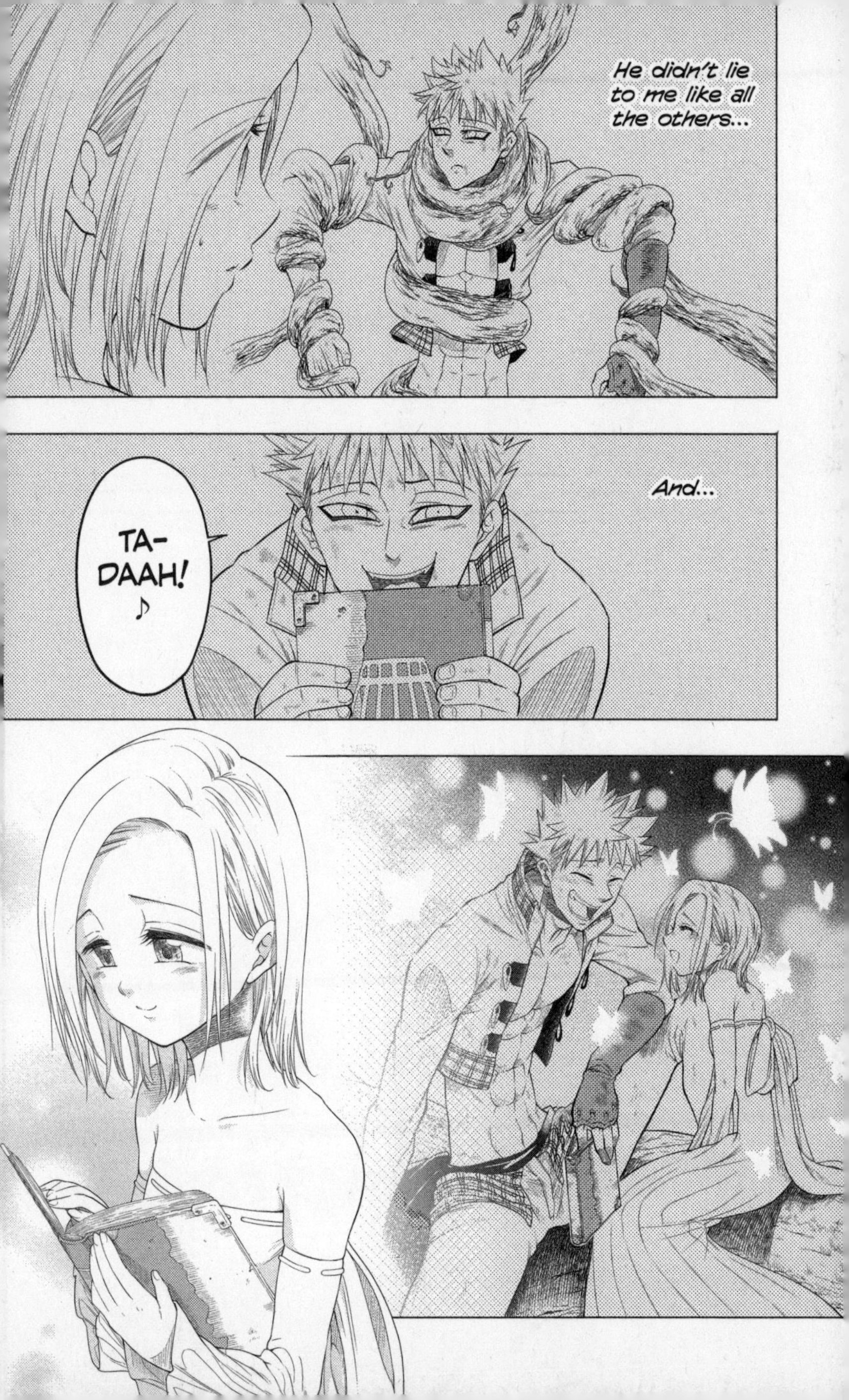
He didn't lie to me like all the others...
And...
TA-DAAH! ♪

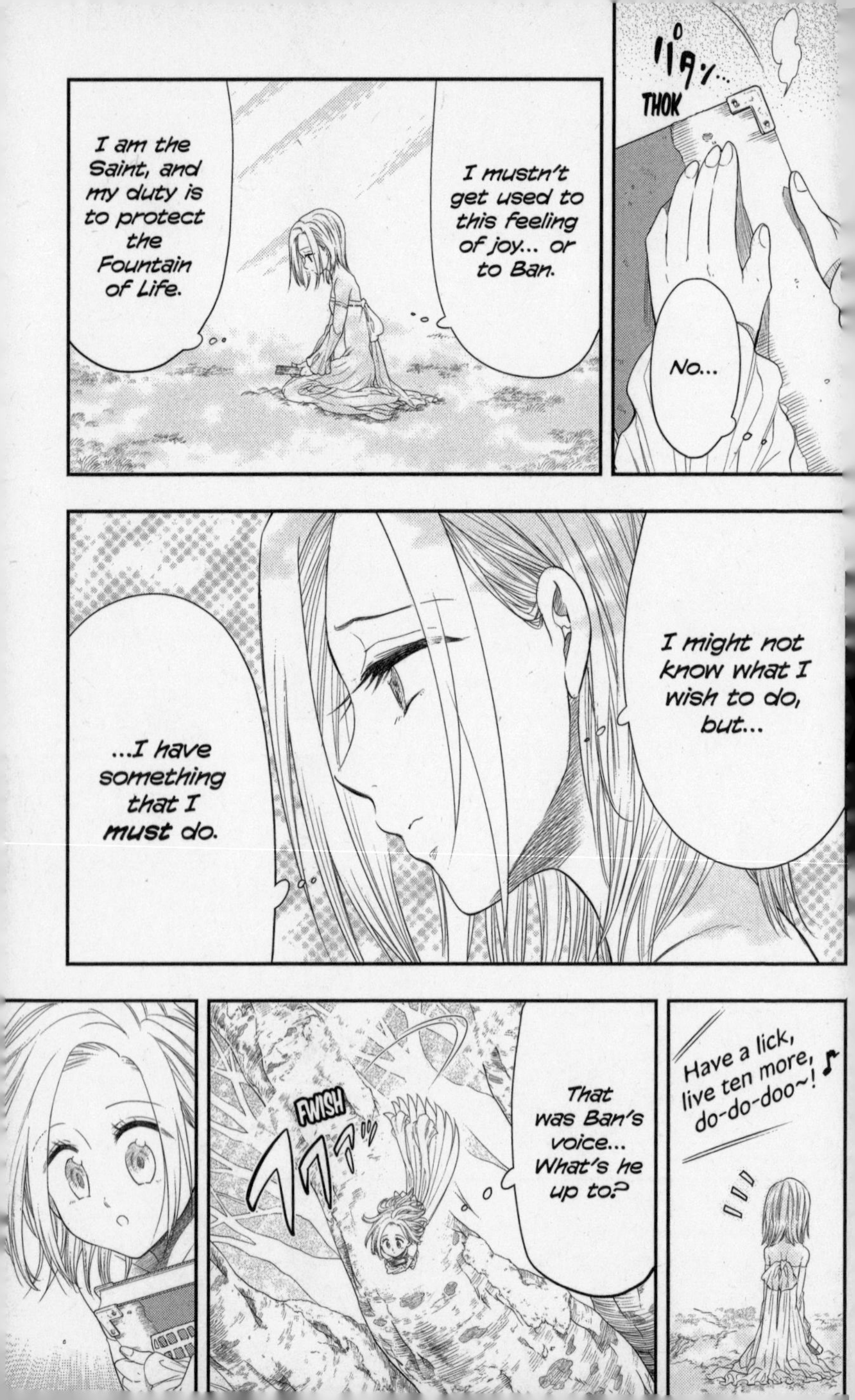
THOK
No...
I mustn't get used to this feeling of joy... or to Ban.
I am the Saint, and my duty is to protect the Fountain of Life.
I might not know what I wish to do, but...
...I have something that I must do.
Have a lick, live ten more, do-do-doo~! ♪
FWISH
That was Ban's voice... What's he up to?

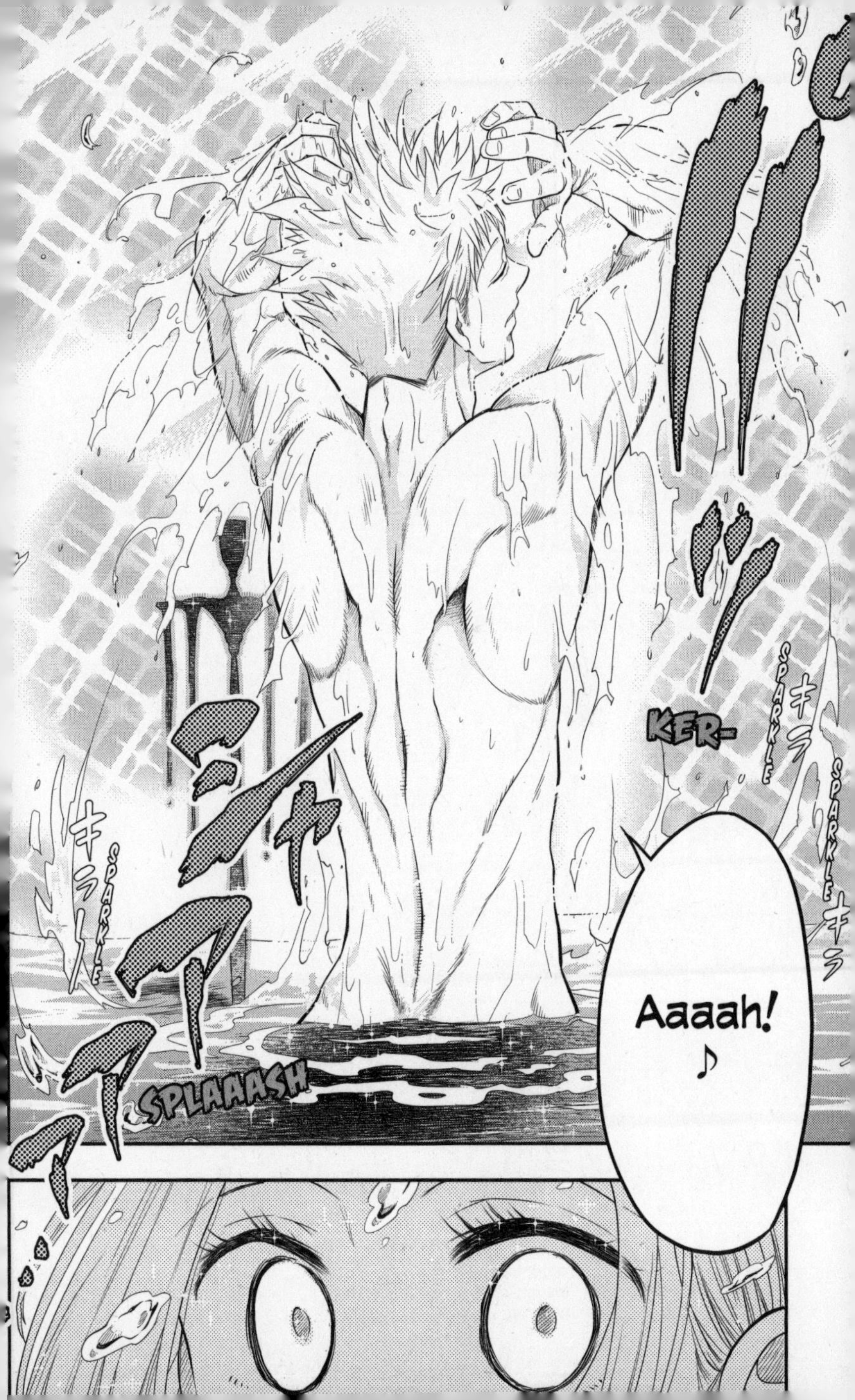

SPARKLE
KER-
SPARKLE
Aaaah! ♪
SPARKLE
SPLAAASH

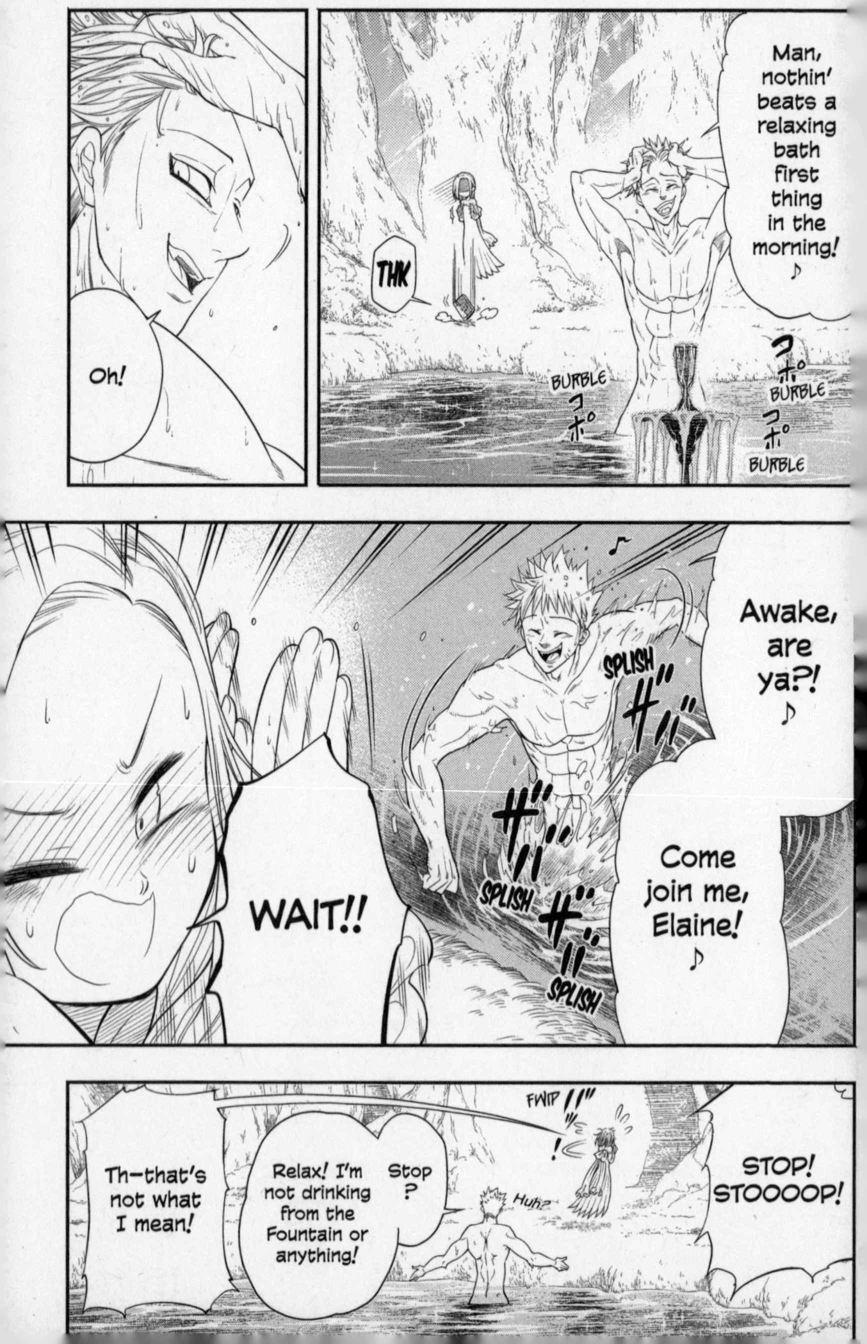

Man, nothin' beats a relaxing bath first thing in the morning! ♪
THK
BURBLE
BURBLE
BURBLE
Oh!
Awake, are ya?! ♪
Come join me, Elaine! ♪
SPLISH
SPLISH
SPLISH
WAIT!!
STOP! STOOOOP!
FWIP
Huh?
Stop?
Relax! I'm not drinking from the Fountain or anything!
Th-that's not what I mean!

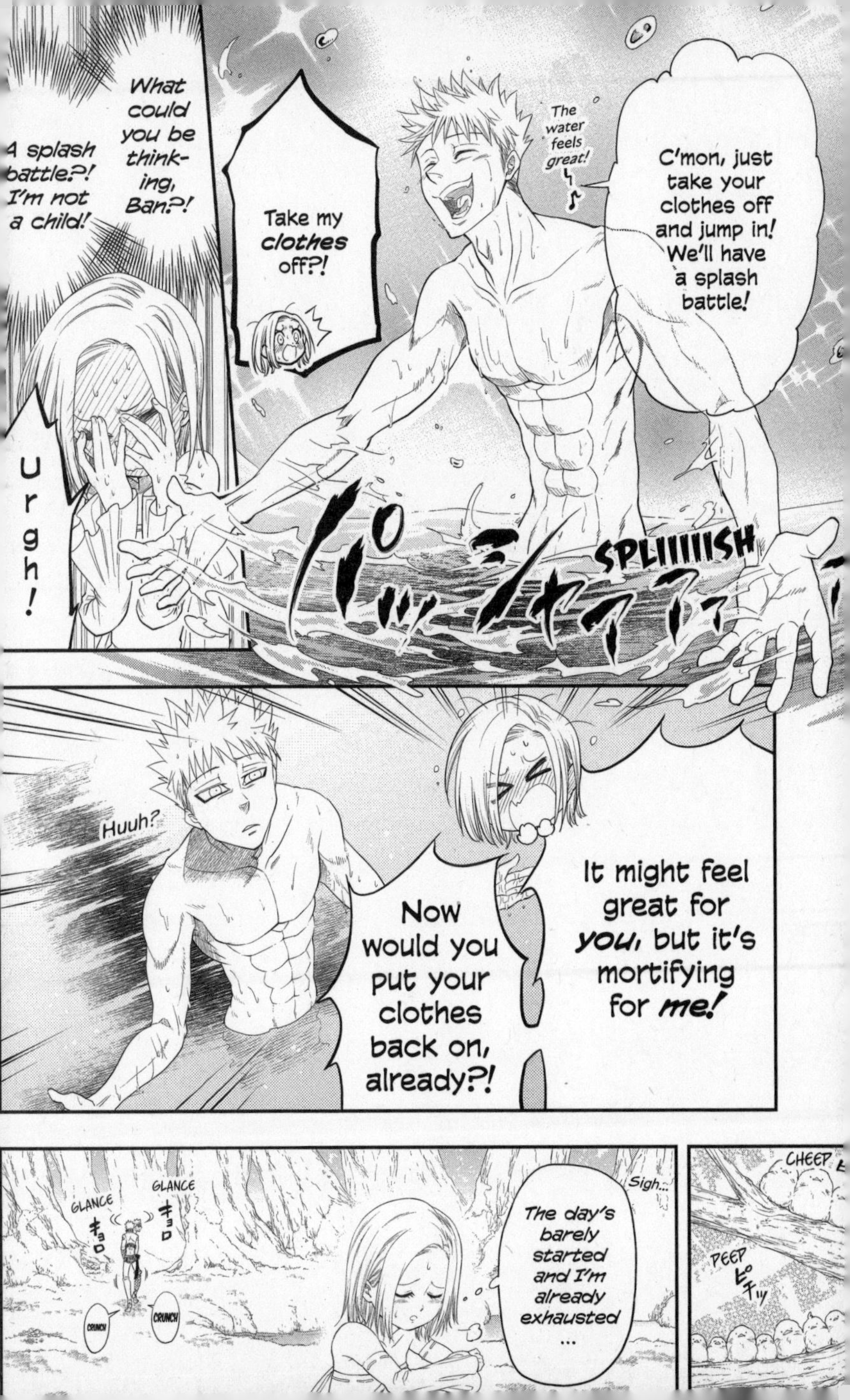
C'mon, just take your clothes off and jump in! We'll have a splash battle!
The water feels great! ♪
Take my clothes off?!
What could you be thinking, Ban?!
A splash battle?! I'm not a child!
Urgh!
SPLIIIIISH
It might feel great for you, but it's mortifying for me!
Now would you put your clothes back on, already?!
Huuh?
CHEEP
PEEP
Sigh...
The day's barely started and I'm already exhausted...
GLANCE
GLANCE
CRUNCH
CRUNCH

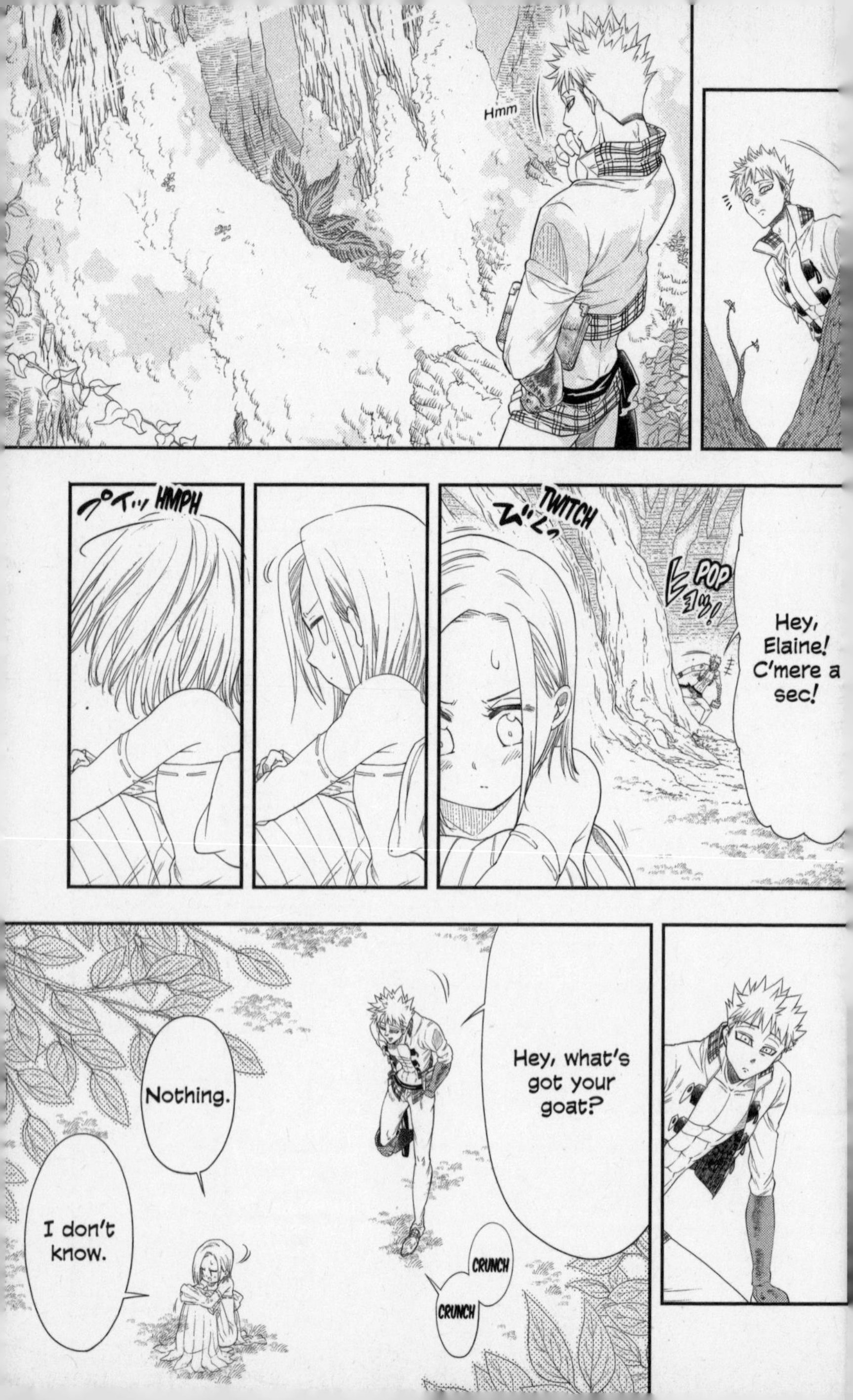

Hmm
Hey, Elaine! C'mere a sec!
POP
TWITCH
HMPH
Hey, what's got your goat?
CRUNCH
CRUNCH
Nothing.
I don't know.

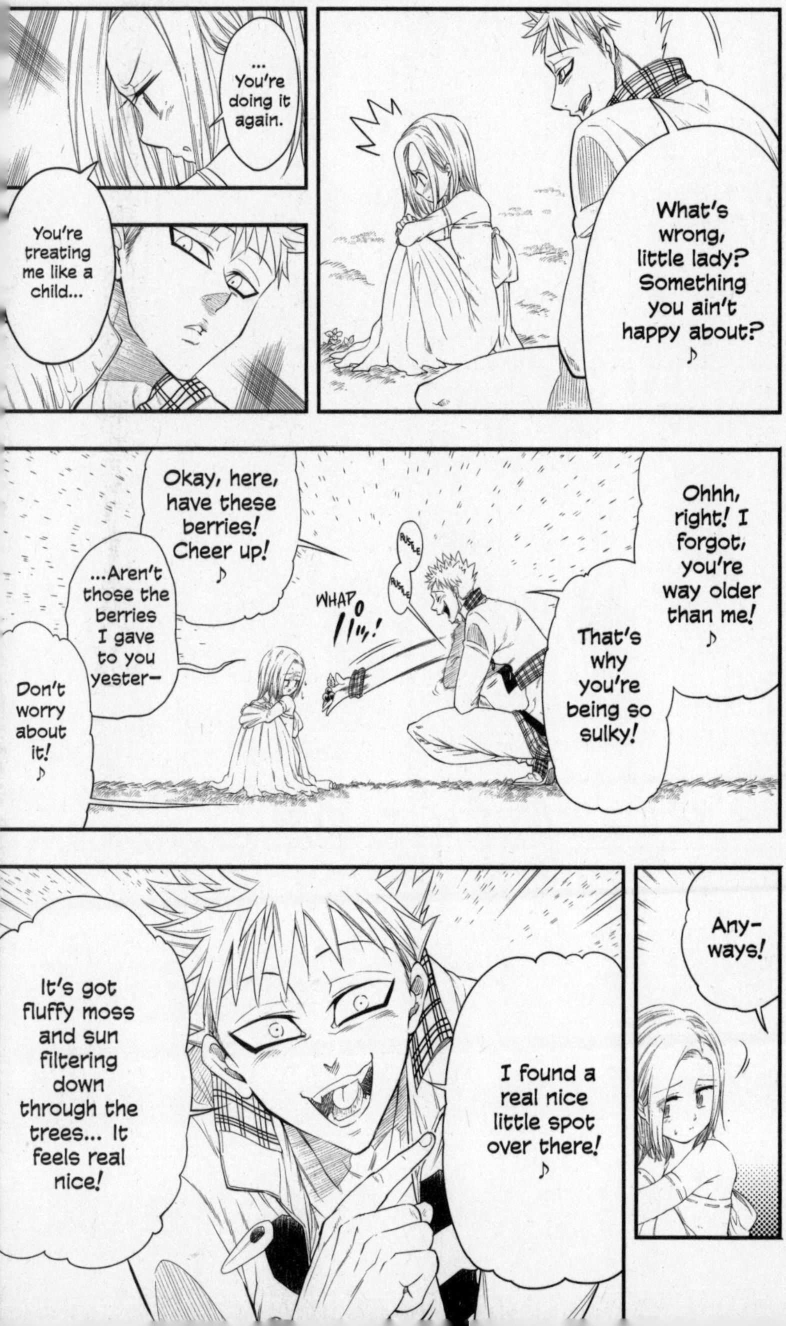
What's wrong, little lady? Something you ain't happy about? ♪
... You're doing it again.
You're treating me like a child...
Ohhh, right! I forgot, you're way older than me! ♪
That's why you're being so sulky!
RUSTLE
RUSTLE
WHAP
Okay, here, have these berries! Cheer up! ♪
...Aren't those the berries I gave to you yester—
Don't worry about it! ♪
Any-ways!
I found a real nice little spot over there! ♪
It's got fluffy moss and sun filtering down through the trees... It feels real nice!

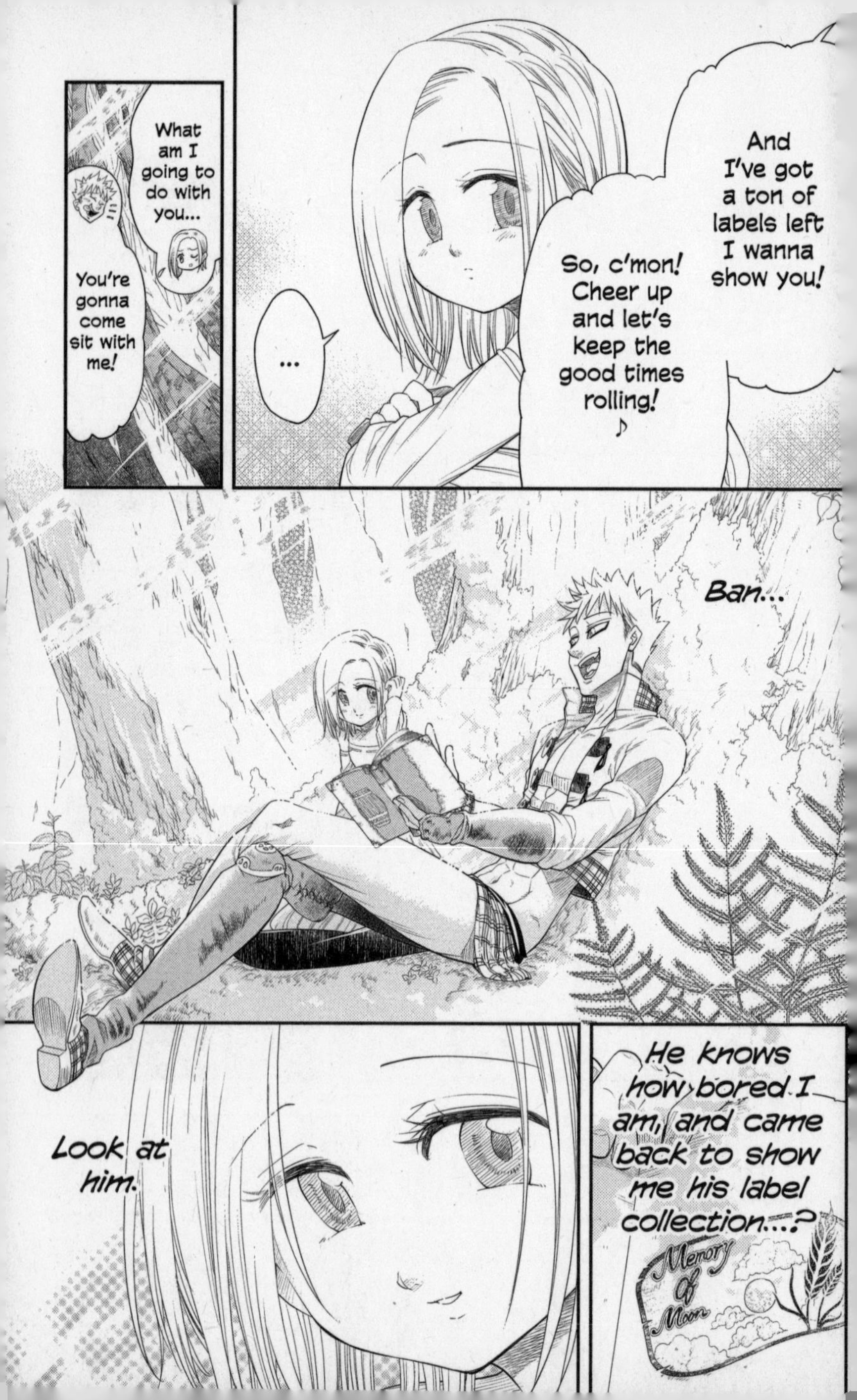
And I've got a ton of labels left I wanna show you!
So, c'mon! Cheer up and let's keep the good times rolling! ♪
...
What am I going to do with you...
You're gonna come sit with me!
Ban...
He knows how bored I am, and came back to show me his label collection...?
Memory Of Moon
Look at him.

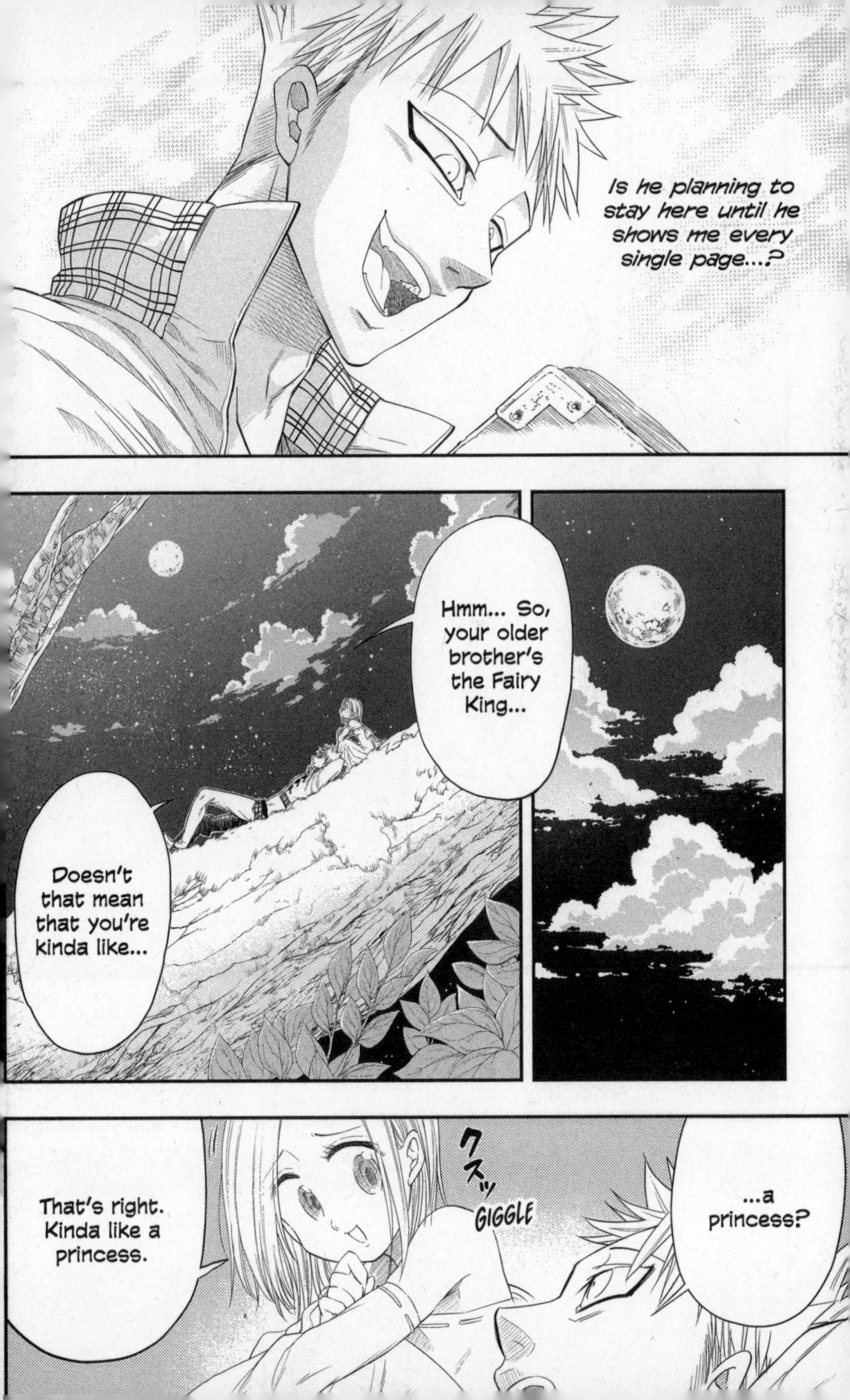
Is he planning to stay here until he shows me every single page...?
Hmm... So, your older brother's the Fairy King...
Doesn't that mean that you're kinda like...
...a princess?
クスッ
GIGGLE
That's right. Kinda like a princess.

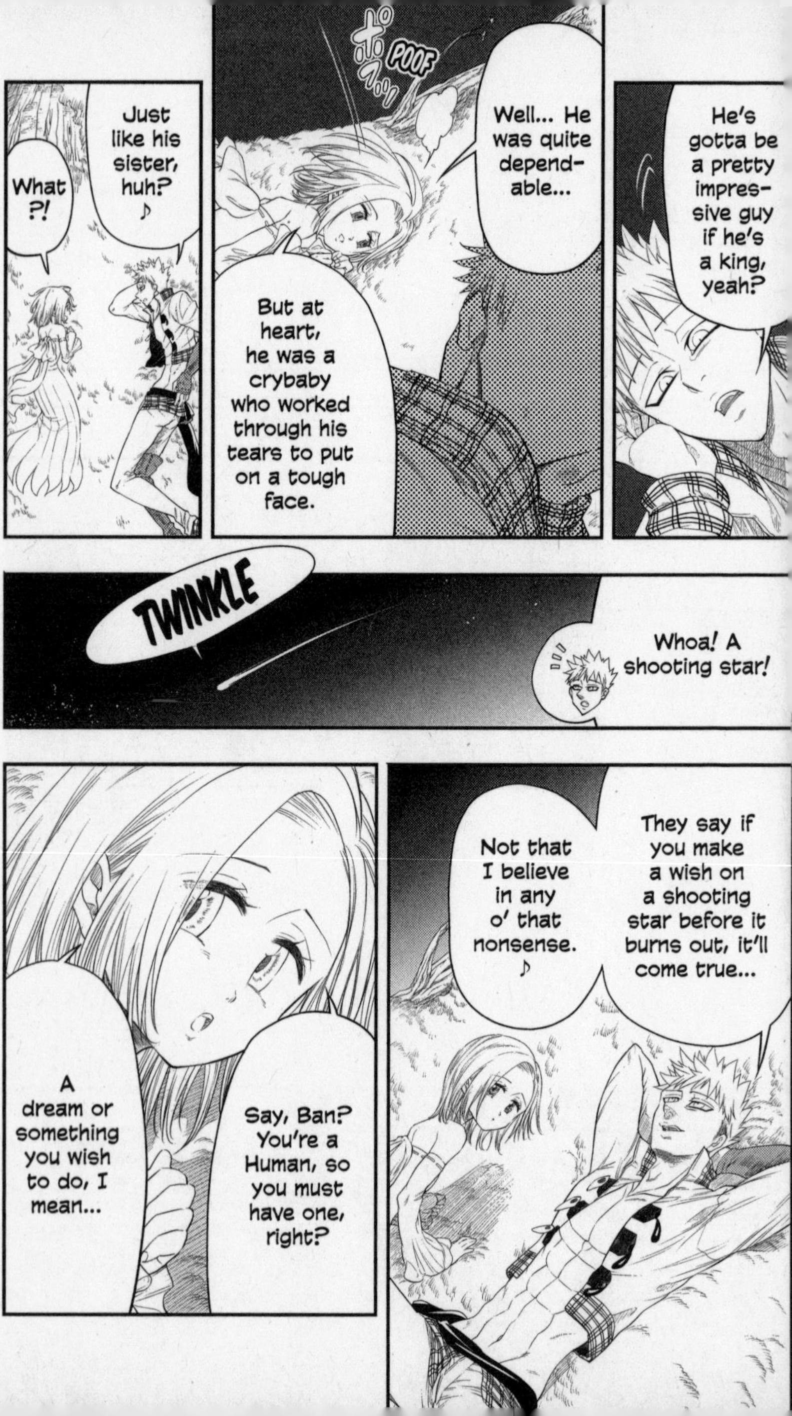
He's gotta be a pretty impressive guy if he's a king, yeah?
POOF
Well... He was quite dependable...
But at heart, he was a crybaby who worked through his tears to put on a tough face.
Just like his sister, huh? ♪
What?!
Whoa! A shooting star!
TWINKLE
They say if you make a wish on a shooting star before it burns out, it'll come true...
Not that I believe in any o' that nonsense. ♪
Say, Ban? You're a Human, so you must have one, right?
A dream or something you wish to do, I mean...

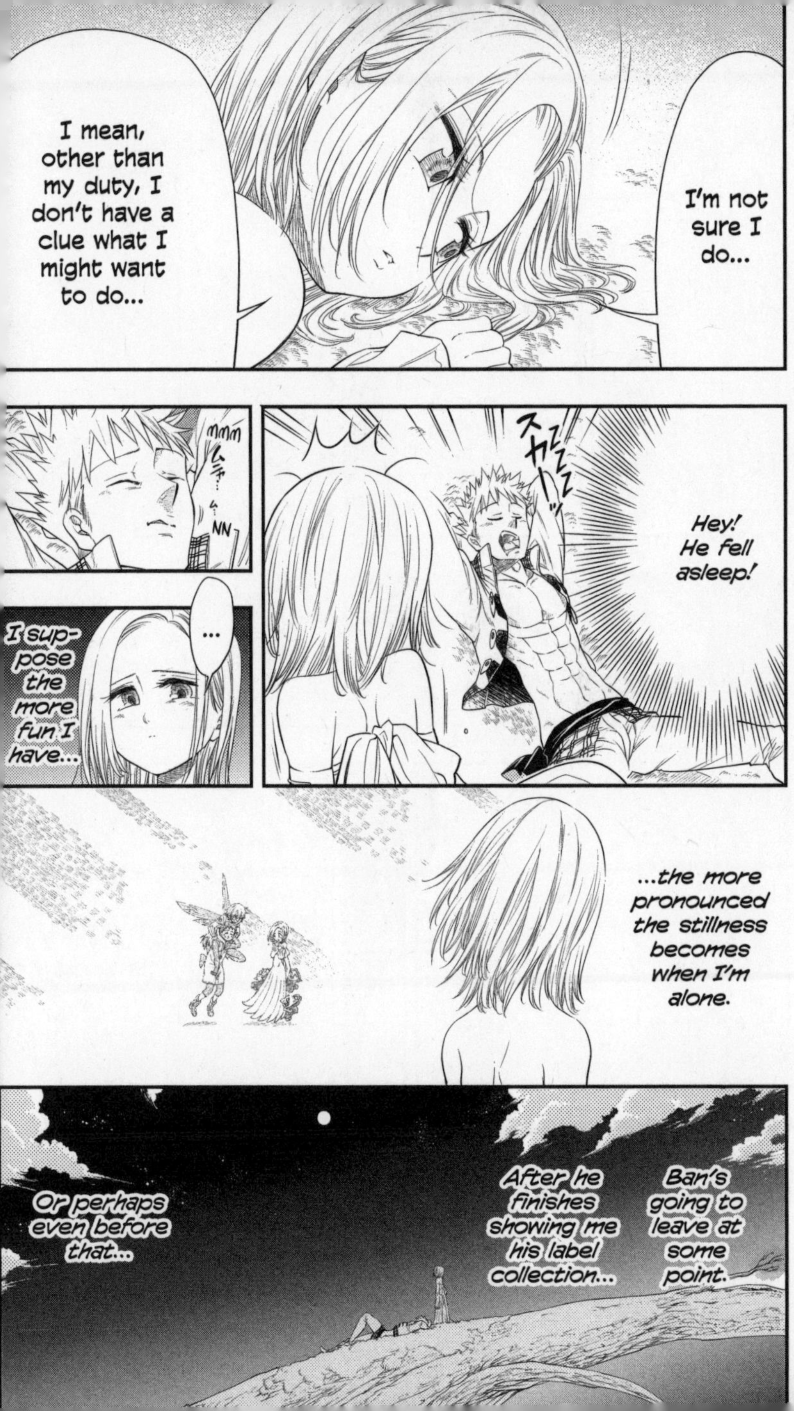
I'm not sure I do...
I mean, other than my duty, I don't have a clue what I might want to do...
Hey! He fell asleep!
ZZZZ
mmm
NN
...
I suppose the more fun I have...
...the more pronounced the stillness becomes when I'm alone.
Ban's going to leave at some point.
After he finishes showing me his label collection...
Or perhaps even before that...

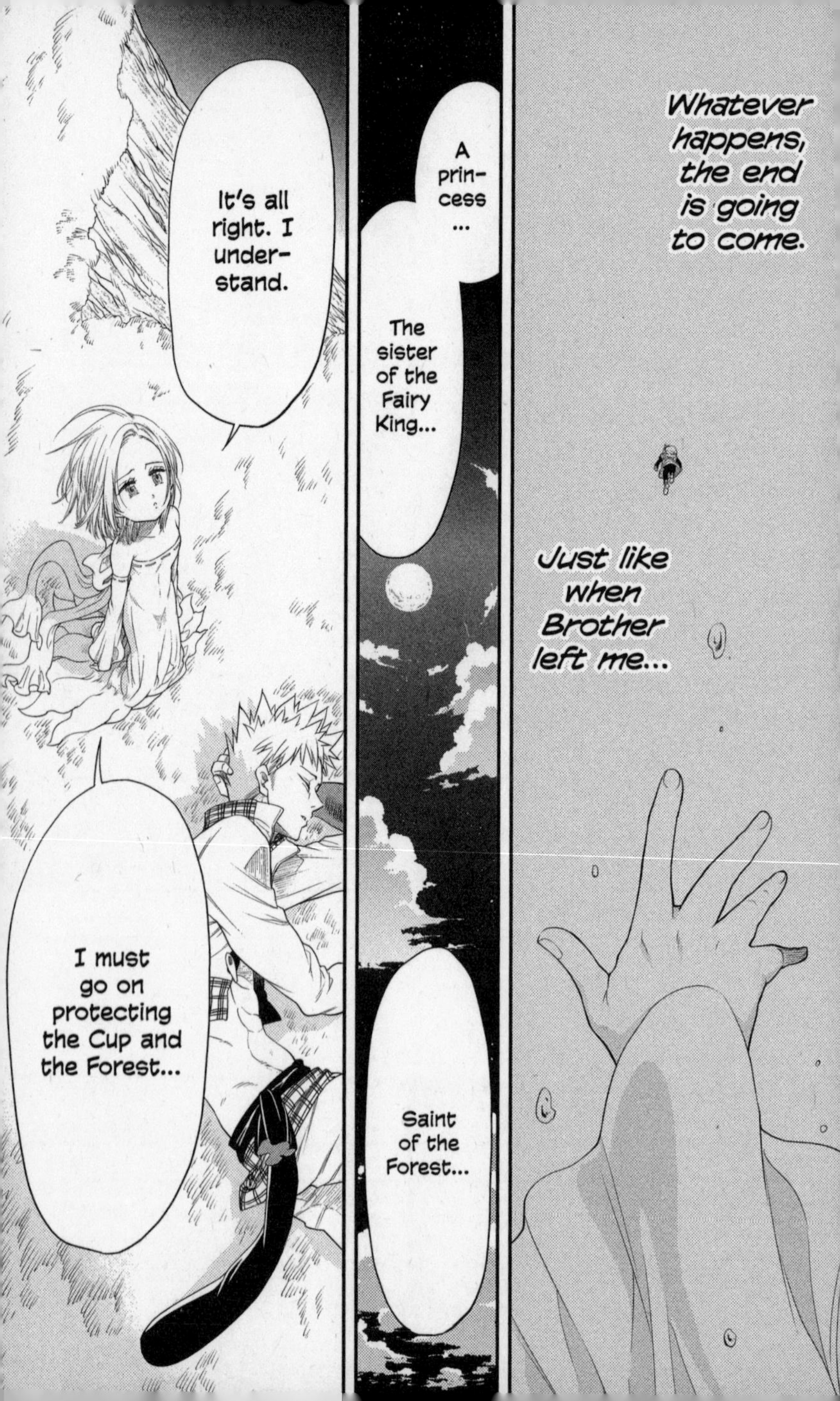
Whatever happens, the end is going to come.
Just like when Brother left me...
A princess...
The sister of the Fairy King...
Saint of the Forest...
It's all right. I understand.
I must go on protecting the Cup and the Forest...

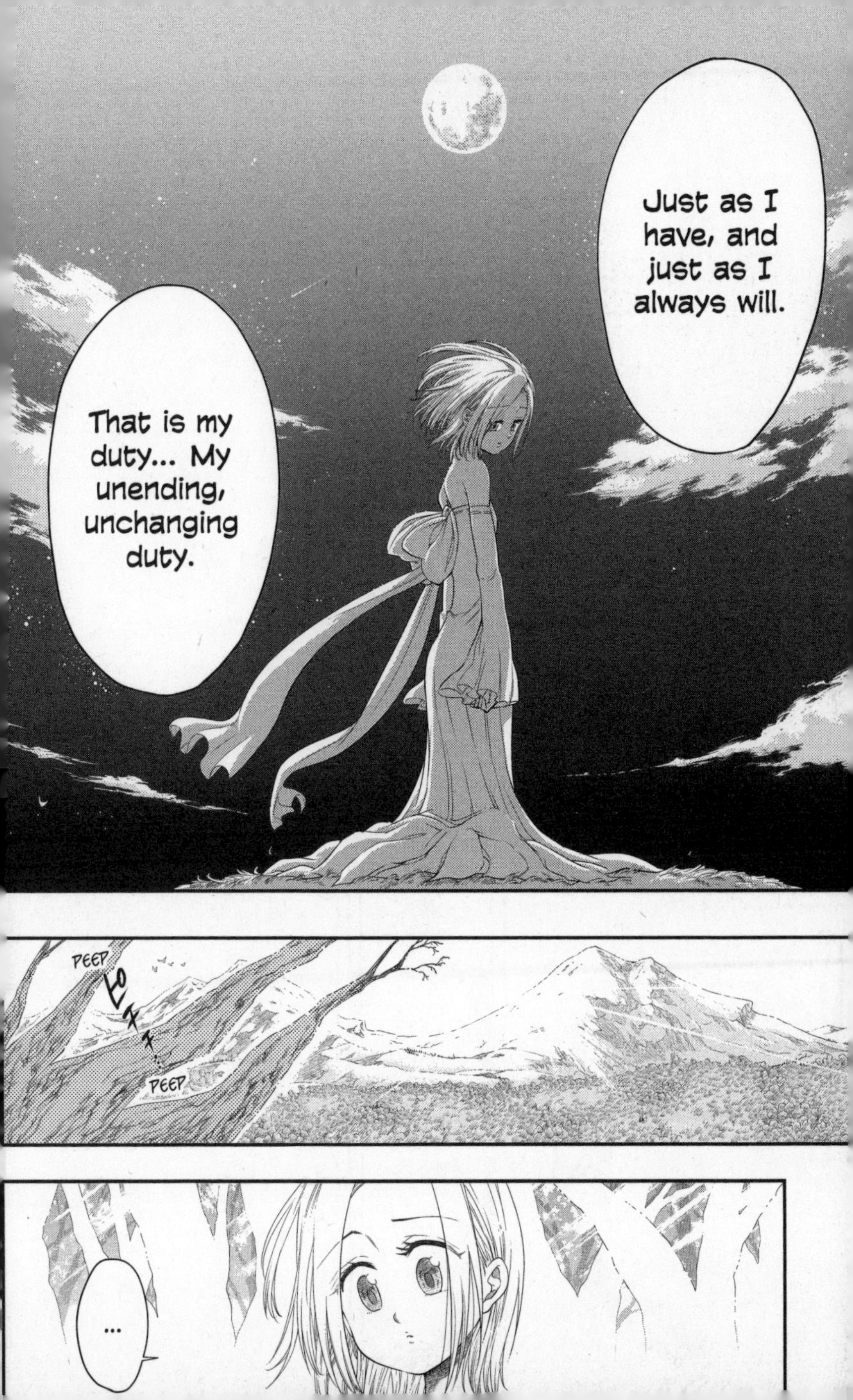
Just as I have, and just as I always will.
That is my duty... My unending, unchanging duty.
PEEP
PEEP
...

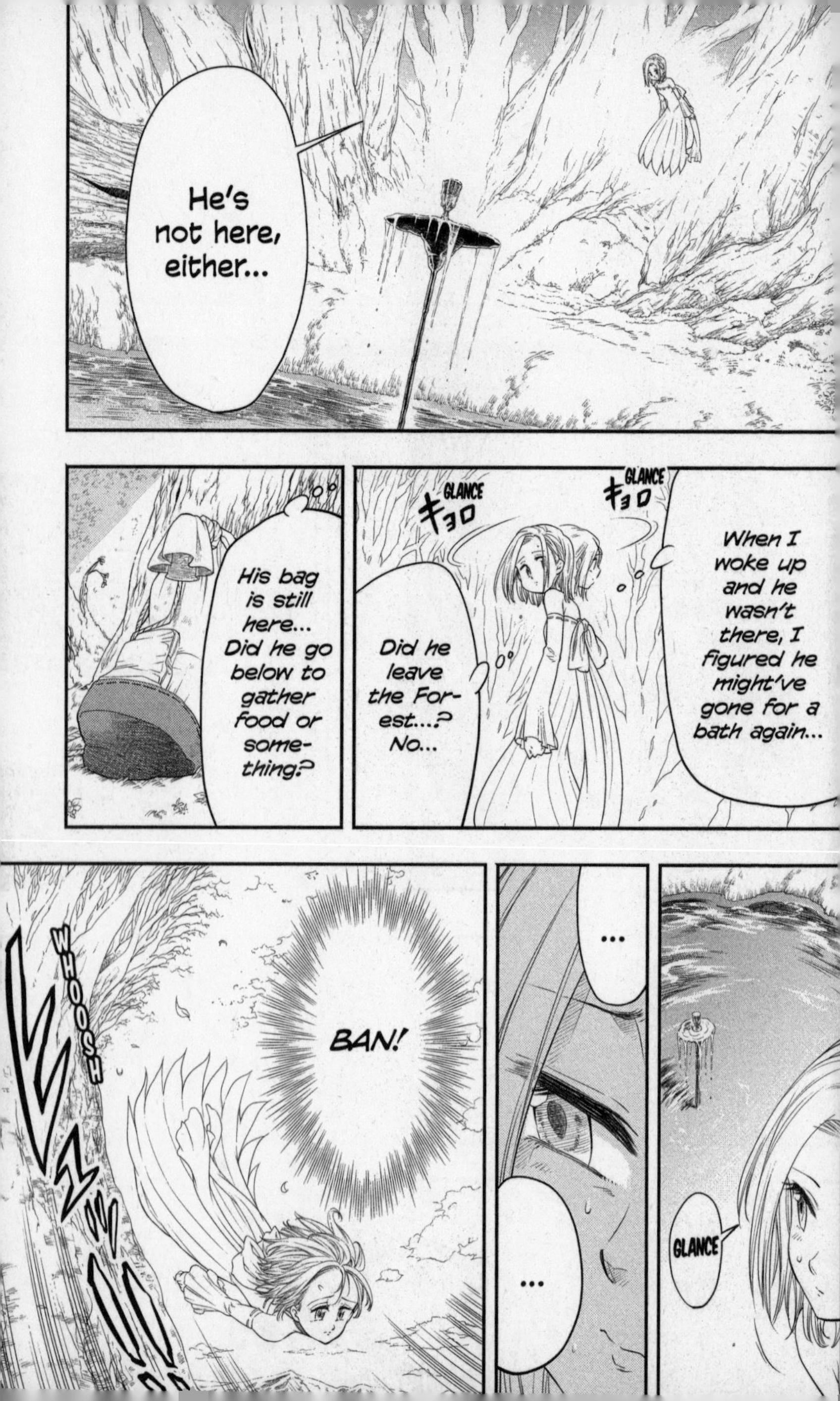
He's not here, either...
When I woke up and he wasn't there, I figured he might've gone for a bath again...
GLANCE
キョロ
GLANCE
キョロ
Did he leave the Forest...? No...
His bag is still here... Did he go below to gather food or something?
GLANCE
...
...
BAN!
WHOOSH

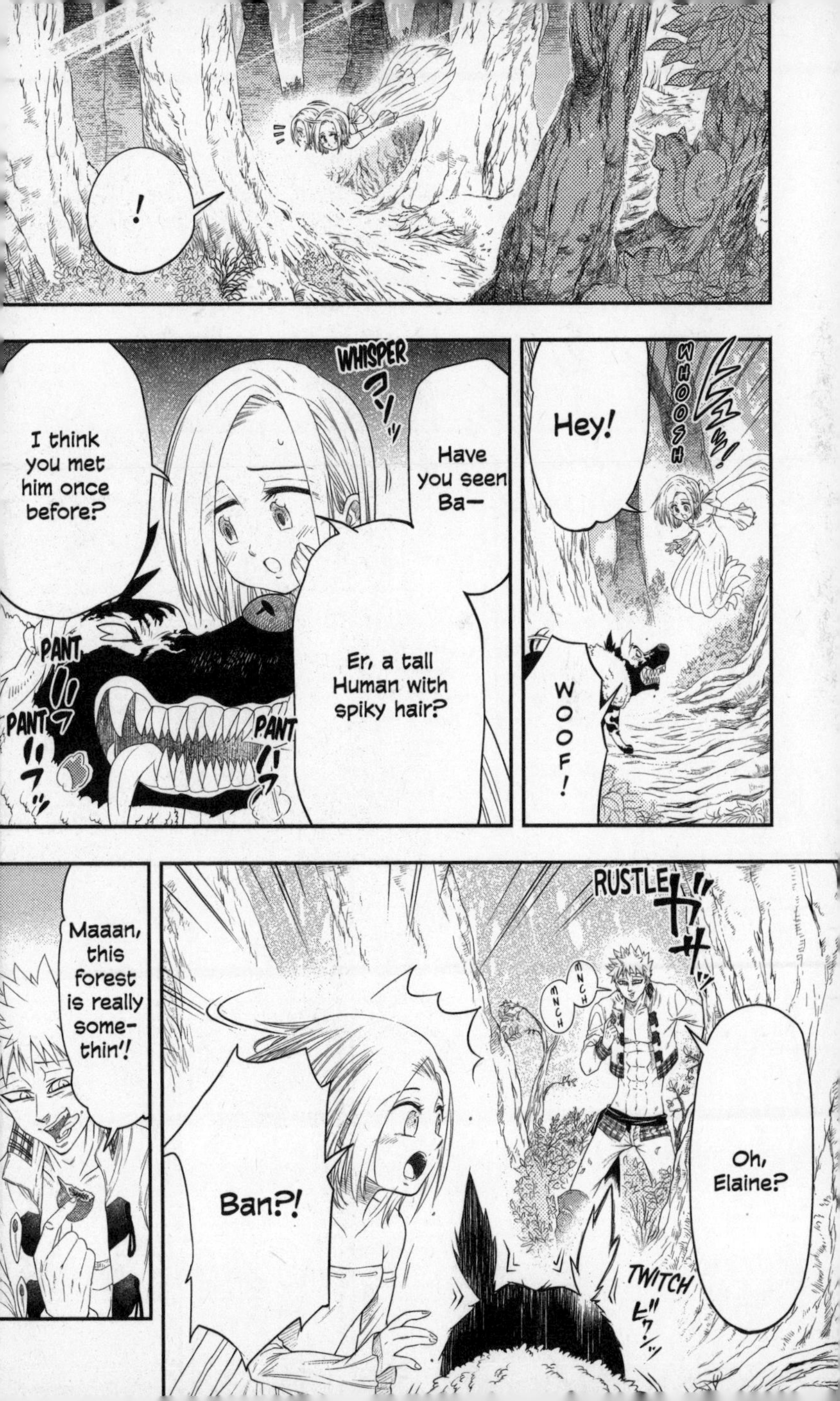
!
WHOOOSH
Hey!
WOOF!
WHISPER
Have you seen Ba–
Er, a tall Human with spiky hair?
I think you met him once before?
PANT
PANT
PANT
RUSTLE
Oh, Elaine?
MNCH MNCH
Ban?!
TWITCH
Maaan, this forest is really somethin'!

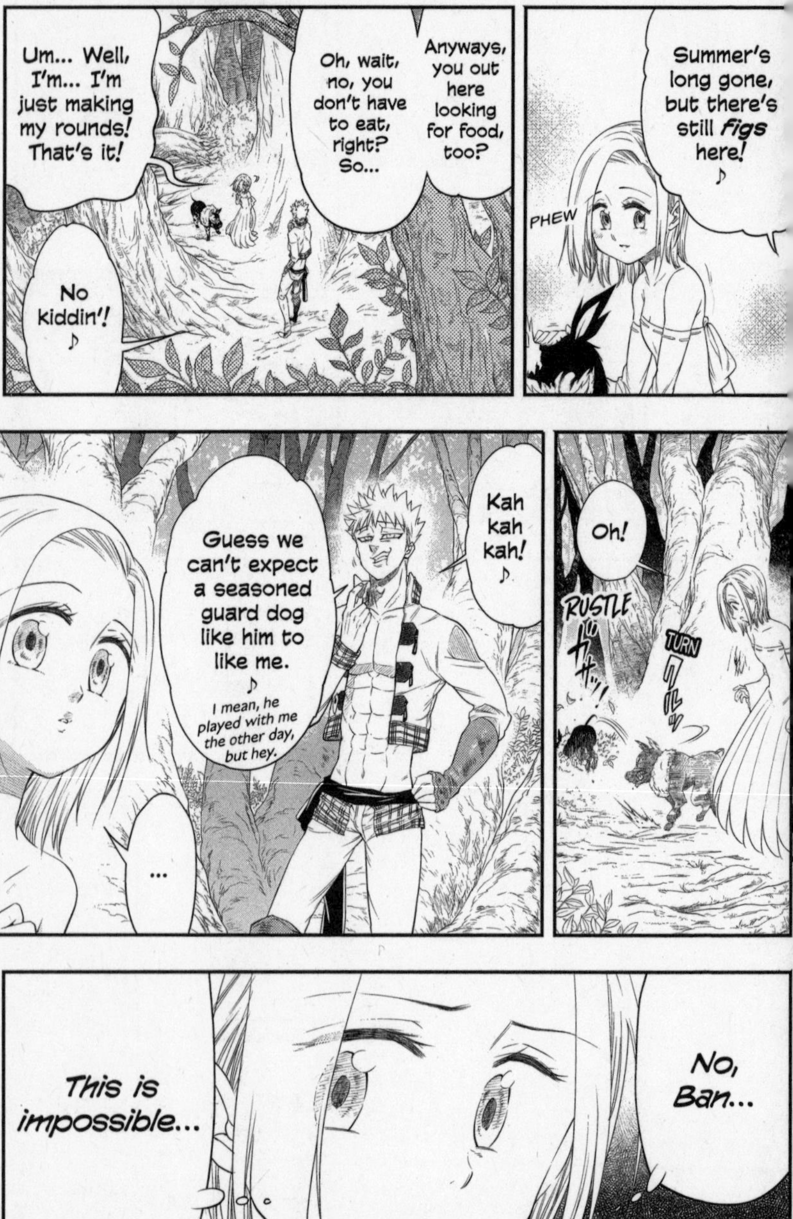
Summer's long gone, but there's still figs here! ♪
PHEW
Anyways, you out here looking for food, too?
Oh, wait, no, you don't have to eat, right? So...
Um... Well, I'm... I'm just making my rounds! That's it!
No kiddin'! ♪
Oh!
RUSTLE
TURN
Kah kah kah! ♪
Guess we can't expect a seasoned guard dog like him to like me. ♪
I mean, he played with me the other day, but hey.
...
No, Ban...
This is impossible...

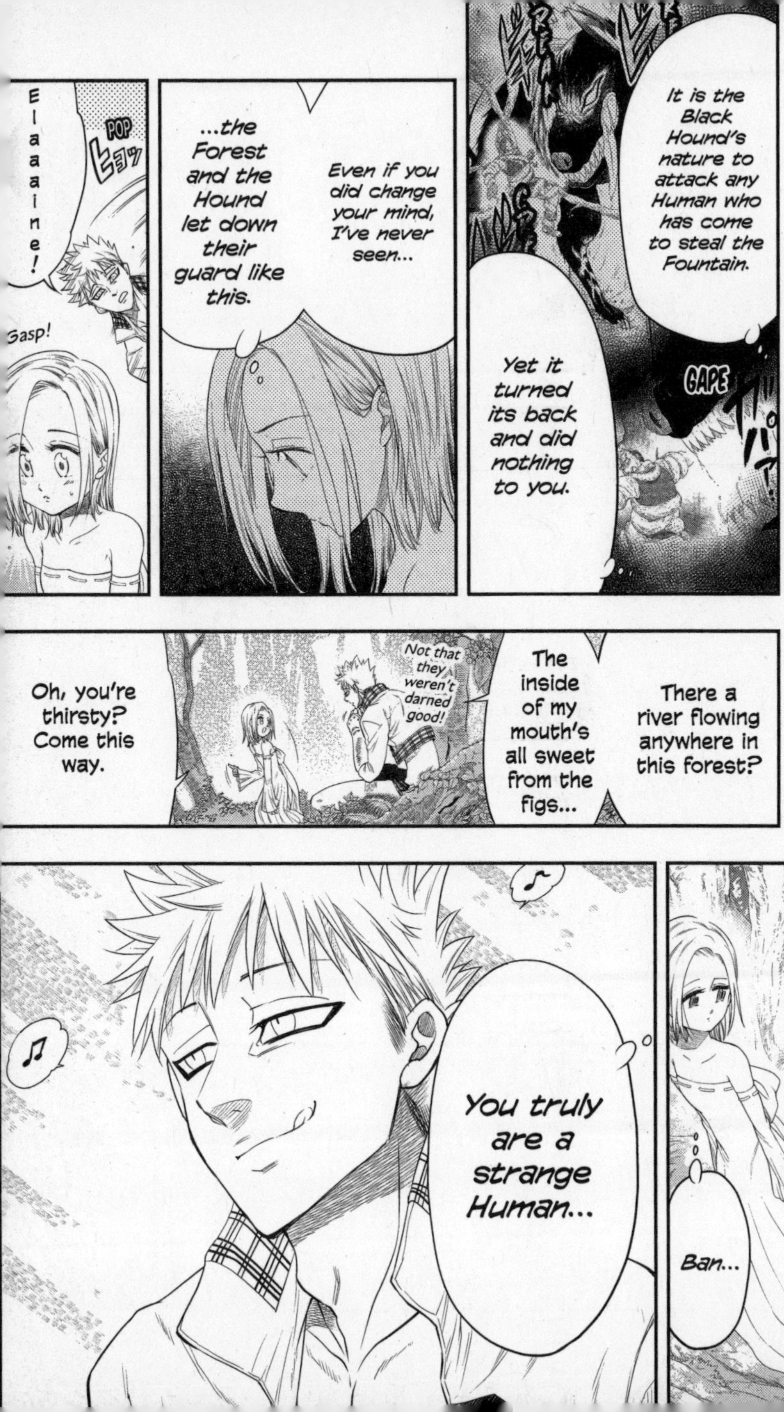

It is the Black Hound's nature to attack any Human who has come to steal the Fountain.
GAPE
Yet it turned its back and did nothing to you.
Even if you did change your mind, I've never seen...
...the Forest and the Hound let down their guard like this.
POP
Elaaaine!
Gasp!
There a river flowing anywhere in this forest?
The inside of my mouth's all sweet from the figs...
Not that they weren't darned good!
Oh, you're thirsty? Come this way.
Ban...
You truly are a strange Human...

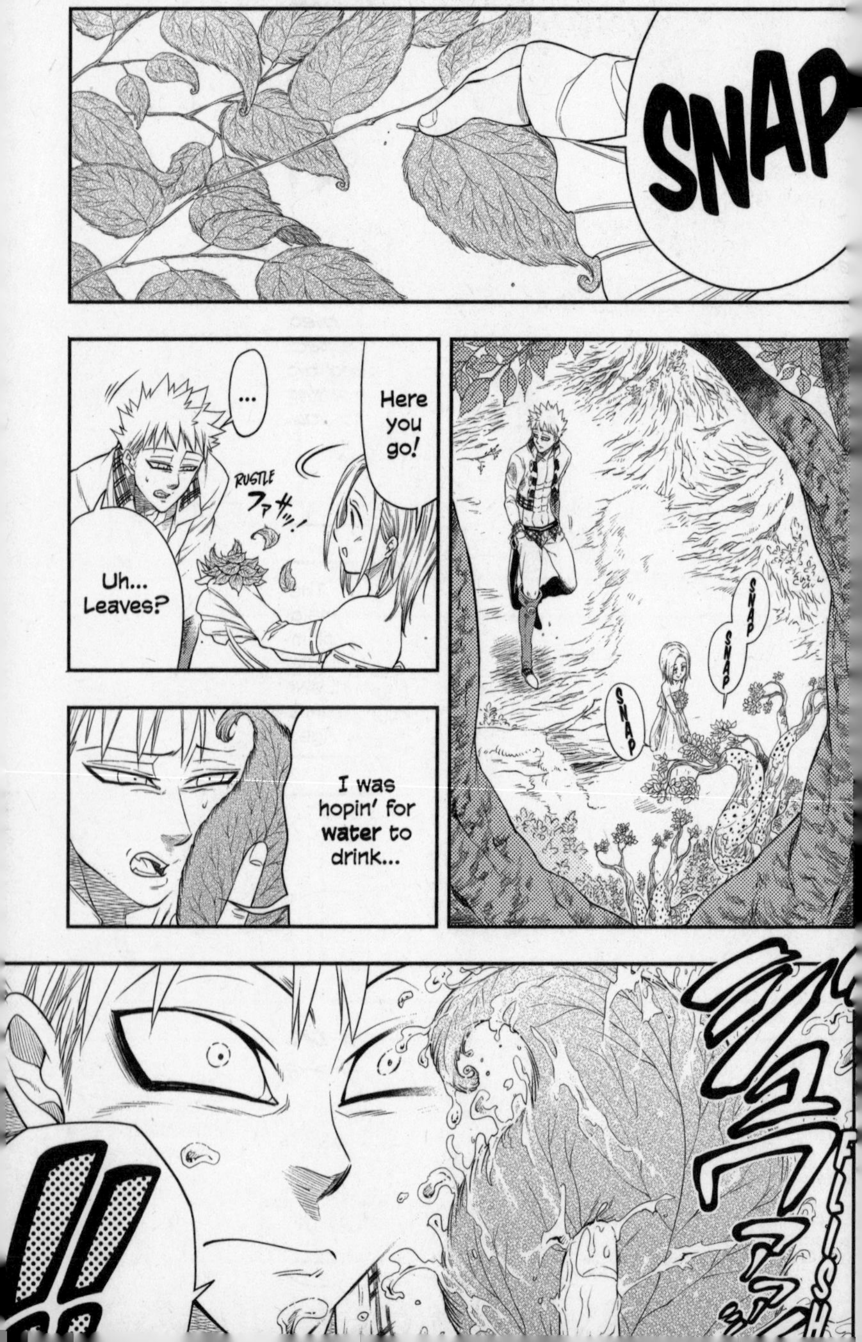
SNAP
SNAP
SNAP
SNAP
Here you go!
RUSTLE ファサッ!
...
Uh... Leaves?
I was hopin' for water to drink...
FLUSH
!!

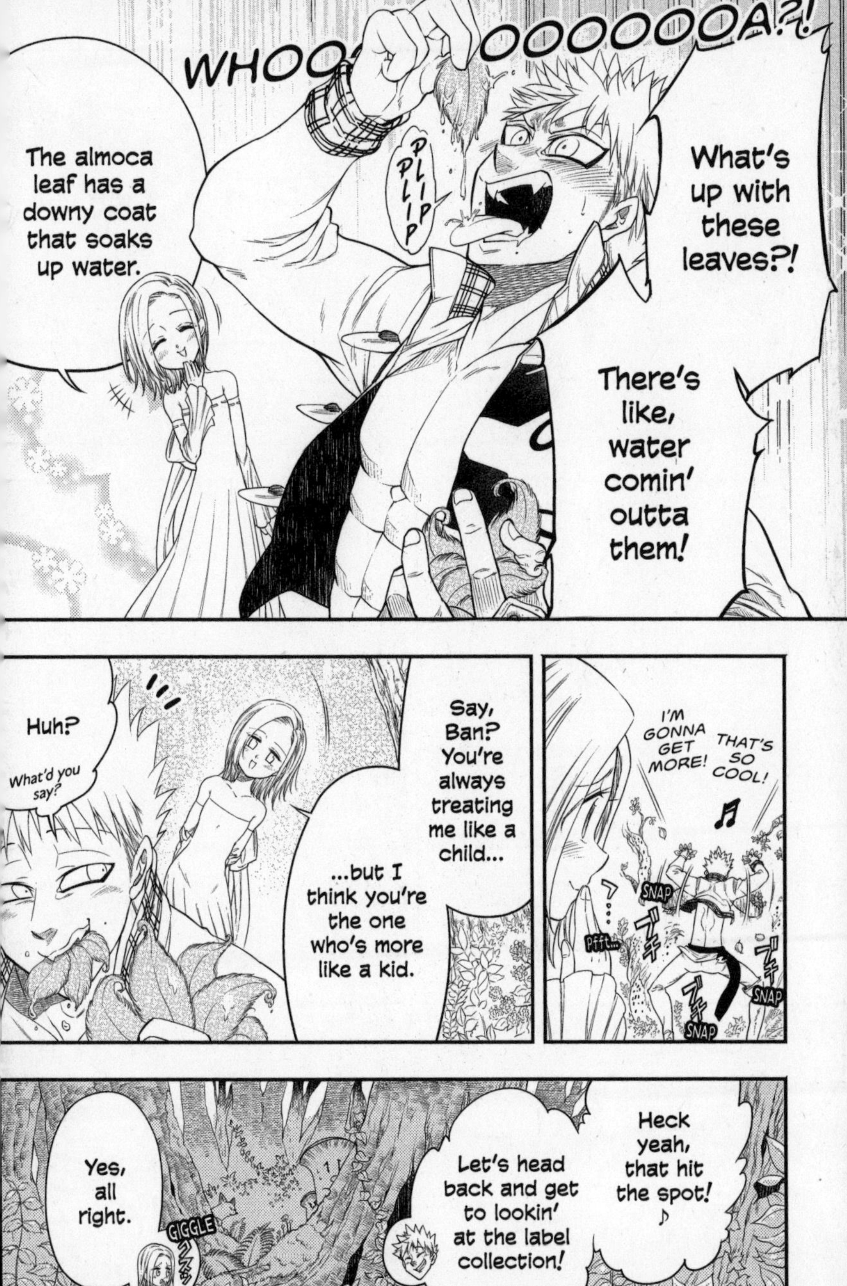
WHOO
OOOOOOA?!
What's up with these leaves?!
There's like, water comin' outta them!
PLIP PLIP
The almoca leaf has a downy coat that soaks up water.
I'M GONNA GET MORE!
THAT'S SO COOL!
♪
SNAP
SNAP
SNAP
Pfft...
Say, Ban? You're always treating me like a child...
...but I think you're the one who's more like a kid.
Huh?
What'd you say?
Heck yeah, that hit the spot! ♪
Let's head back and get to lookin' at the label collection!
Yes, all right.
GIGGLE

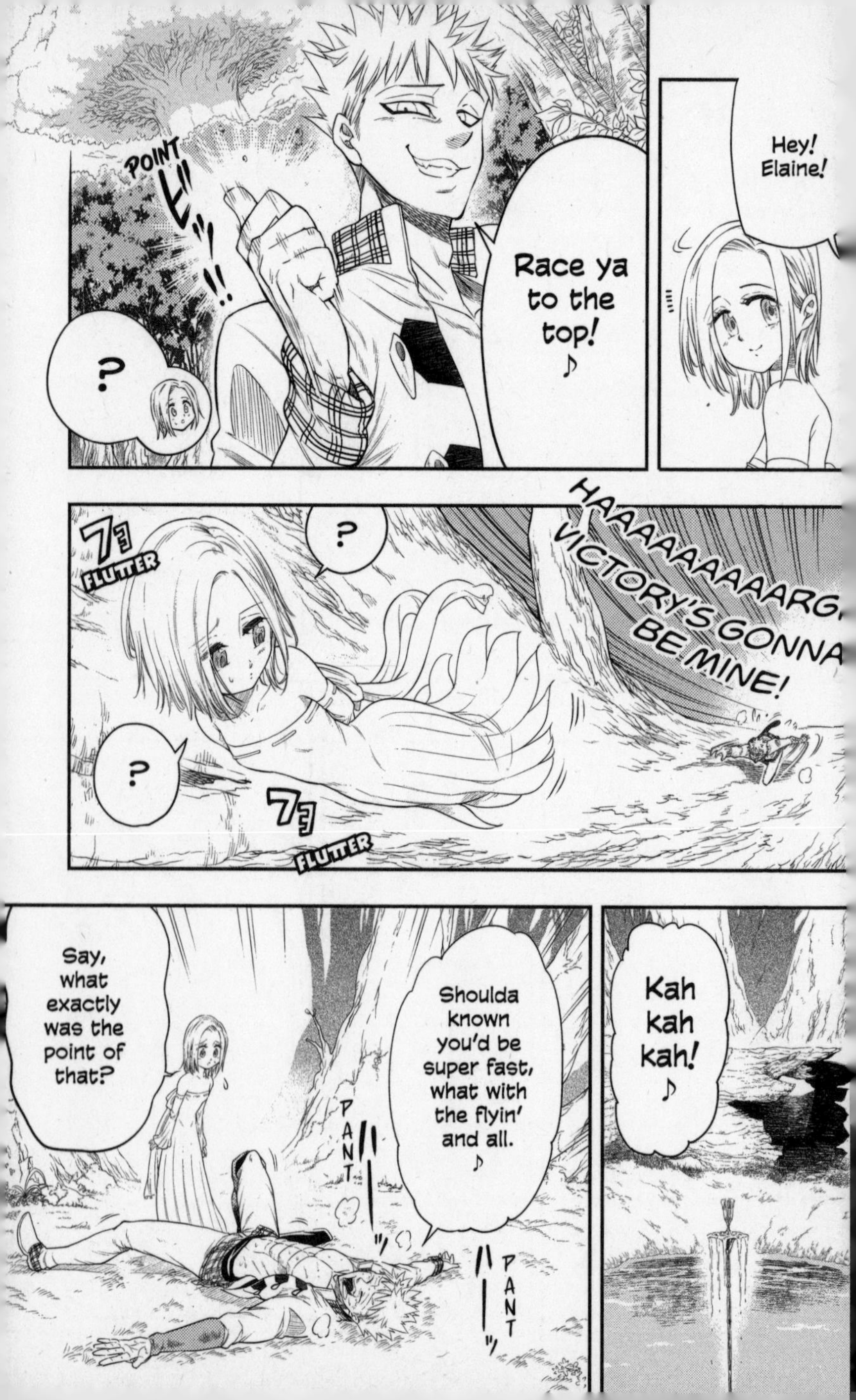
Hey! Elaine!
POINT
Race ya to the top! ♪
?
HAAAAAAAAAARG! VICTORY'S GONNA BE MINE!
?
FLUTTER
?
FLUTTER
Kah kah kah! ♪
PANT
Shoulda known you'd be super fast, what with the flyin' and all. ♪
PANT
Say, what exactly was the point of that?

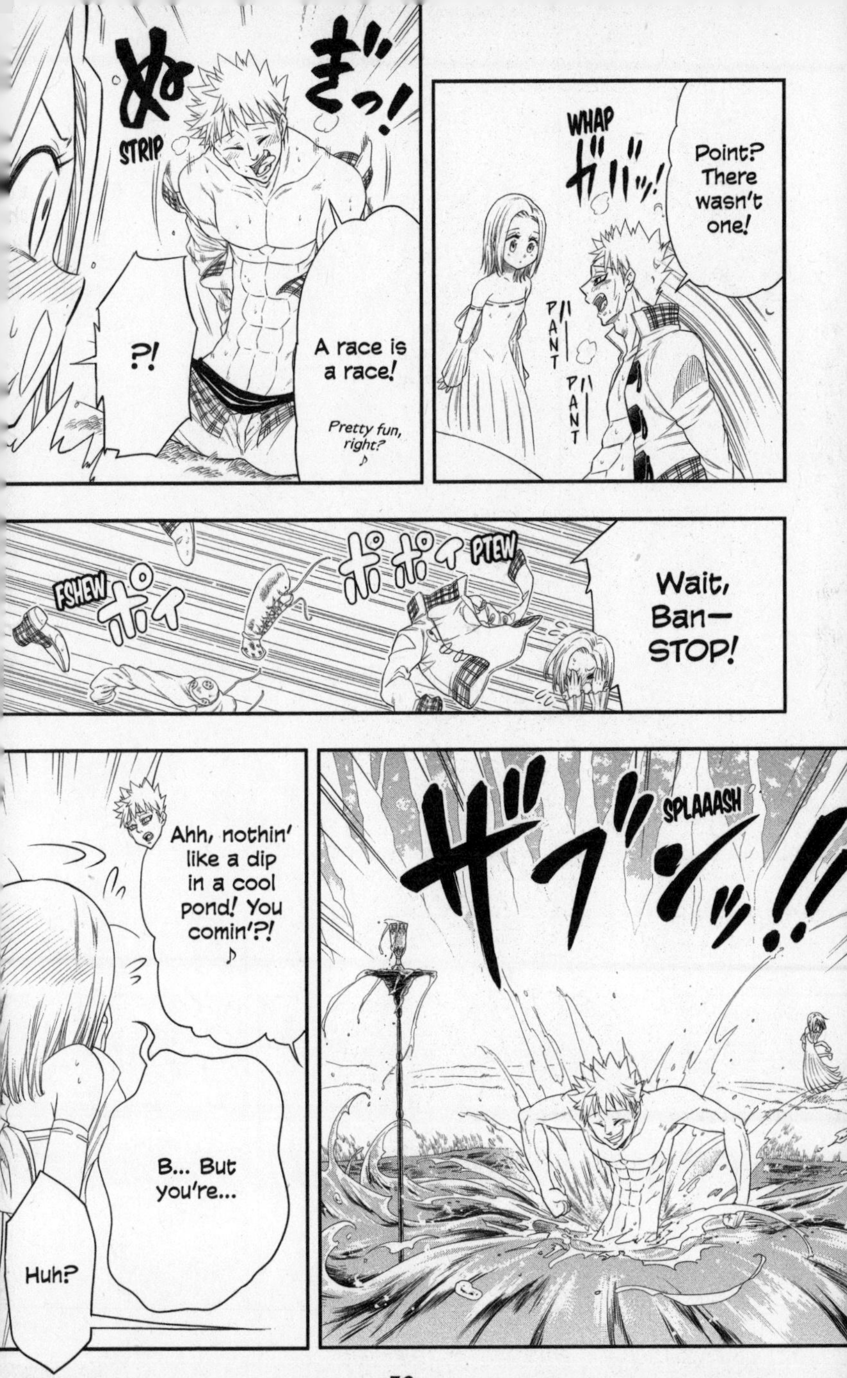
Point? There wasn't one!
WHAP
ガッ!
PANT PANT
ぬぎっ!
STRIP
A race is a race!
Pretty fun, right? ♪
?!
Wait, Ban—STOP!
PTEW
ポポイ
FSHEW
ポイ
SPLAAASH
ザブンッ!!
Ahh, nothin' like a dip in a cool pond! You comin'?! ♪
B... But you're...
Huh?

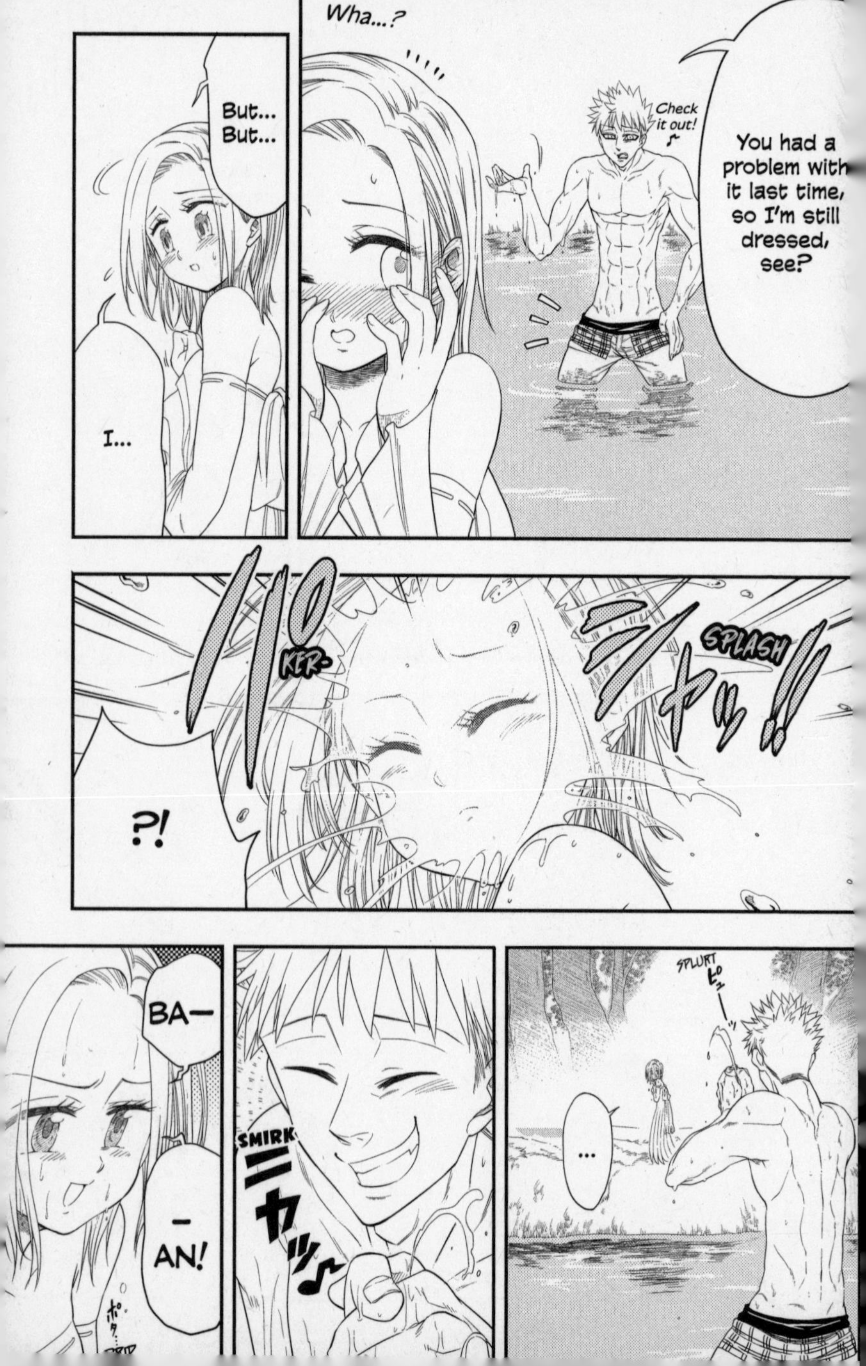

You had a problem with it last time, so I'm still dressed, see?
Check it out! ♪
Wha...?
But... But...
I...
SPLASH
KER-
?!
SPLURT
...
SMIRK
BA—
–AN!

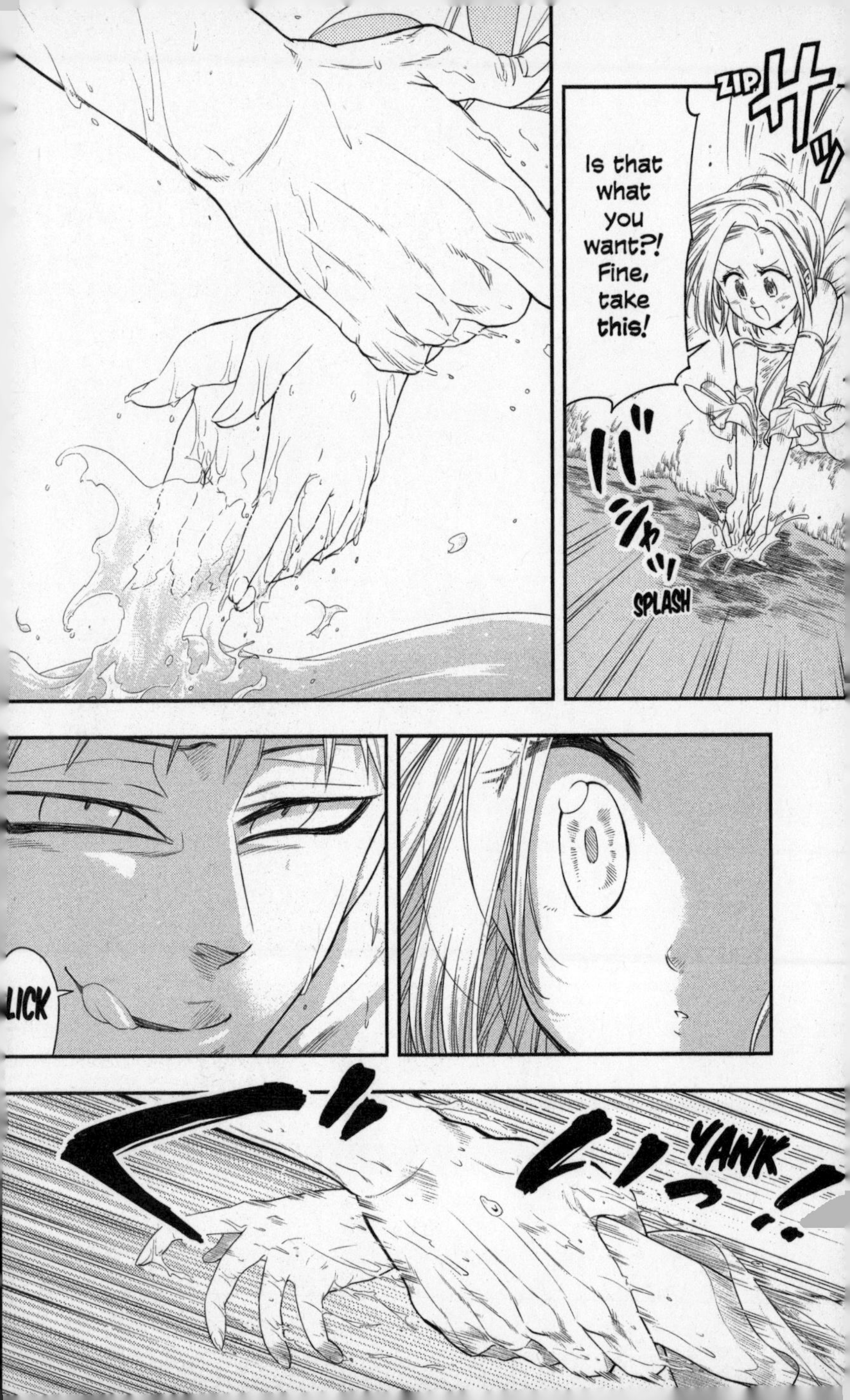
ZIP
Is that what you want?! Fine, take this!
SPLASH
LICK
YANK

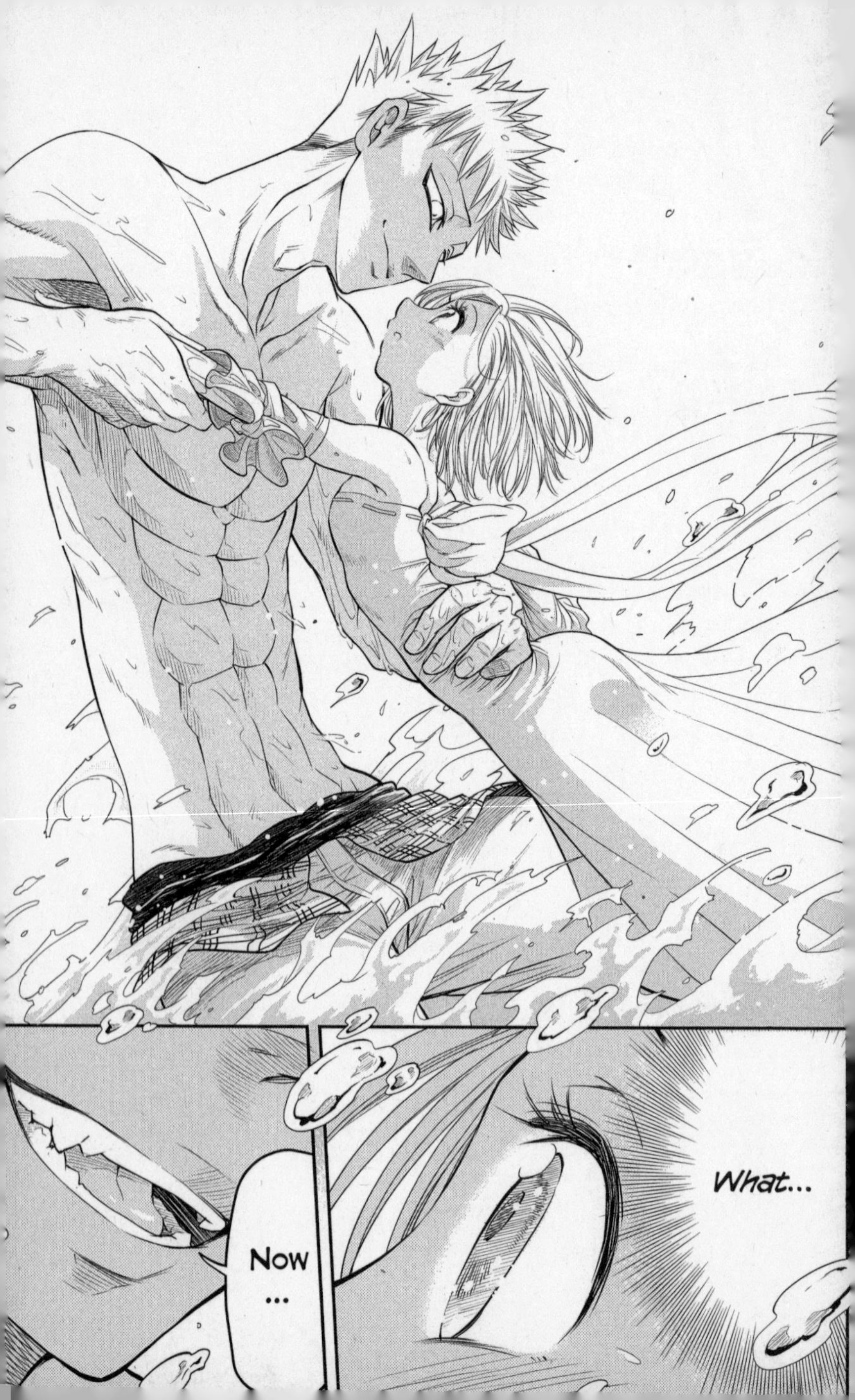
What...
Now ...

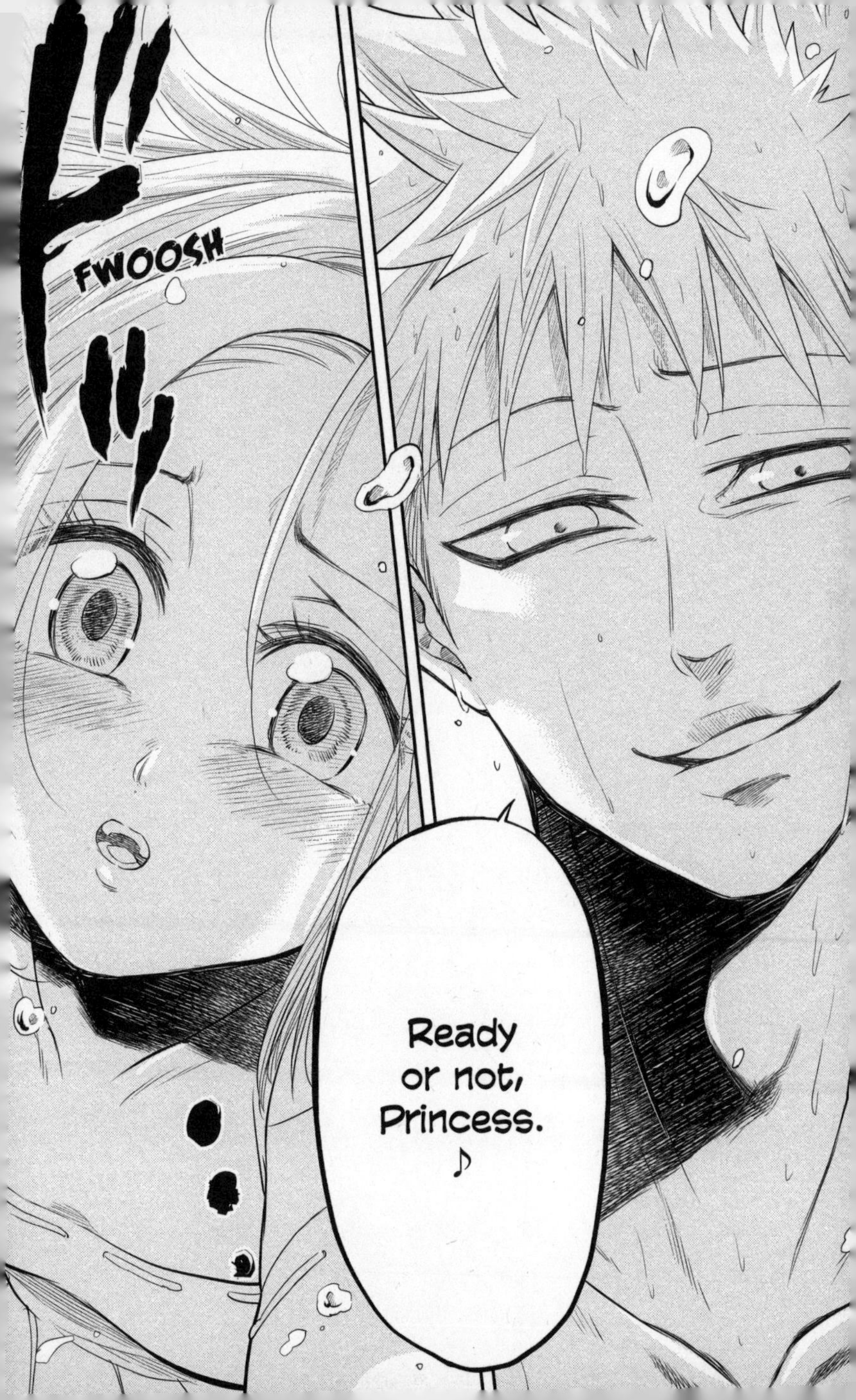
FWOOSH
Ready or not, Princess. ♪

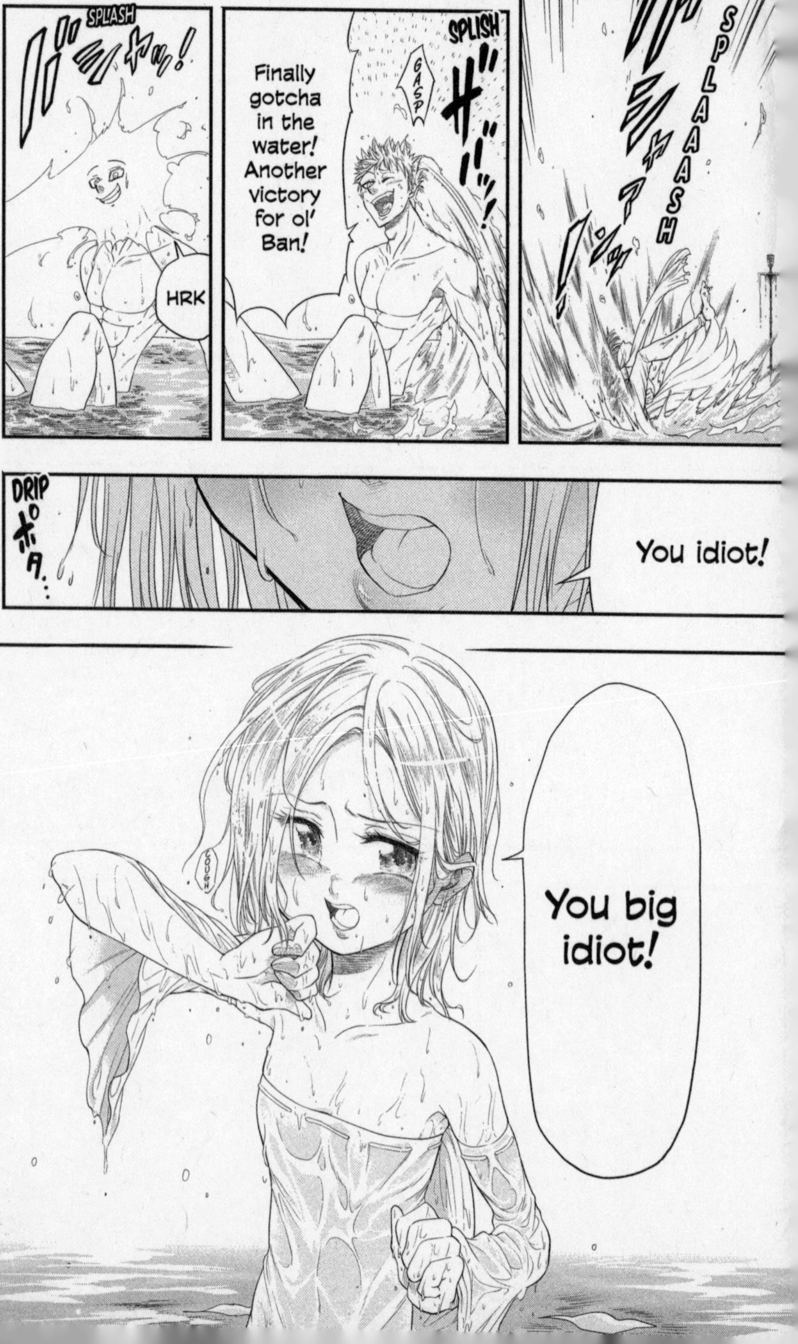
SPLAAAASH
SPLISH
GASP
Finally gotcha in the water! Another victory for ol' Ban!
SPLASH
HRK
You idiot!
DRIP
COUGH
You big idiot!

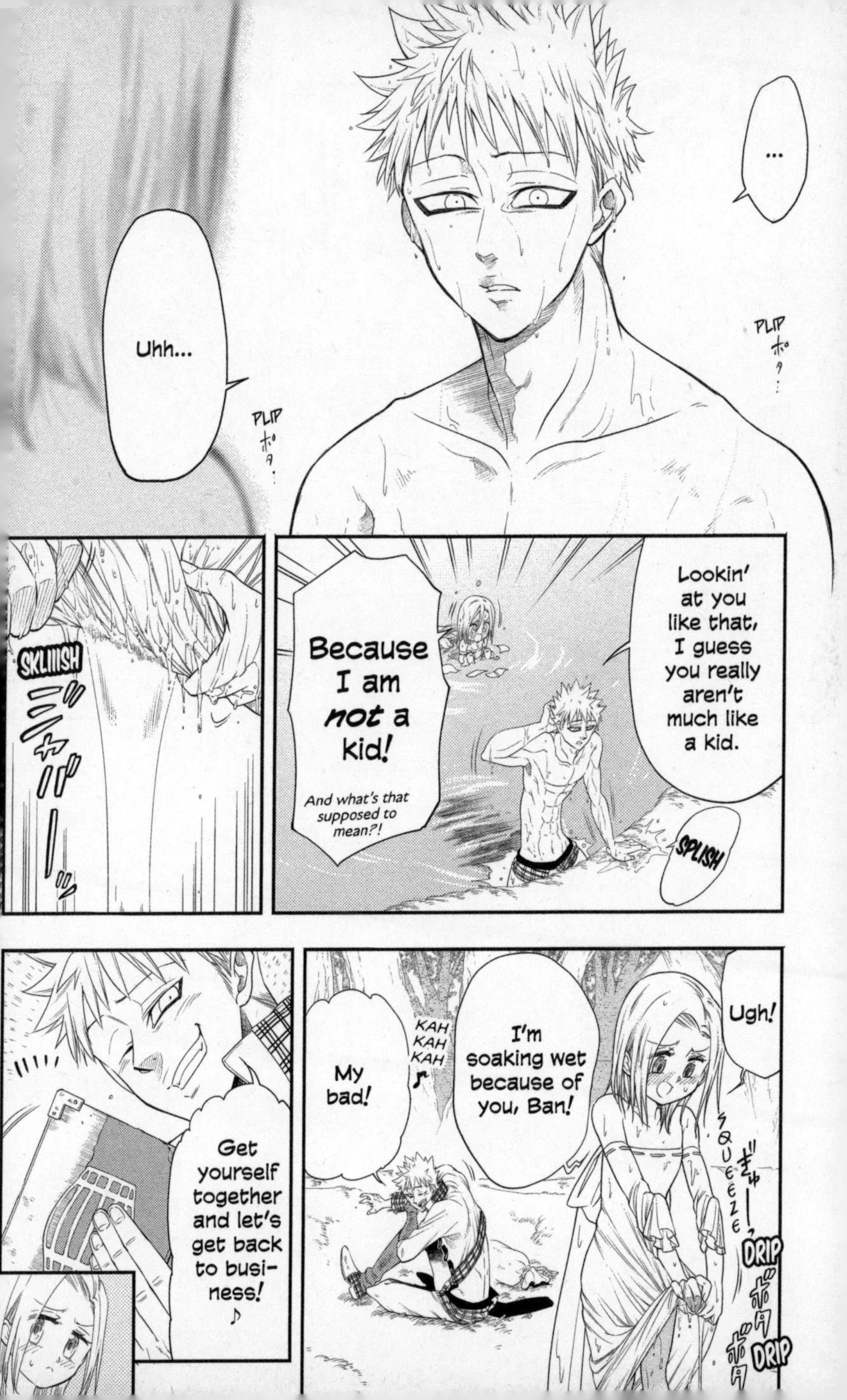
...
PLIP
Uhh...
PLIP
Lookin' at you like that, I guess you really aren't much like a kid.
SPLISH
Because I am *not* a kid!
And what's that supposed to mean?!
SKLIIISH
Ugh!
I'm soaking wet because of you, Ban!
KAH KAH KAH ♪
My bad!
SQUEEZE
DRIP
DRIP
Get yourself together and let's get back to business! ♪

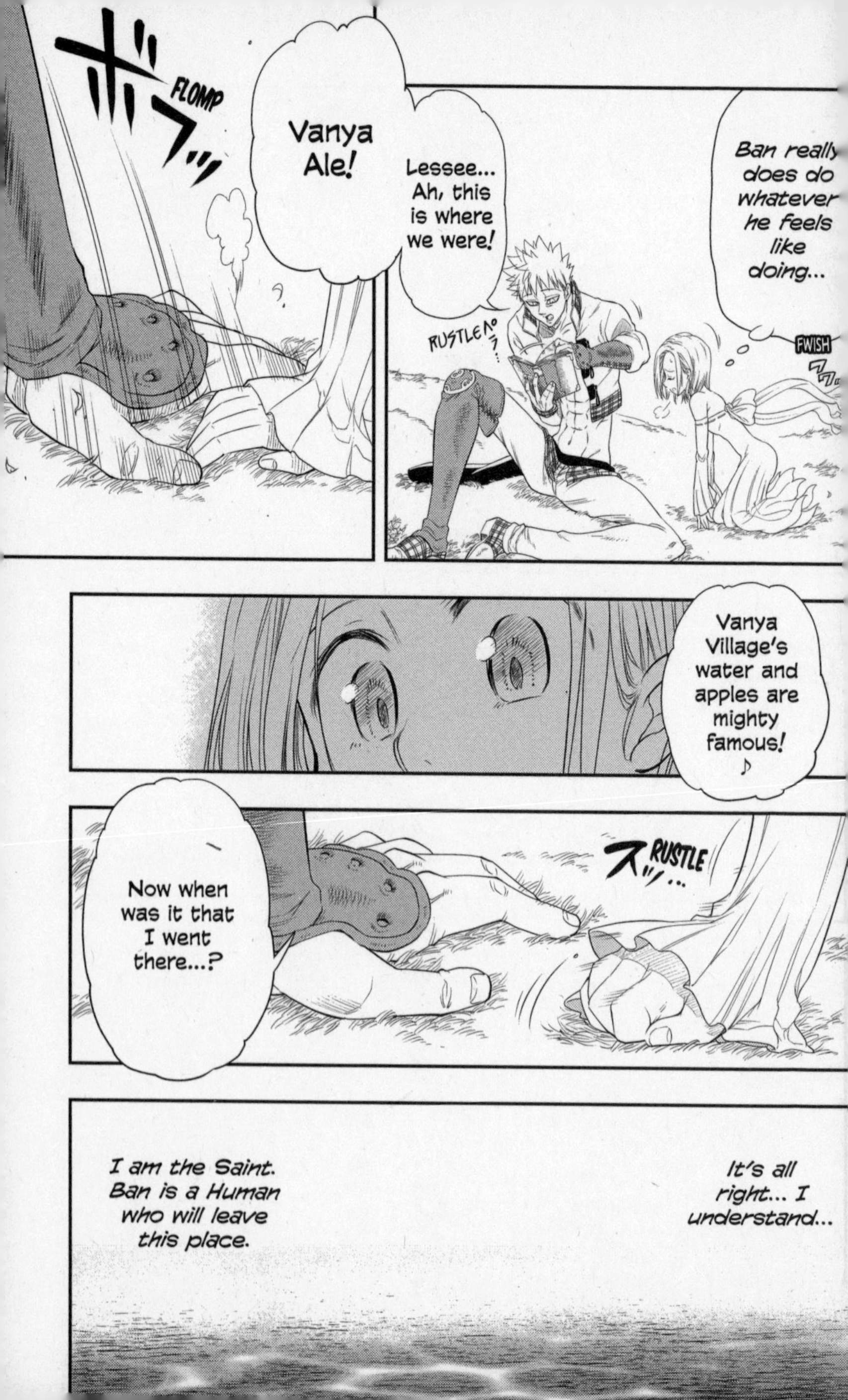
Ban really does do whatever he feels like doing...
FWISH
Lessee... Ah, this is where we were!
RUSTLE
Vanya Ale!
FLOMP
Vanya Village's water and apples are mighty famous! ♪
RUSTLE...
Now when was it that I went there...?
It's all right... I understand...
I am the Saint. Ban is a Human who will leave this place.

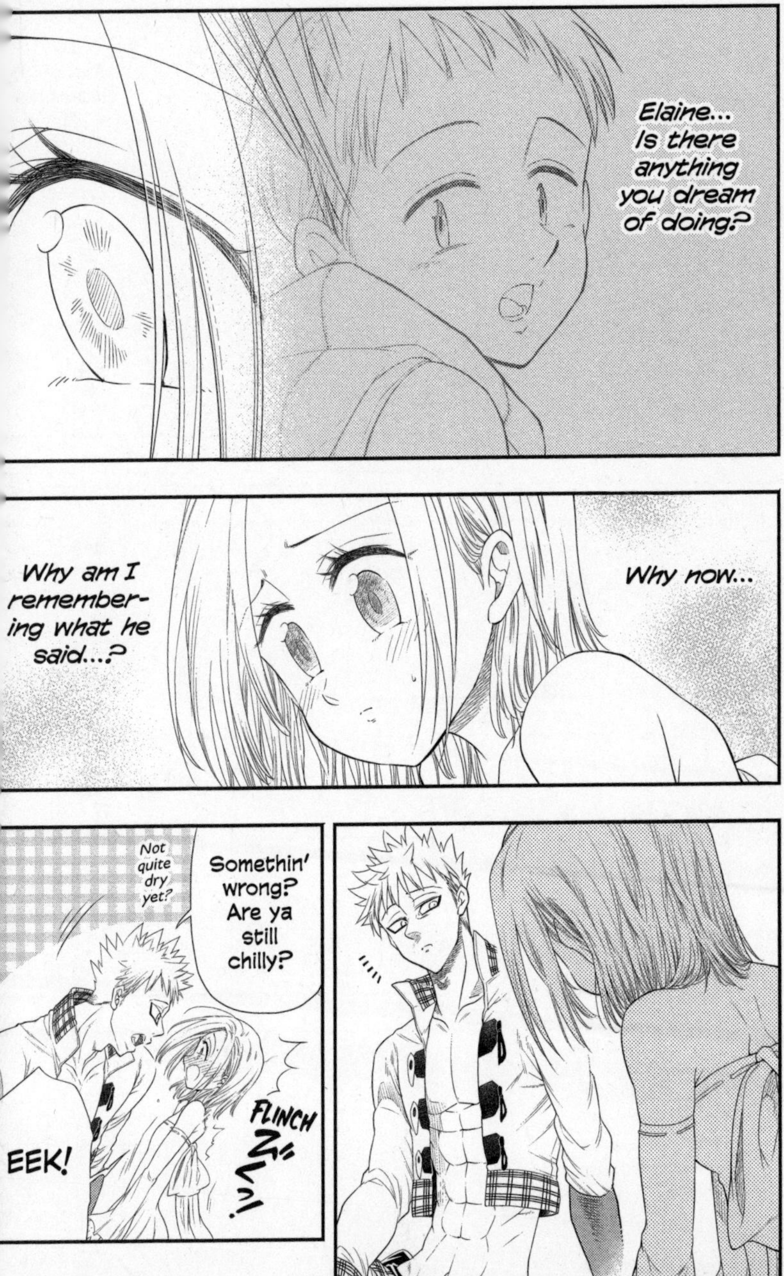
Elaine... Is there anything you dream of doing?
Why now...
Why am I remembering what he said...?
Somethin' wrong? Are ya still chilly?
Not quite dry yet?
FLINCH
EEK!

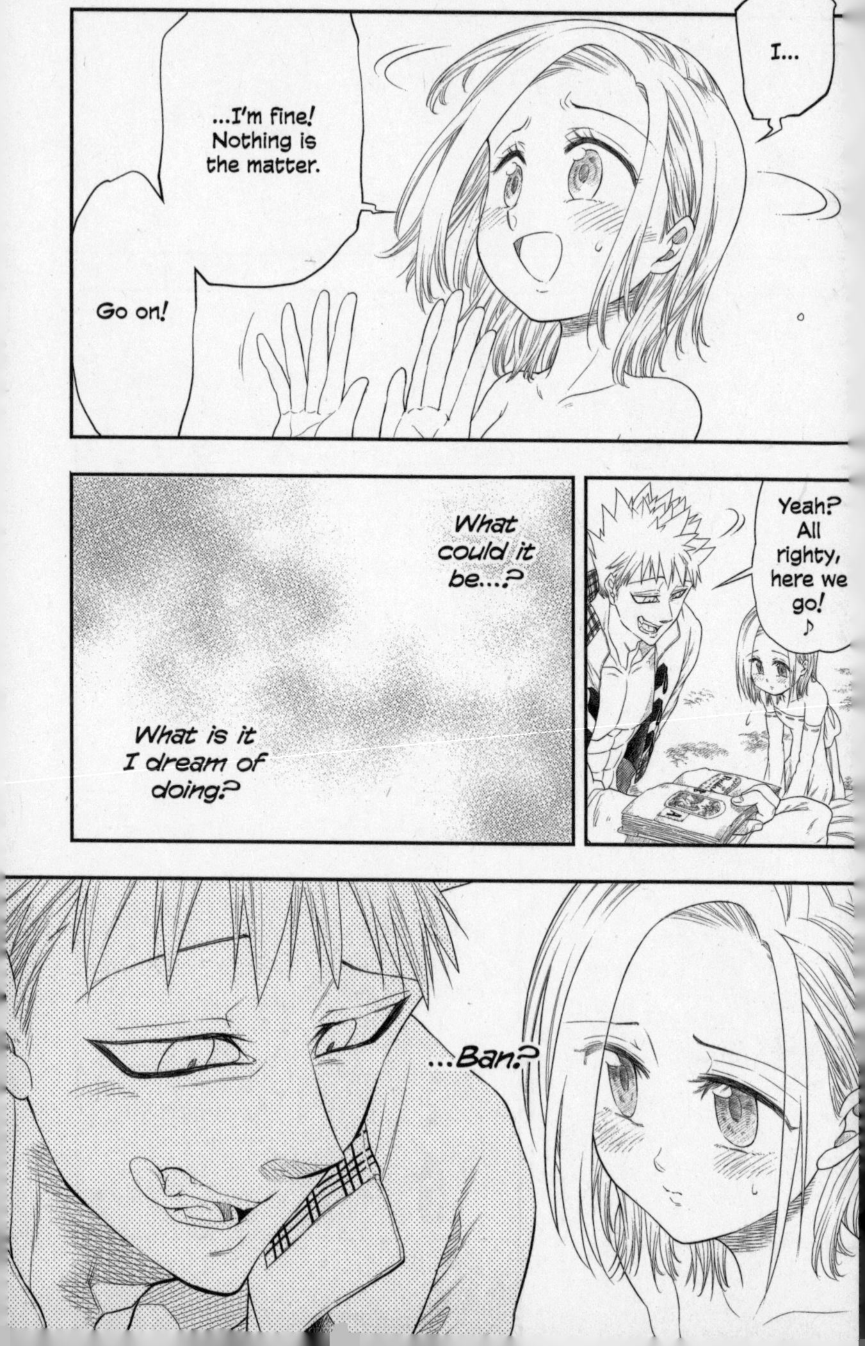
I...
...I'm fine! Nothing is the matter.
Go on!
Yeah? All righty, here we go! ♪
What could it be...?
What is it I dream of doing?
...Ban?

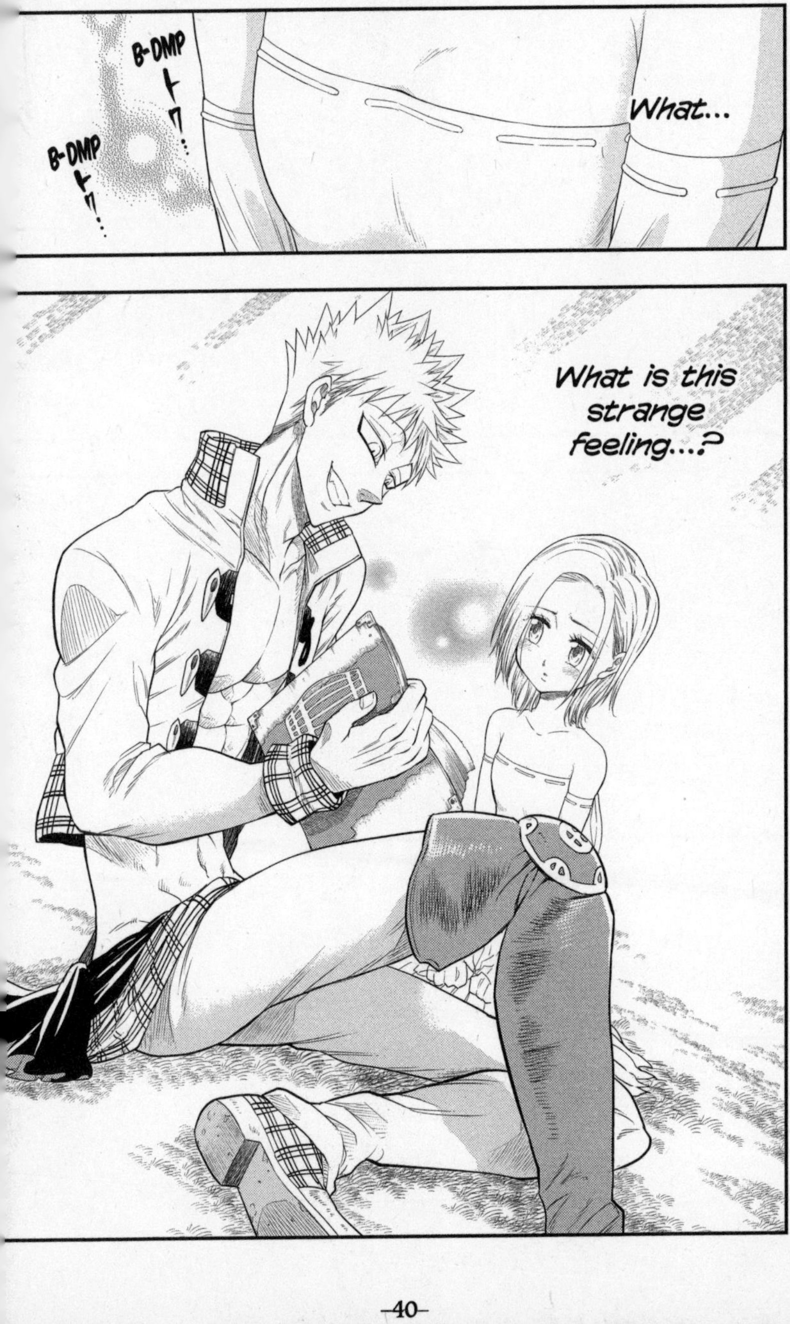
What...
B-DMP
B-DMP
What is this strange feeling...?

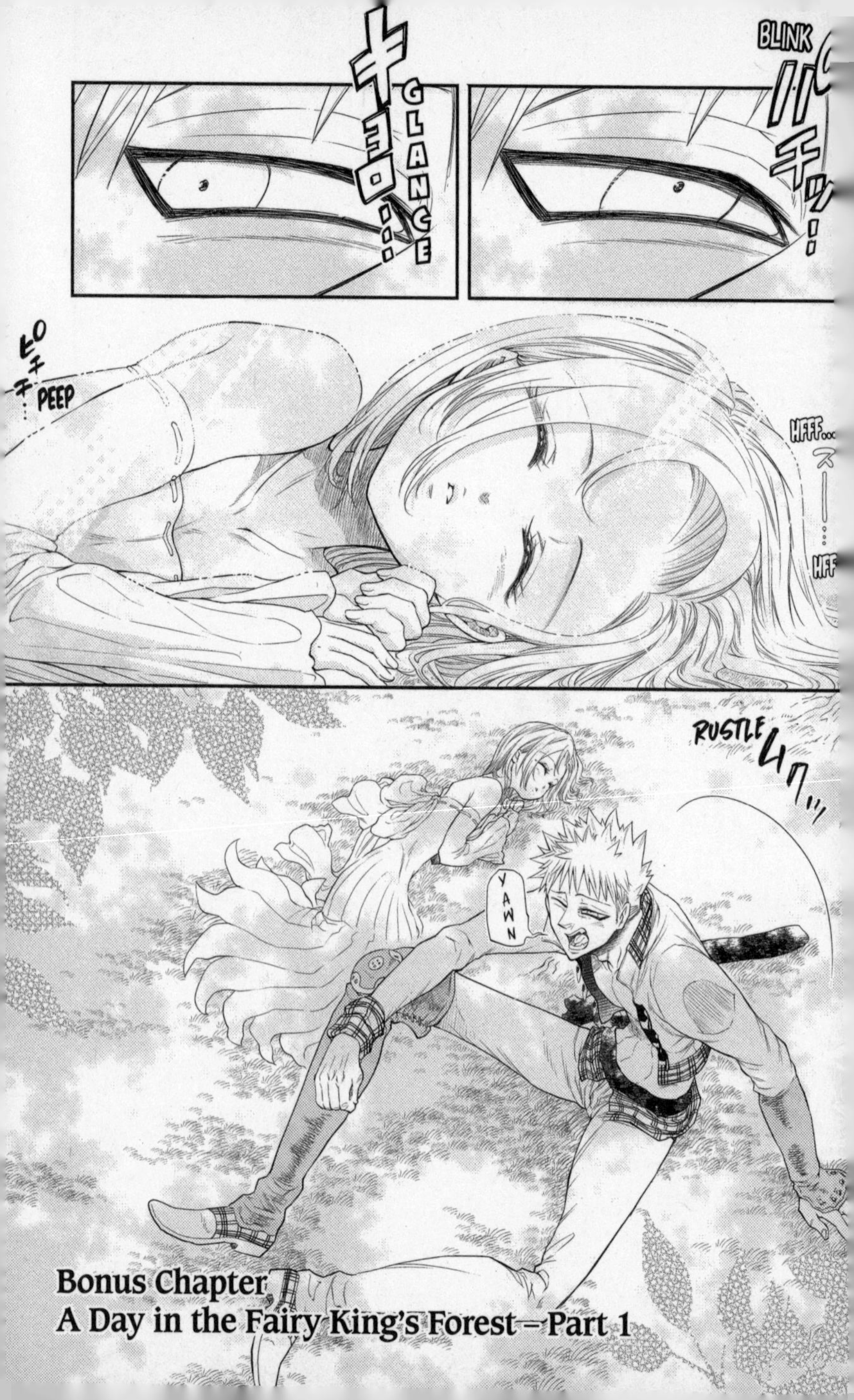
BLINK
パチッ!!
GLANCE
キョロ…
HFFF…
スー…
HFF
PEEP
ピチチ…
RUSTLE
ムクッ
YAWN

Bonus Chapter
A Day in the Fairy King's Forest—Part 1

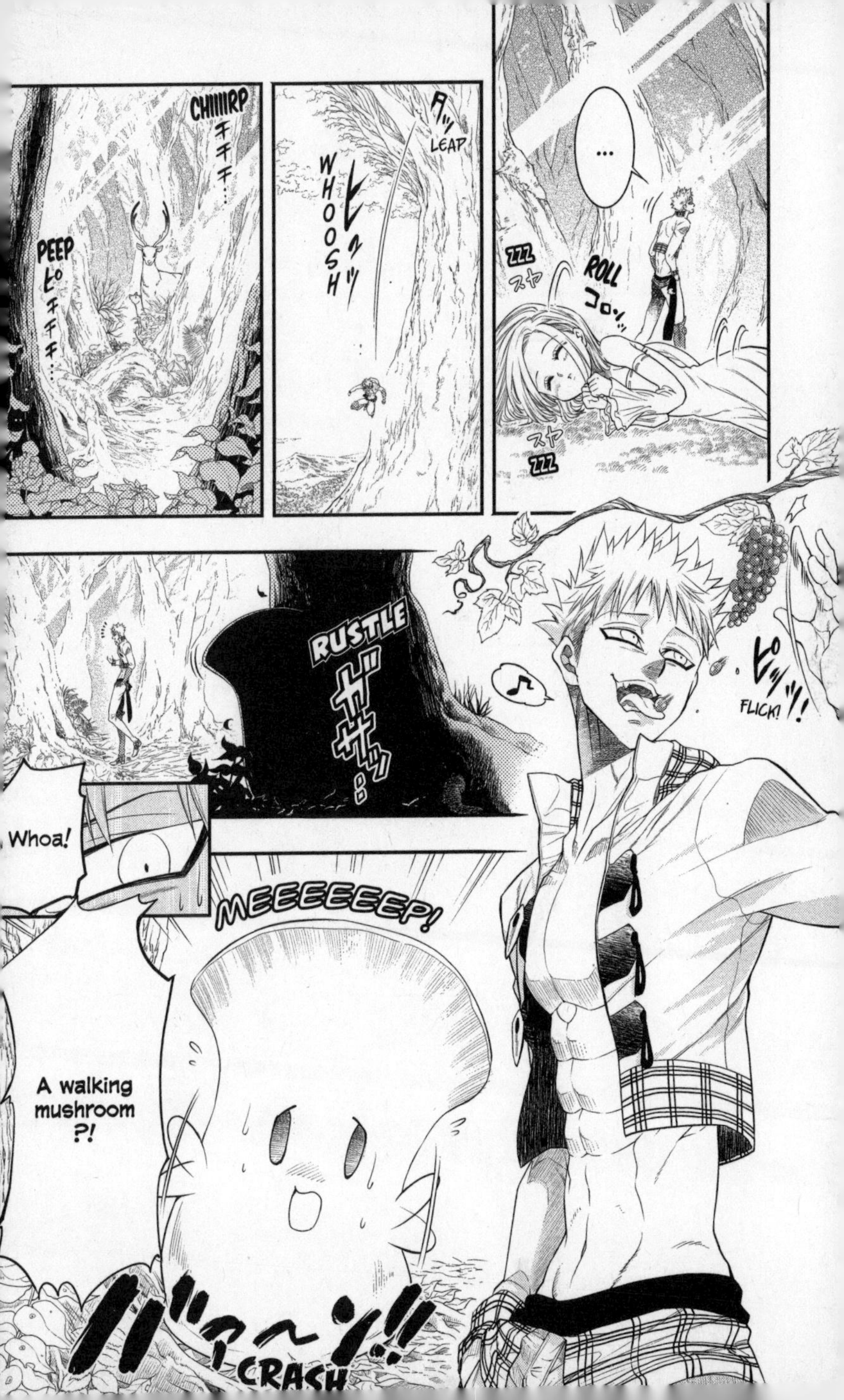

…
ZZZ
スヤ
ROLL
コロッ
スヤ
ZZZ
LEAP
WHOOSH
CHIIIIRP
チチチ…
PEEP
ピチチチ…
♪
FLICK!
RUSTLE
Whoa!
MEEEEEEEP!
A walking mushroom?!
CRASH

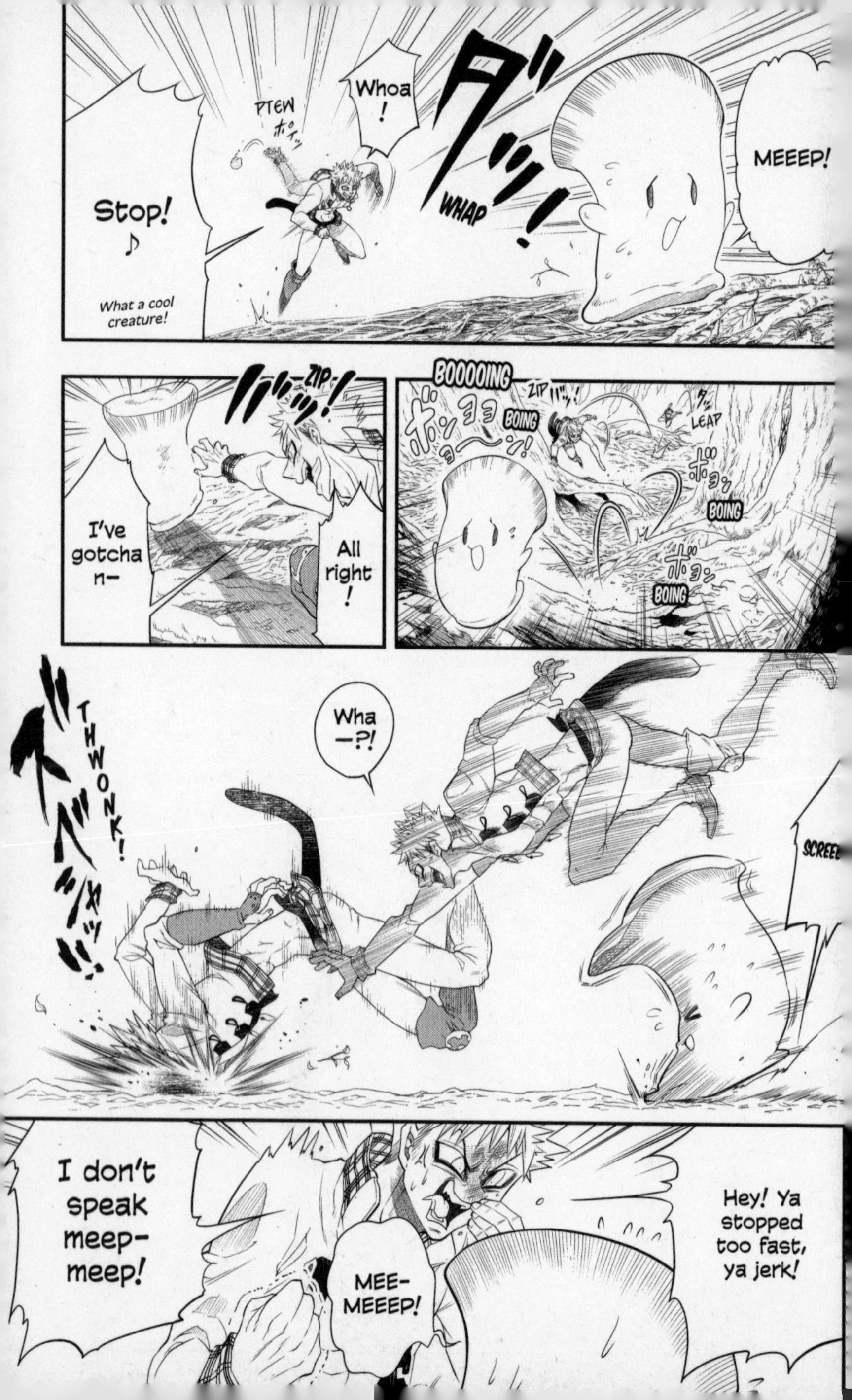
MEEEP!
WHAP
Whoa!
PTEW
Stop! ♪
What a cool creature!
BOOOOING
ZIP
LEAP
BOING
BOING
BOING
ZIP
All right!
I've gotcha n–
SCREE
Wha–?!
THWONK!
Hey! Ya stopped too fast, ya jerk!
MEE-MEEEP!
I don't speak meep-meep!

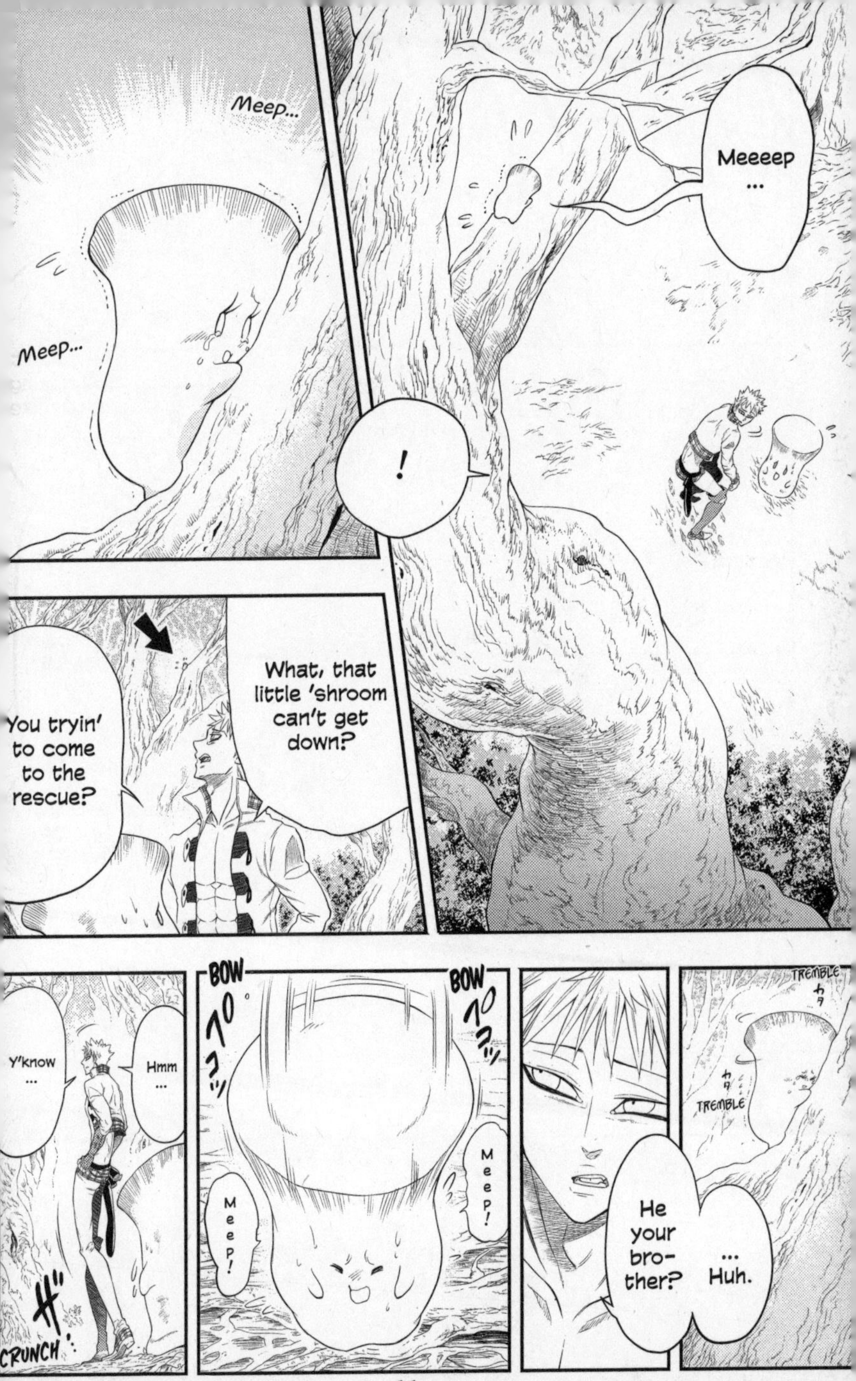
Meeeep ...
!
Meep...
Meep...
What, that little 'shroom can't get down?
You tryin' to come to the rescue?
TREMBLE
TREMBLE
... Huh.
He your bro-ther?
BOW
BOW
Meep!
Meep!
Hmm ...
Y'know ...
CRUNCH

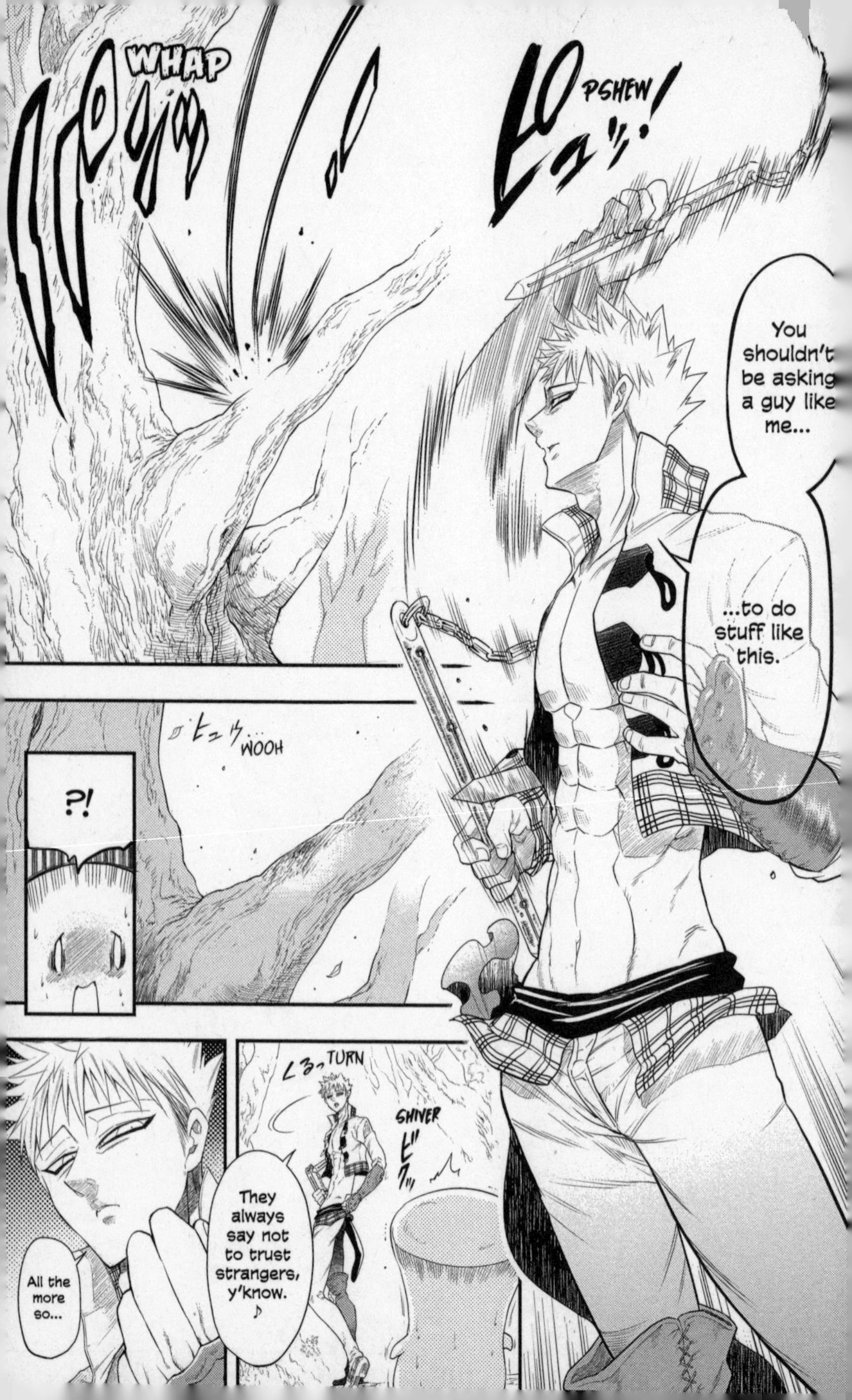
PSHEW!
WHAP
You shouldn't be asking a guy like me...
...to do stuff like this.
WOOH
?!
TURN
SHIVER
They always say not to trust strangers, y'know. ♪
All the more so...

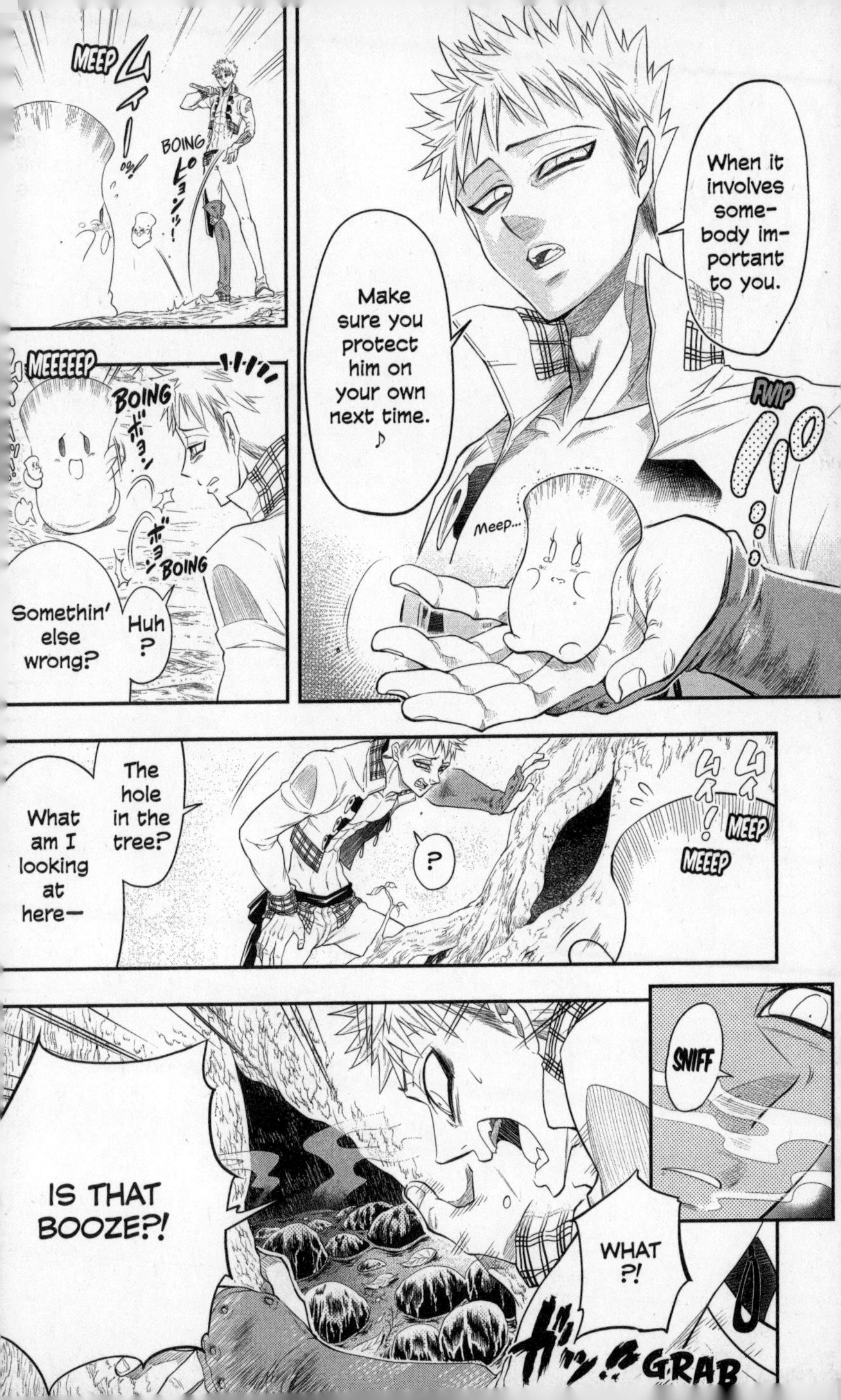
When it involves some-body im-portant to you.
Make sure you protect him on your own next time. ♪
FWIP
Meep...
MEEP
BOING
MEEEEEP
BOING
BOING
Huh?
Somethin' else wrong?
MEEP
MEEEP
?
The hole in the tree?
What am I looking at here—
SNIFF
WHAT?!
GRAB
IS THAT BOOZE?!

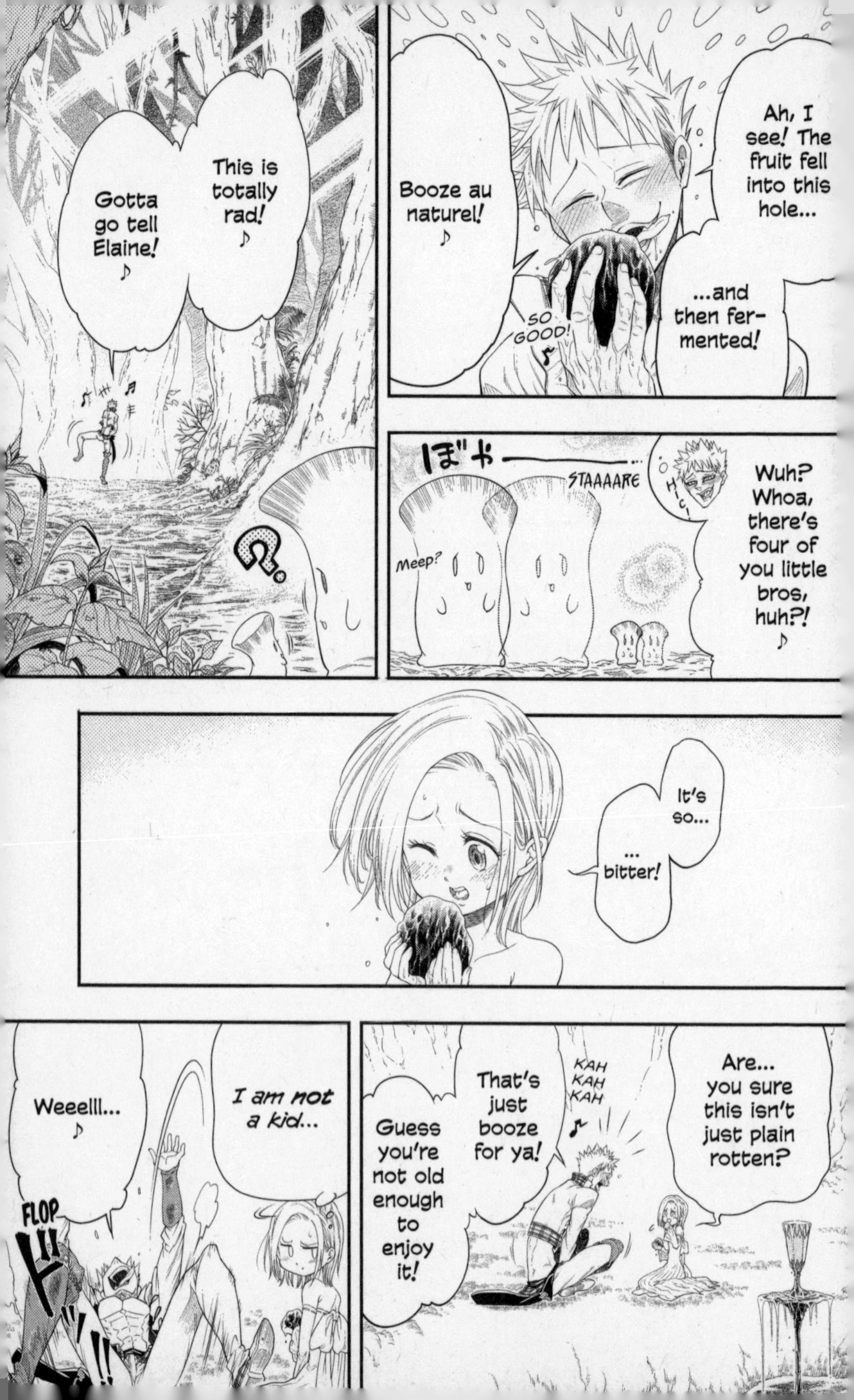
Ah, I see! The fruit fell into this hole...
...and then fermented!
SO GOOD! ♪
Booze au naturel! ♪
Wuh? Whoa, there's four of you little bros, huh?! ♪
HIC
STAAAARE
Meep?
This is totally rad! ♪
Gotta go tell Elaine! ♪
It's so...
...bitter!
Are... you sure this isn't just plain rotten?
KAH KAH KAH ♪
That's just booze for ya!
Guess you're not old enough to enjoy it!
I am *not* a kid...
Weeelll... ♪
FLOP

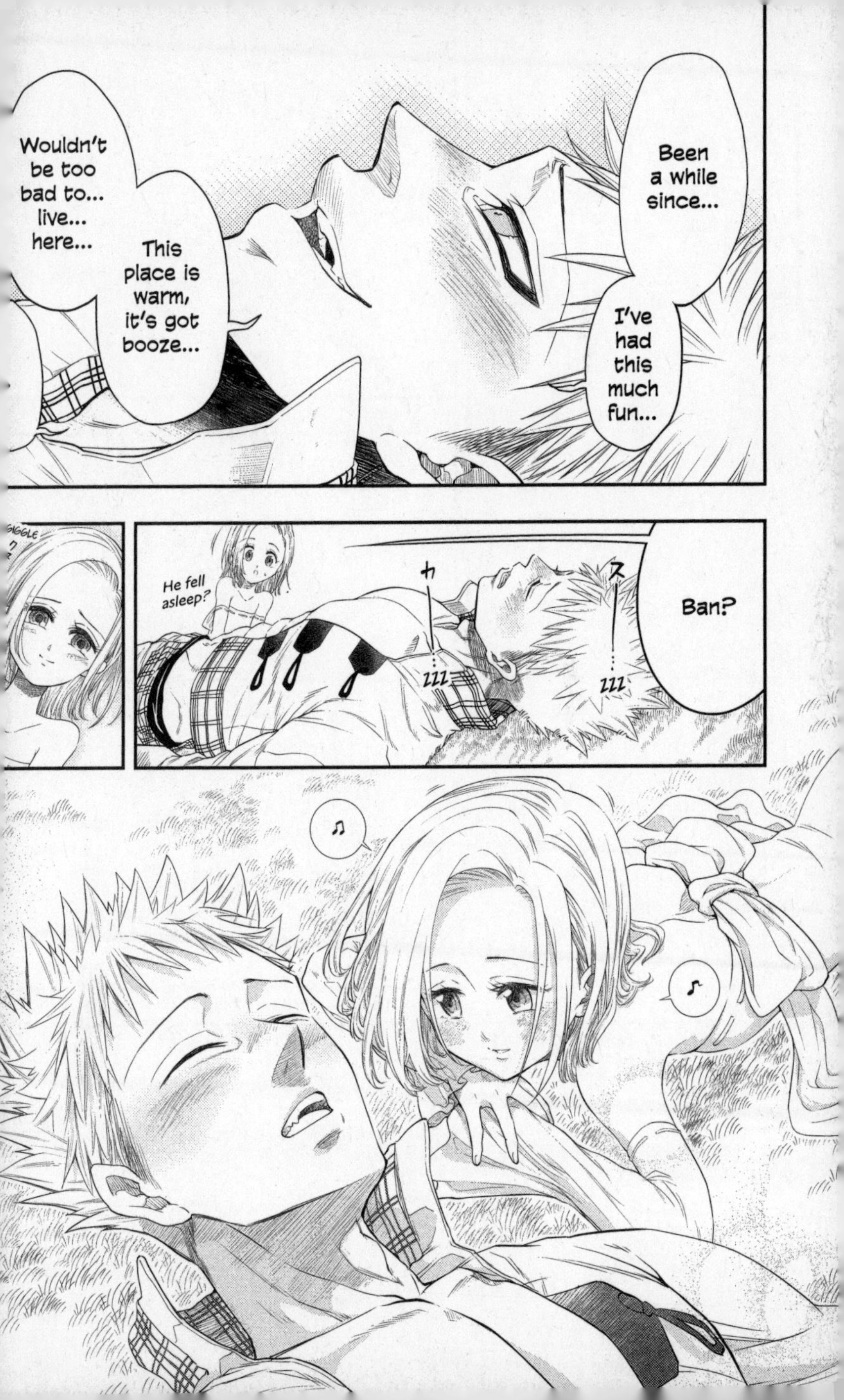
Been a while since...
I've had this much fun...
This place is warm, it's got booze...
Wouldn't be too bad to... live... here...
Ban?
ス
zzz
カ
zzz
He fell asleep?
GIGGLE
♪
♪

Chapter 5
Wings of Freedom

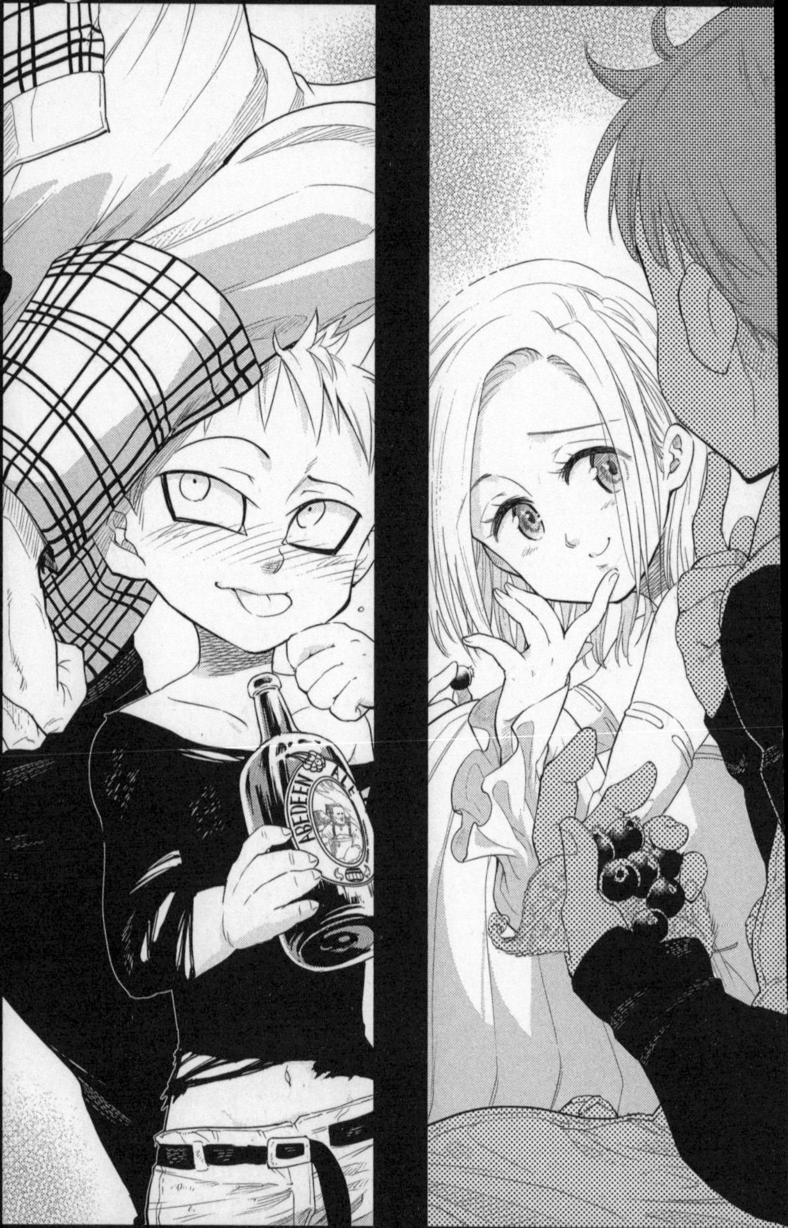

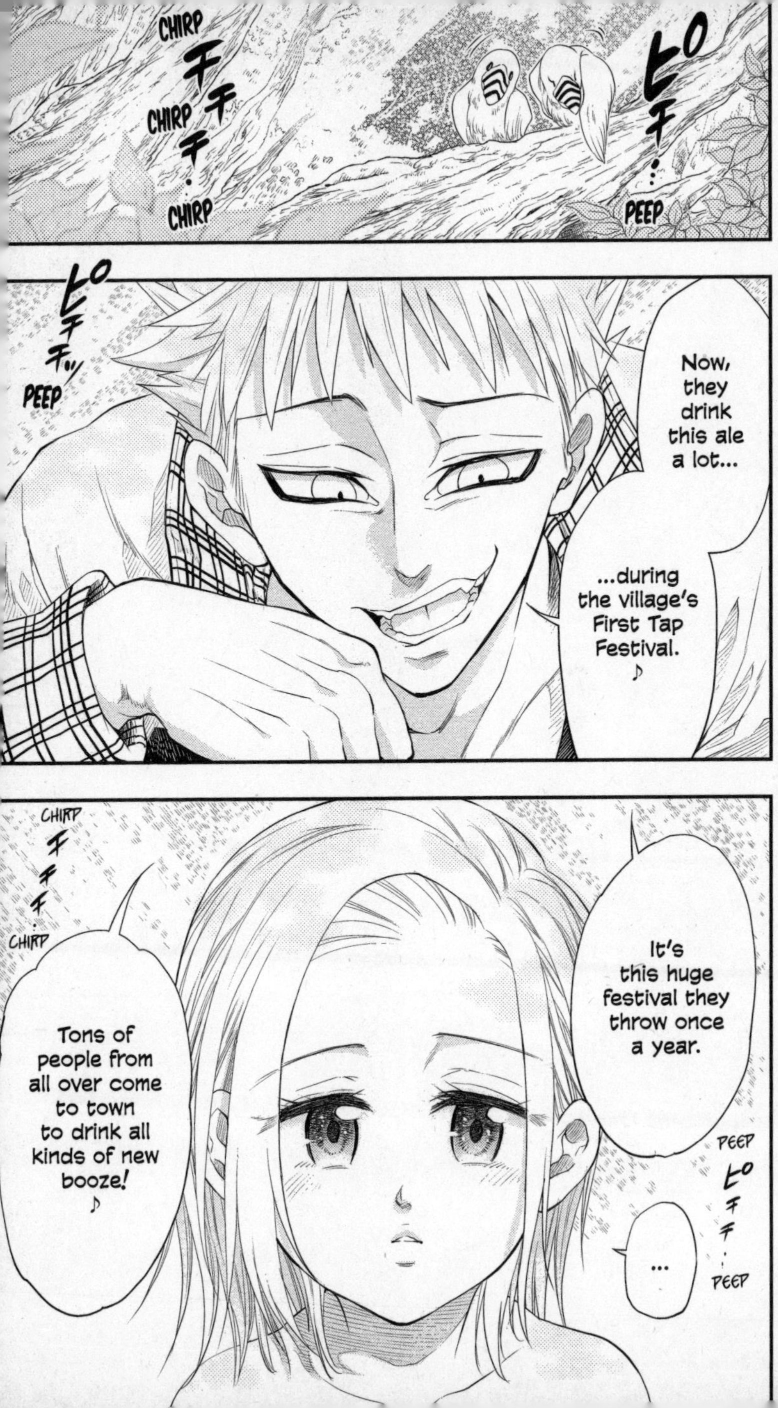
ピロチ…
PEEP
CHIRP
チチ
CHIRP
チ・
CHIRP
Now, they drink this ale a lot...
...during the village's First Tap Festival. ♪
ピロチチッ
PEEP
It's this huge festival they throw once a year.
PEEP
ピロチチ・
PEEP
...
Tons of people from all over come to town to drink all kinds of new booze! ♪
CHIRP
チチチ・
CHIRP

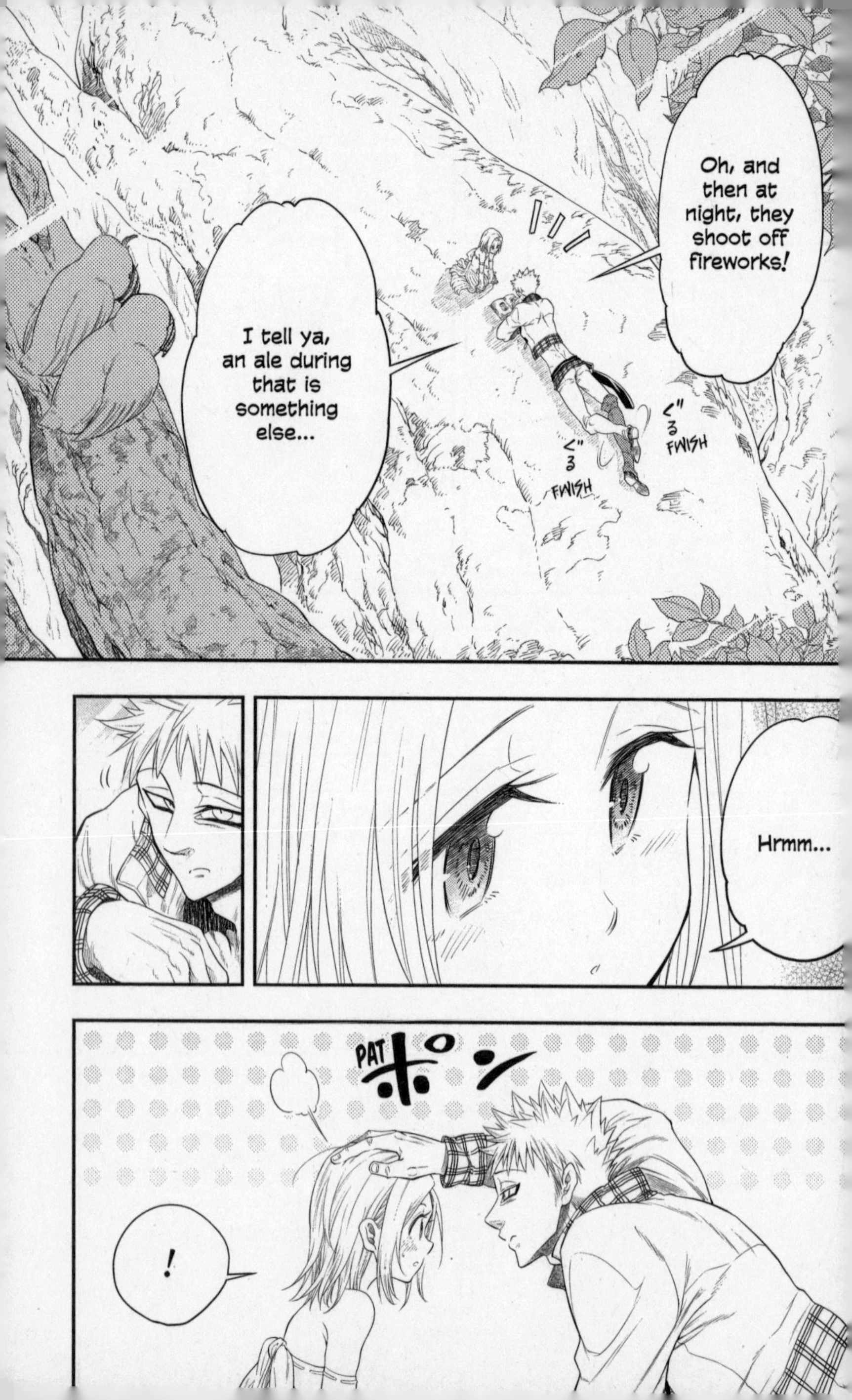
Oh, and then at night, they shoot off fireworks!
I tell ya, an ale during that is something else...
ぐる FWISH
ぐる FWISH
Hrmm...
PAT ポン
!

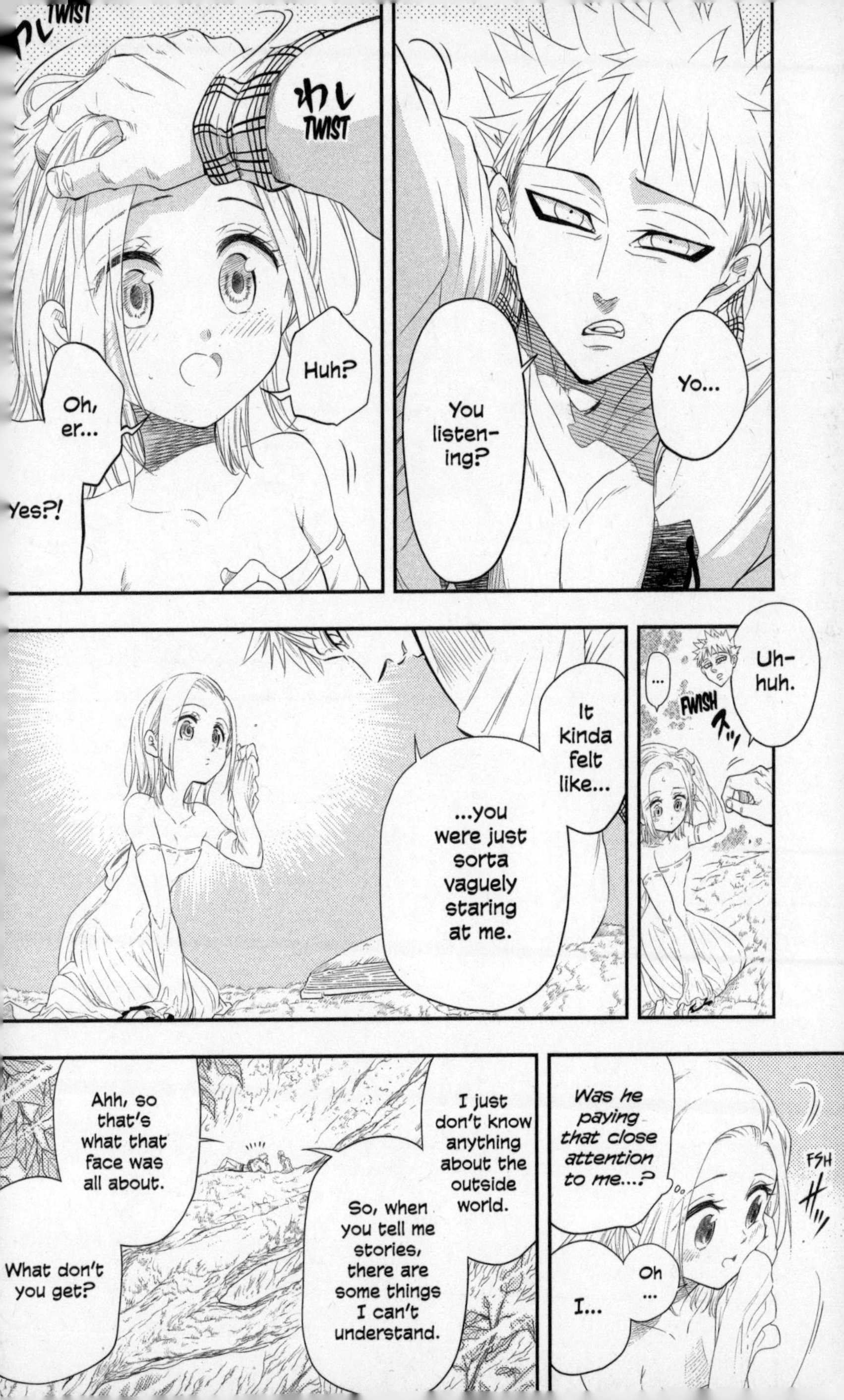
Yo...
You listening?
わし TWIST
TWIST
Huh?
Oh, er...
Yes?!
Uh-huh.
...
FWISH スッ
It kinda felt like...
...you were just sorta vaguely staring at me.
Was he paying that close attention to me...?
FSH
Oh...
I...
I just don't know anything about the outside world.
So, when you tell me stories, there are some things I can't understand.
Ahh, so that's what that face was all about.
What don't you get?

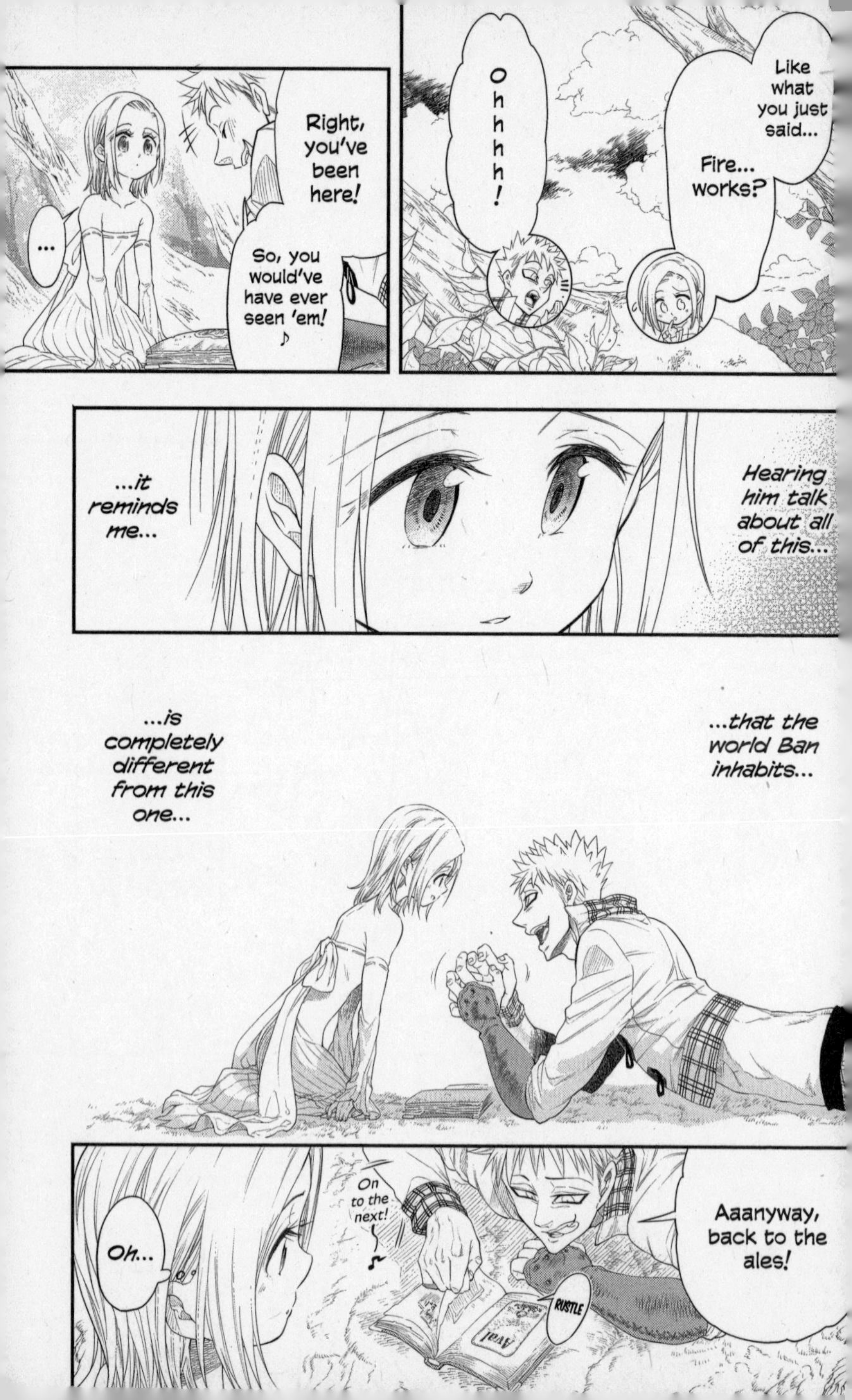
Like what you just said...
Fire... works?
Ohhhh!
Right, you've been here!
So, you would've have ever seen 'em! ♪
...
Hearing him talk about all of this...
...it reminds me...
...that the world Ban inhabits...
...is completely different from this one...
Aaanyway, back to the ales!
On to the next! ♪
RUSTLE
Oh...

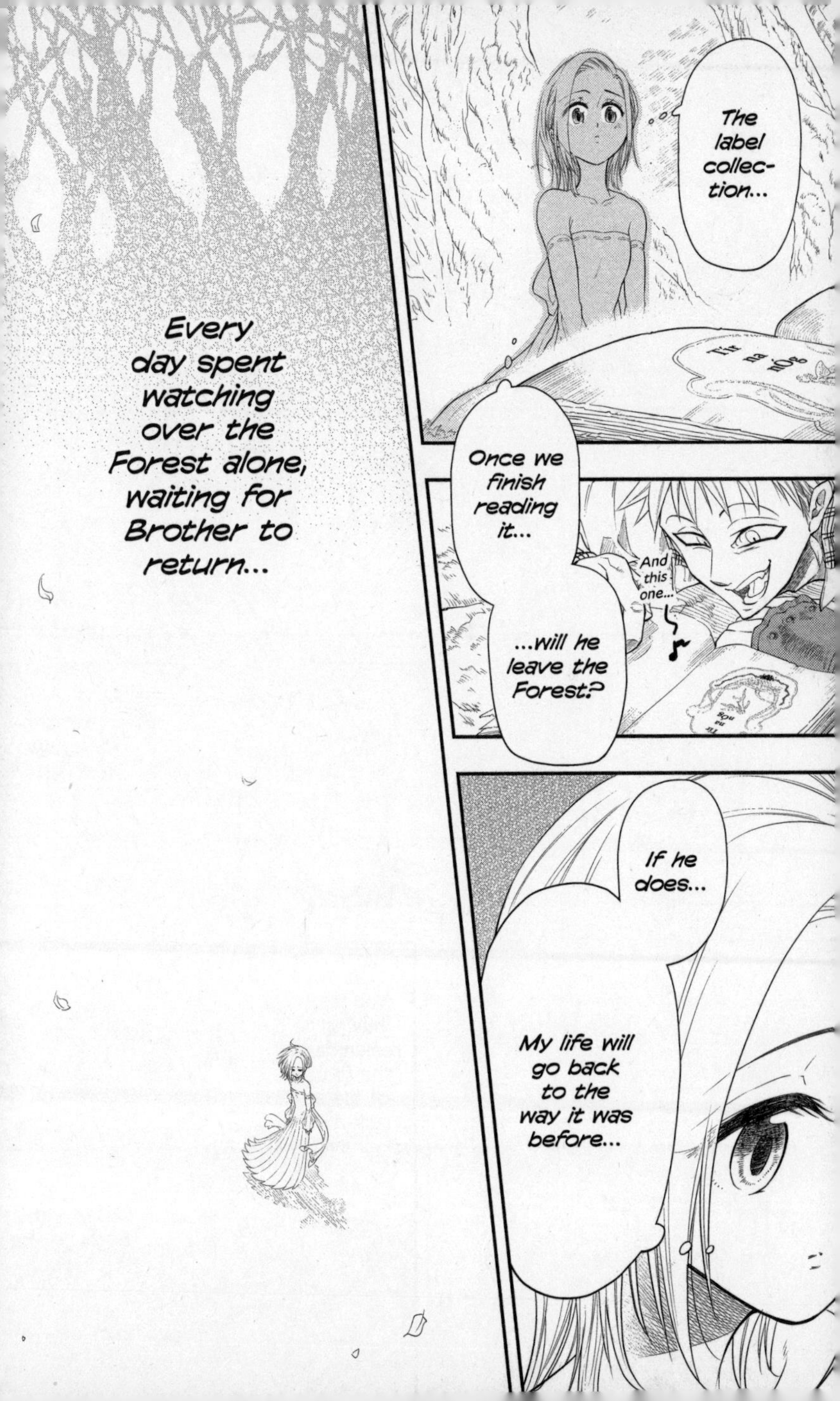

The label collec-tion...
Once we finish reading it...
...will he leave the Forest?
And this one...
If he does...
My life will go back to the way it was before...
Every day spent watching over the Forest alone, waiting for Brother to return...

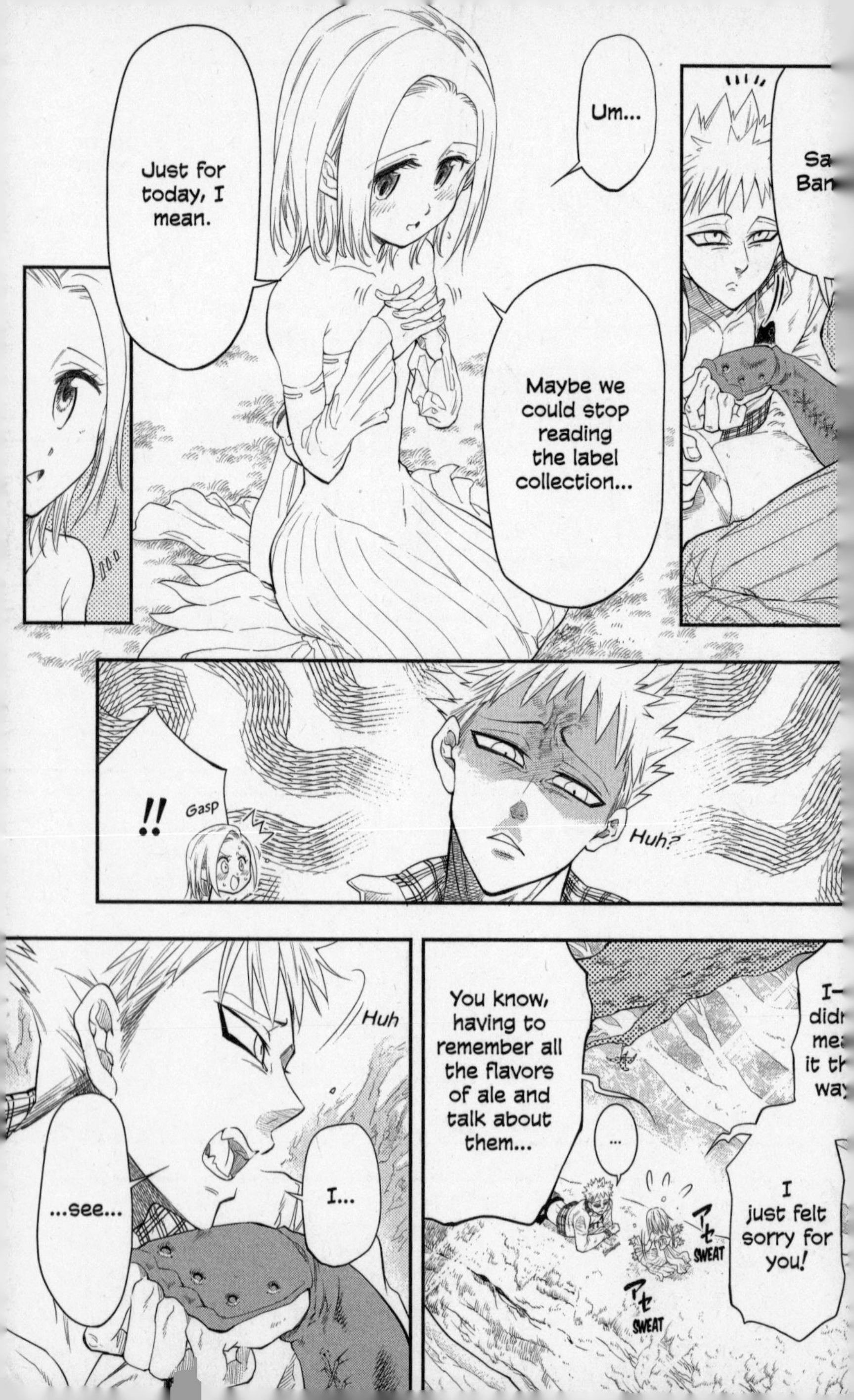
Sa Ban
Um...
Maybe we could stop reading the label collection...
Just for today, I mean.
Huh?
!! Gasp
I— didr mea it th way
I just felt sorry for you!
SWEAT
You know, having to remember all the flavors of ale and talk about them...
...
SWEAT
Huh
I...
...see...

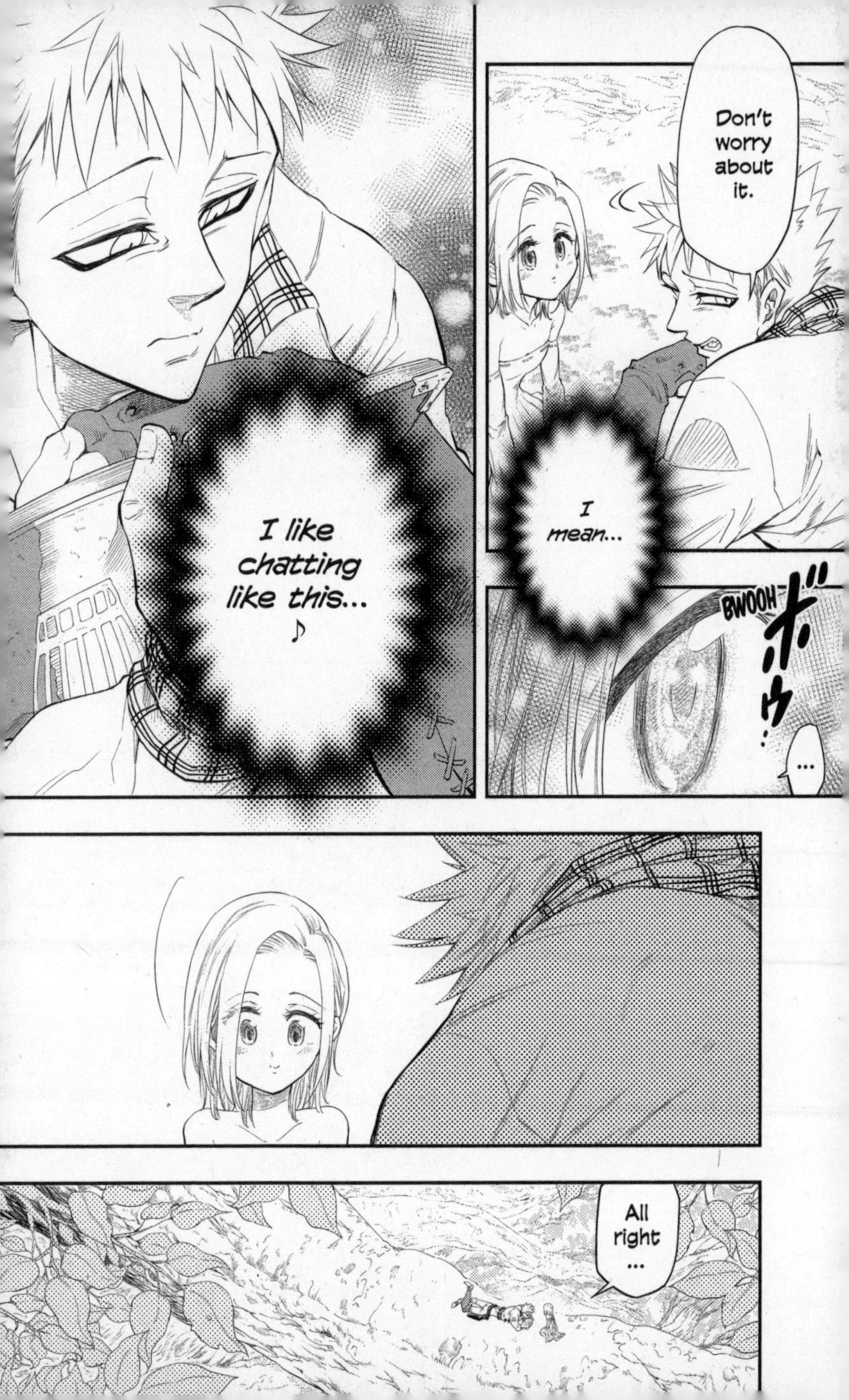
Don't worry about it.
I mean...
BWOOH
...
I like chatting like this... ♪
All right ...

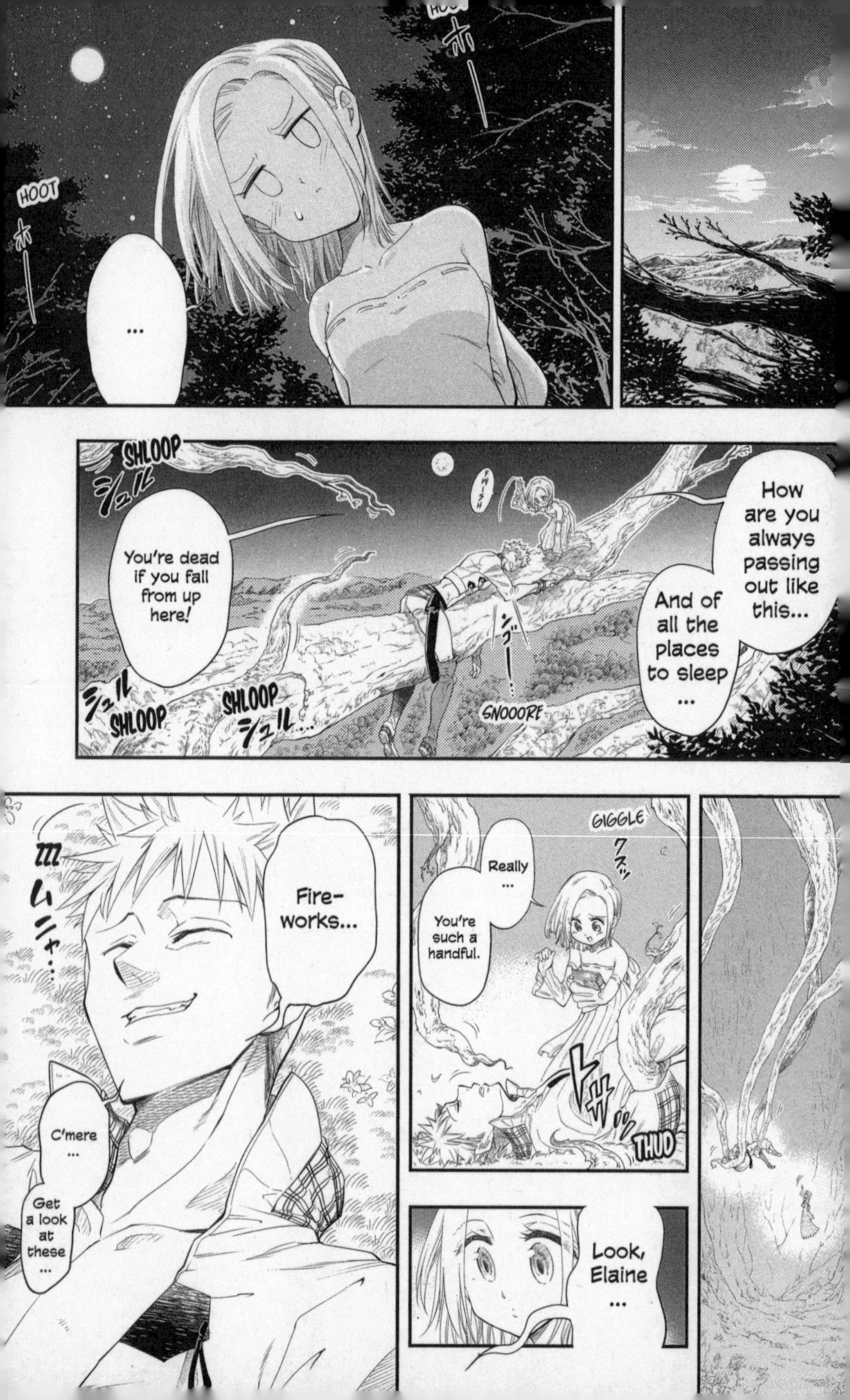
HOOT
ホー
HOOT
ホー
...
How are you always passing out like this...
And of all the places to sleep ...
FWISH
SNOOORE
You're dead if you fall from up here!
SHLOOP
シュル
SHLOOP
シュル
SHLOOP
シュル...
GIGGLE
クスッ
Really ...
You're such a handful.
THUD
Look, Elaine ...
Fire-works...
zzz
ムニャ...
C'mere ...
Get a look at these ...

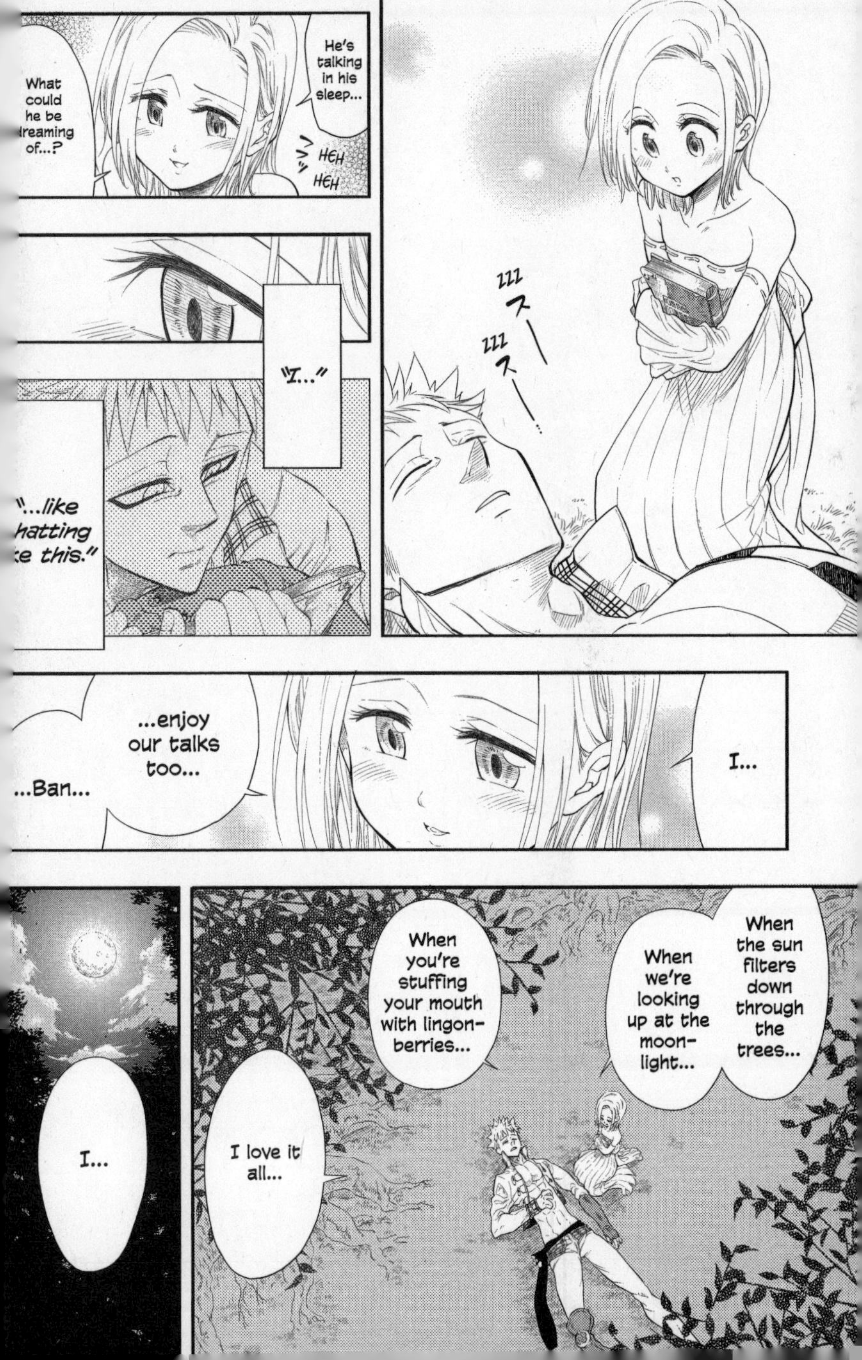

ZZZ
ス—
ZZZ
ス—
He's talking in his sleep...
What could he be dreaming of...?
HEH HEH
"I..."
"...like
hatting
e this."
I...
...enjoy our talks too...
...Ban...
When the sun filters down through the trees...
When we're looking up at the moon-light...
When you're stuffing your mouth with lingon-berries...
I love it all...
I...

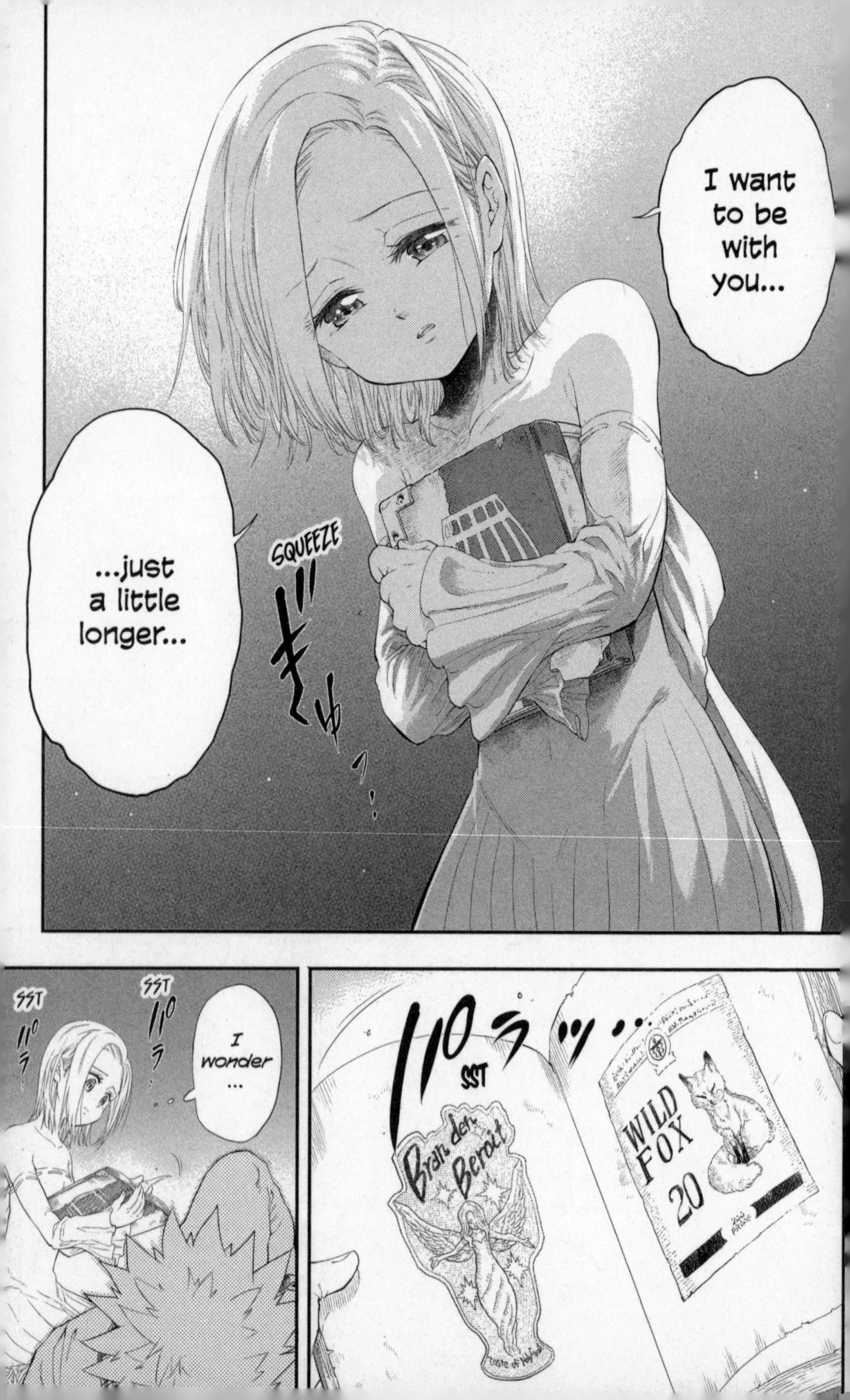
I want to be with you...
...just a little longer...
SQUEEZE
SST
Bran den Beroit
WILD FOX
20
SST
SST
I wonder ...

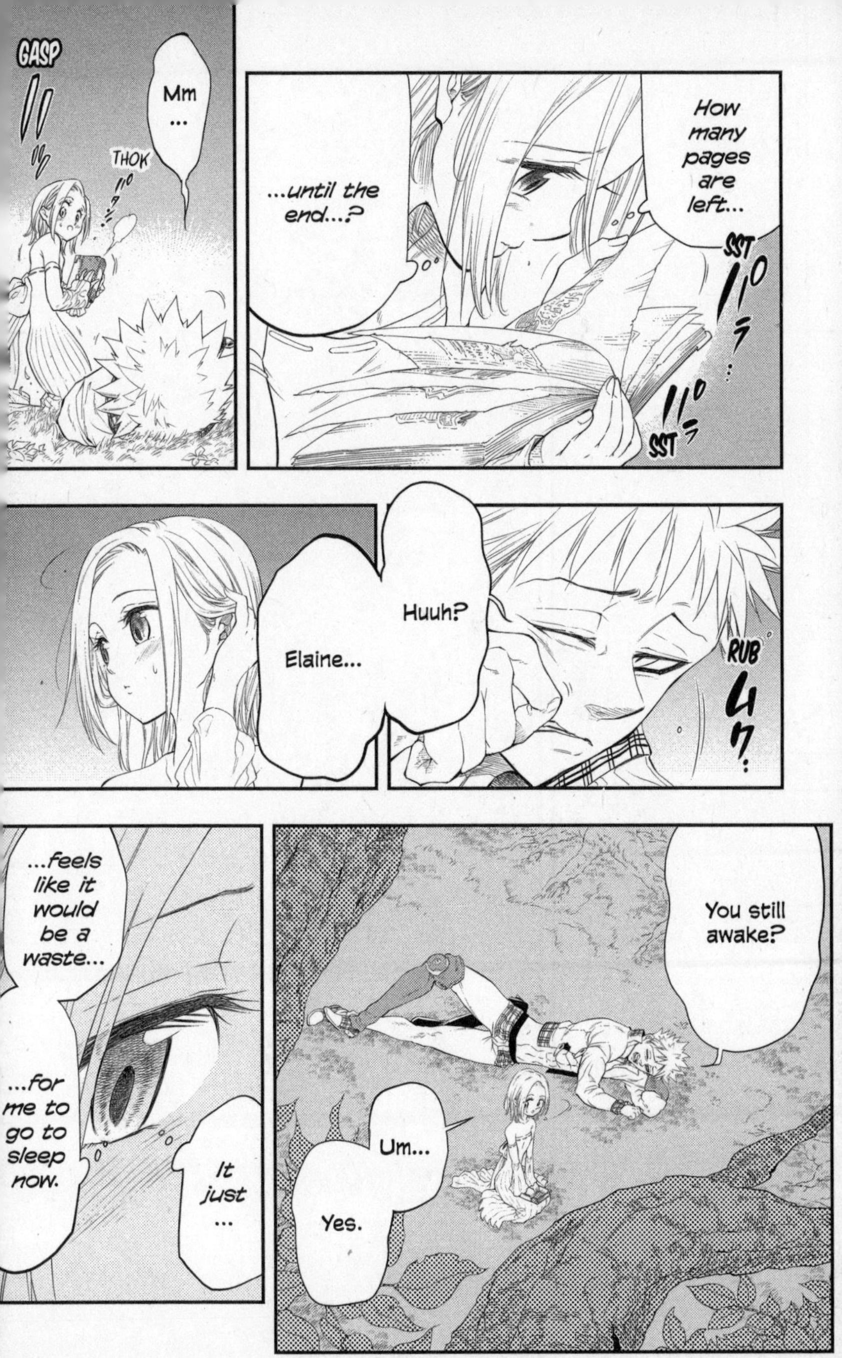
How many pages are left...
...until the end...?
SST
SST
Mm...
GASP
THOK
Huuh?
Elaine...
RUB
You still awake?
Um...
Yes.
It just...
...feels like it would be a waste...
...for me to go to sleep now.

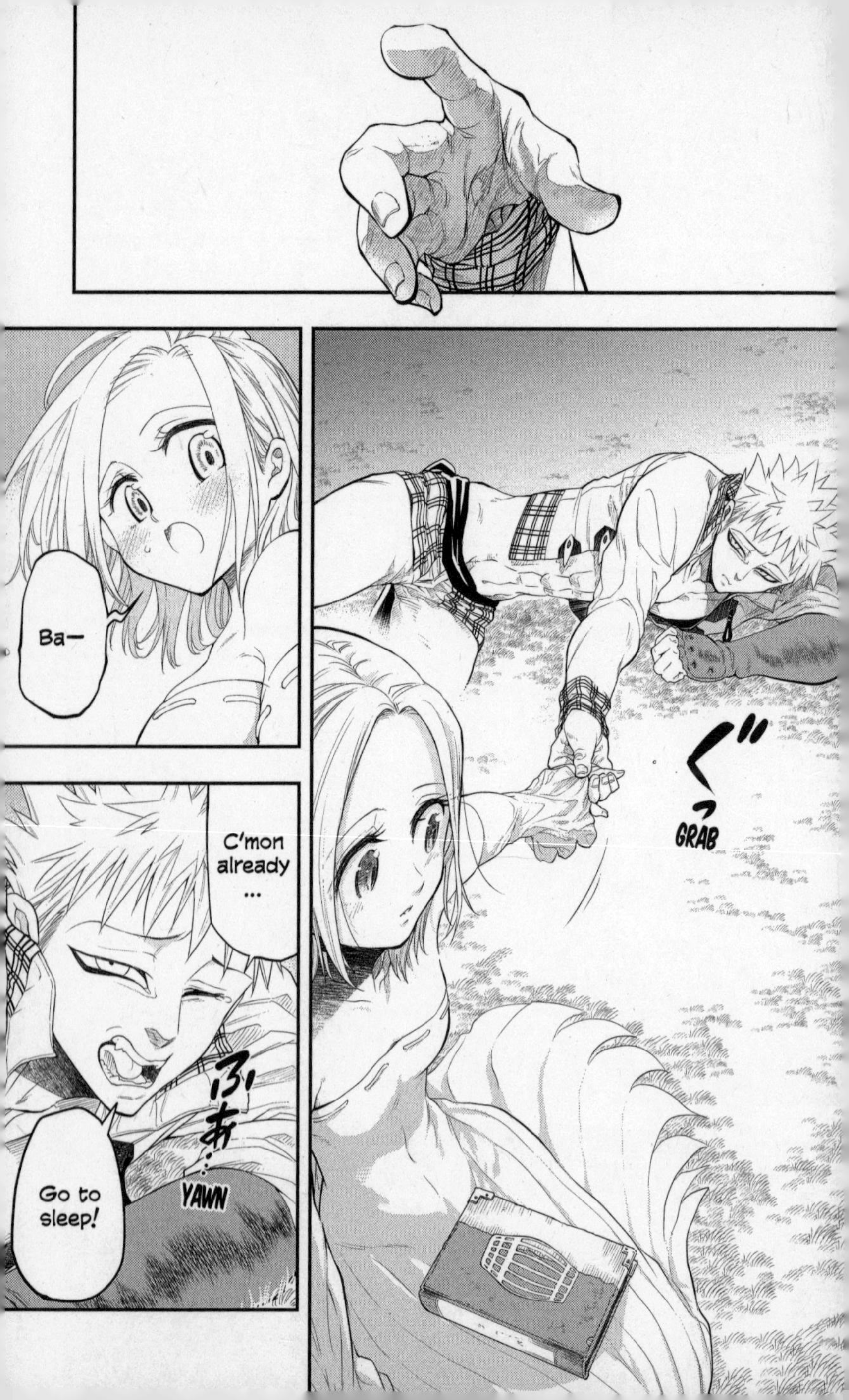
GRAB
Ba—
C'mon already ...
Go to sleep!
YAWN

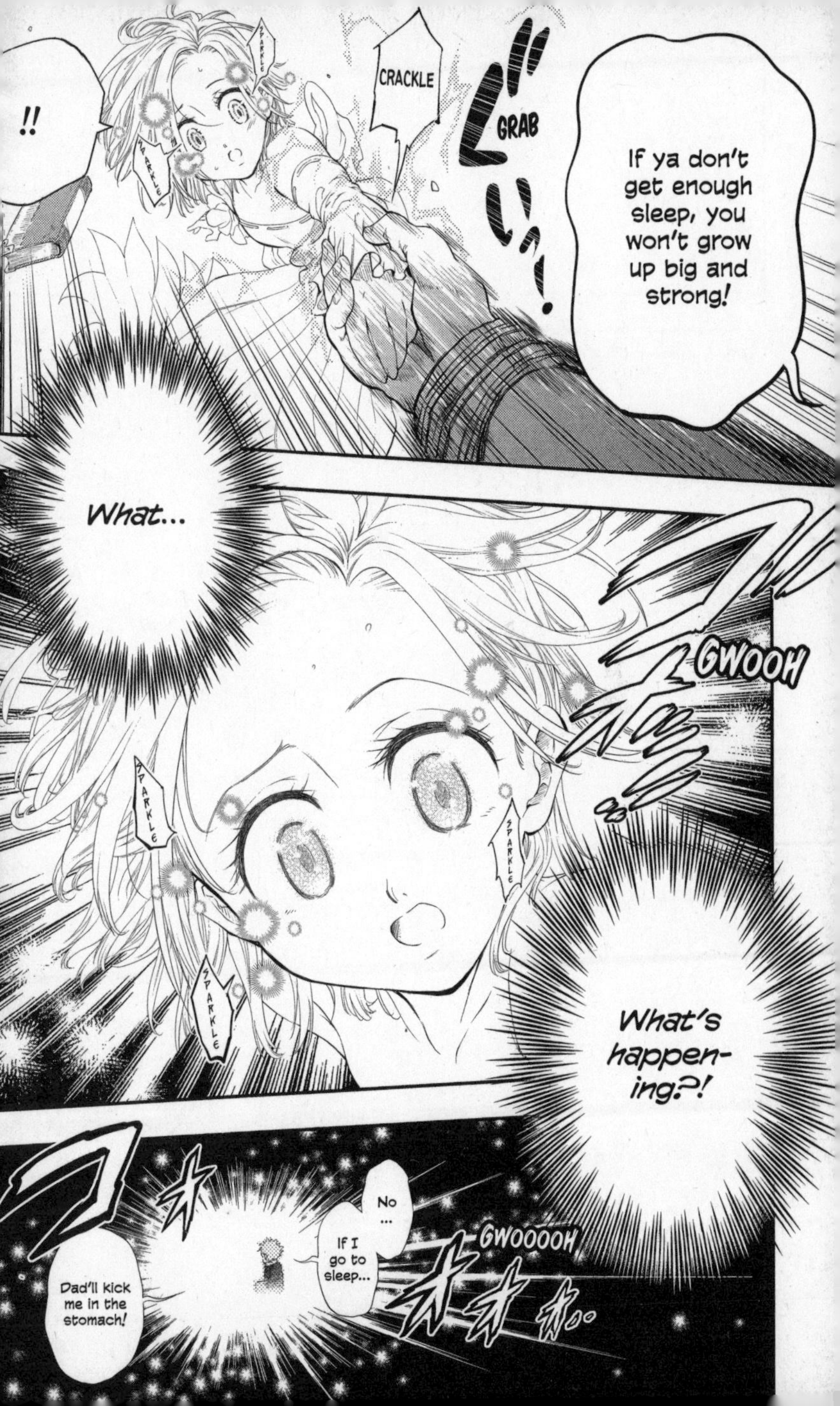
If ya don't get enough sleep, you won't grow up big and strong!
GRAB
CRACKLE
SPARKLE
SPARKLE
!!
What...
GWOOH
SPARKLE
SPARKLE
SPARKLE
What's happen-ing?!
GWOOOOH
No ...
If I go to sleep...
Dad'll kick me in the stomach!

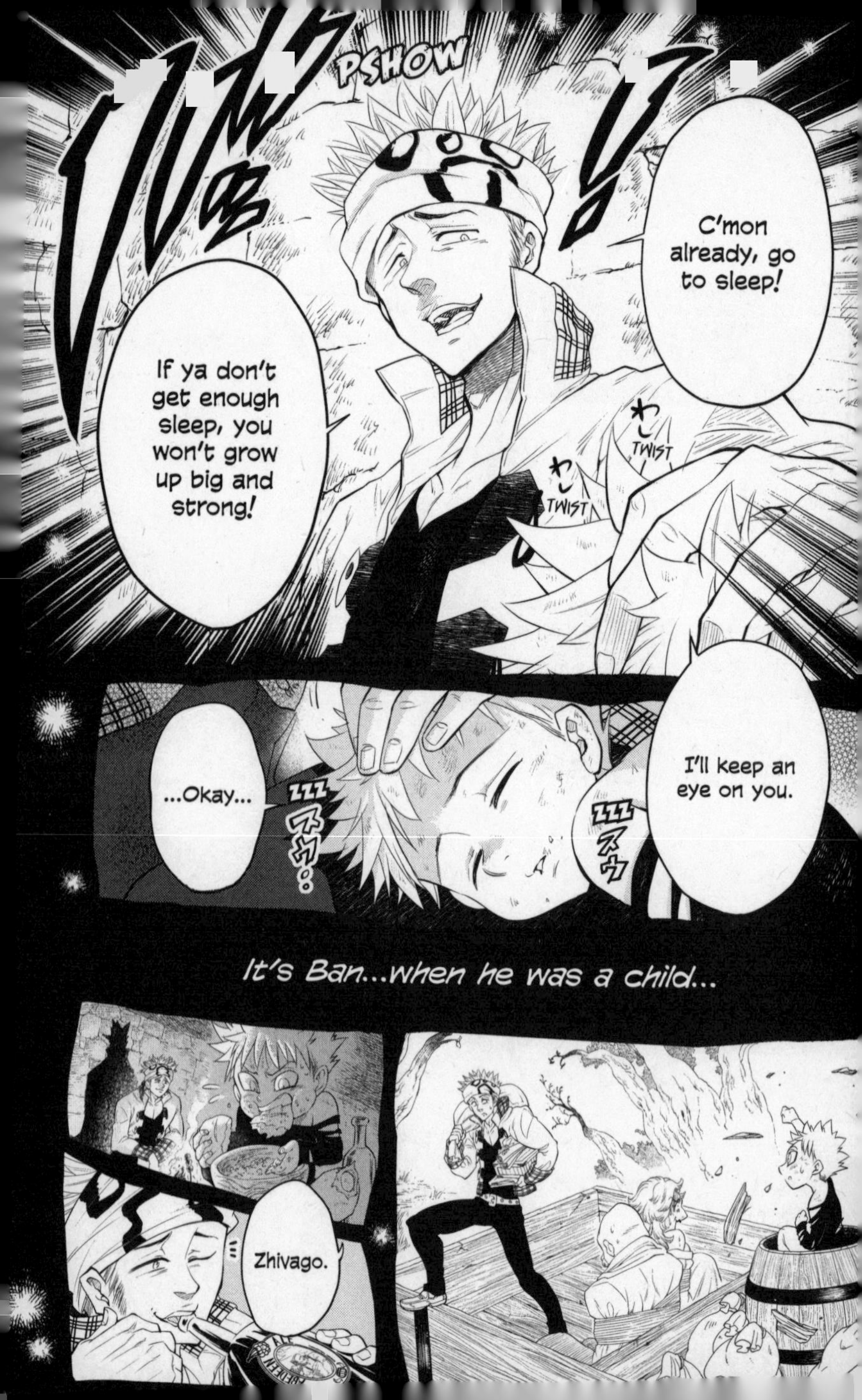
PSHOW
C'mon already, go to sleep!
If ya don't get enough sleep, you won't grow up big and strong!
TWIST
TWIST
I'll keep an eye on you.
ZZZ
...Okay...
ZZZ
It's Ban...when he was a child...
Zhivago.

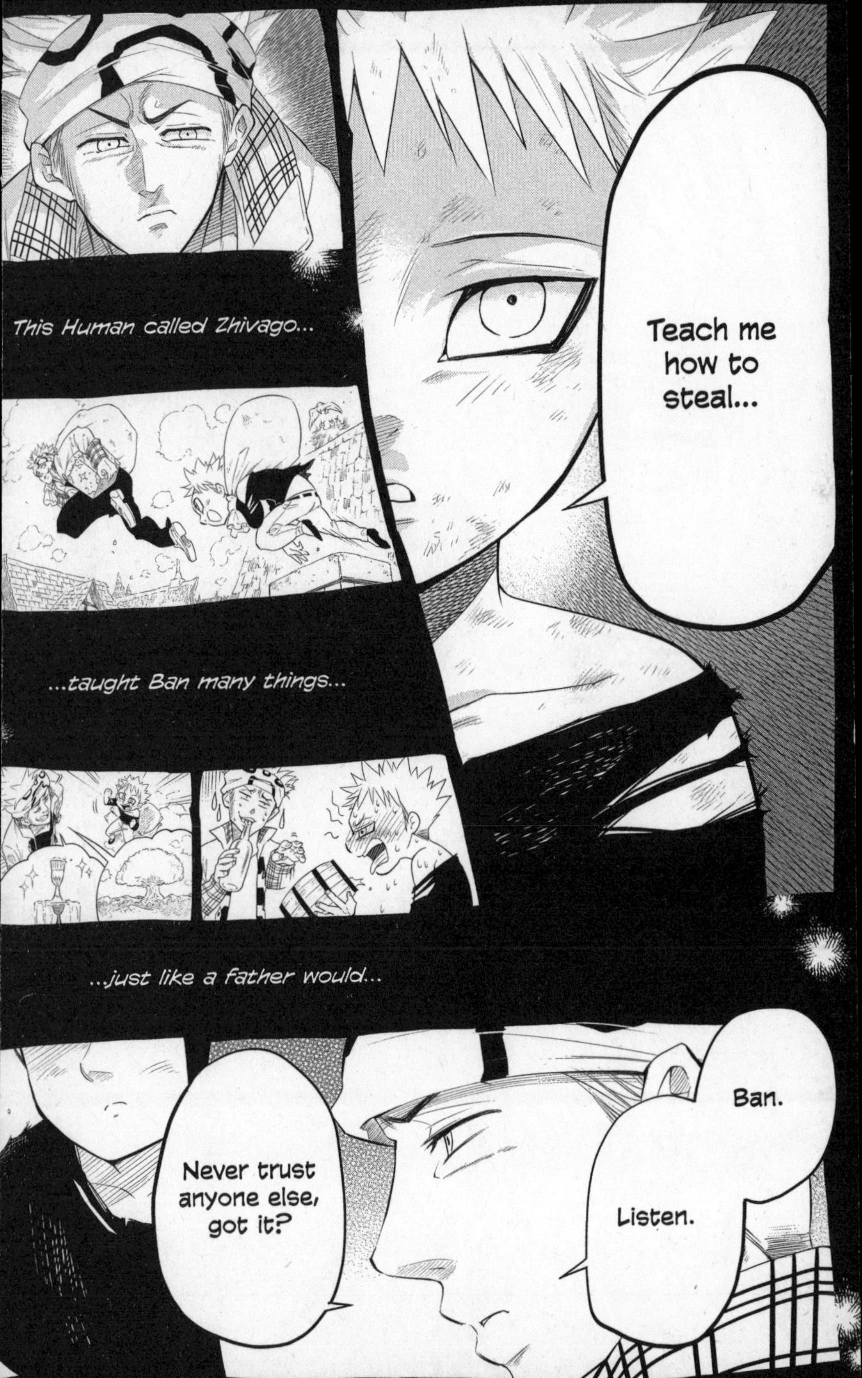
Teach me how to steal...
This Human called Zhivago...
...taught Ban many things...
...just like a father would...
Ban.
Listen.
Never trust anyone else, got it?

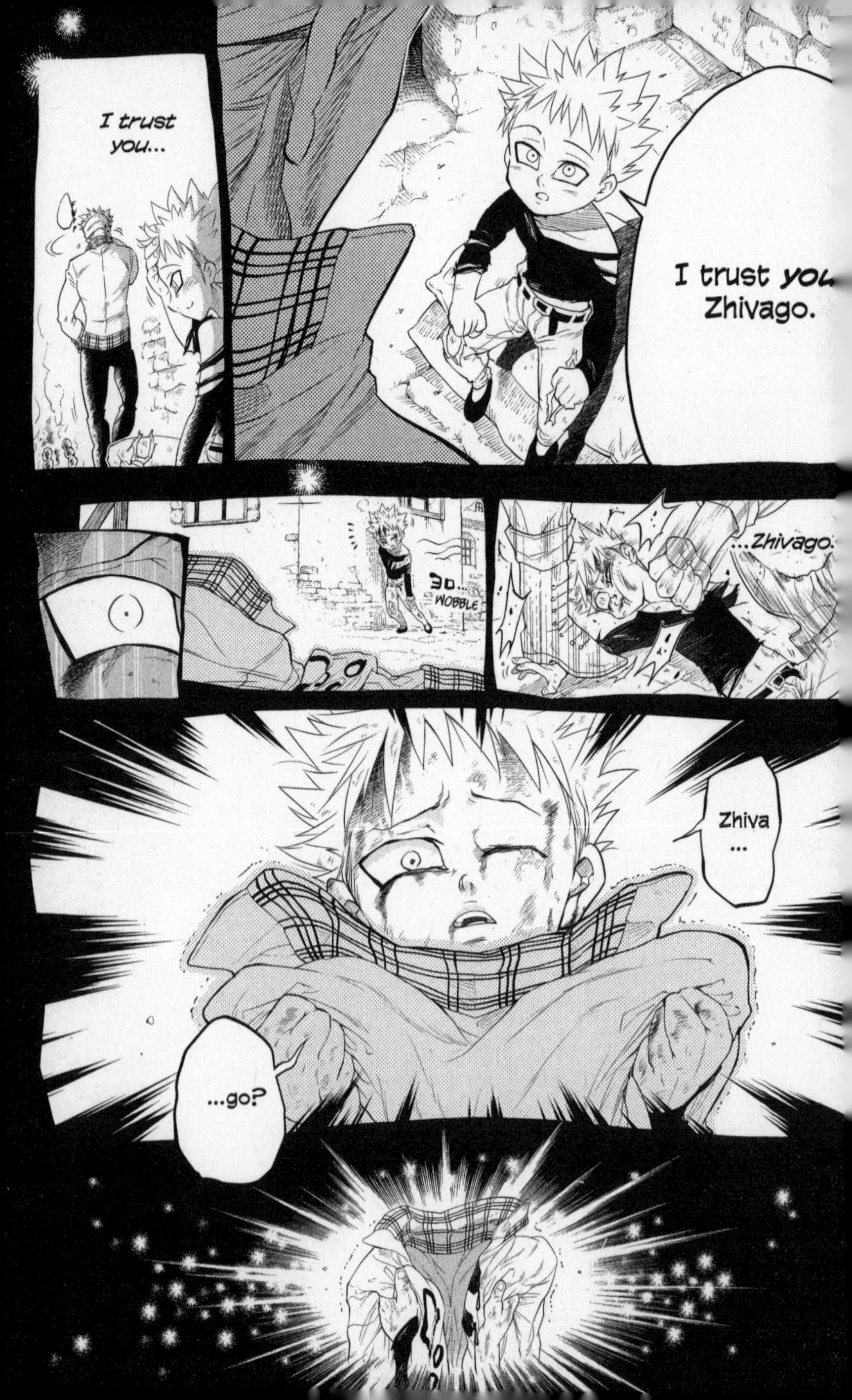
I trust you Zhivago.
I trust you...
...Zhivago...
WOBBLE
Zhiva ...
...go?

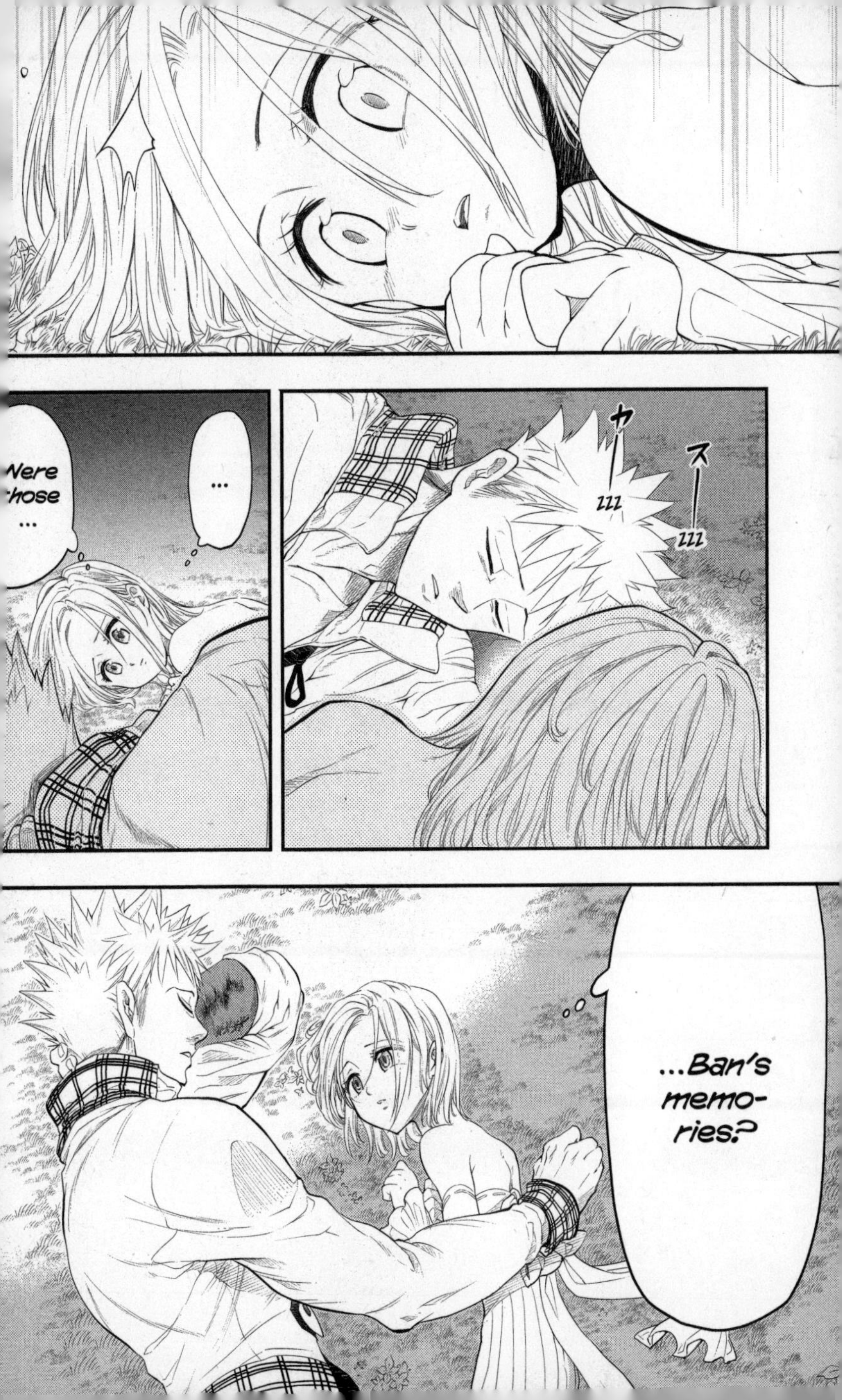
ヤ
ZZZ
ス
ZZZ
...
Were those ...
...Ban's memories?

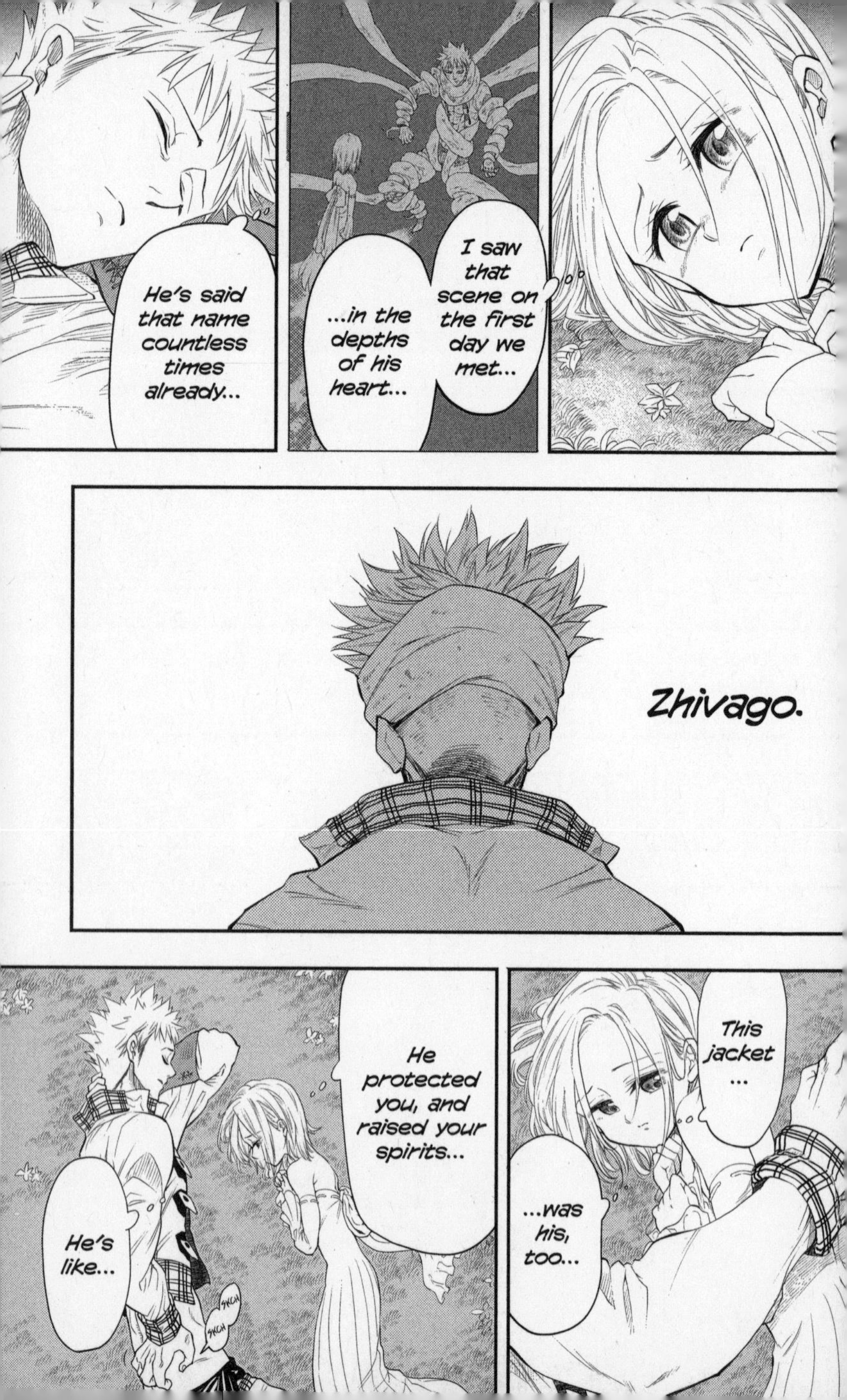
I saw that scene on the first day we met...
...in the depths of his heart...
He's said that name countless times already...
Zhivago.
This jacket ...
...was his, too...
He protected you, and raised your spirits...
He's like...
SKCH
SKCH

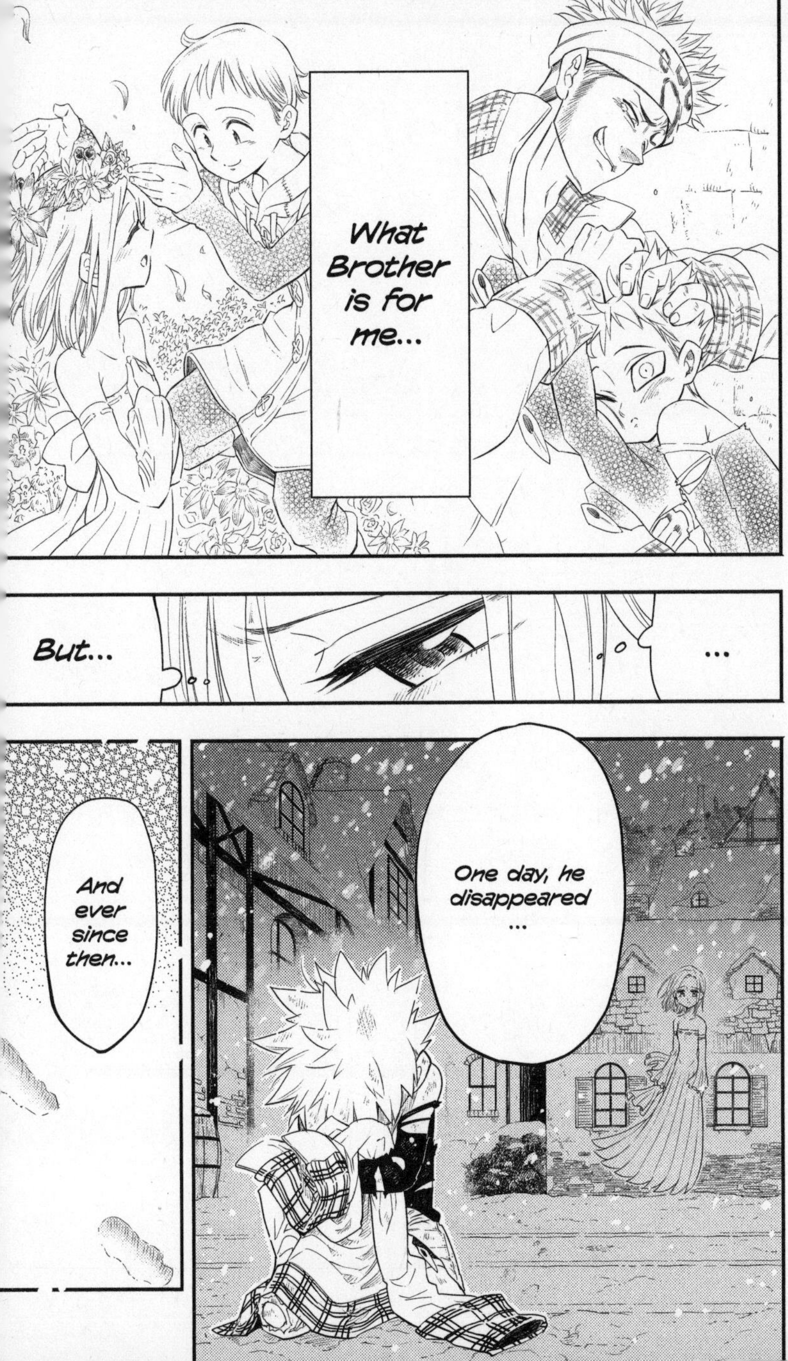
What Brother is for me...
...
But...
One day, he disappeared ...
And ever since then...

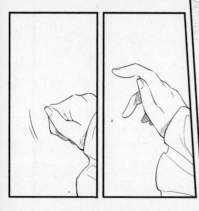

...Ban has lived entirely on his own.

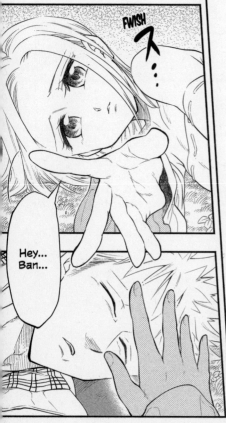

FWISH

Hey... Ban...

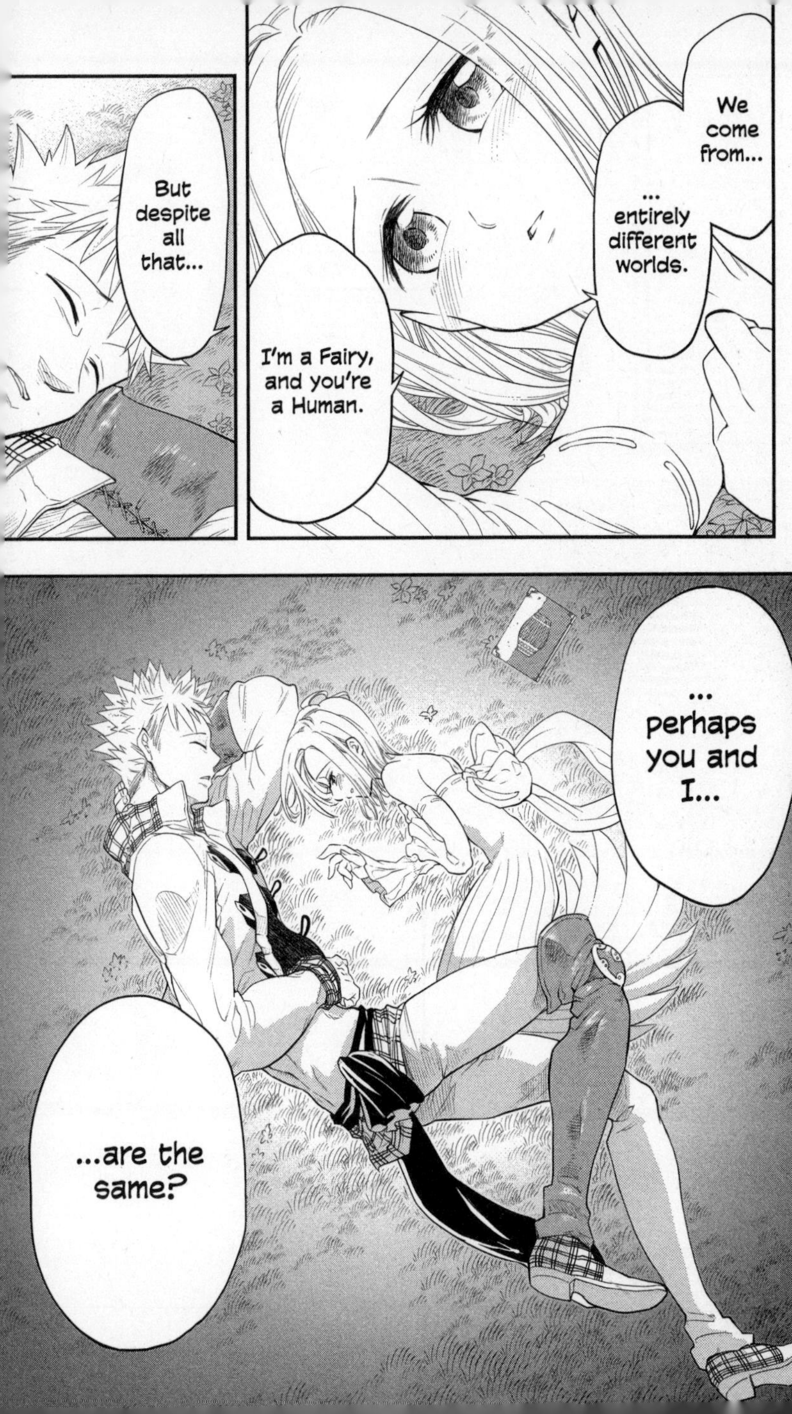
We come from...
...entirely different worlds.
I'm a Fairy, and you're a Human.
But despite all that...
...perhaps you and I...
...are the same?

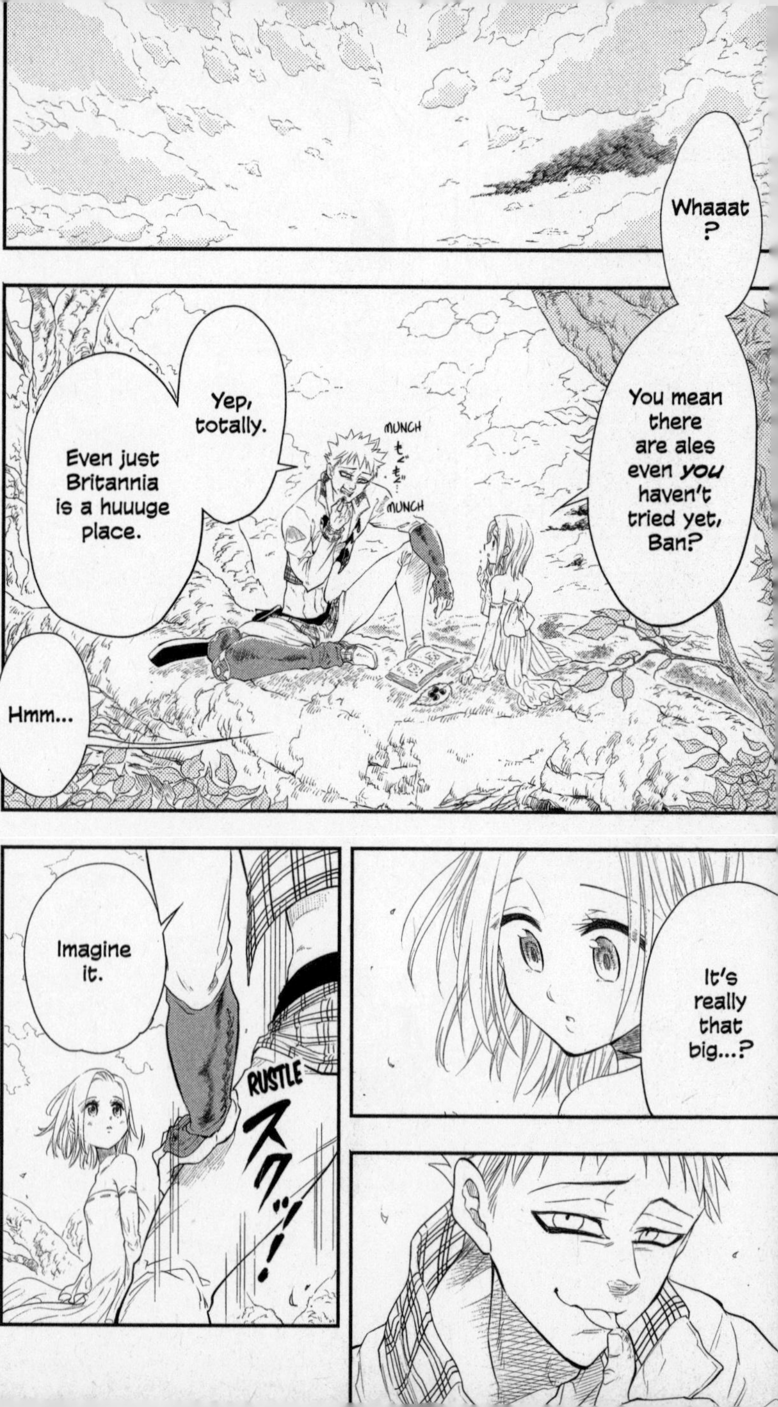
Whaaat?
You mean there are ales even *you* haven't tried yet, Ban?
Yep, totally.
MUNCH
もぐもぐ…
MUNCH
Even just Britannia is a huuuge place.
Hmm...
It's really that big...?
Imagine it.
RUSTLE
スクッ!

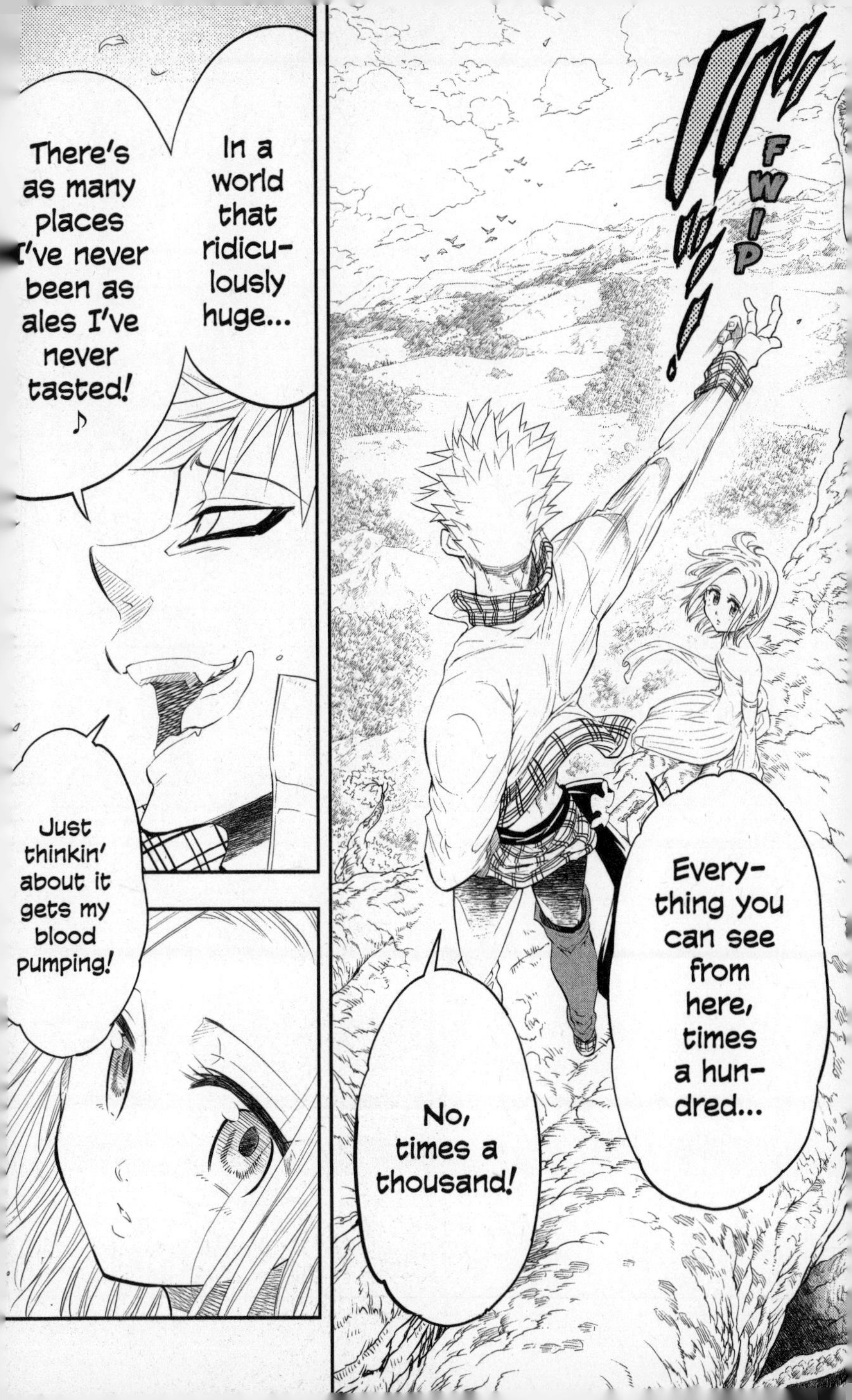
FWIP
Every-thing you can see from here, times a hun-dred...
No, times a thousand!
In a world that ridicu-lously huge...
There's as many places I've never been as ales I've never tasted! ♪
Just thinkin' about it gets my blood pumping!

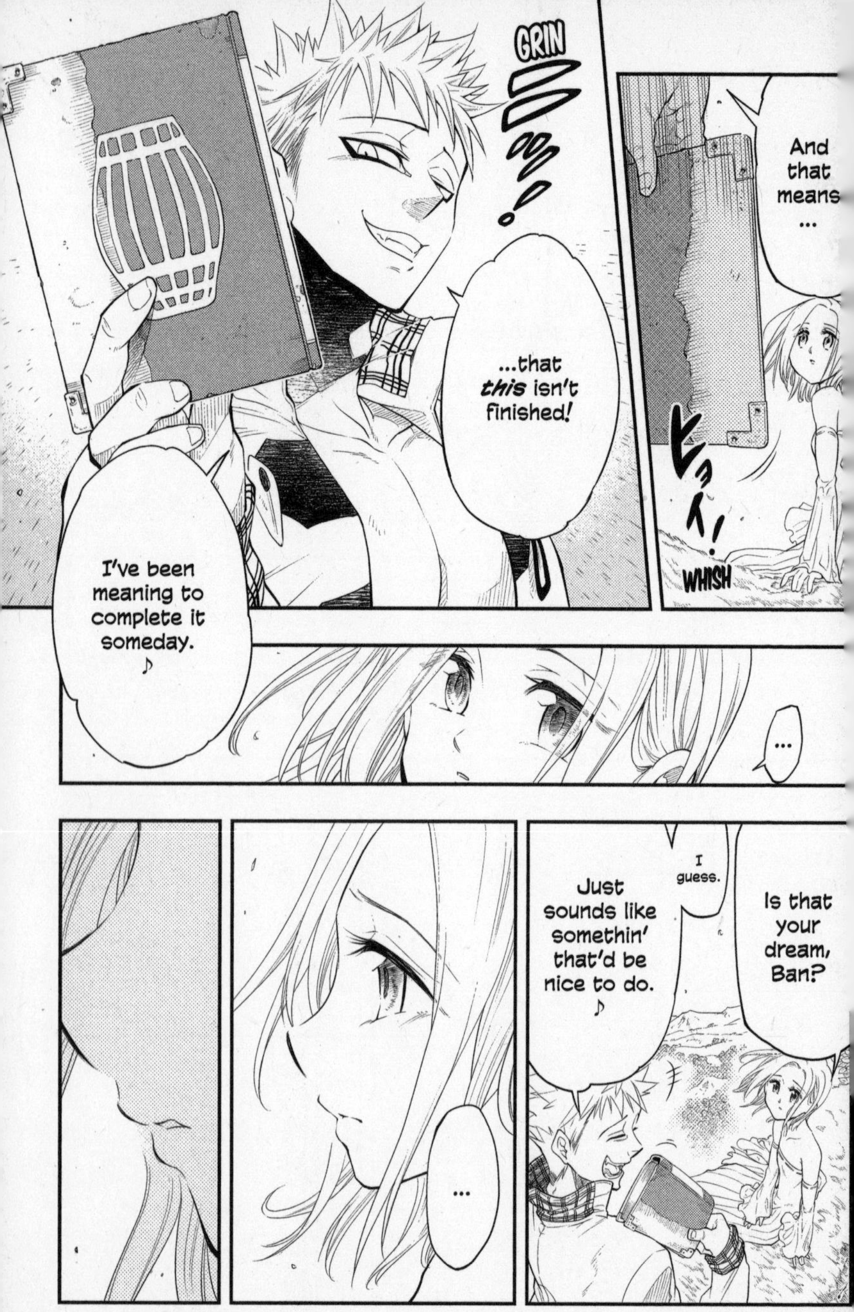
And that means ...
ヒョイ!
WHISH
GRIN
...that *this* isn't finished!
I've been meaning to complete it someday. ♪
...
Is that your dream, Ban?
I guess.
Just sounds like somethin' that'd be nice to do. ♪
...

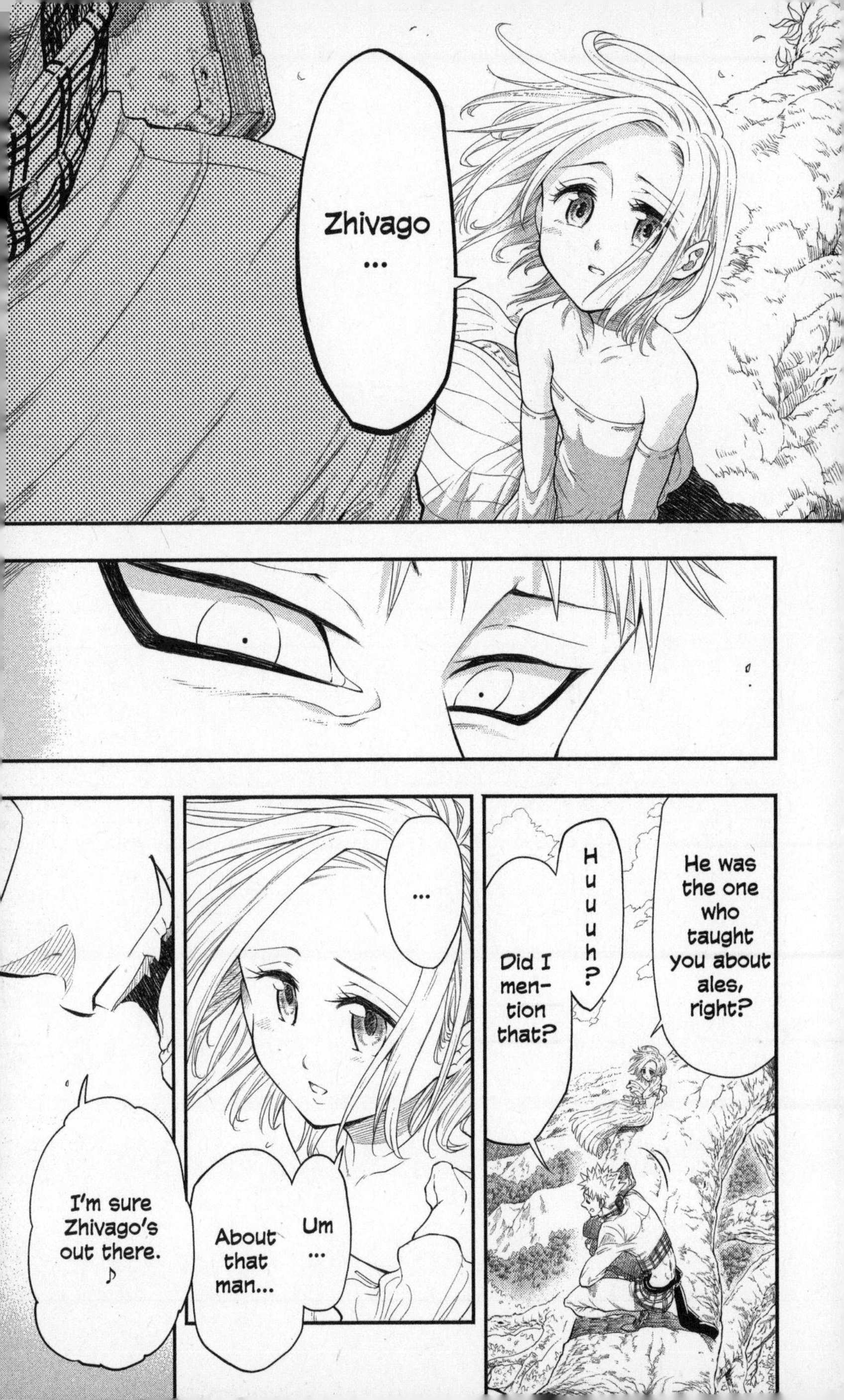
Zhivago ...
He was the one who taught you about ales, right?
Huuuh?
Did I mention that?
...
Um ...
About that man...
I'm sure Zhivago's out there. ♪

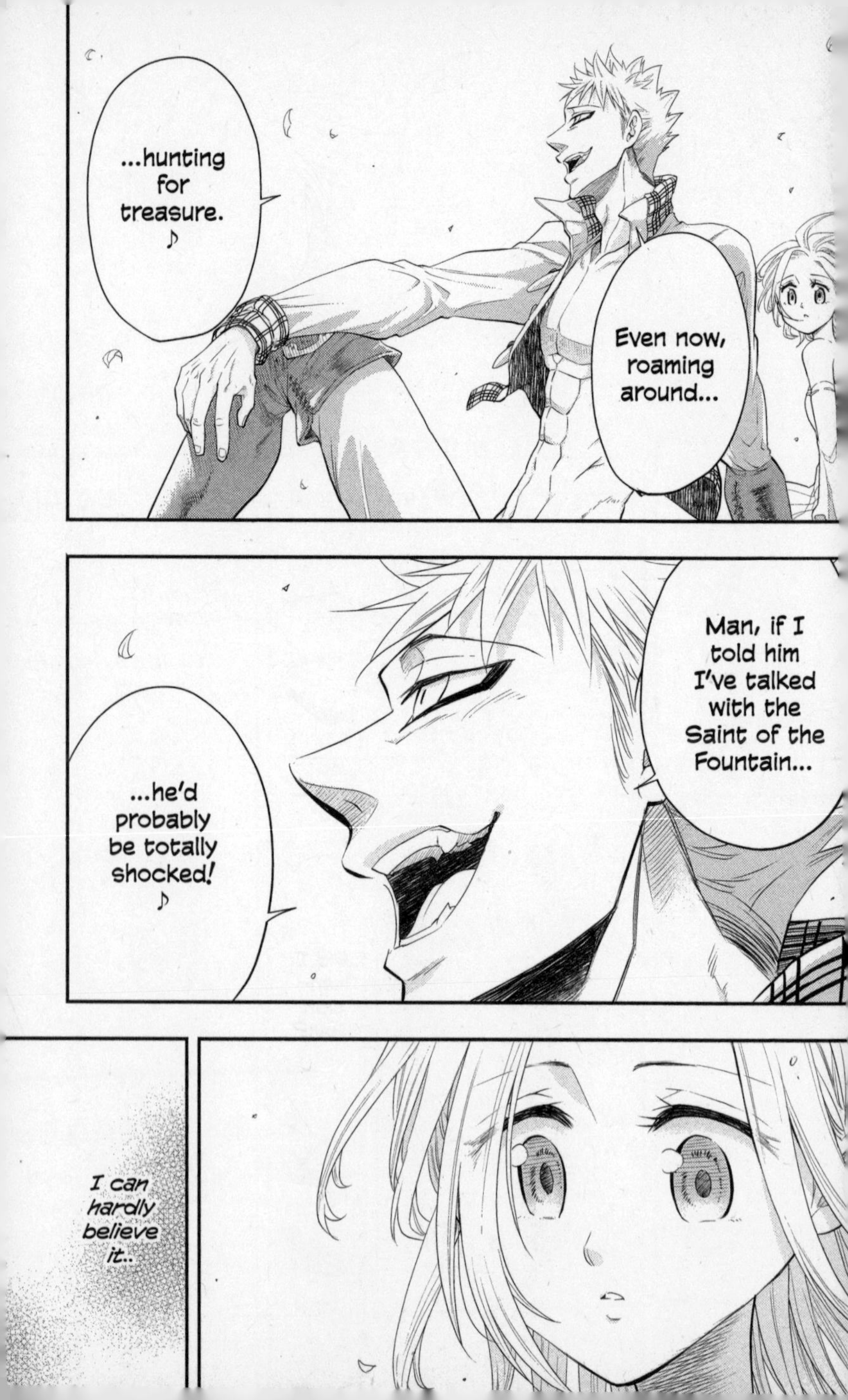
Even now, roaming around...
...hunting for treasure. ♪
Man, if I told him I've talked with the Saint of the Fountain...
...he'd probably be totally shocked! ♪
I can hardly believe it..

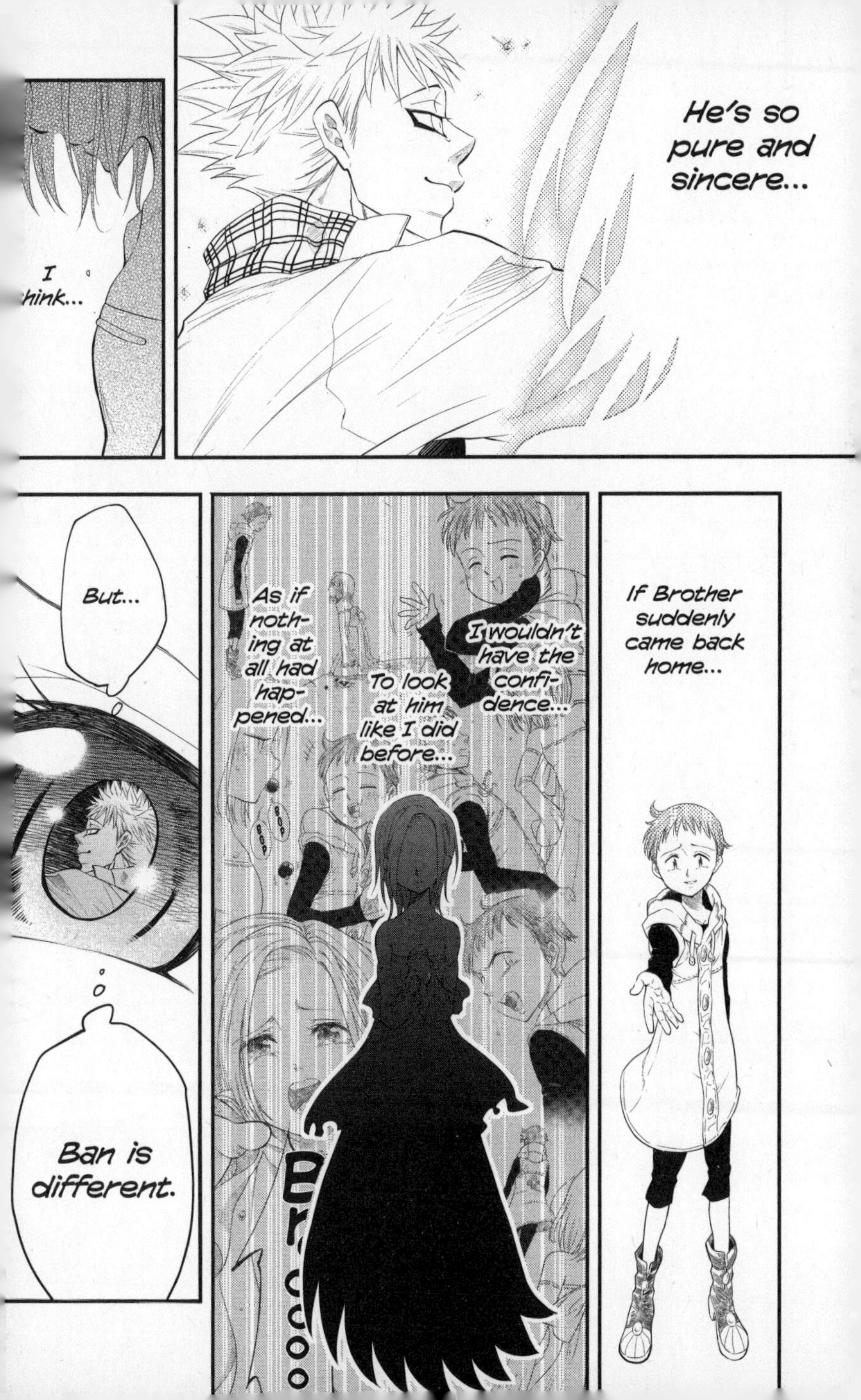
He's so pure and sincere...
I
hink...
If Brother suddenly came back home...
I wouldn't have the confidence...
To look at him like I did before...
As if nothing at all had happened...
But...
Ban is different.

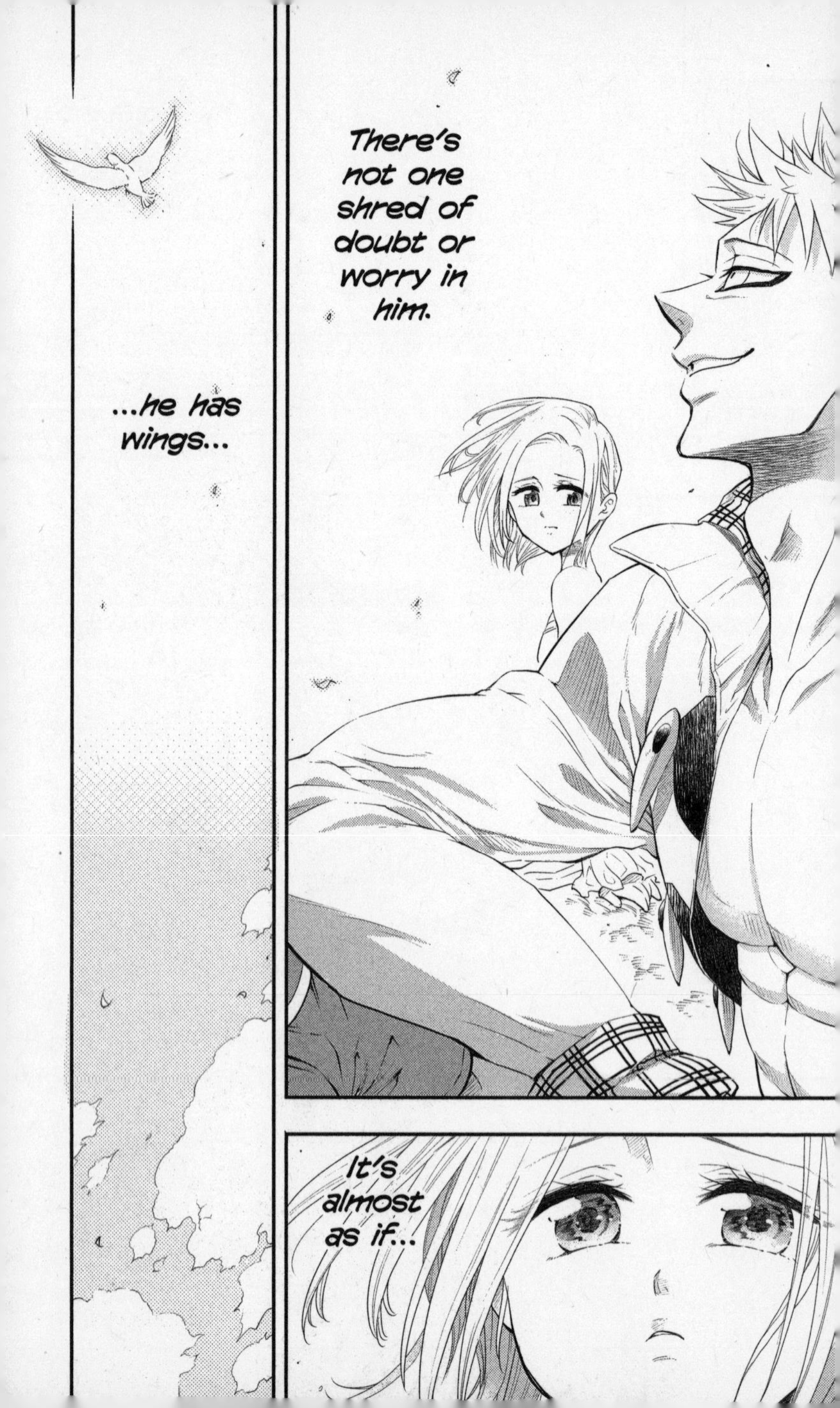

There's not one shred of doubt or worry in him.
It's almost as if...
...he has wings...

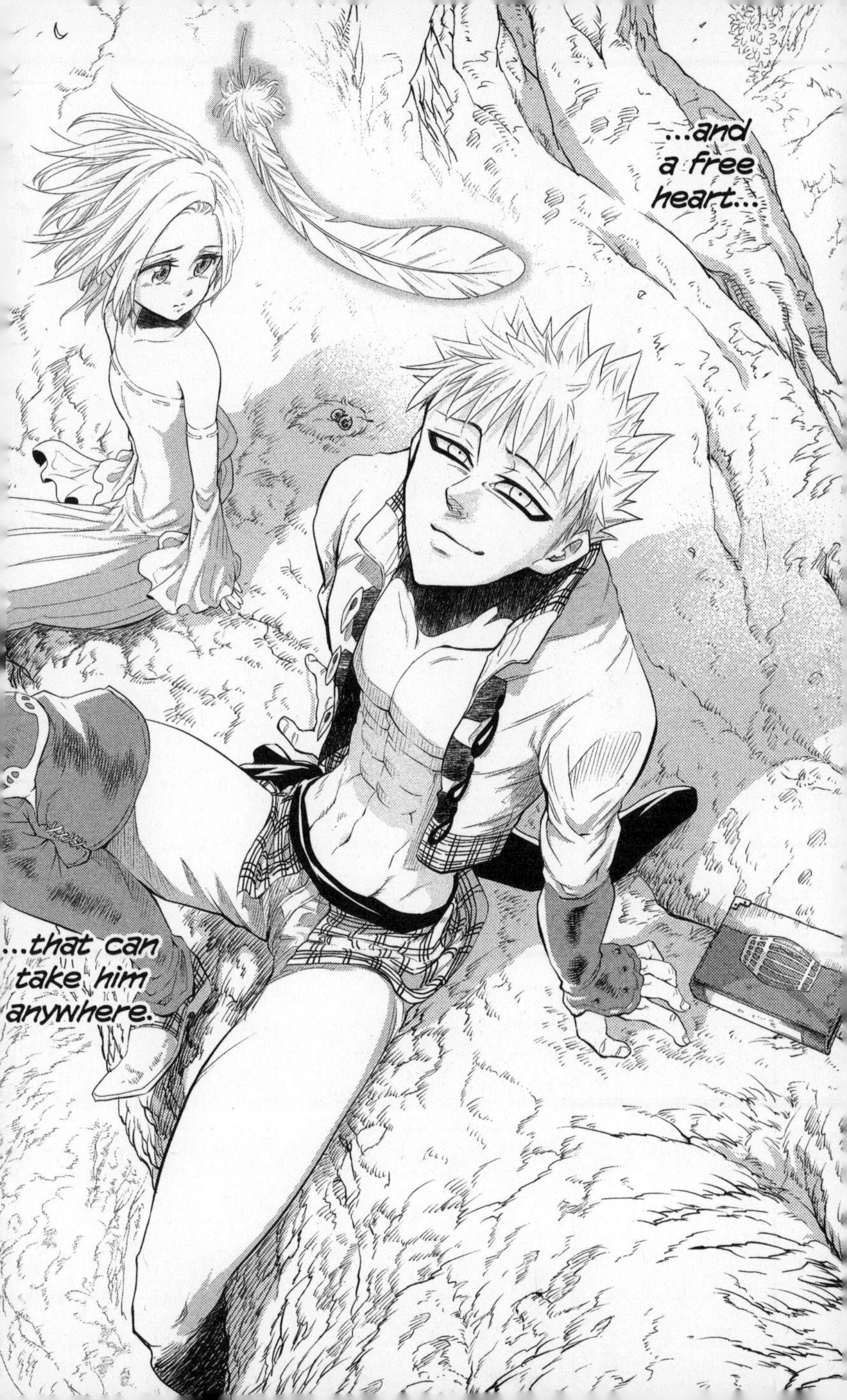
...and
a free
heart...
...that can
take him
anywhere.

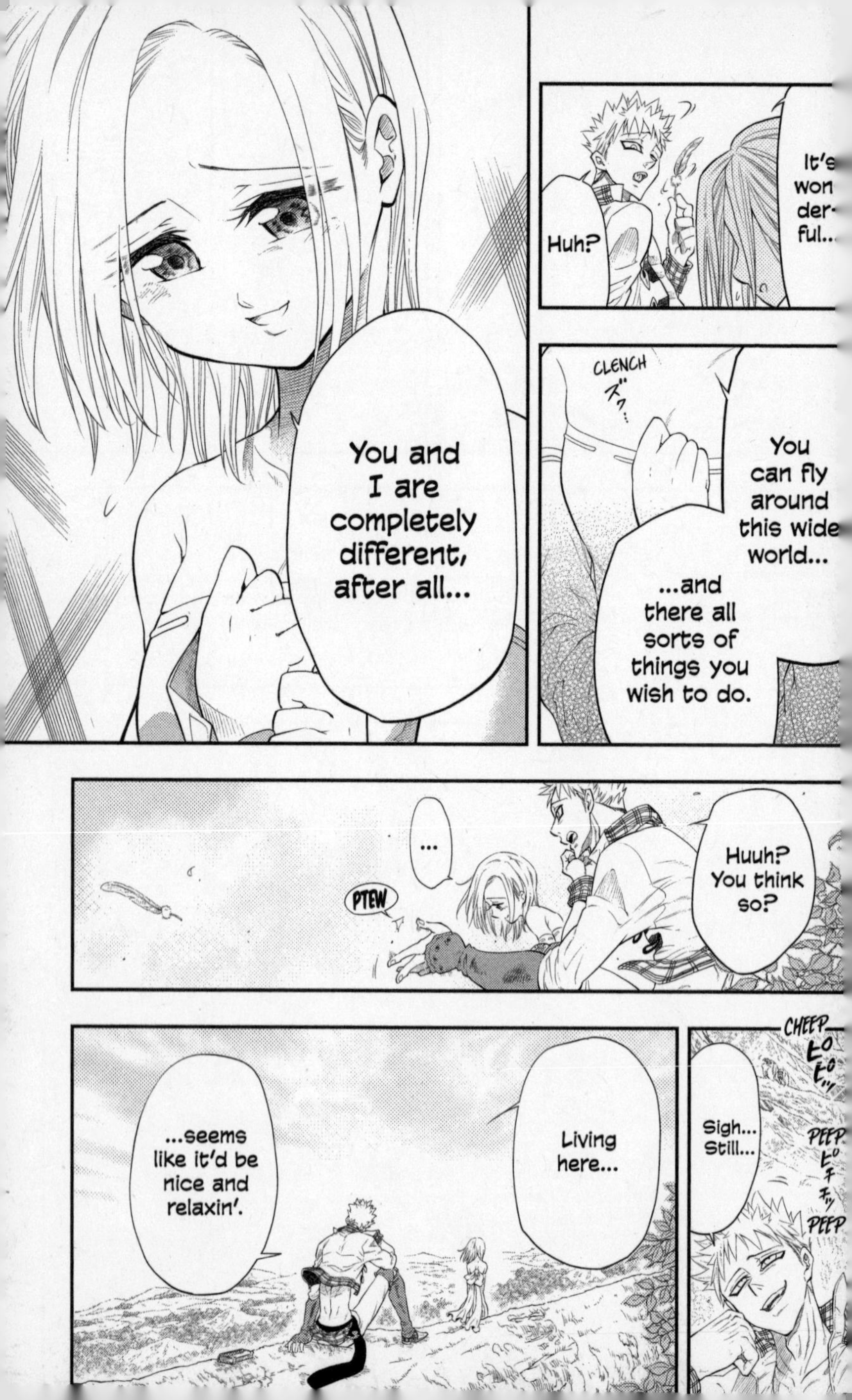
It's won der- ful...
Huh?
CLENCH
You can fly around this wide world...
...and there all sorts of things you wish to do.
You and I are completely different, after all...
Huuh? You think so?
PTEW
...
CHEEP
Sigh... Still...
PEEP
PEEP
Living here...
...seems like it'd be nice and relaxin'.

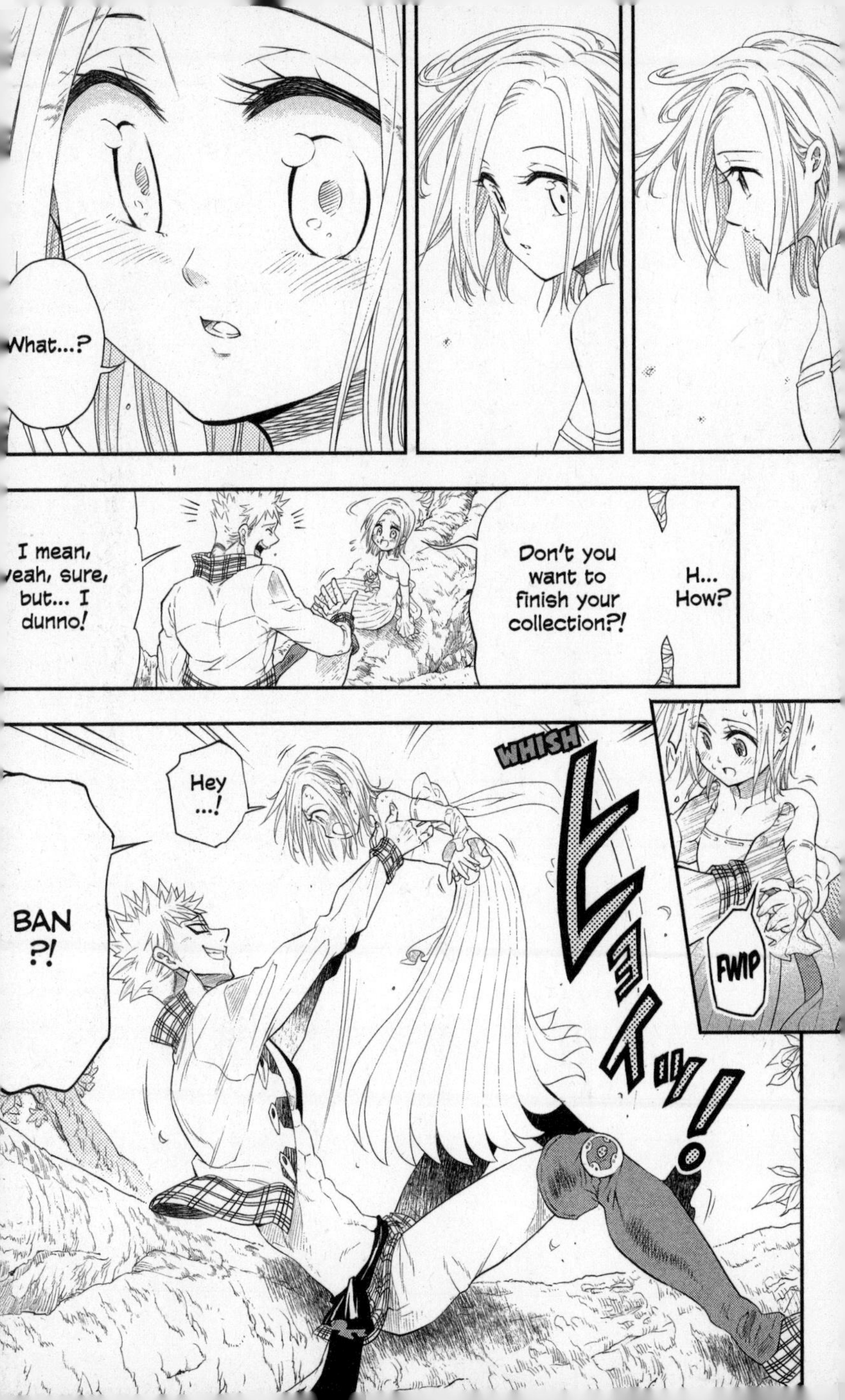
What...?
H... How?
Don't you want to finish your collection?!
I mean, yeah, sure, but... I dunno!
FWIP
WHISH
ヒョイッ!
Hey ...!
BAN ?!

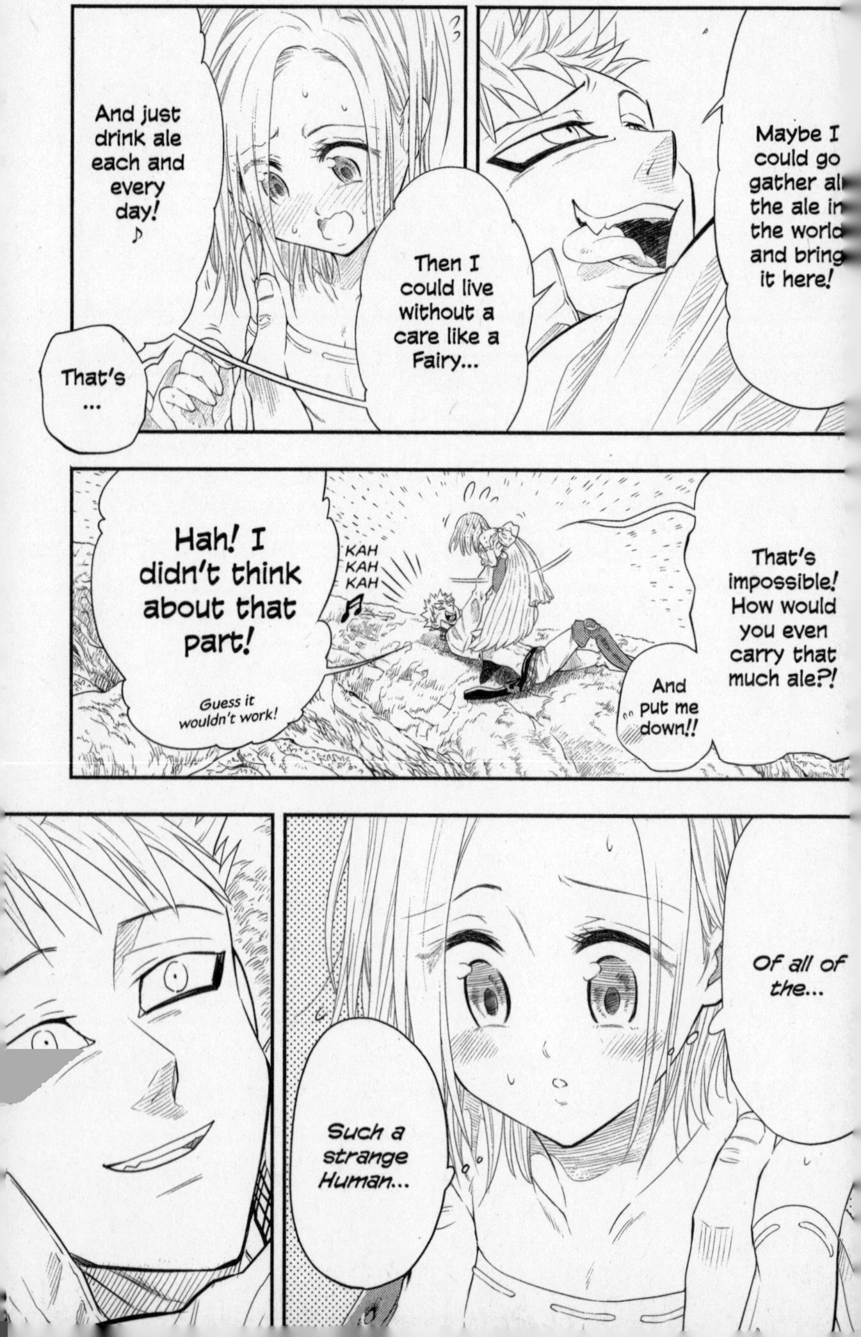
Maybe I could go gather all the ale in the world and bring it here!
Then I could live without a care like a Fairy...
And just drink ale each and every day! ♪
That's ...
That's impossible! How would you even carry that much ale?!
And put me down!!
KAH KAH KAH ♪
Hah! I didn't think about that part!
Guess it wouldn't work!
Of all of the...
Such a strange Human...

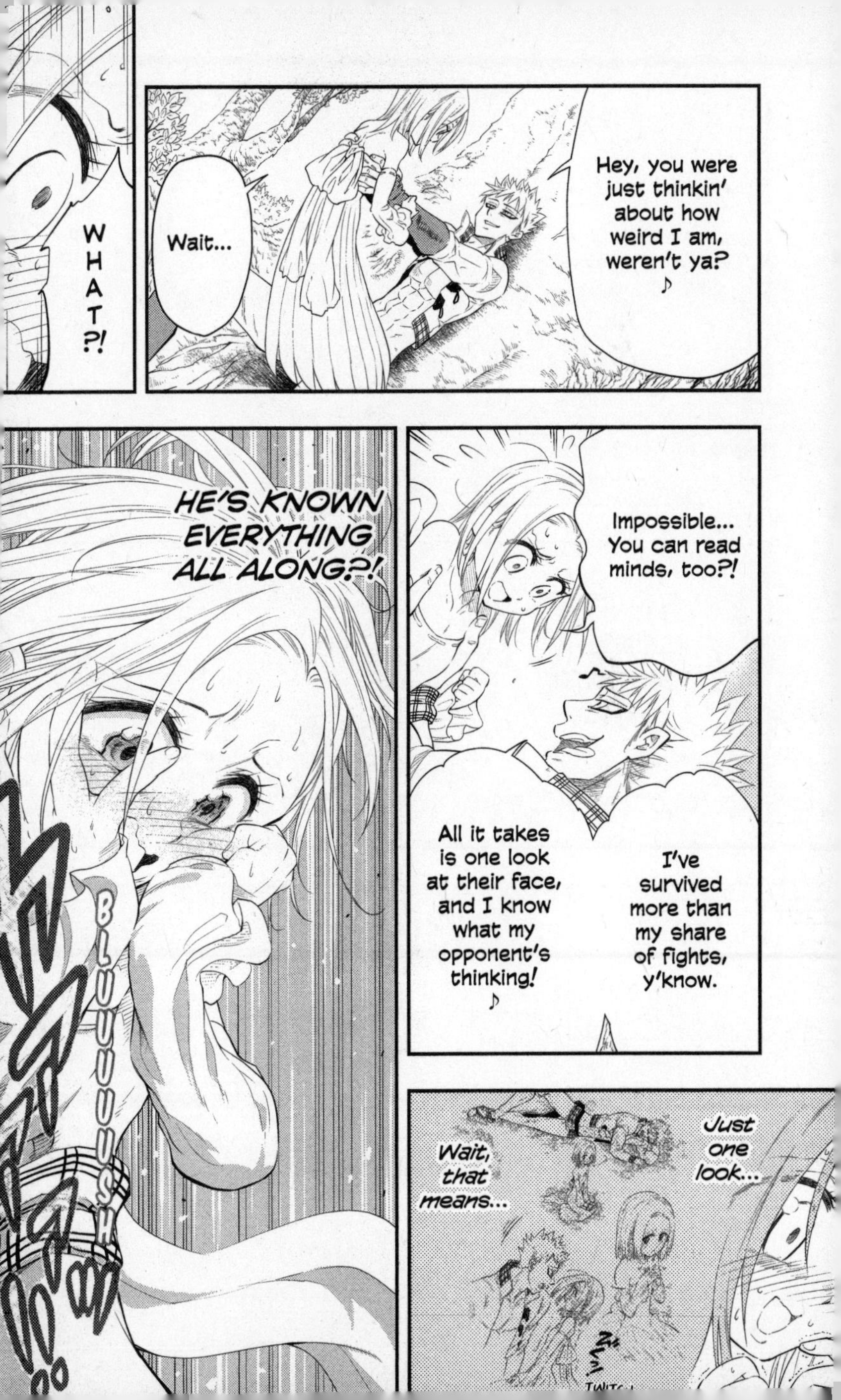

Hey, you were just thinkin' about how weird I am, weren't ya? ♪
Wait...
WHAT?!
Impossible... You can read minds, too?!
I've survived more than my share of fights, y'know.
All it takes is one look at their face, and I know what my opponent's thinking! ♪
Just one look...
Wait, that means...
HE'S KNOWN EVERYTHING ALL ALONG?!
BLUUUUUUSH

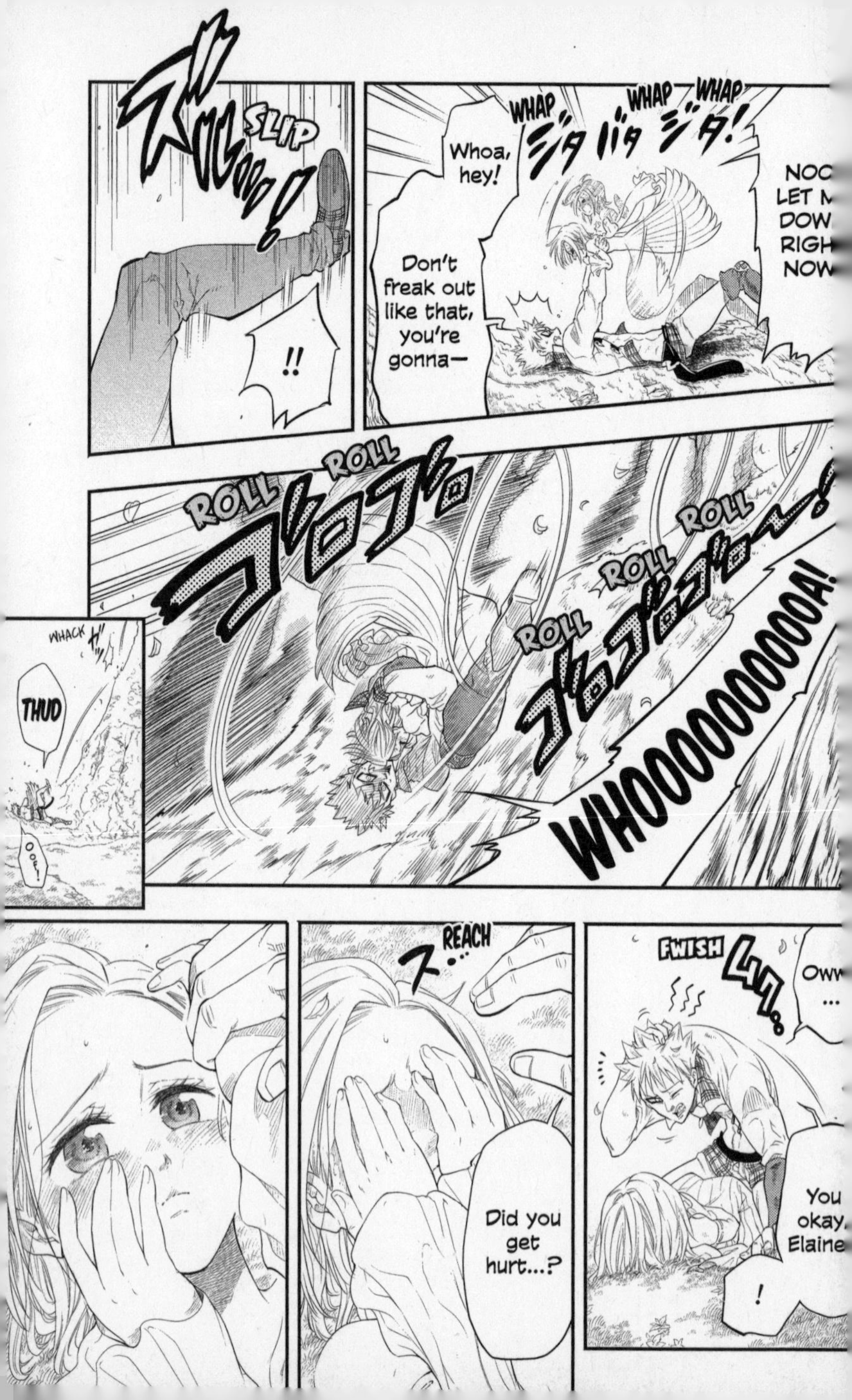
NOO
LET M
DOW
RIGH
NOW
WHAP WHAP WHAP
ジタバタジタ!
Whoa, hey!
Don't freak out like that, you're gonna—
SLIP
!!
ROLL ROLL
ROLL ROLL ROLL ROLL
WHOOOOOOOOOOA!
WHACK
THUD
Oof!
FWISH
Oww ...
You okay, Elaine
!
REACH
Did you get hurt...?

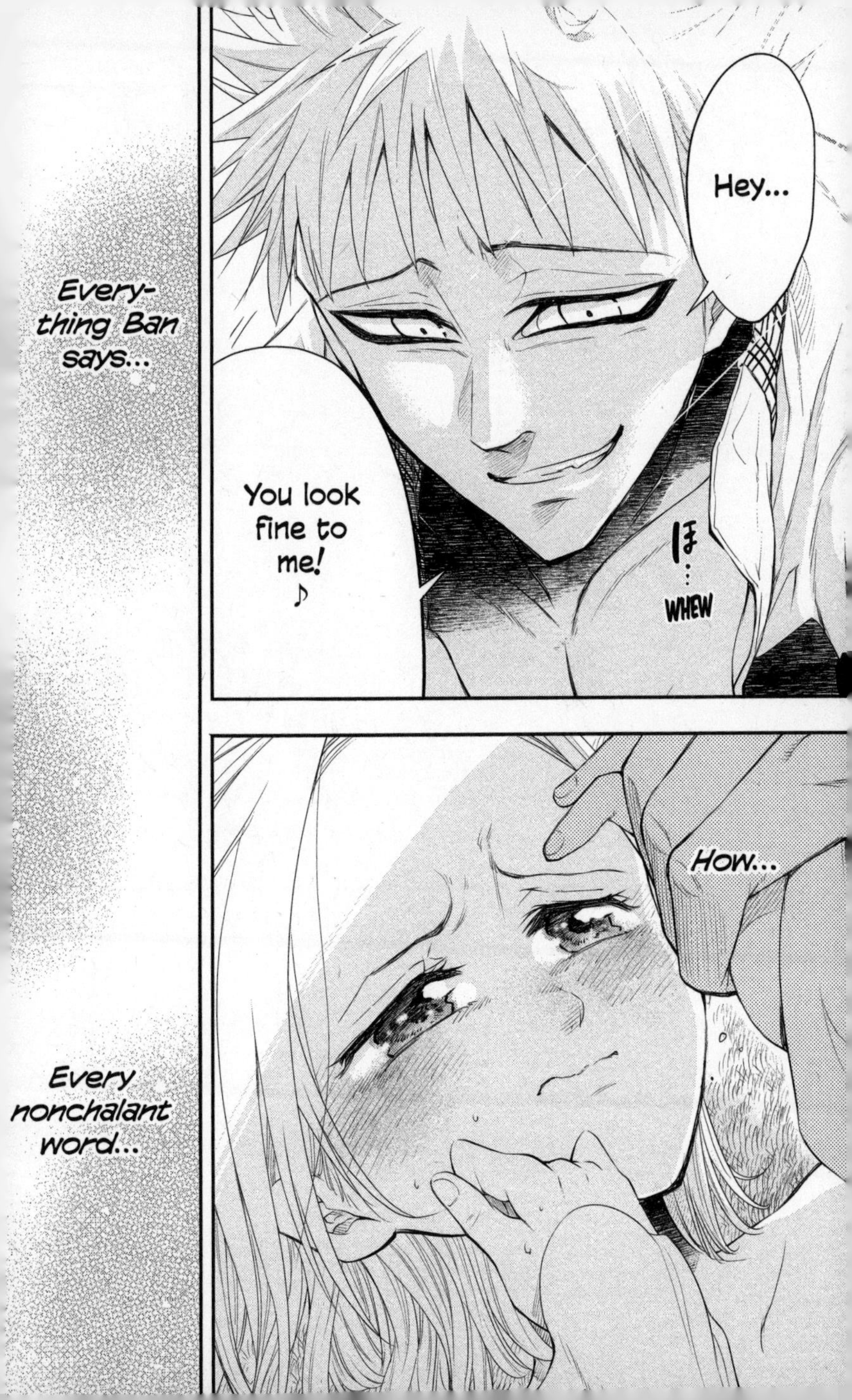
Hey...
You look fine to me! ♪
ほ…
WHEW
Every-thing Ban says...
How...
Every nonchalant word...

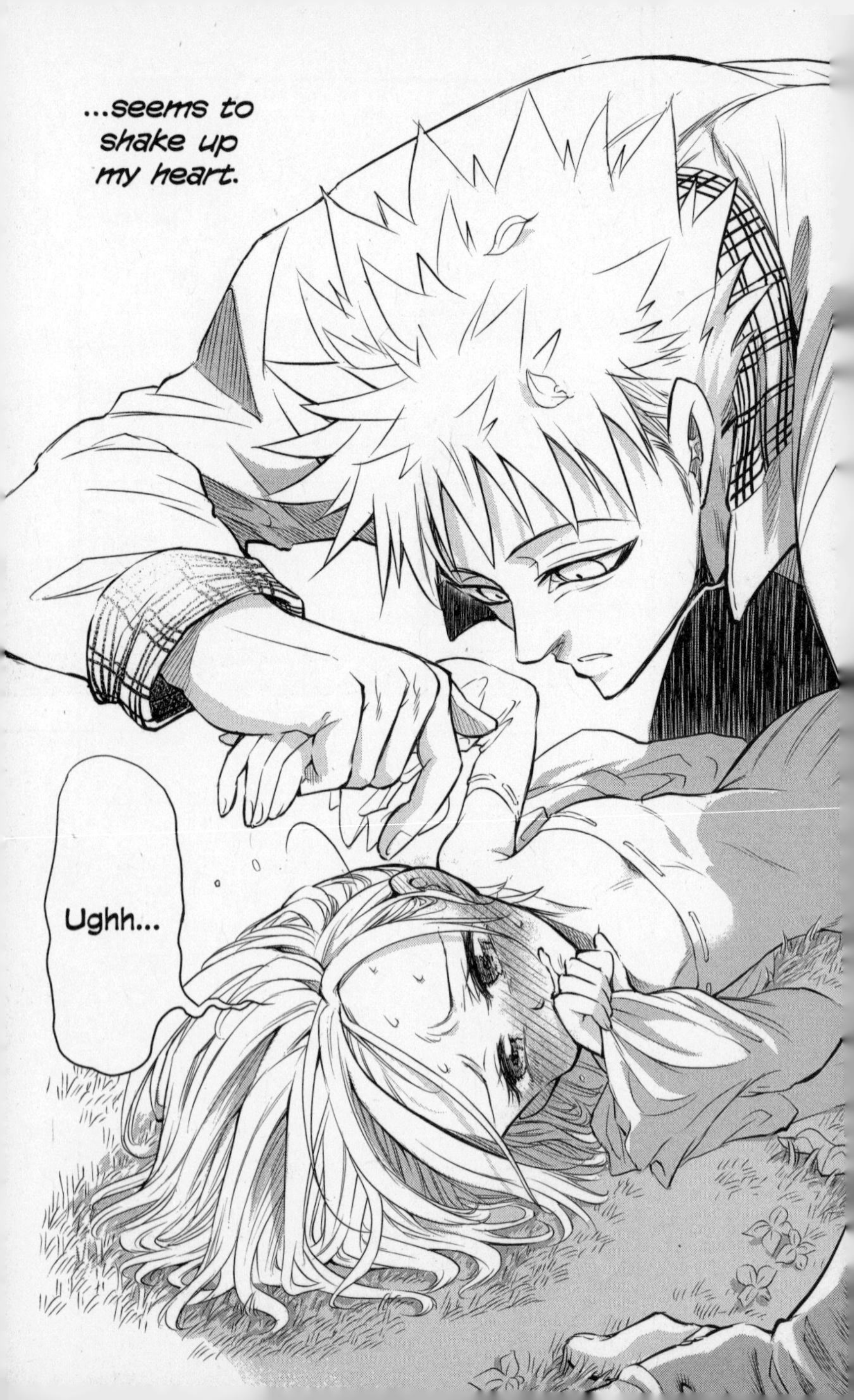
...seems to shake up my heart.
Ughh...

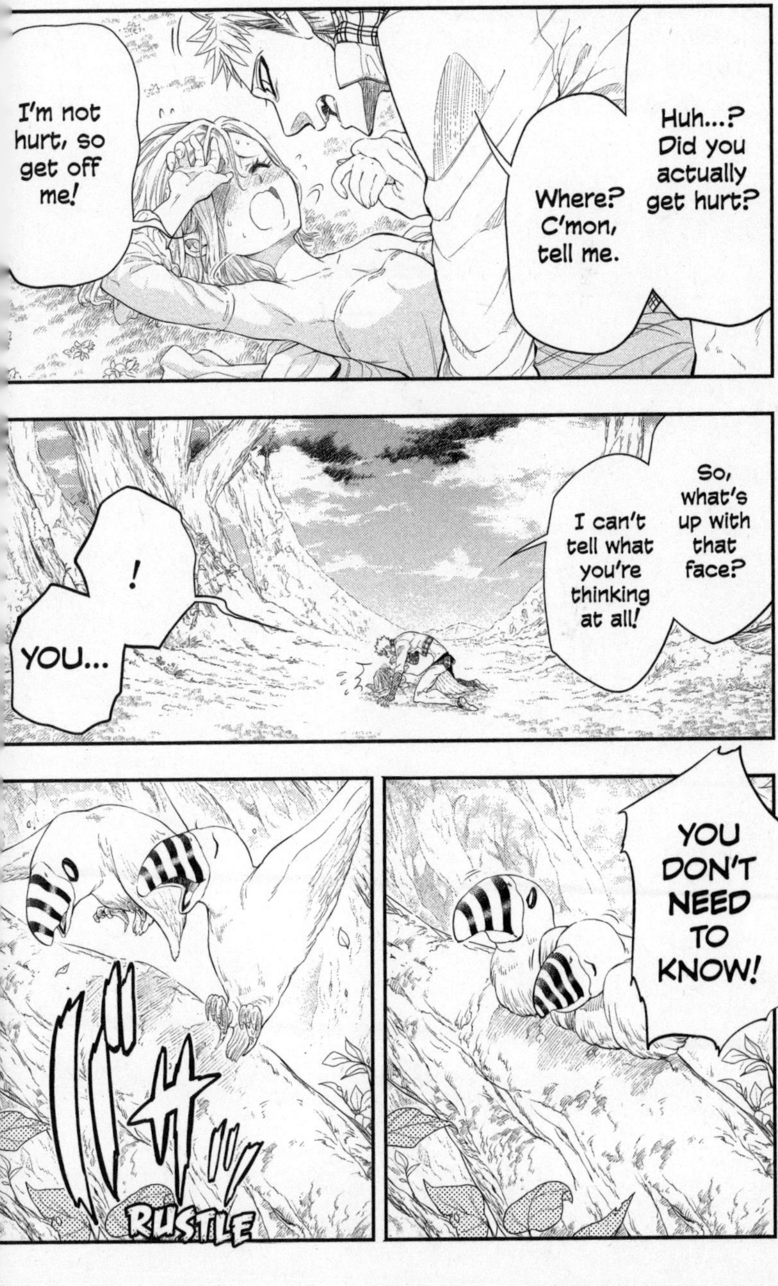
Huh...? Did you actually get hurt?
Where? C'mon, tell me.
I'm not hurt, so get off me!
So, what's up with that face?
I can't tell what you're thinking at all!
!
YOU...
YOU DON'T NEED TO KNOW!
RUSTLE

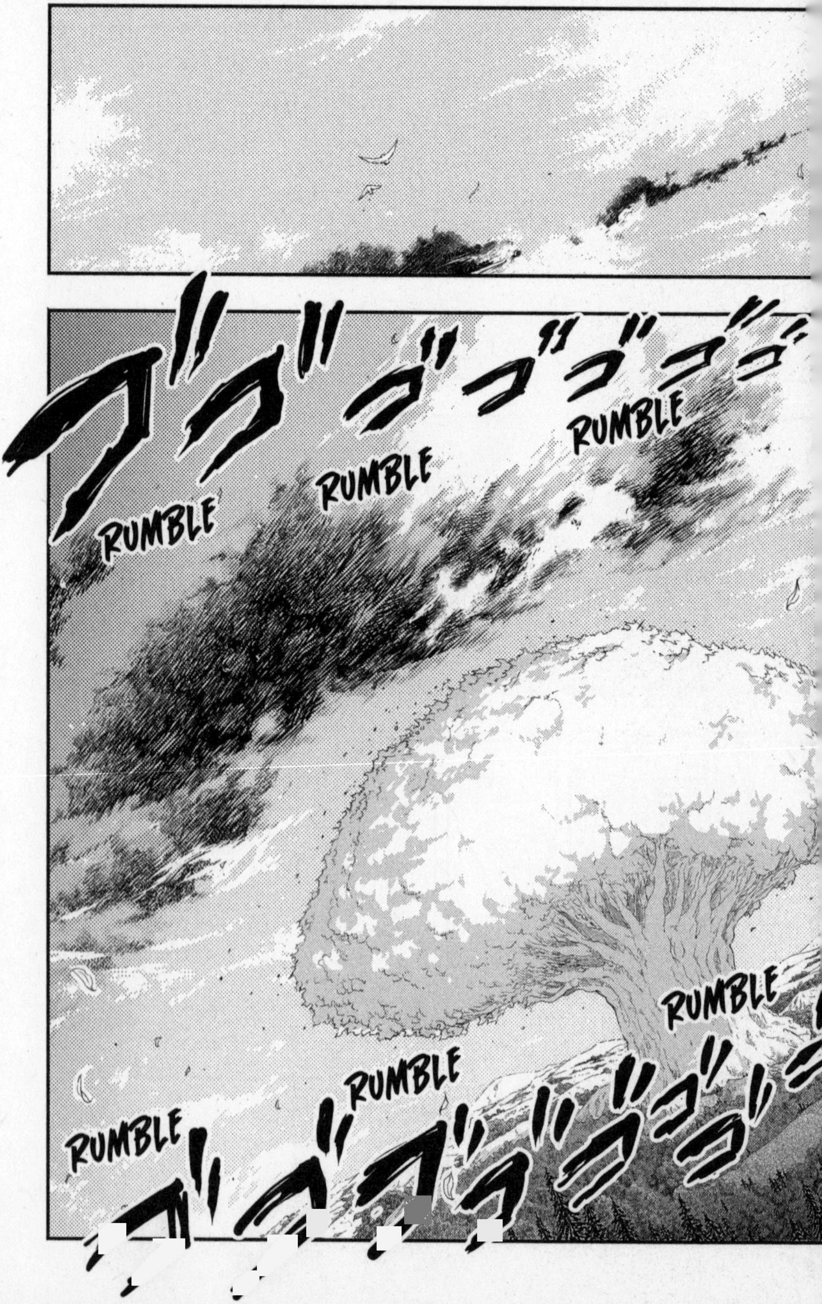
ゴゴゴゴゴゴ
RUMBLE
RUMBLE
RUMBLE
RUMBLE
RUMBLE
RUMBLE

onus Chapter
Day in the Fairy King's Forest – Part 2

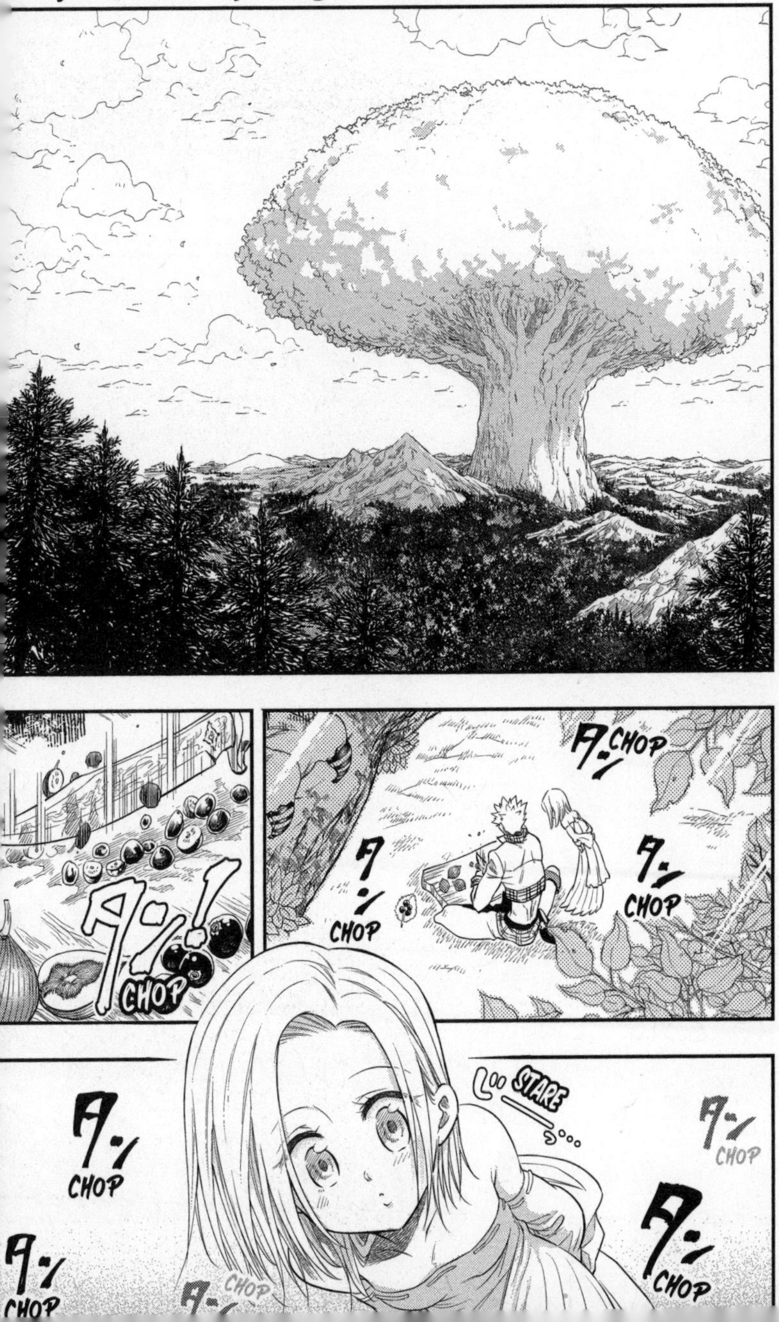
CHOP
CHOP
CHOP
CHOP
STARE
CHOP
CHOP
CHOP
CHOP
CHOP

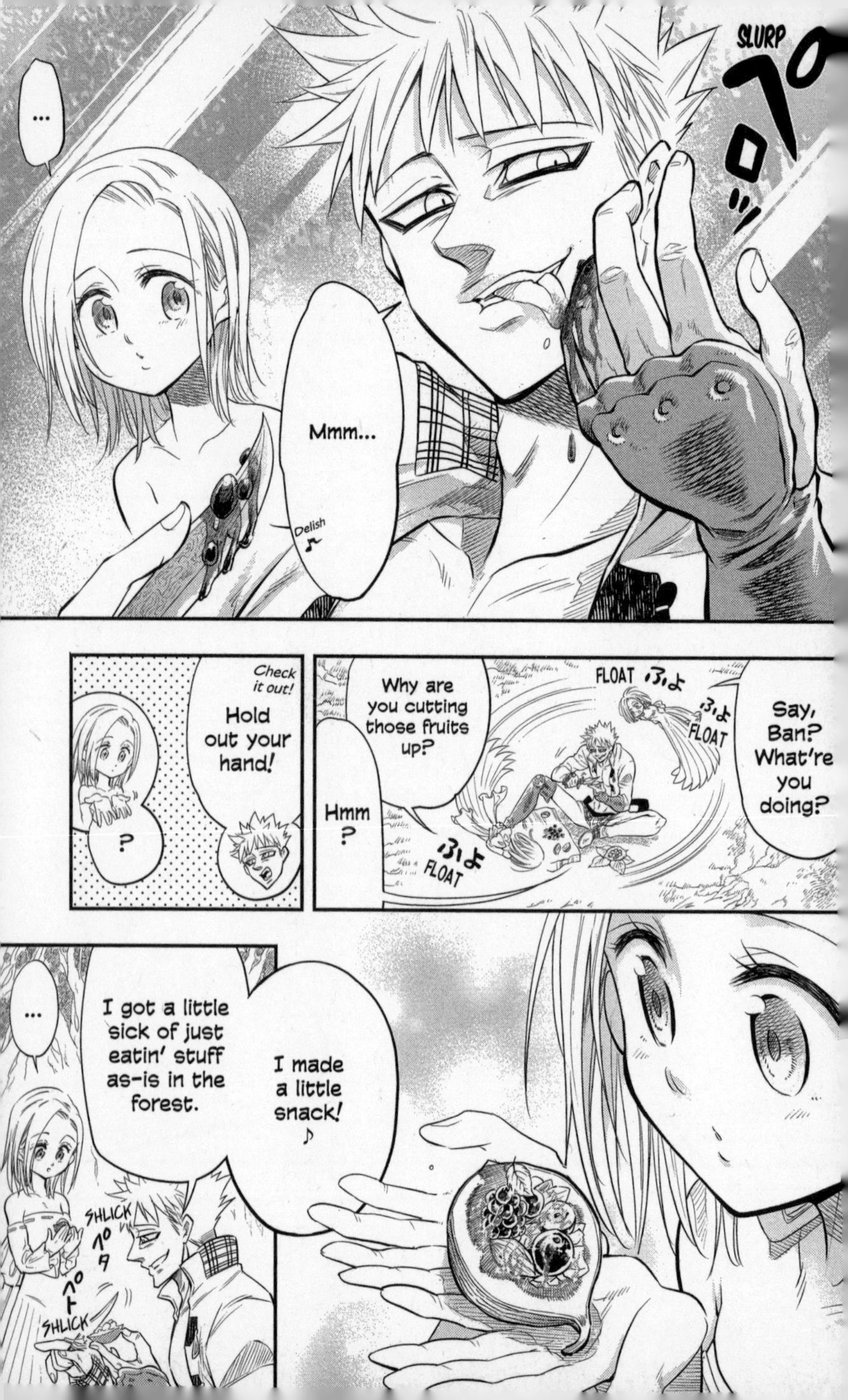
SLURP
ペロッ
Mmm...
Delish ♪
...
Say, Ban? What're you doing?
FLOAT ふよ
ふよ FLOAT
Why are you cutting those fruits up?
Hmm?
ふよ FLOAT
Check it out! Hold out your hand!
?
I got a little sick of just eatin' stuff as-is in the forest.
I made a little snack! ♪
...
SHLICK ペタ
ペト SHLICK

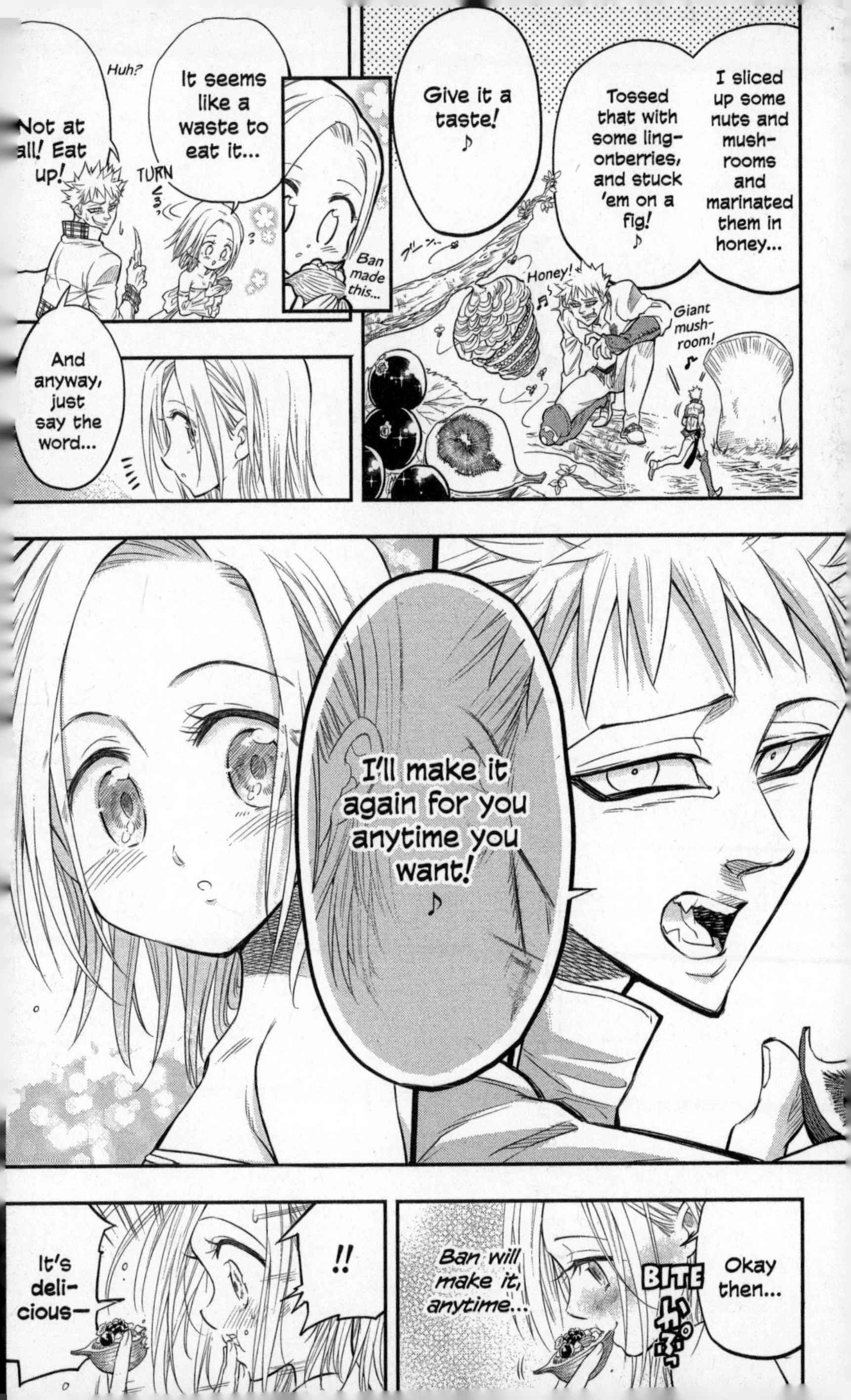
I sliced up some nuts and mushrooms and marinated them in honey...
Tossed that with some lingonberries, and stuck 'em on a fig! ♪
Give it a taste! ♪
Honey! ♪
Giant mushroom! ♪
Ban made this...
It seems like a waste to eat it...
Huh?
TURN
Not at all! Eat up!
And anyway, just say the word...
I'll make it again for you anytime you want! ♪
Okay then...
BITE
Ban will make it, anytime...
!!
It's delicious—

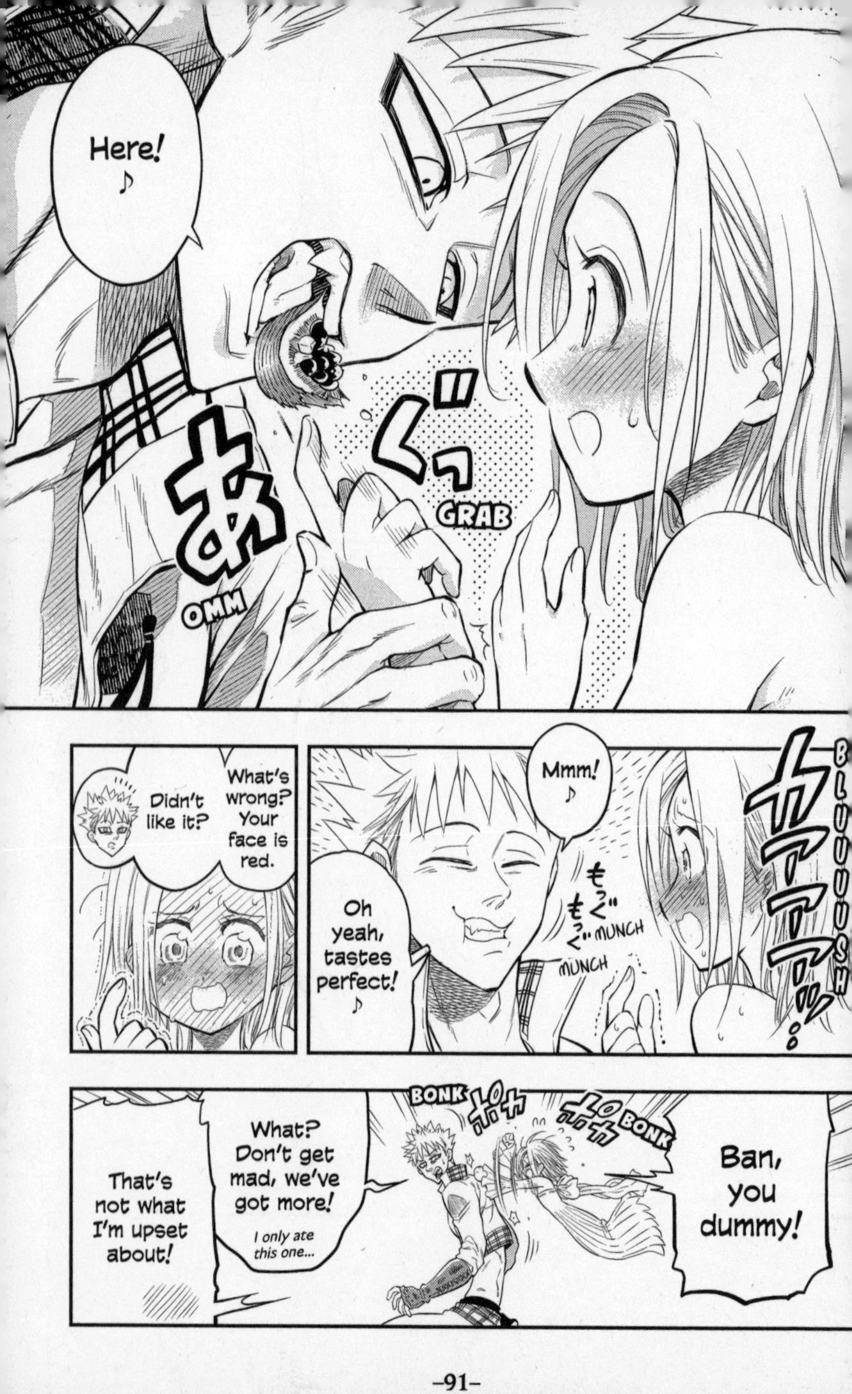

Here! ♪
ぐっ
GRAB
あ
OMM
カァァァッ
BLUUUUSH
Mmm! ♪
もぐ もぐ
MUNCH MUNCH
Oh yeah, tastes perfect! ♪
What's wrong? Your face is red.
Didn't like it?
Ban, you dummy!
ポカ
BONK
ポカ
BONK
What? Don't get mad, we've got more!
I only ate this one...
That's not what I'm upset about!

hapter 6
he Wish

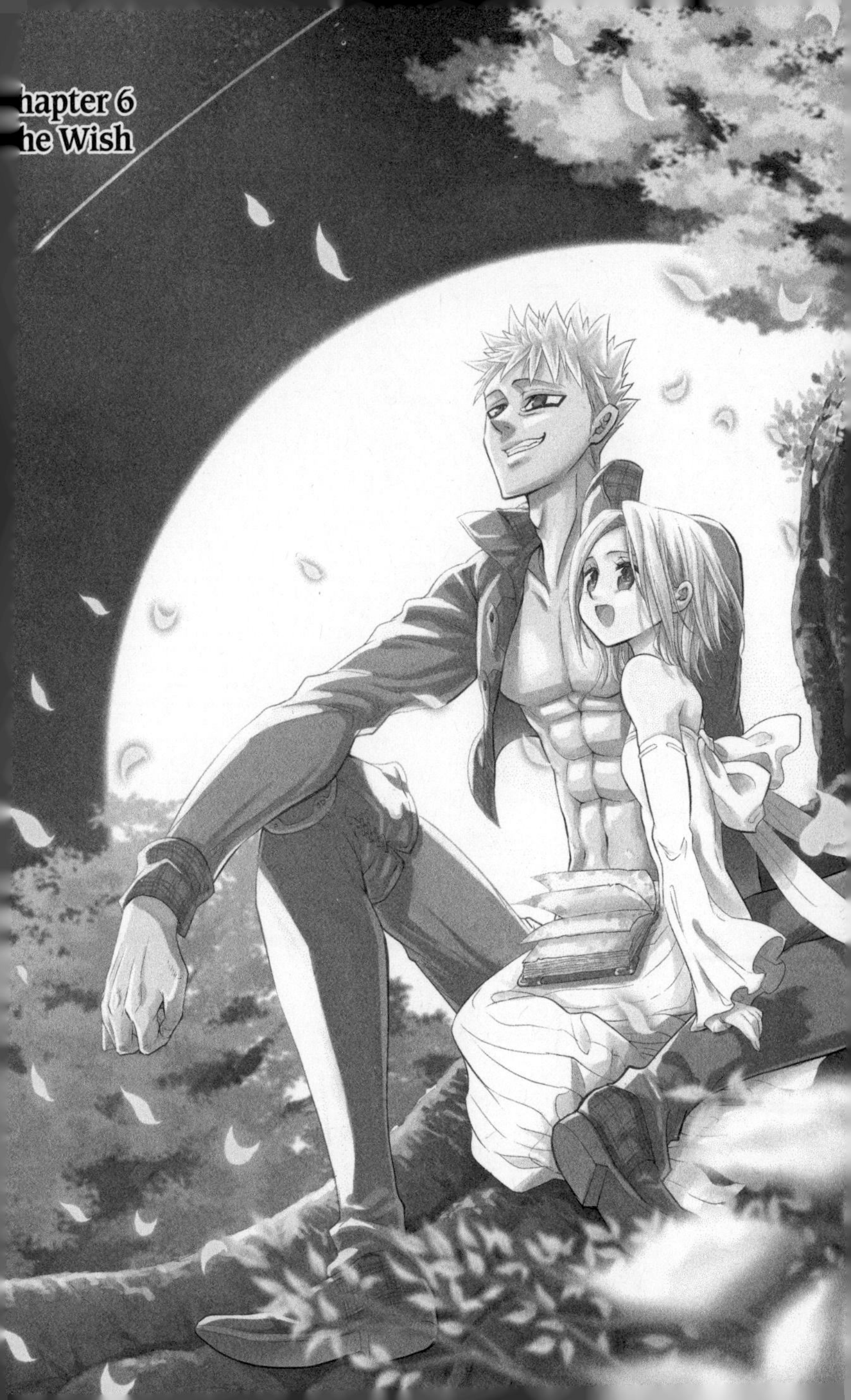

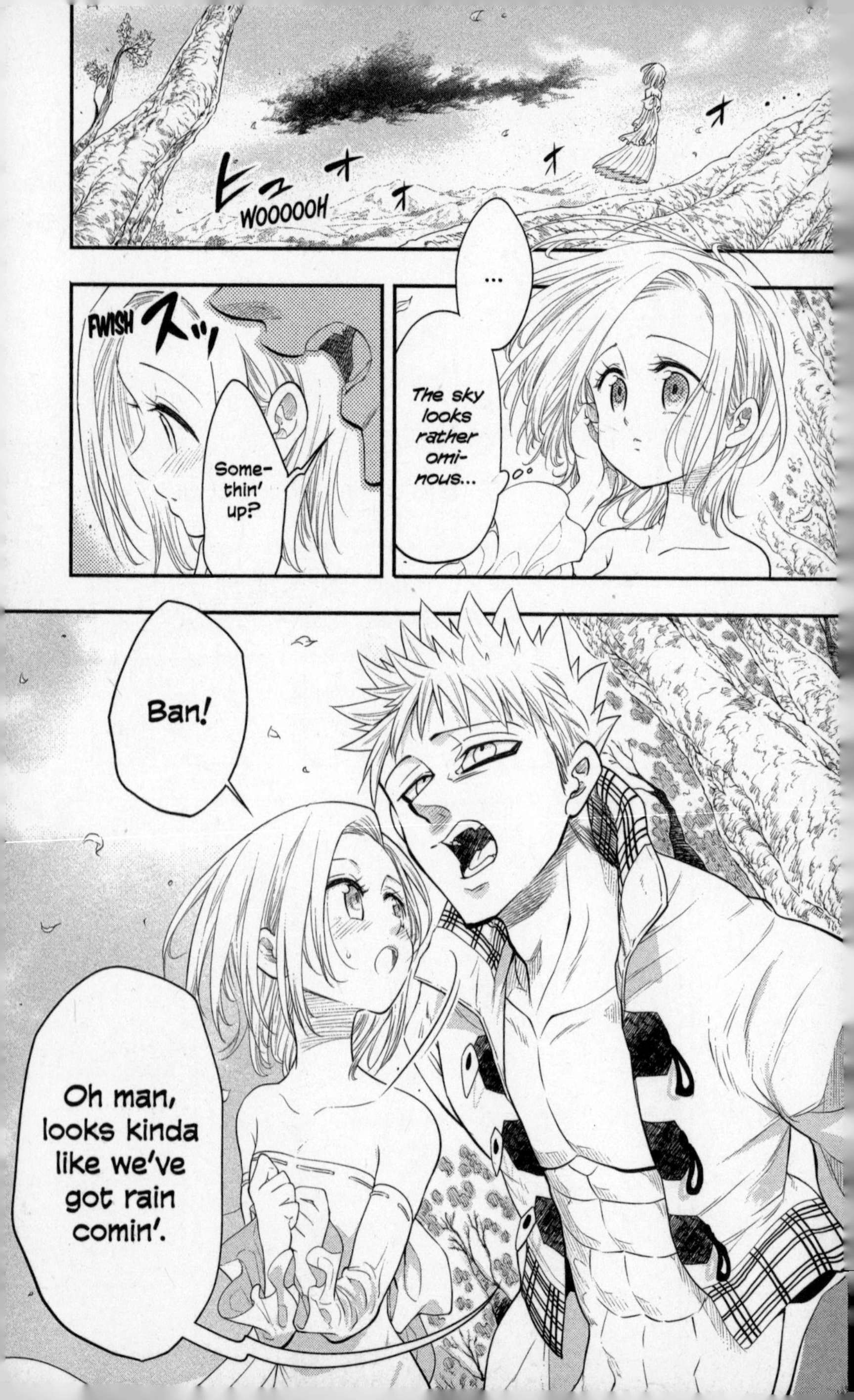
ヒュオオオ…
WOOOOOH
...
The sky looks rather omi-nous...
FWISH ズッ
Some-thin' up?
Ban!
Oh man, looks kinda like we've got rain comin'.

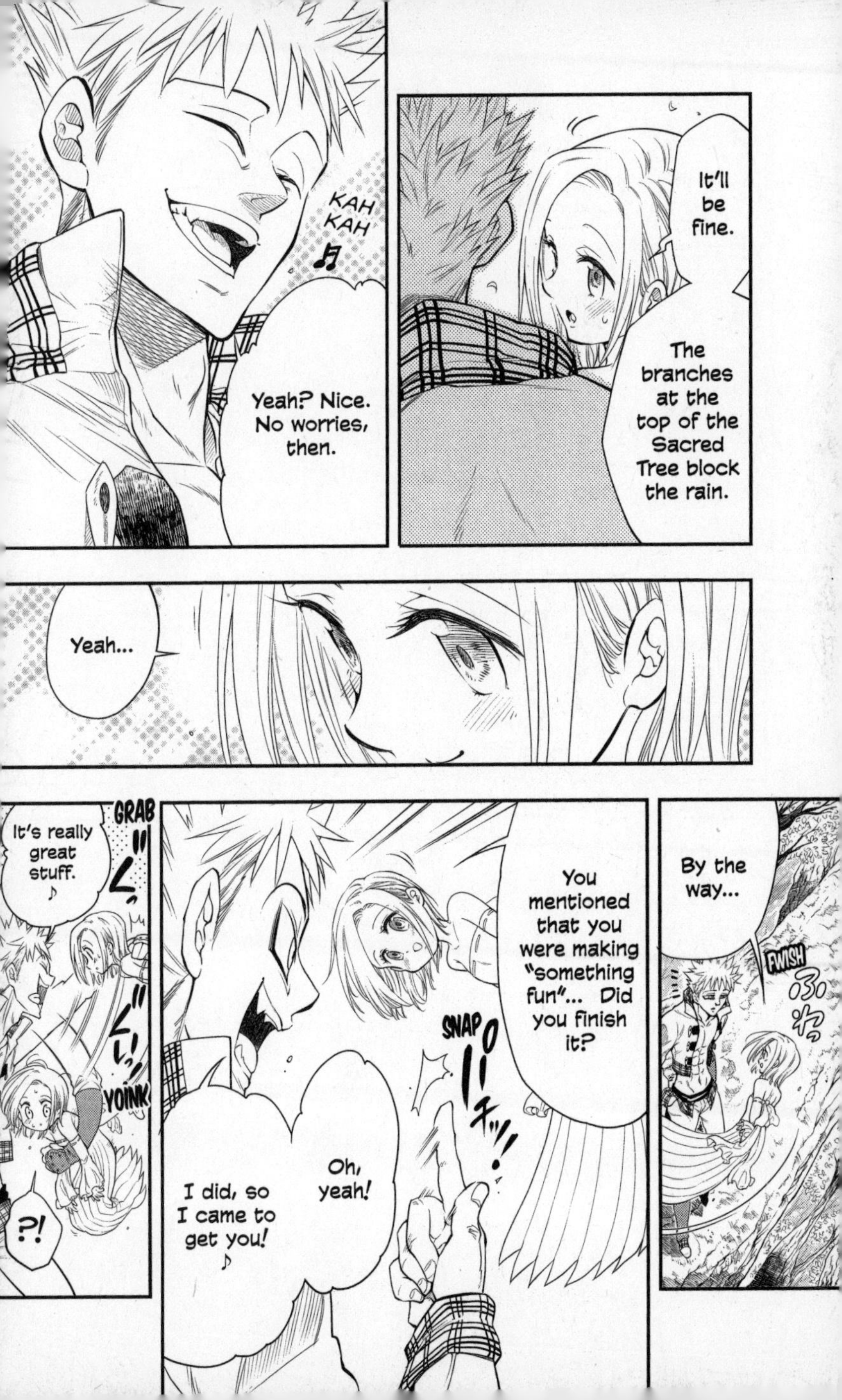
It'll be fine.
The branches at the top of the Sacred Tree block the rain.
KAH KAH ♪
Yeah? Nice. No worries, then.
Yeah...
By the way...
FWISH
You mentioned that you were making "something fun"... Did you finish it?
SNAP
Oh, yeah!
I did, so I came to get you! ♪
GRAB
It's really great stuff. ♪
YOINK
?!

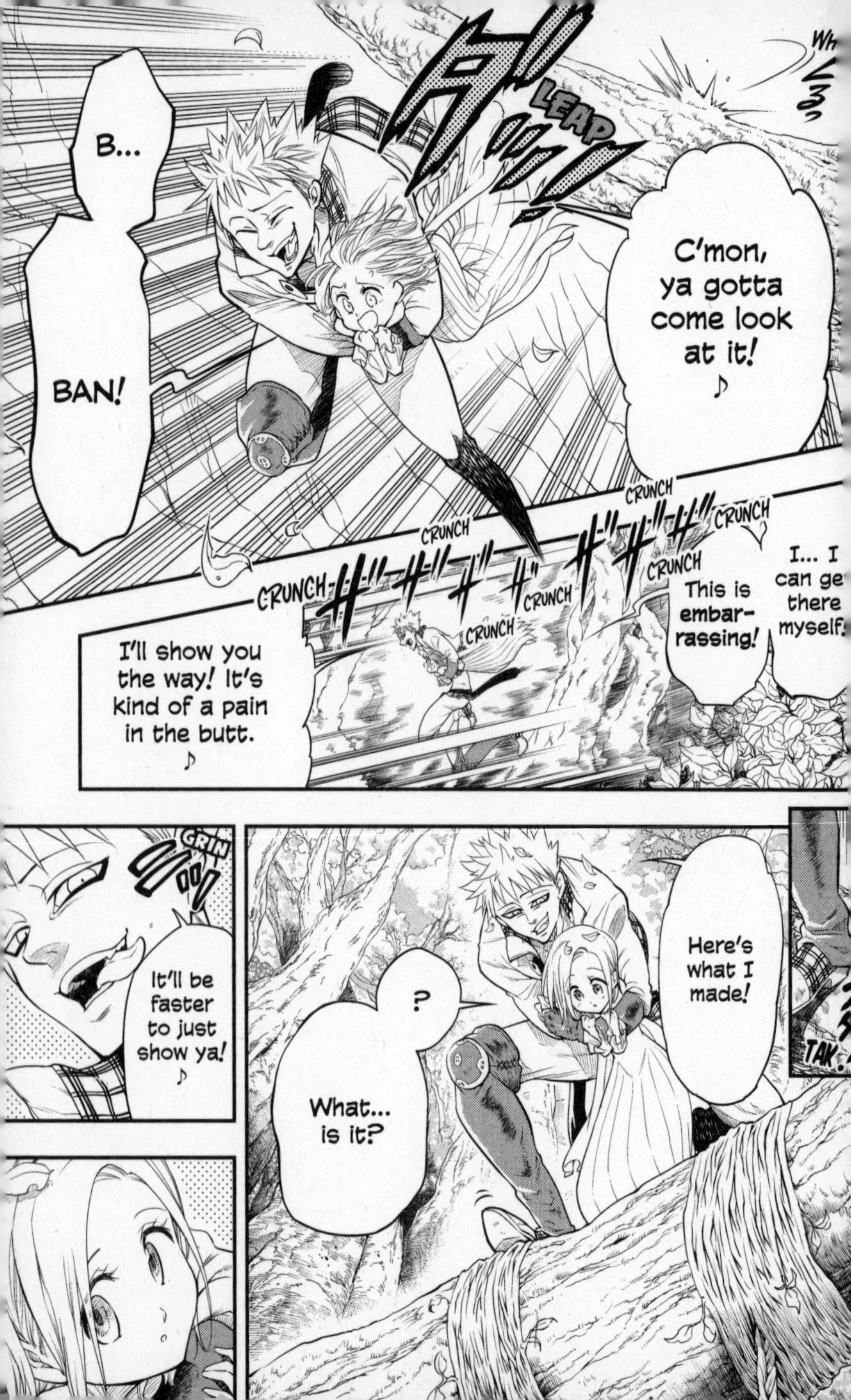
LEAP
C'mon, ya gotta come look at it! ♪
B...
BAN!
CRUNCH
CRUNCH
CRUNCH
CRUNCH
CRUNCH
CRUNCH
I... I can ge there myself!
This is embar-rassing!
I'll show you the way! It's kind of a pain in the butt. ♪
TAK
Here's what I made!
?
What... is it?
GRIN
It'll be faster to just show ya! ♪

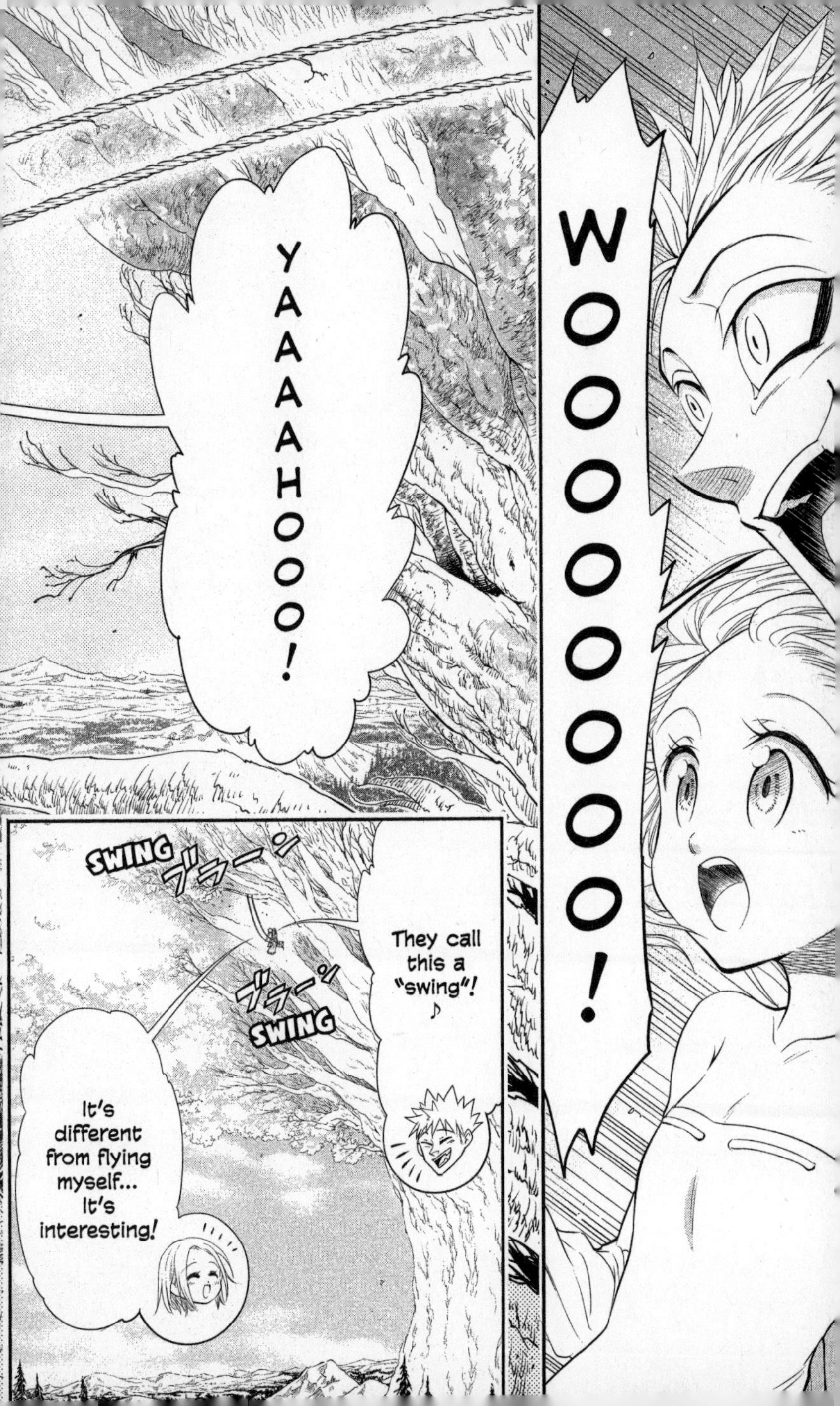
WOOOOOOOO!
YAAAHOOO!
SWING
SWING
They call this a "swing"! ♪
It's different from flying myself... It's interesting!

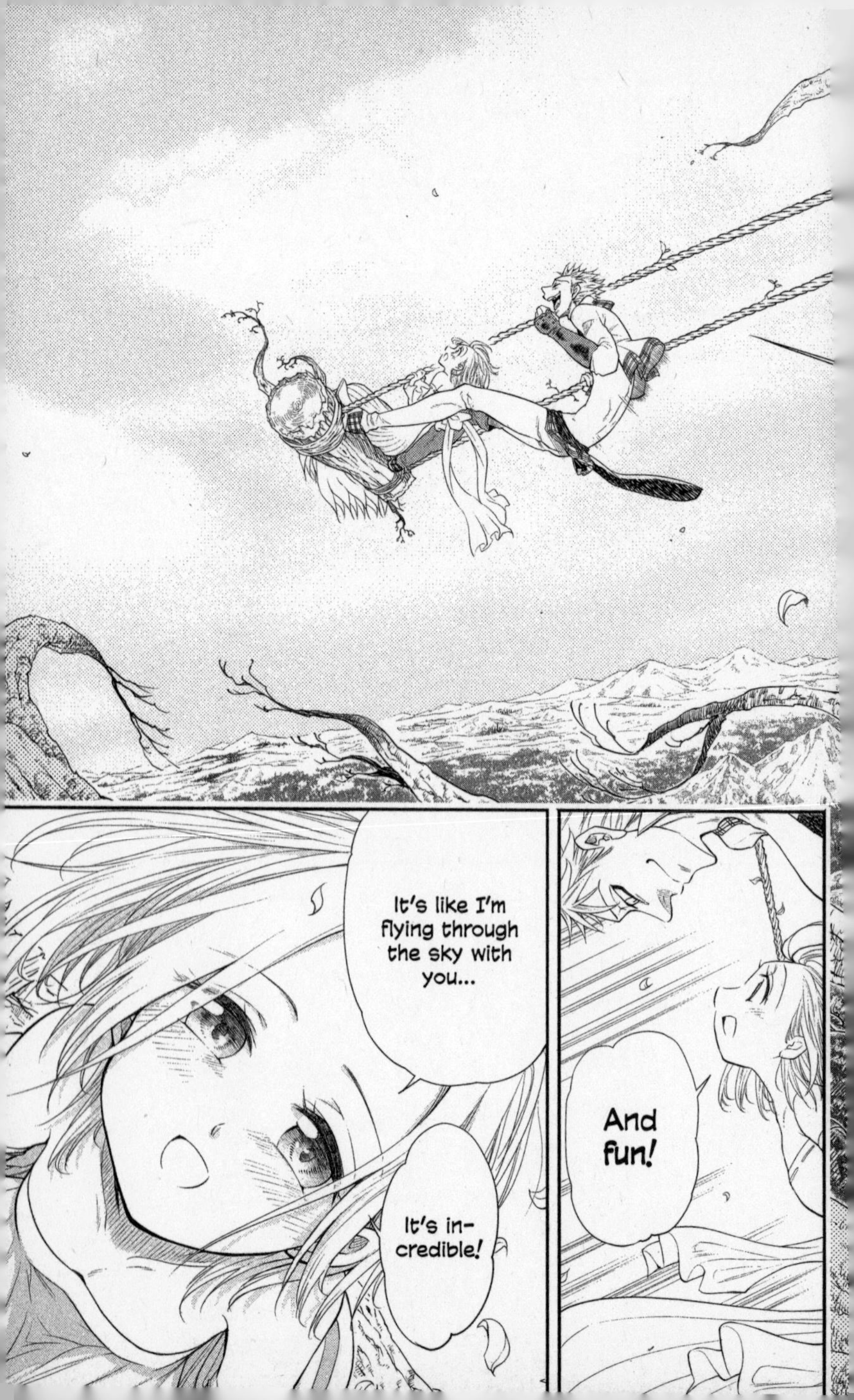

It's like I'm flying through the sky with you...
It's incredible!
And fun!

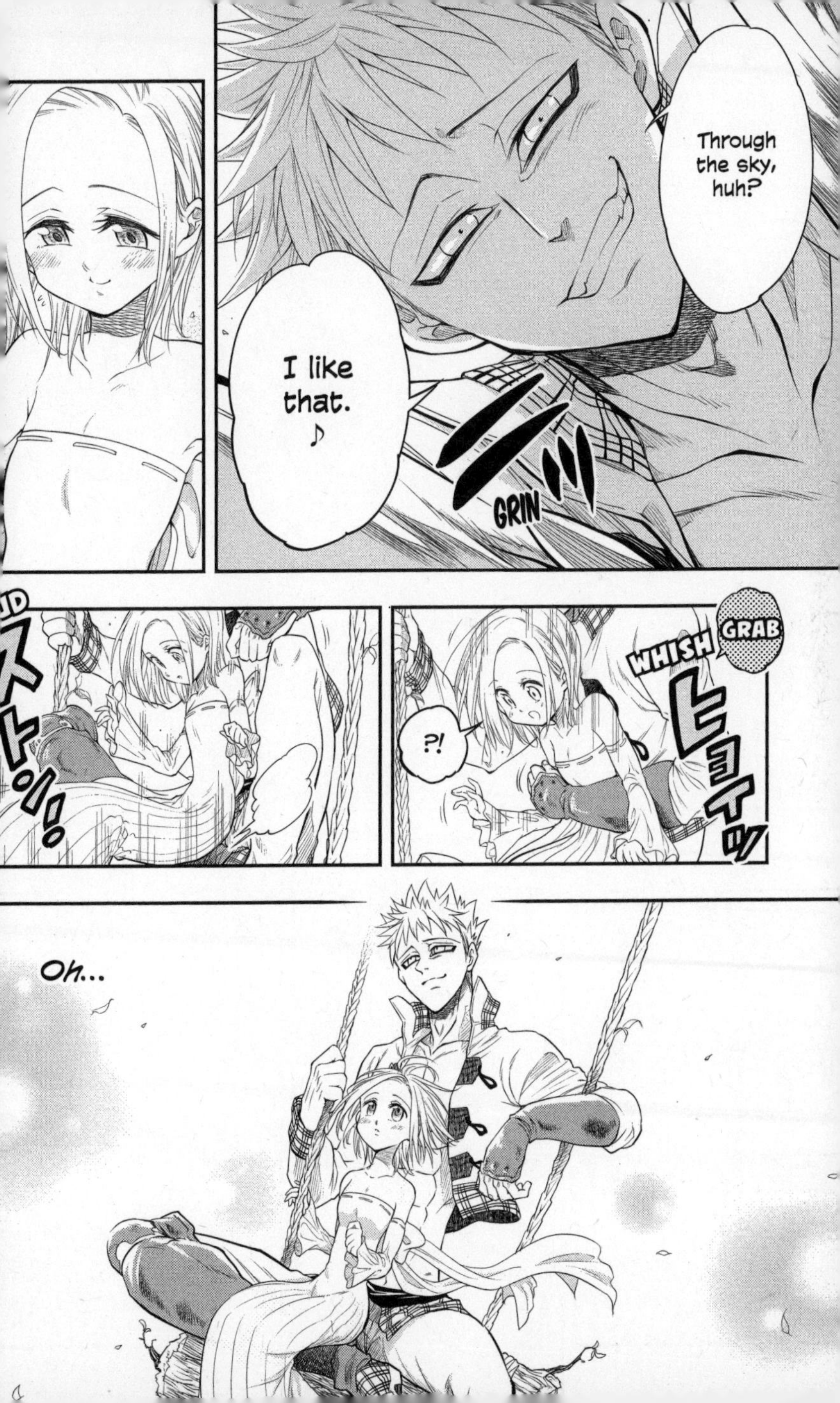
Through the sky, huh?
I like that. ♪
GRIN
GRAB
WHISH
ヒョイッ
?!
ストッ!!
Oh...

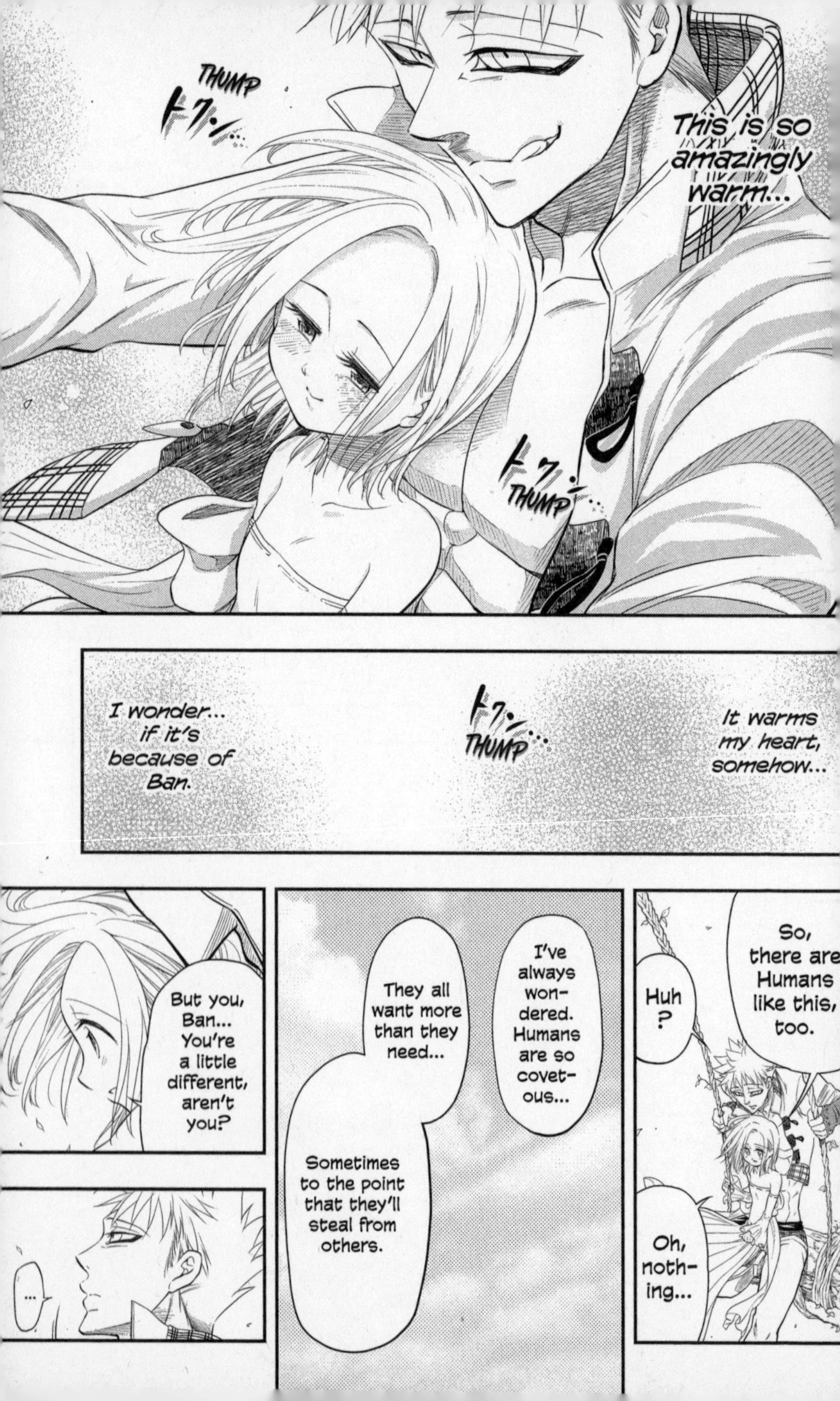
This is so amazingly warm...
THUMP
トク
トク
THUMP
It warms my heart, somehow...
トク
THUMP
I wonder... if it's because of Ban.
So, there are Humans like this, too.
Huh?
Oh, nothing...
I've always wondered. Humans are so covetous...
They all want more than they need...
Sometimes to the point that they'll steal from others.
But you, Ban... You're a little different, aren't you?
...

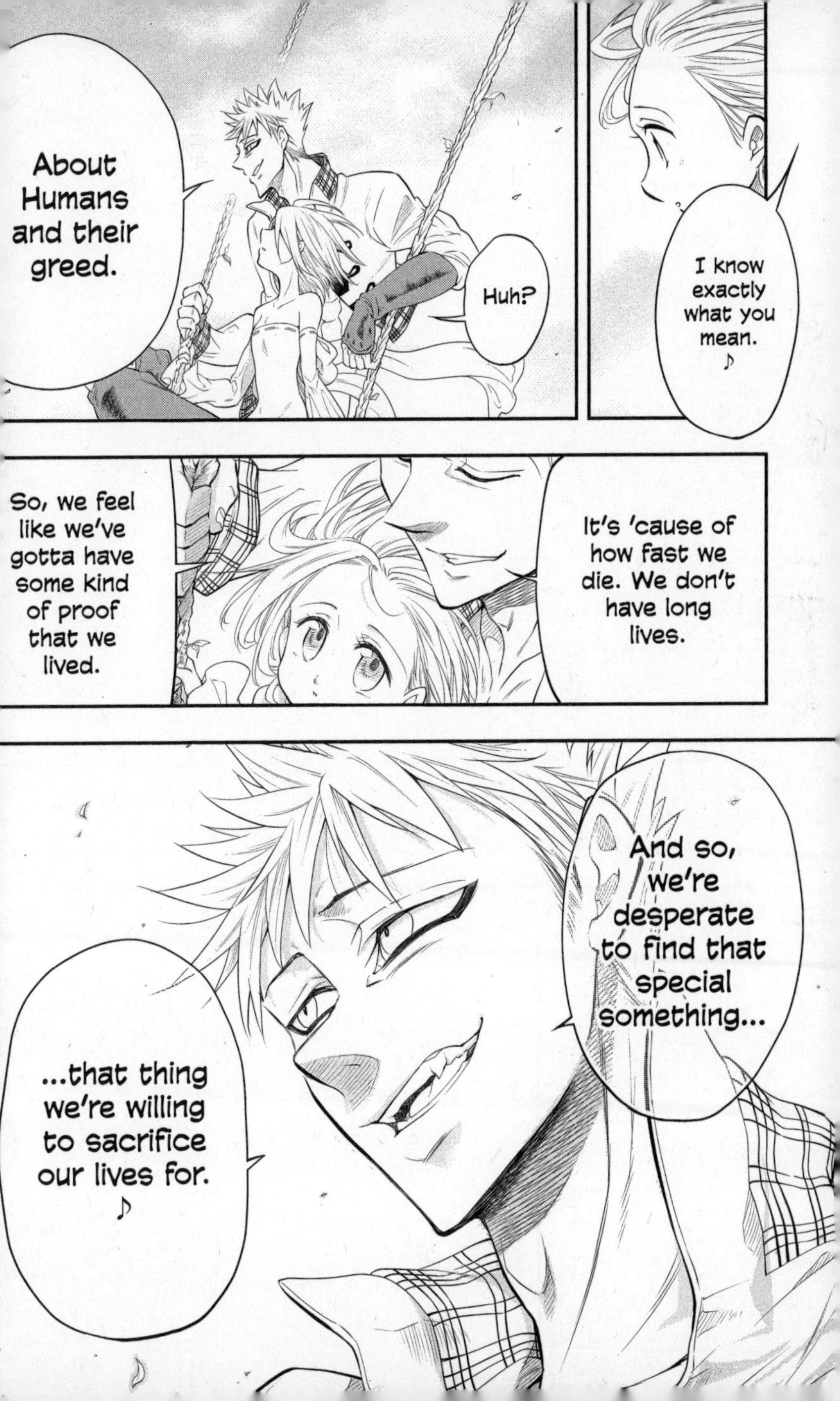
I know exactly what you mean. ♪
About Humans and their greed.
Huh?
It's 'cause of how fast we die. We don't have long lives.
So, we feel like we've gotta have some kind of proof that we lived.
And so, we're desperate to find that special something...
...that thing we're willing to sacrifice our lives for. ♪

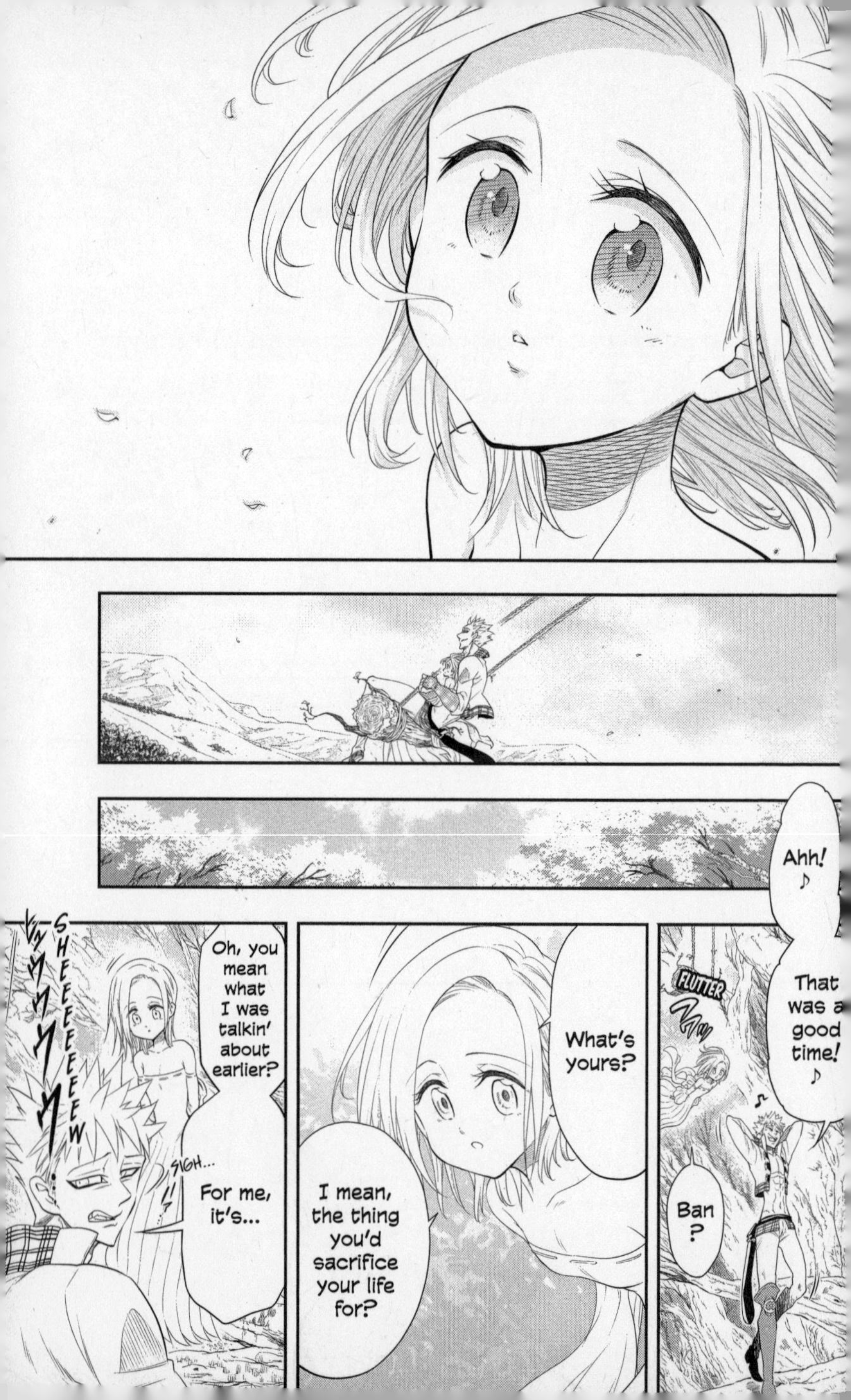
Ahh! ♪
That was a good time! ♪
FLUTTER
Ban?
What's yours?
I mean, the thing you'd sacrifice your life for?
Oh, you mean what I was talkin' about earlier?
SHEEEEEEEEW
SIGH...
For me, it's...

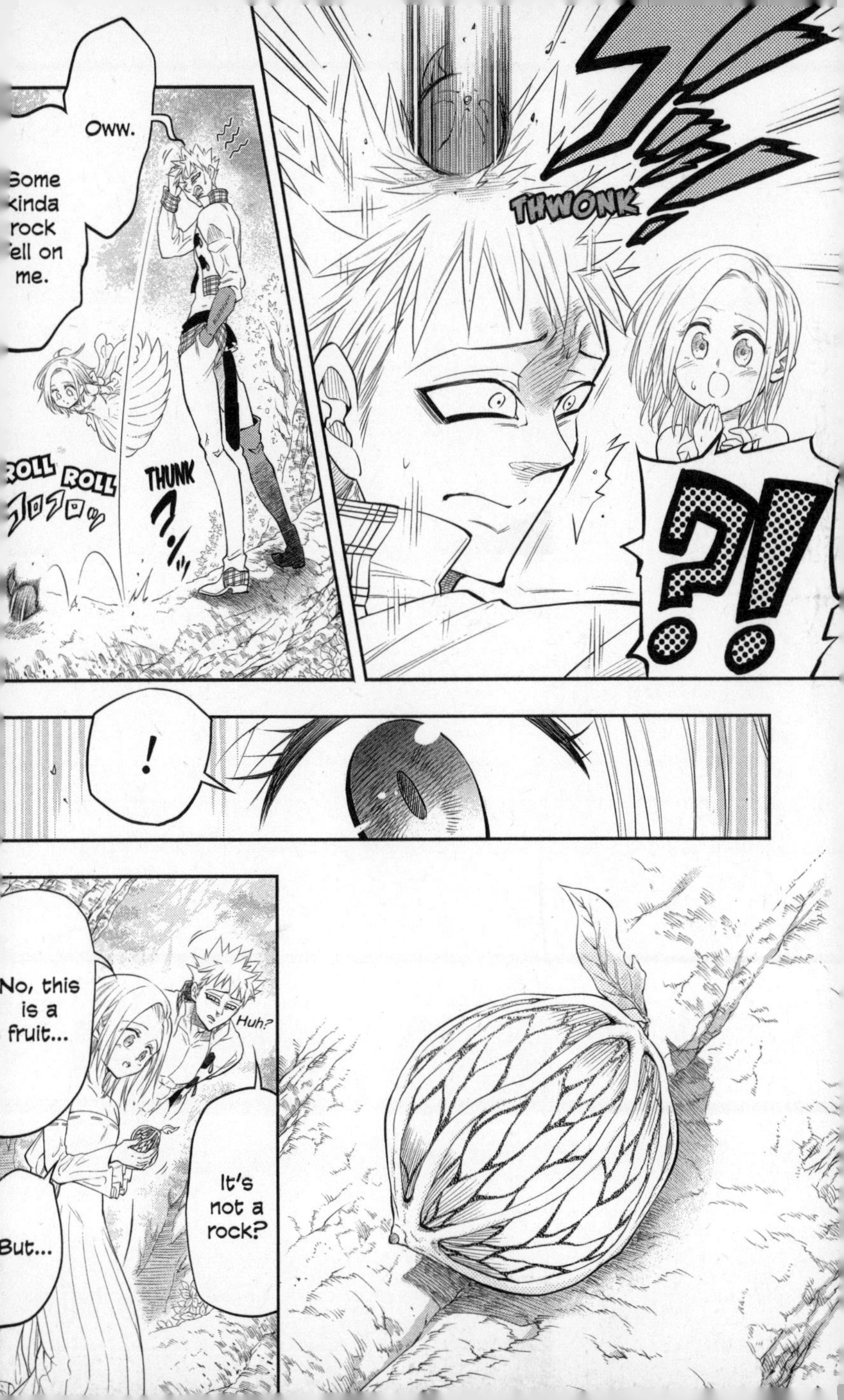

THWONK
?!!
Oww.
Some kinda rock fell on me.
THUNK
ROLL ROLL
コロコロッ
!
Huh?
It's not a rock?
No, this is a fruit...
But...

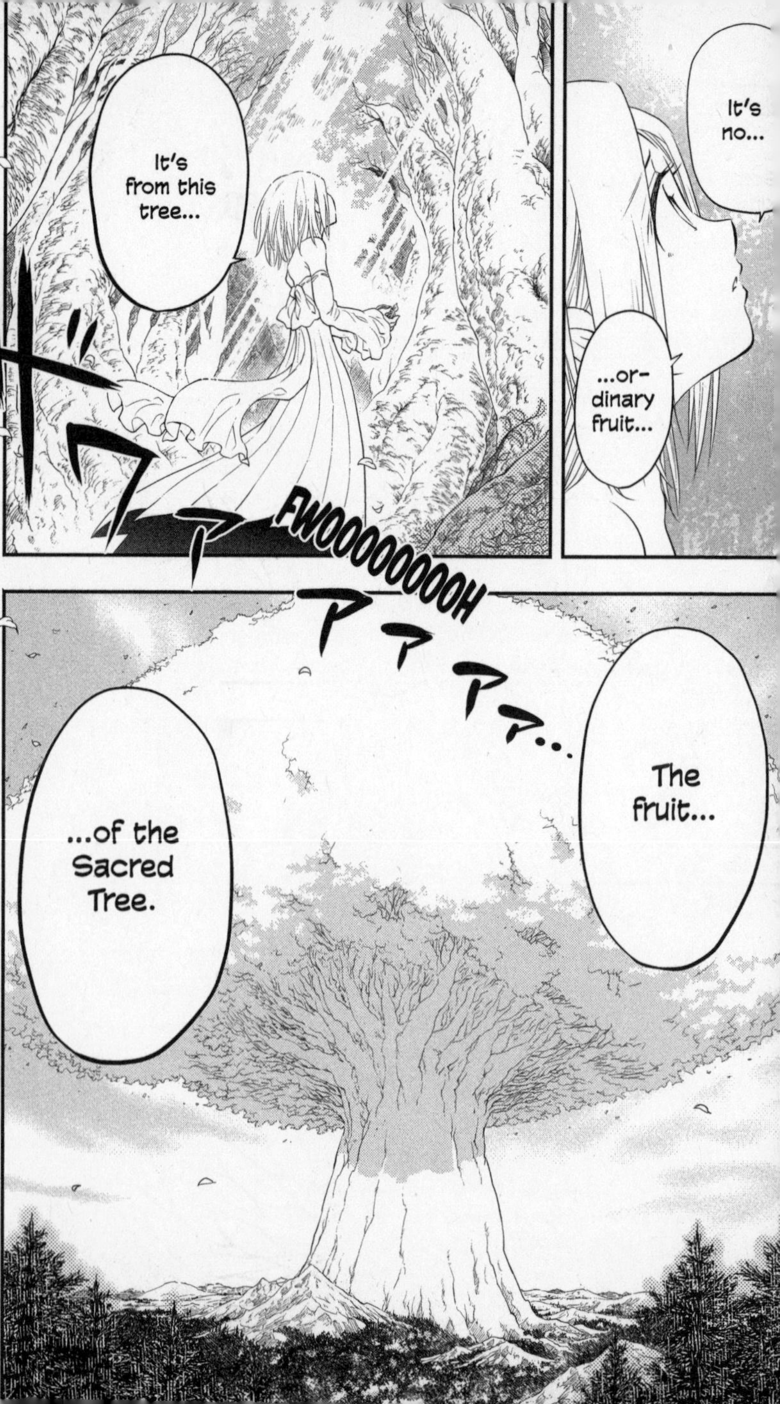
It's no...
...or-dinary fruit...
It's from this tree...
FWOOOOOOOOOOH
The fruit...
...of the Sacred Tree.

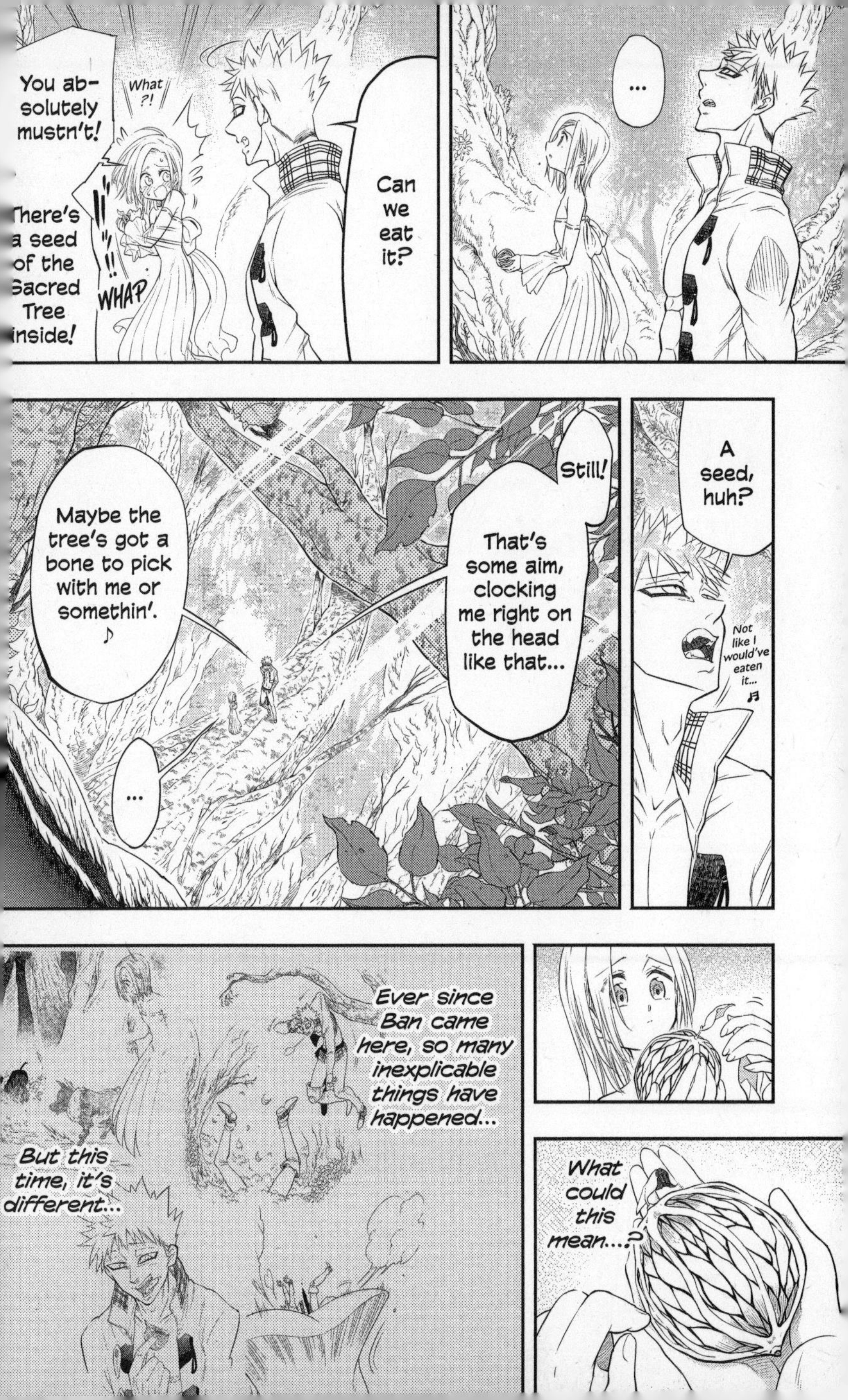
...
Can we eat it?
What ?!
You ab-solutely mustn't!
There's a seed of the Sacred Tree inside!
WHAP
A seed, huh?
Not like I would've eaten it... ♬
Still!
That's some aim, clocking me right on the head like that...
Maybe the tree's got a bone to pick with me or somethin'. ♪
...
What could this mean...?
Ever since Ban came here, so many inexplicable things have happened...
But this time, it's different...

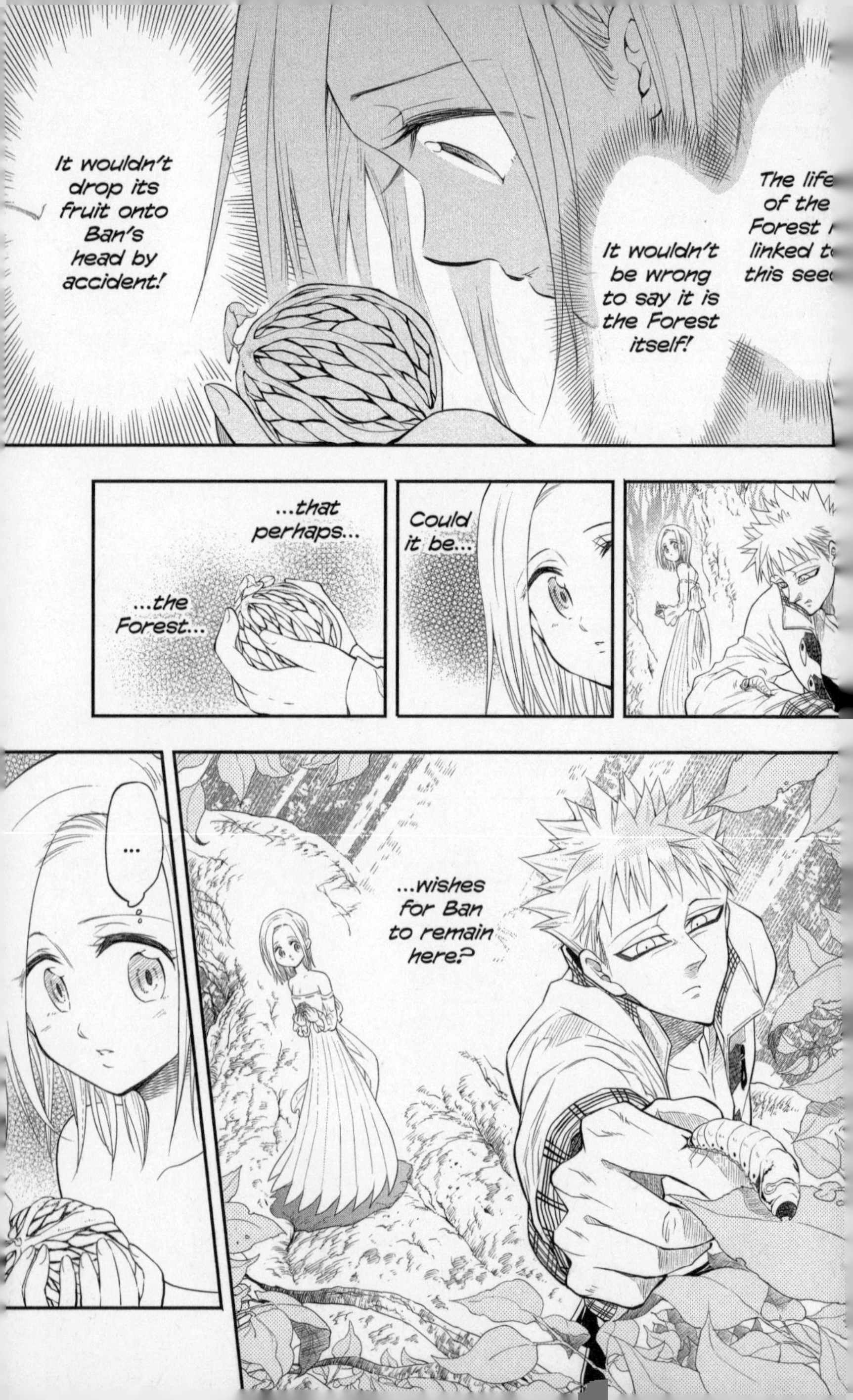
The life of the Forest linked t this see
It wouldn't be wrong to say it is the Forest itself!
It wouldn't drop its fruit onto Ban's head by accident!
Could it be...
...that perhaps...
...the Forest...
...wishes for Ban to remain here?
...

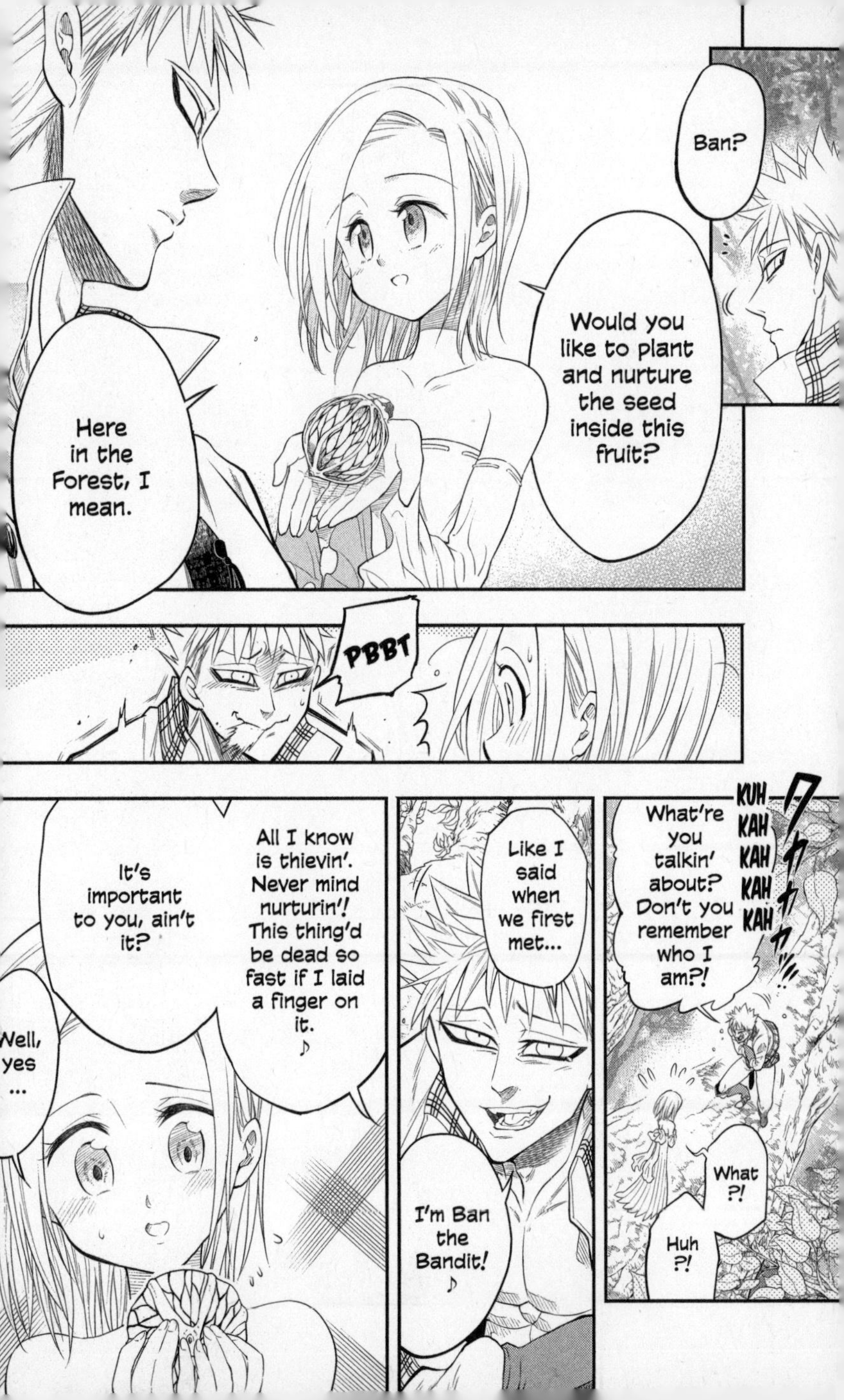
Ban?
Would you like to plant and nurture the seed inside this fruit?
Here in the Forest, I mean.
PBBT
What're you talkin' about? Don't you remember who I am?!
KUH KAH KAH KAH KAH
What ?!
Huh ?!
Like I said when we first met...
I'm Ban the Bandit! ♪
All I know is thievin'. Never mind nurturin'! This thing'd be dead so fast if I laid a finger on it. ♪
It's important to you, ain't it?
Well, yes ...

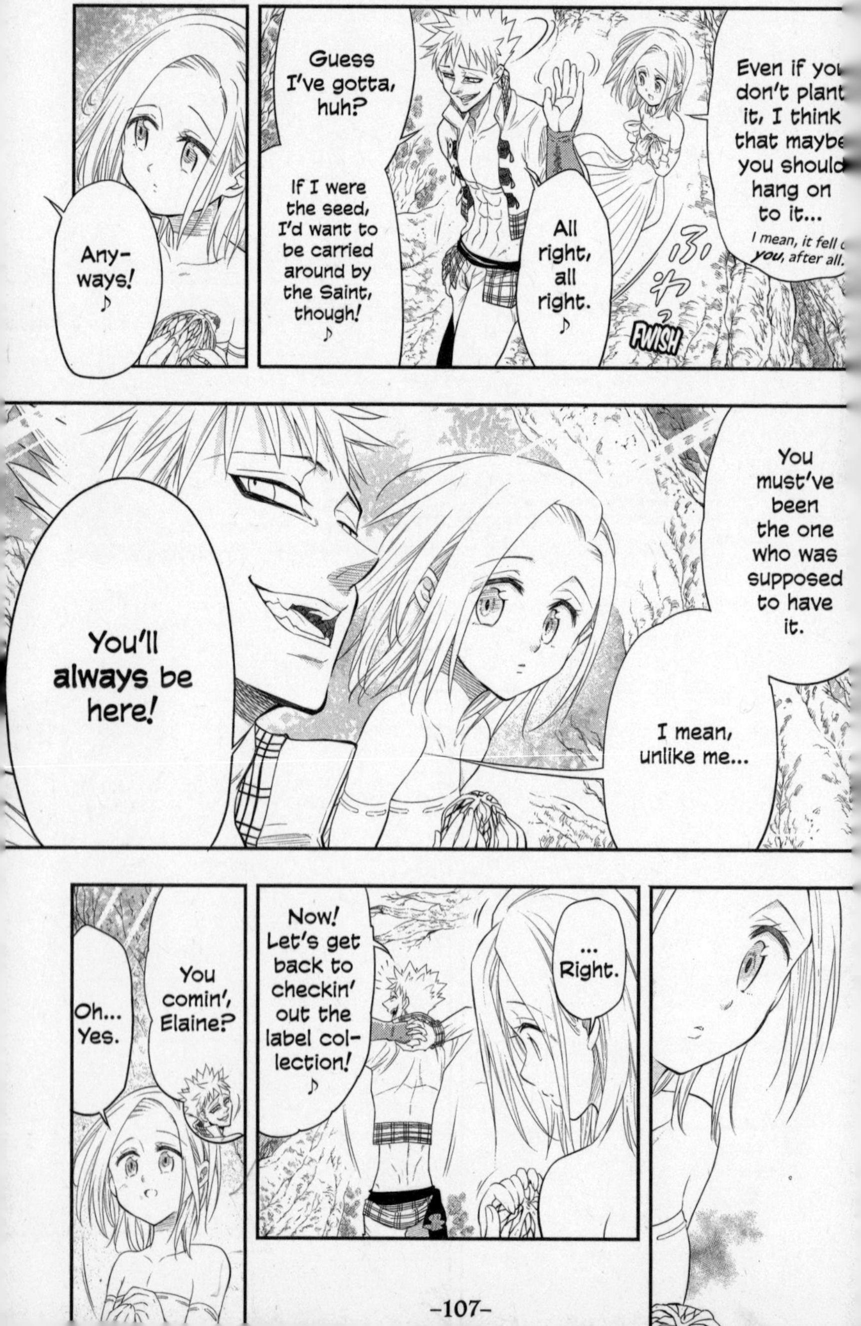
Even if you don't plant it, I think that maybe you should hang on to it...
I mean, it fell on you, after all.
FWISH
All right, all right. ♪
Guess I've gotta, huh?
If I were the seed, I'd want to be carried around by the Saint, though! ♪
Any-ways! ♪
You must've been the one who was supposed to have it.
I mean, unlike me...
You'll always be here!
... Right.
Now! Let's get back to checkin' out the label col-lection! ♪
You comin', Elaine?
Oh... Yes.

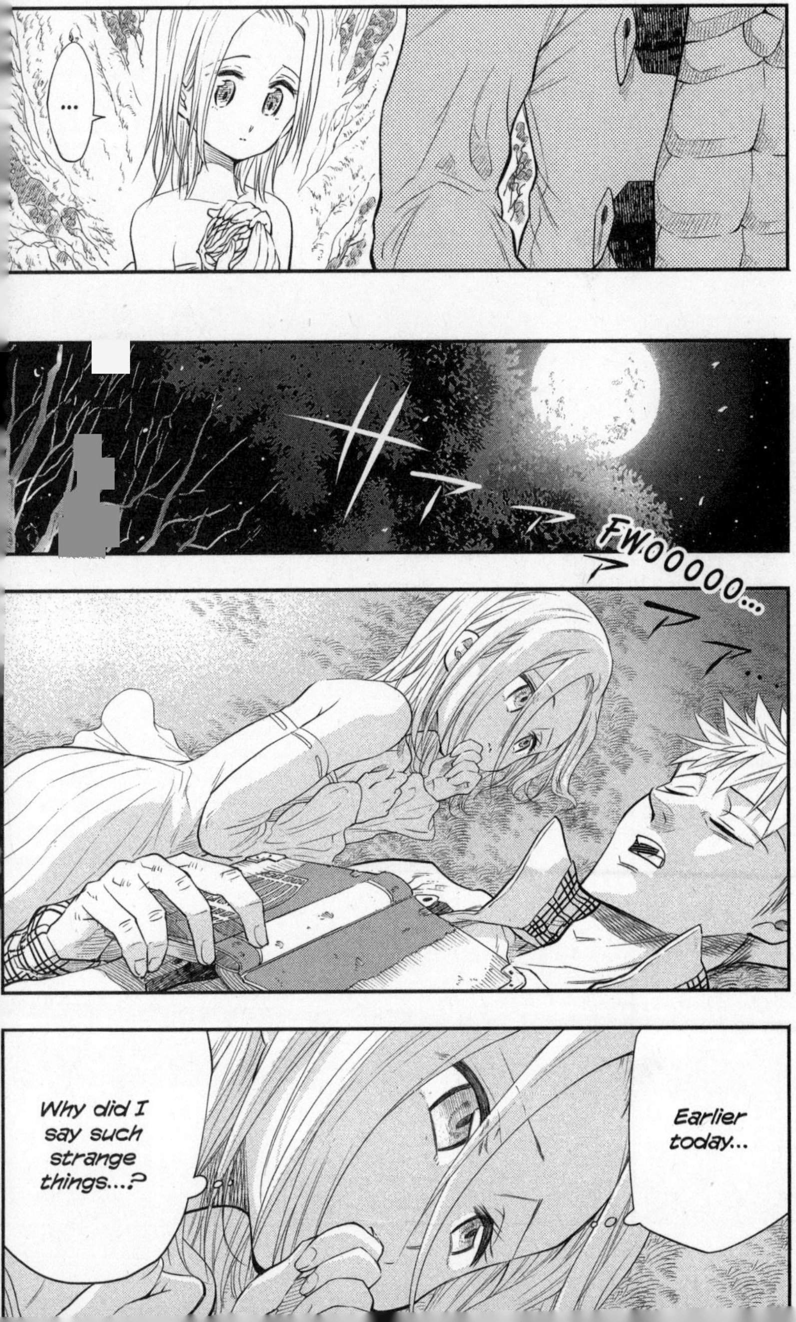
...
FWOOOOO...
Earlier today...
Why did I say such strange things...?

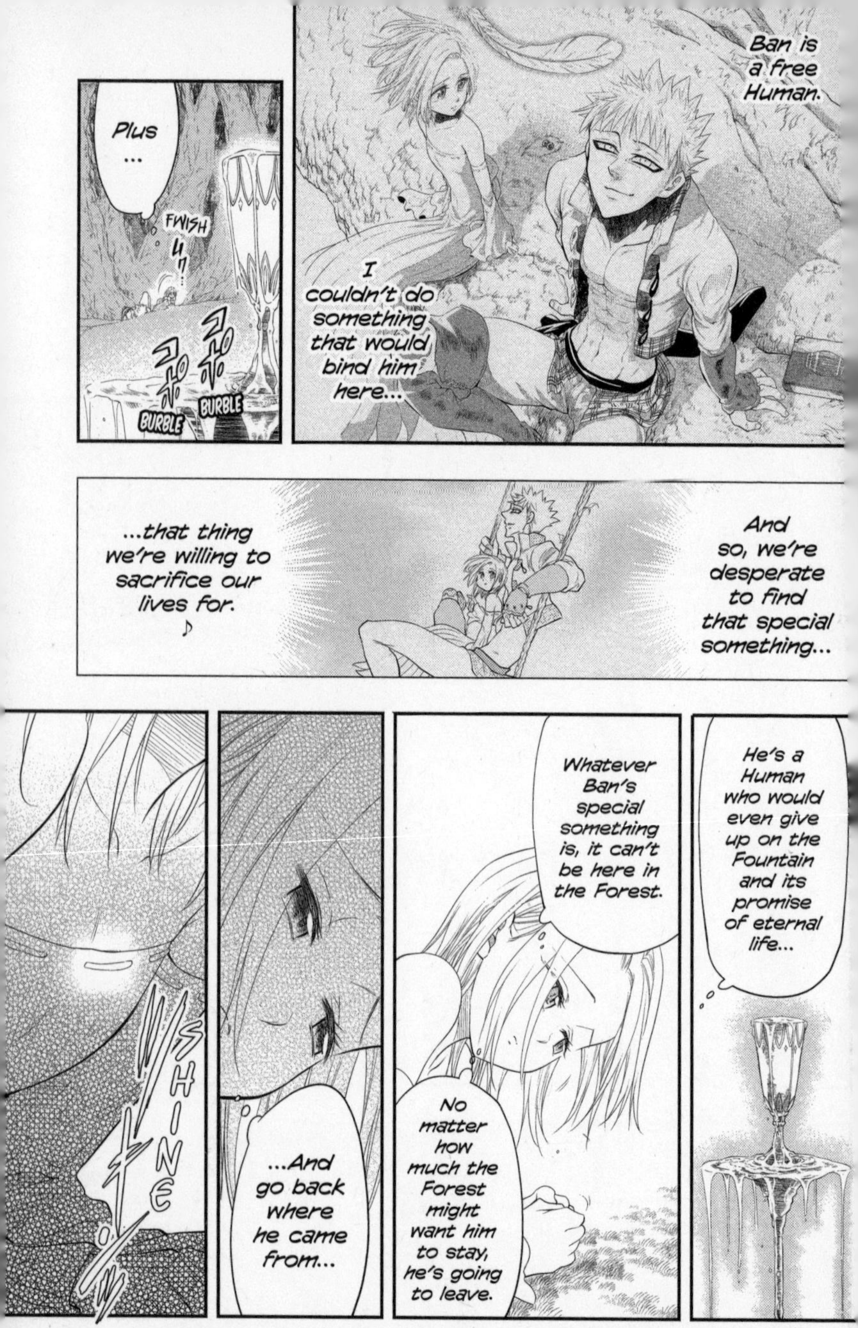
Ban is a free Human.
I couldn't do something that would bind him here...
Plus...
FWISH
BURBLE
BURBLE
And so, we're desperate to find that special something...
...that thing we're willing to sacrifice our lives for. ♪
He's a Human who would even give up on the Fountain and its promise of eternal life...
Whatever Ban's special something is, it can't be here in the Forest.
No matter how much the Forest might want him to stay, he's going to leave.
...And go back where he came from...
SHINE

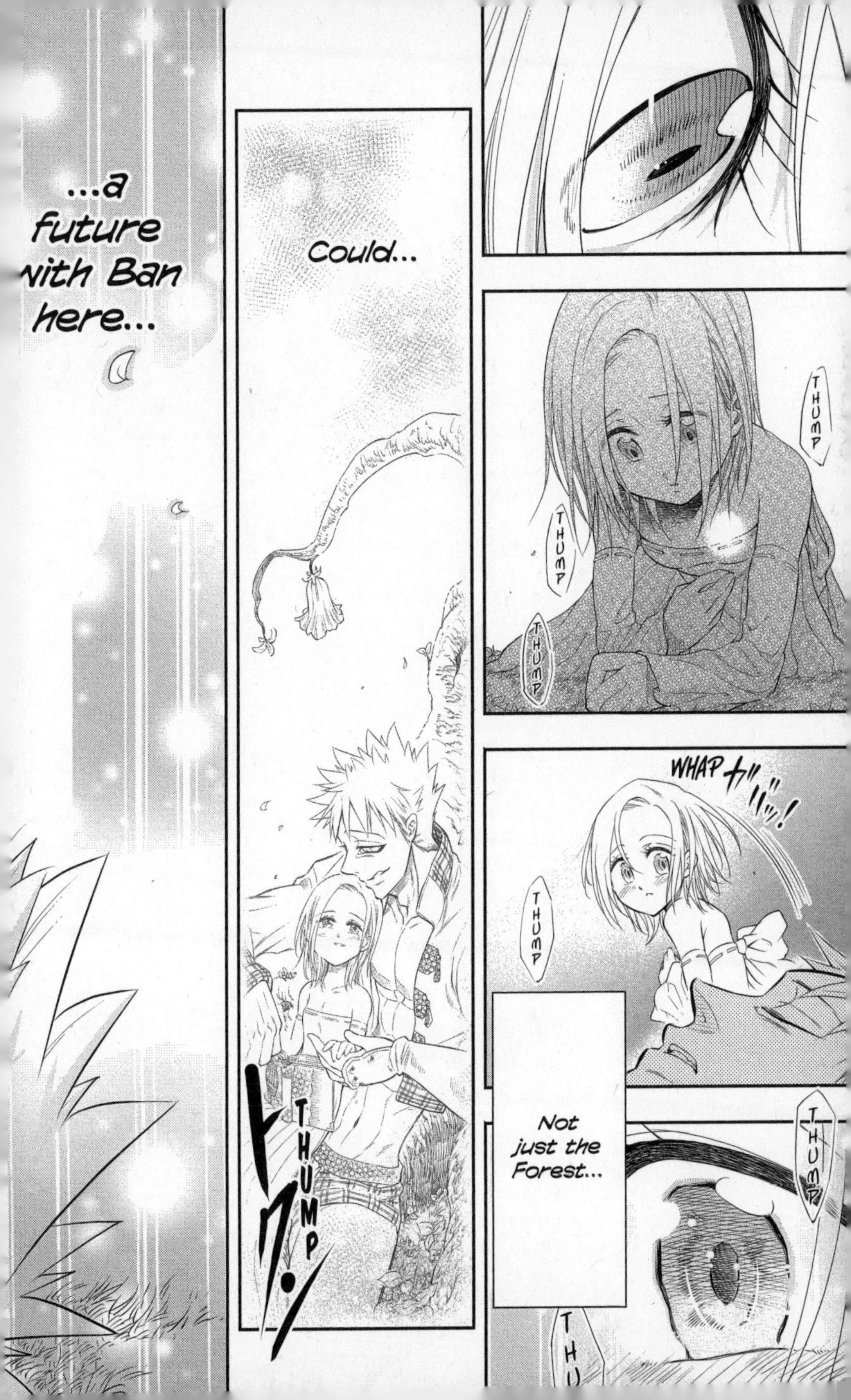
THUMP
THUMP
THUMP
WHAP
THUMP
Not just the Forest...
THUMP
THU
Could...
THUMP
...a future with Ban here...

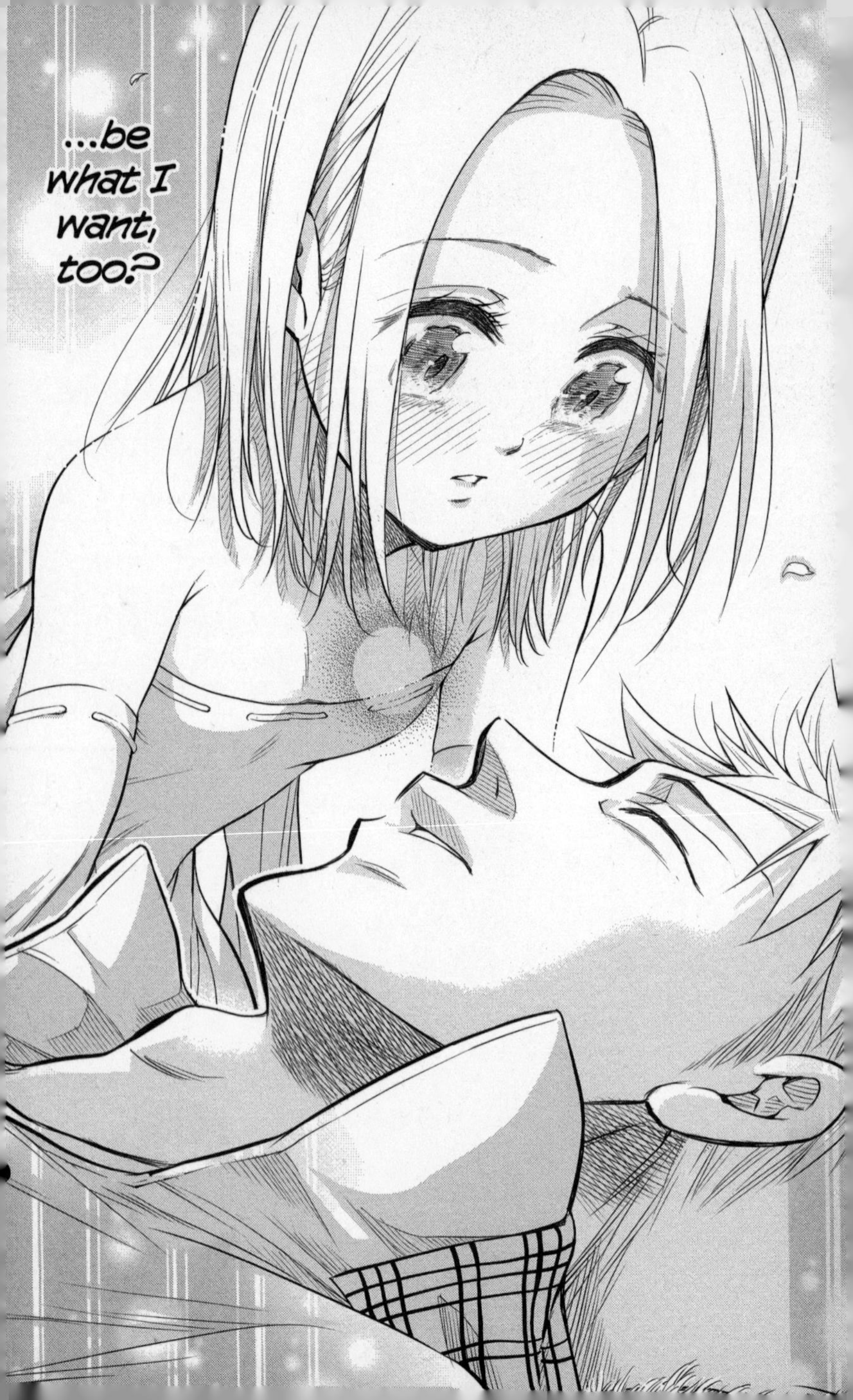
...be what I want, too?

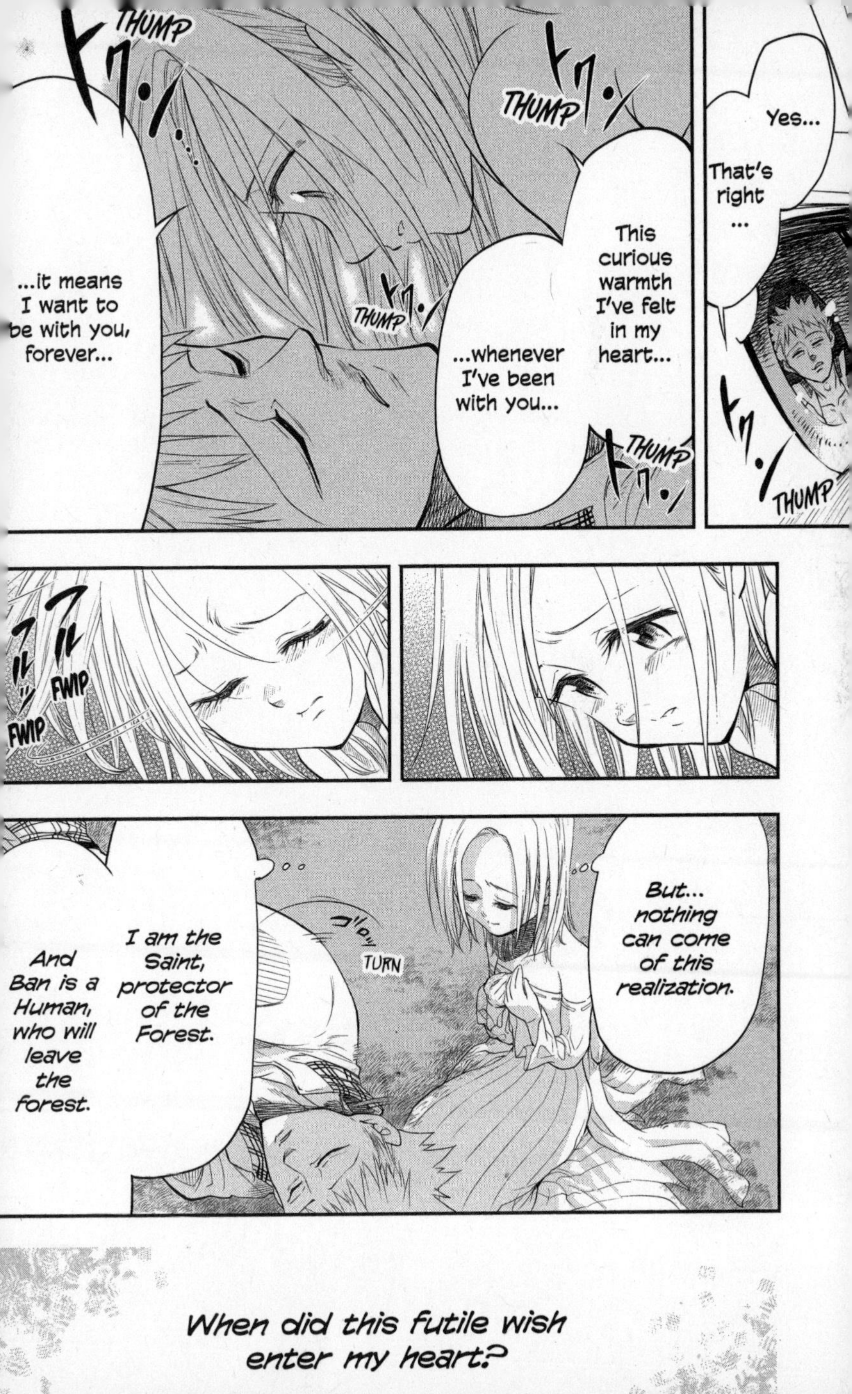
Yes...
That's right...
THUMP
This curious warmth I've felt in my heart...
THUMP
...whenever I've been with you...
THUMP
...it means I want to be with you, forever...
THUMP
THUMP
FWIP FWIP
But... nothing can come of this realization.
TURN
I am the Saint, protector of the Forest.
And Ban is a Human, who will leave the forest.
When did this futile wish enter my heart?

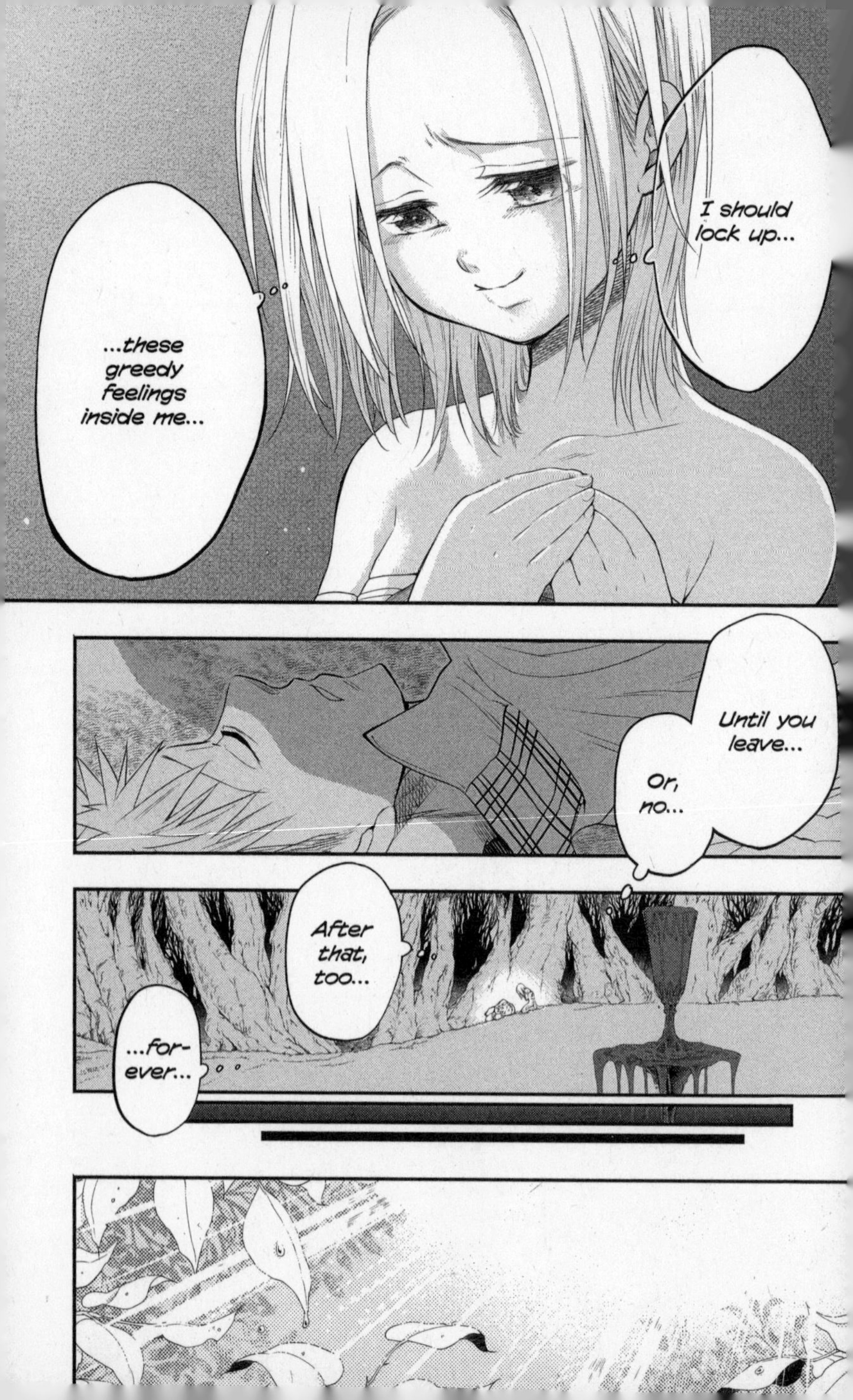
I should lock up...
...these greedy feelings inside me...
Until you leave...
Or, no...
After that, too...
...for-ever...

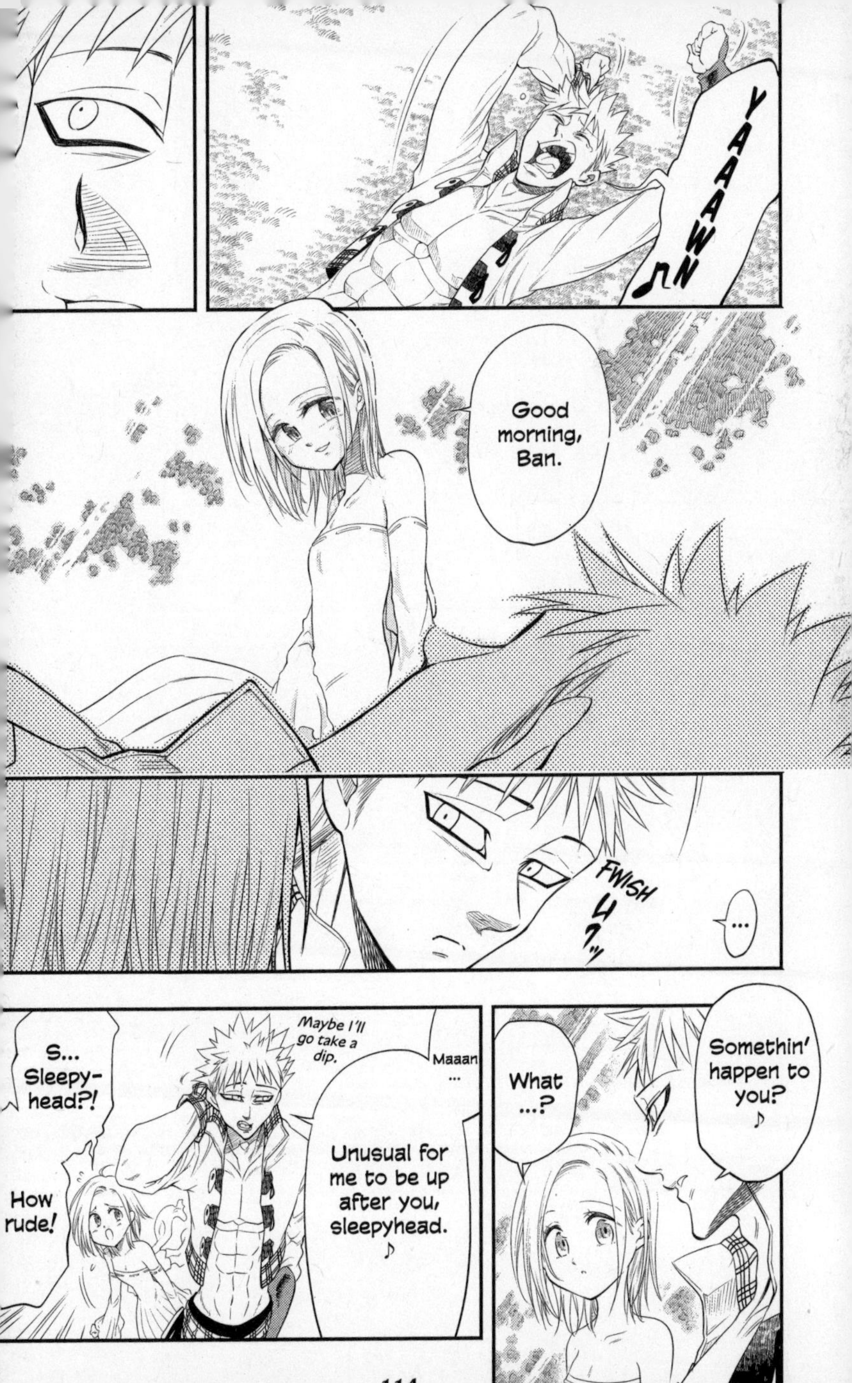
YAAAAWN ♪
Good morning, Ban.
FWISH
...
Somethin' happen to you? ♪
What ...?
Maaan ...
Maybe I'll go take a dip.
Unusual for me to be up after you, sleepyhead. ♪
S... Sleepy-head?!
How rude!

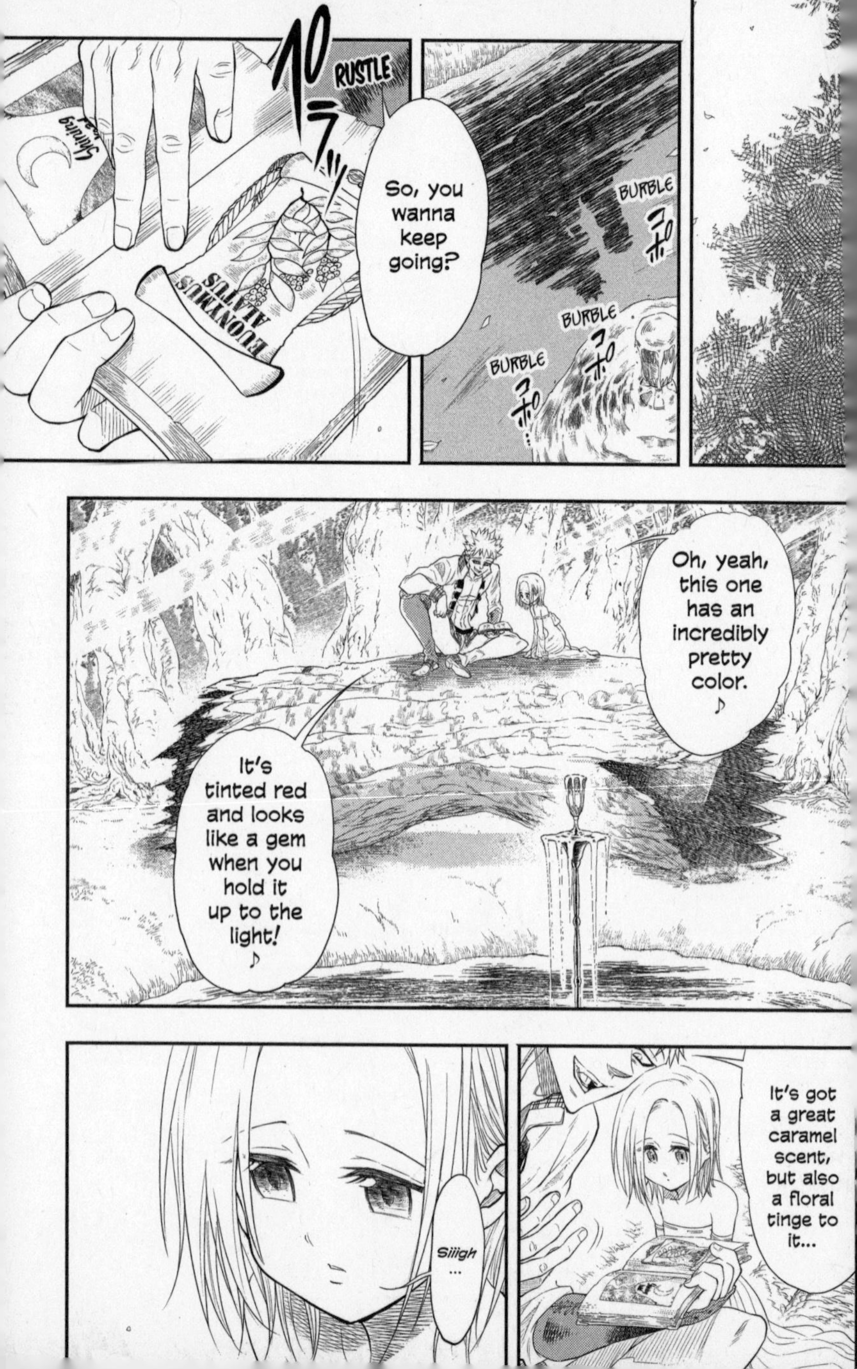
BURBLE
BURBLE
BURBLE
RUSTLE
So, you wanna keep going?
EUONYMUS ALATUS
Oh, yeah, this one has an incredibly pretty color. ♪
It's tinted red and looks like a gem when you hold it up to the light! ♪
It's got a great caramel scent, but also a floral tinge to it...
Siiigh ...

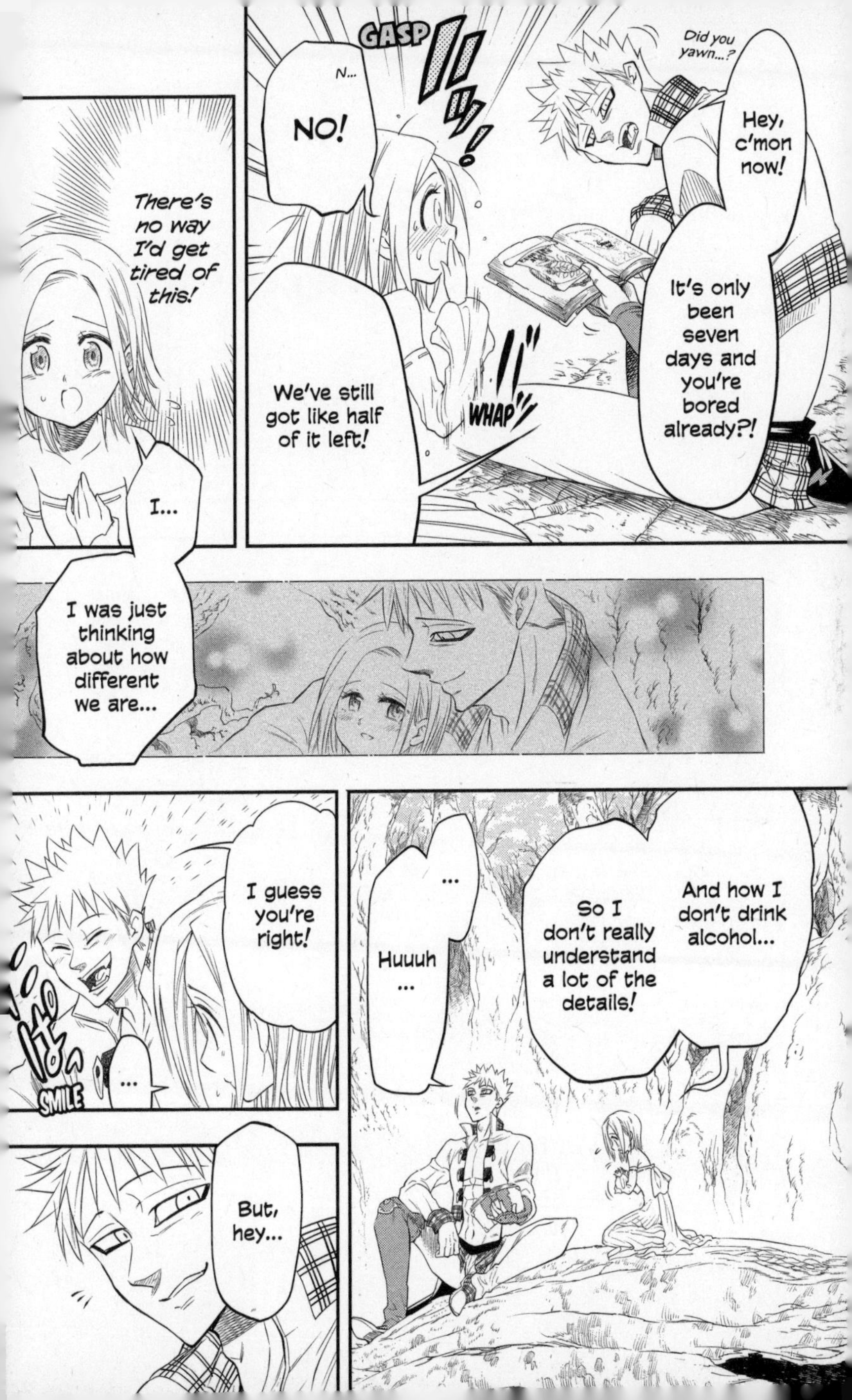
Did you yawn...?
Hey, c'mon now!
It's only been seven days and you're bored already?!
GASP
N...
NO!
WHAP
We've still got like half of it left!
There's no way I'd get tired of this!
I...
I was just thinking about how different we are...
And how I don't drink alcohol...
So I don't really understand a lot of the details!
...
Huuuh...
I guess you're right!
SMILE
...
But, hey...

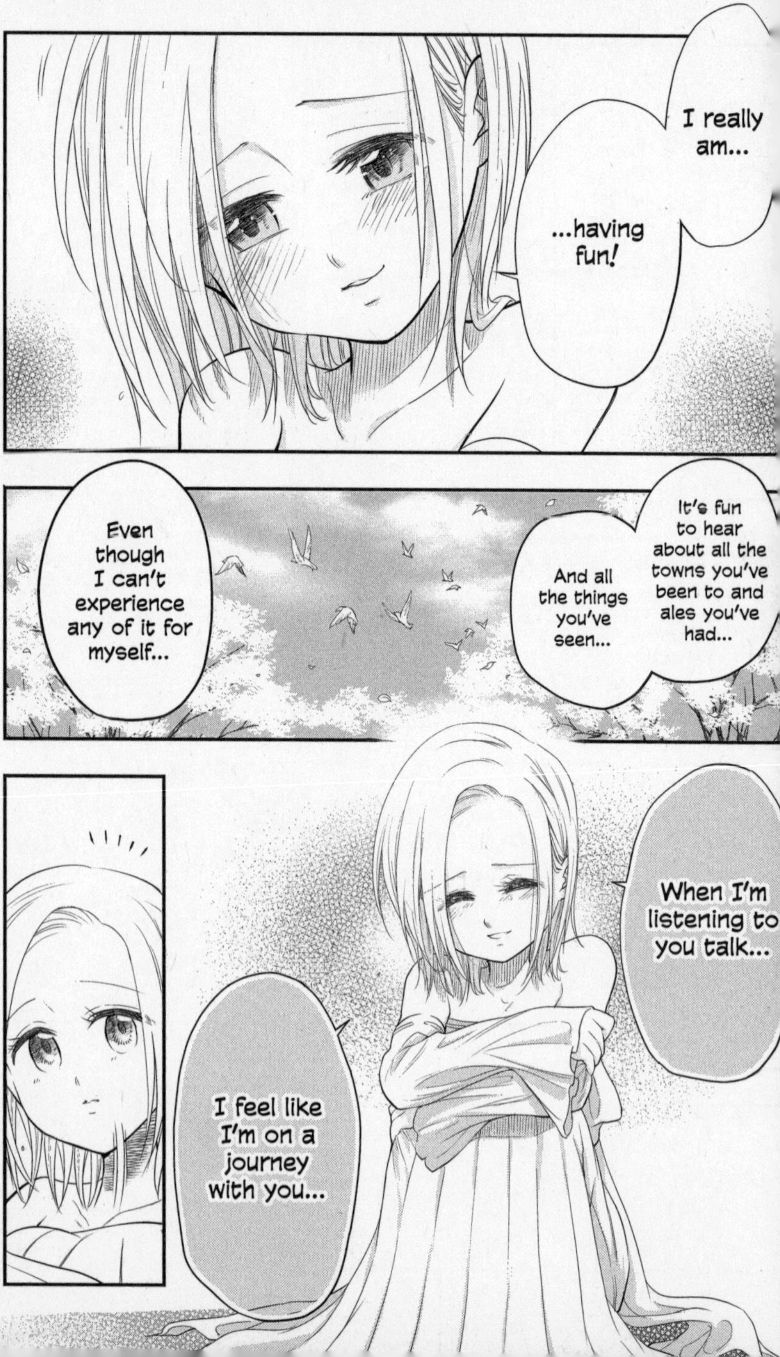
I really am...
...having fun!
It's fun to hear about all the towns you've been to and ales you've had...
And all the things you've seen...
Even though I can't experience any of it for myself...
When I'm listening to you talk...
I feel like I'm on a journey with you...

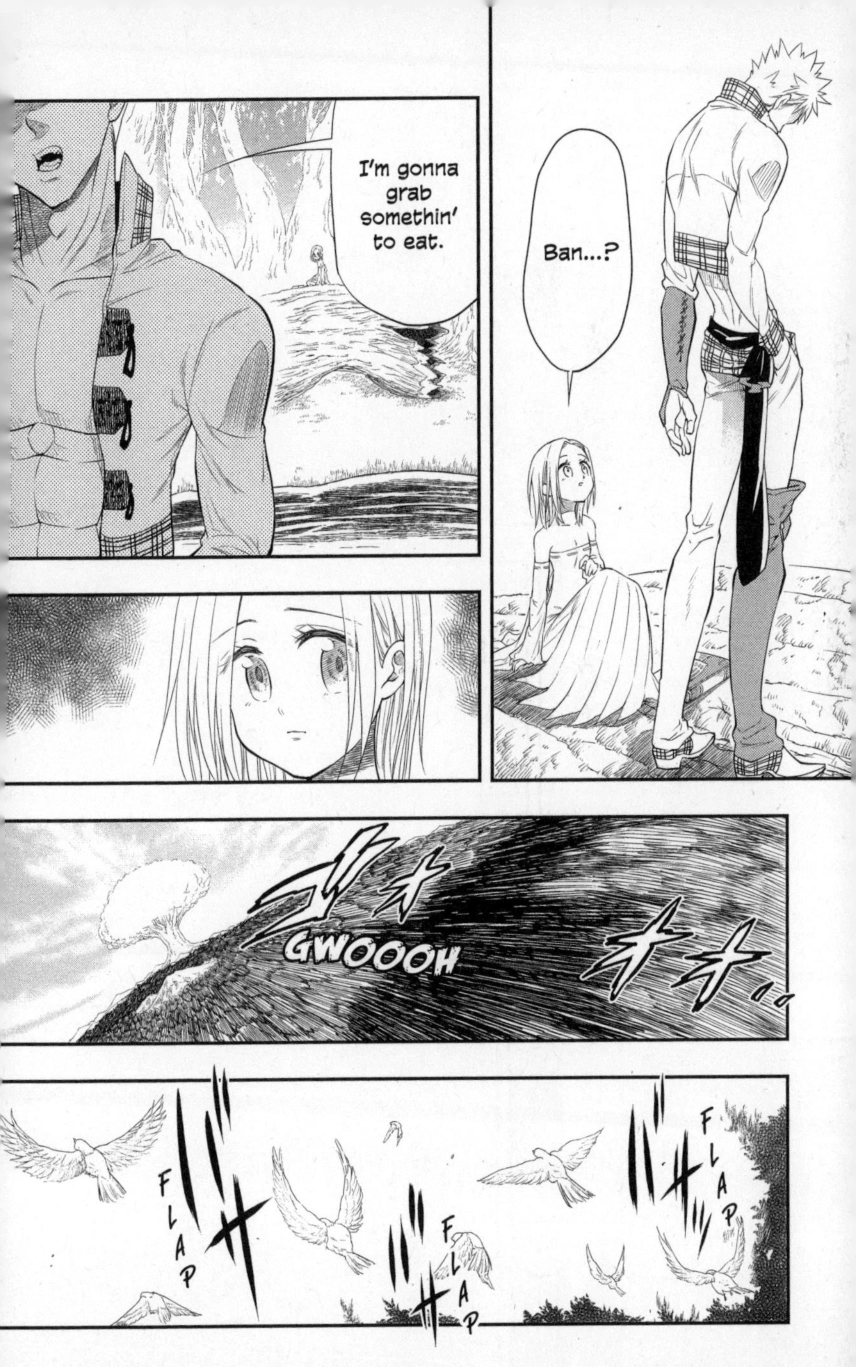

Ban...?
I'm gonna grab somethin' to eat.
GWOOOH
FLAP
FLAP
FLAP
FLAP

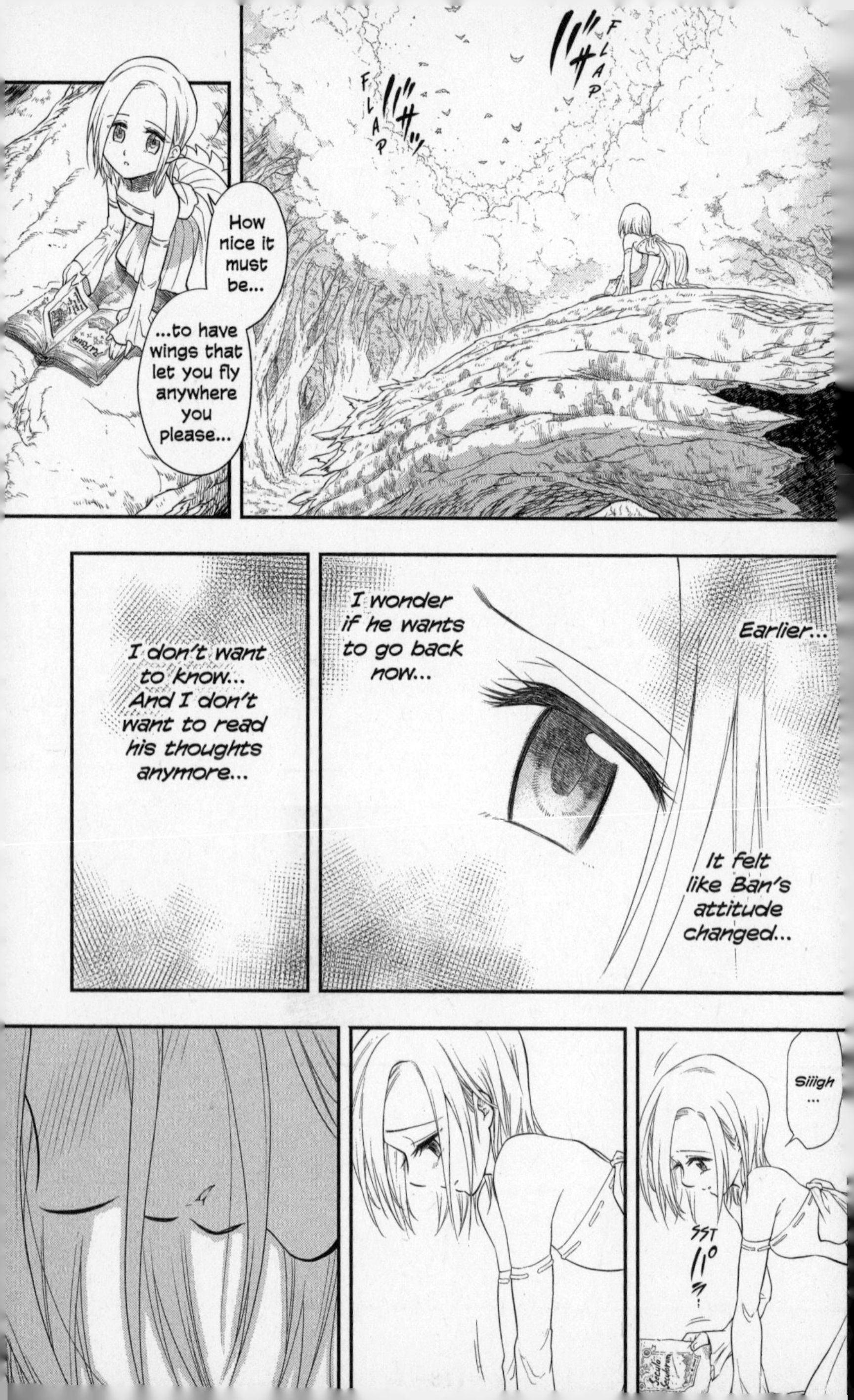
FLAP
FLAP
How nice it must be...
...to have wings that let you fly anywhere you please...
Earlier...
It felt like Ban's attitude changed...
I wonder if he wants to go back now...
I don't want to know... And I don't want to read his thoughts anymore...
Siiigh ...
SST

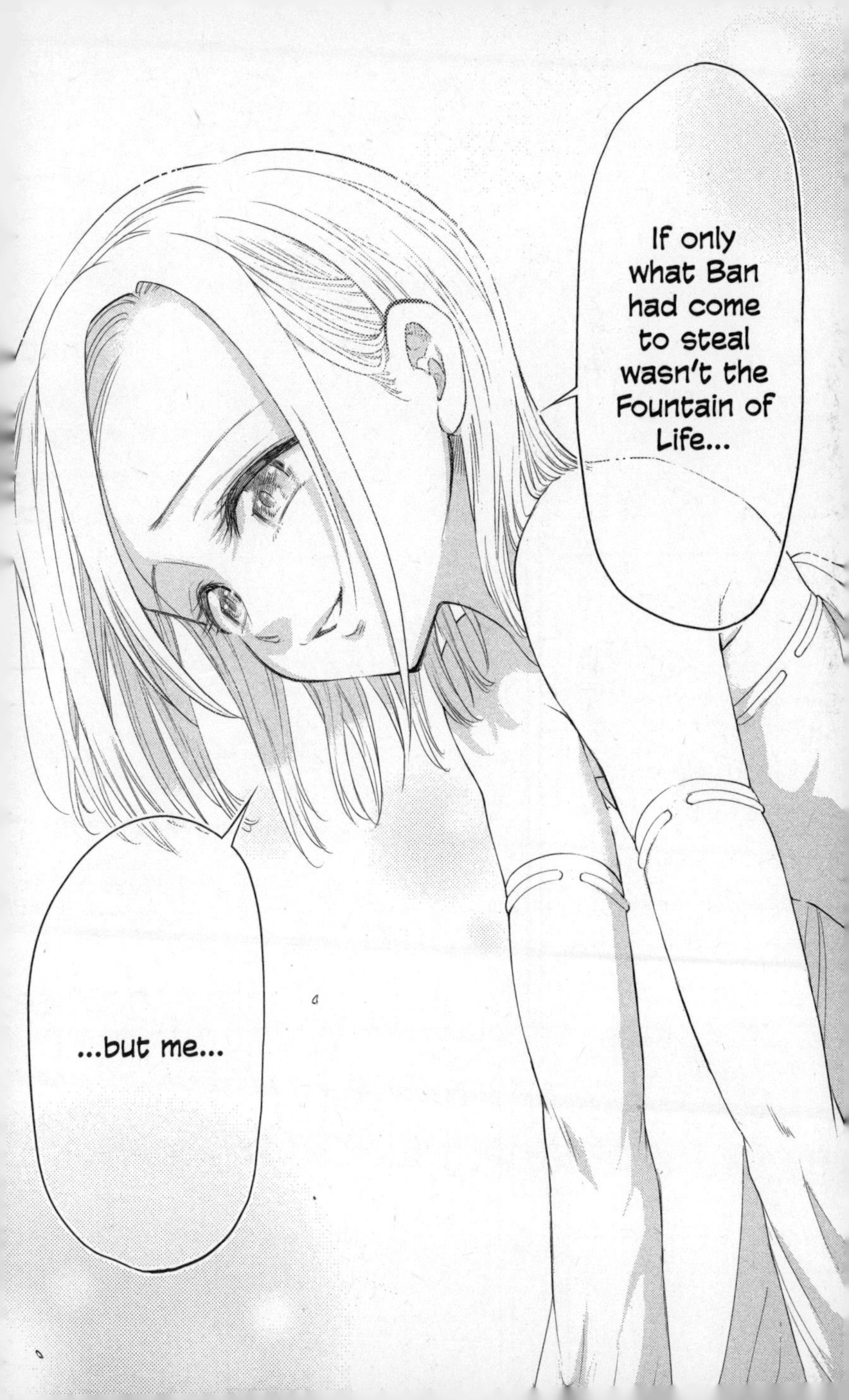
If only what Ban had come to steal wasn't the Fountain of Life...
...but me...

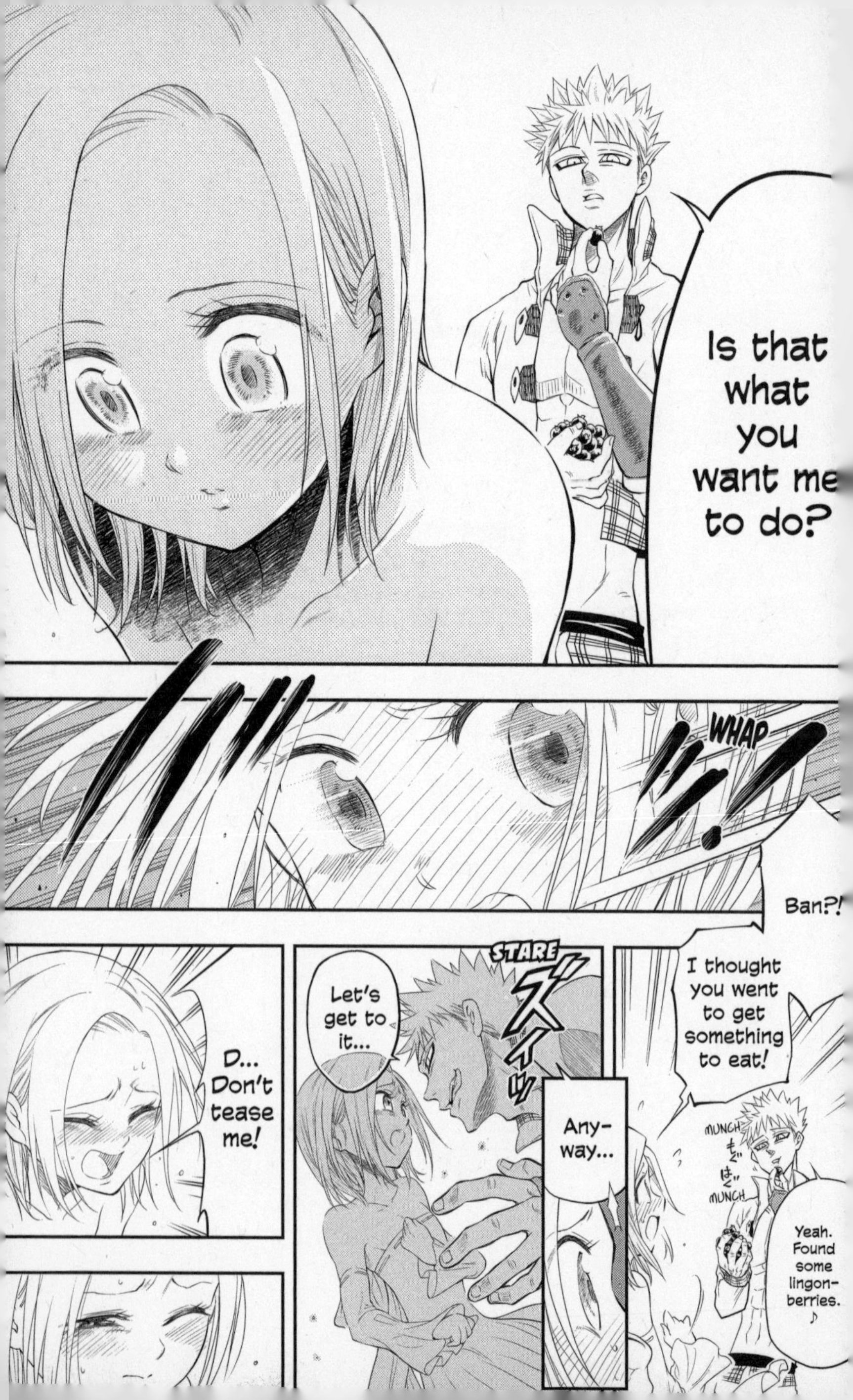
Is that what you want me to do?
WHAP
Ban?!
I thought you went to get something to eat!
MUNCH
もぐ
はぐ
MUNCH
Yeah. Found some lingon-berries. ♪
Any-way...
STARE
ズイッ
Let's get to it...
D... Don't tease me!

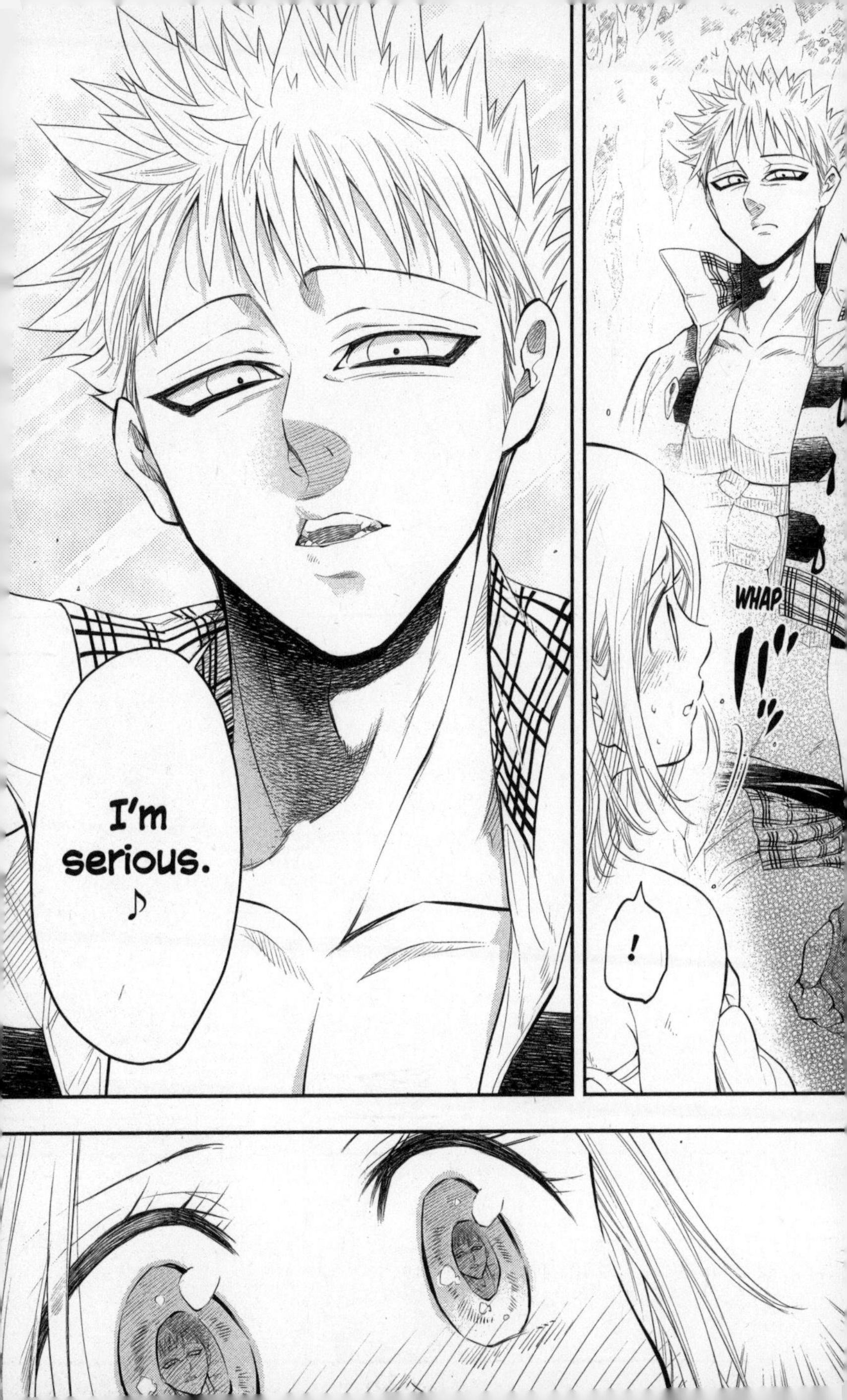
WHAP
!
I'm serious. ♪

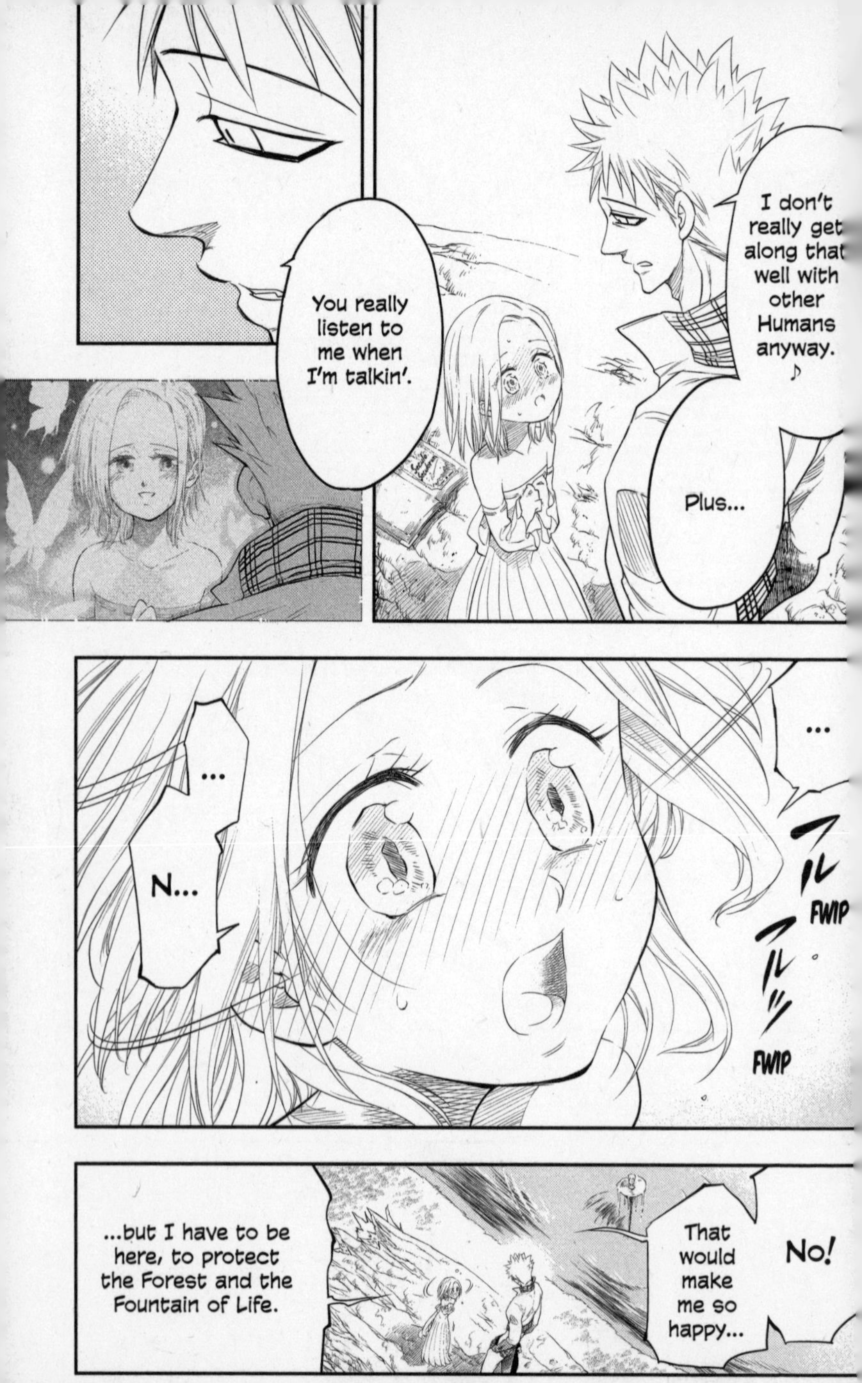
I don't really get along that well with other Humans anyway. ♪
Plus...
You really listen to me when I'm talkin'.
...
フル FWIP
フルッ FWIP
...
N...
No!
That would make me so happy...
...but I have to be here, to protect the Forest and the Fountain of Life.

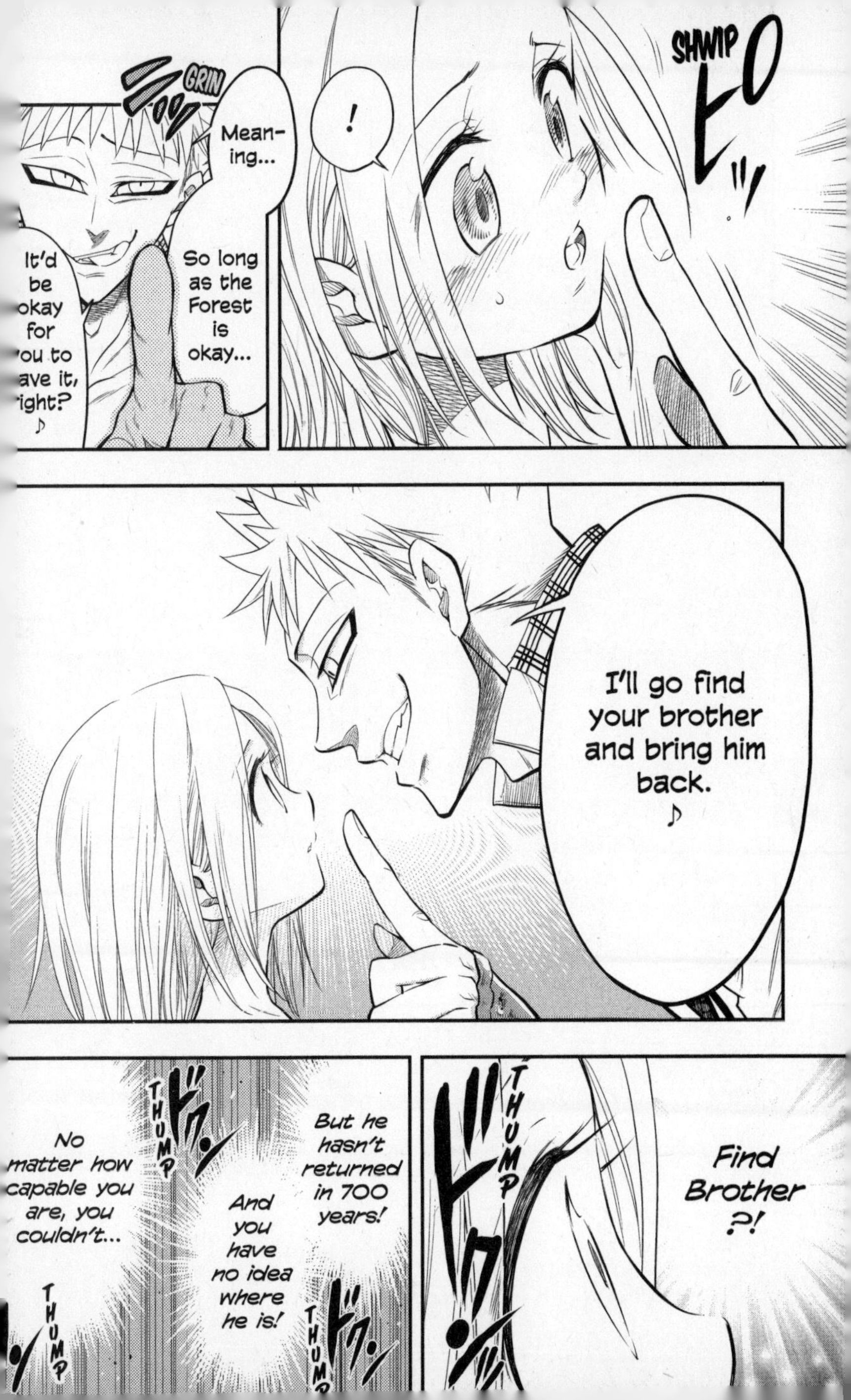
SHWIP
!
GRIN
Mean-ing...
So long as the Forest is okay...
It'd be okay for ou to ave it, ight? ♪
I'll go find your brother and bring him back. ♪
THUMP
Find Brother ?!
THUMP
But he hasn't returned in 700 years!
And you have no idea where he is!
THUMP
No matter how capable you are, you couldn't...
THUMP
THUMP

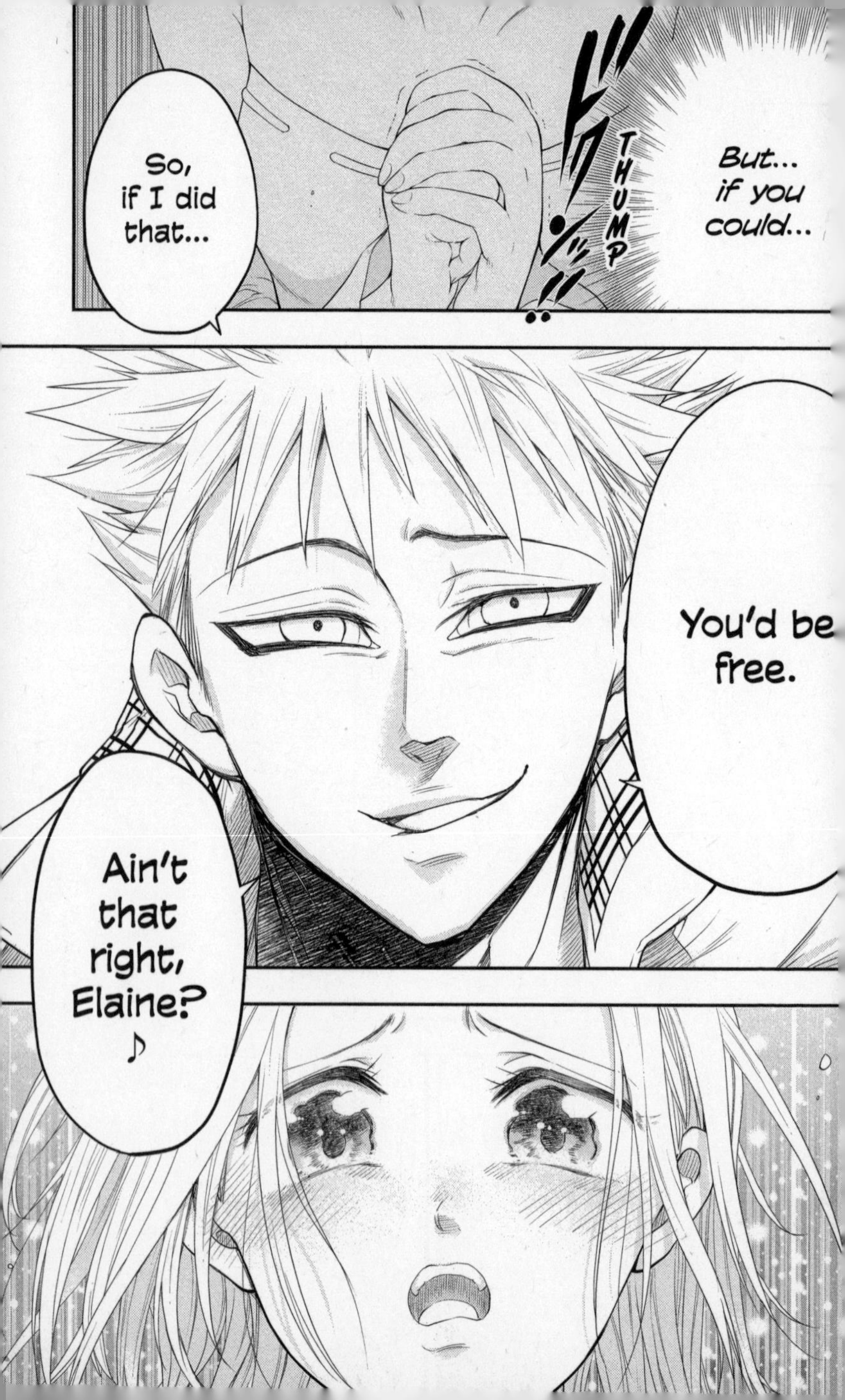
But... if you could...
THUMP
So, if I did that...
You'd be free.
Ain't that right, Elaine? ♪

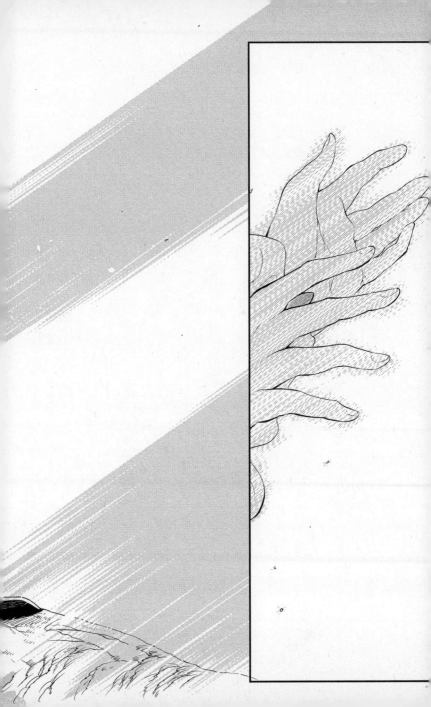

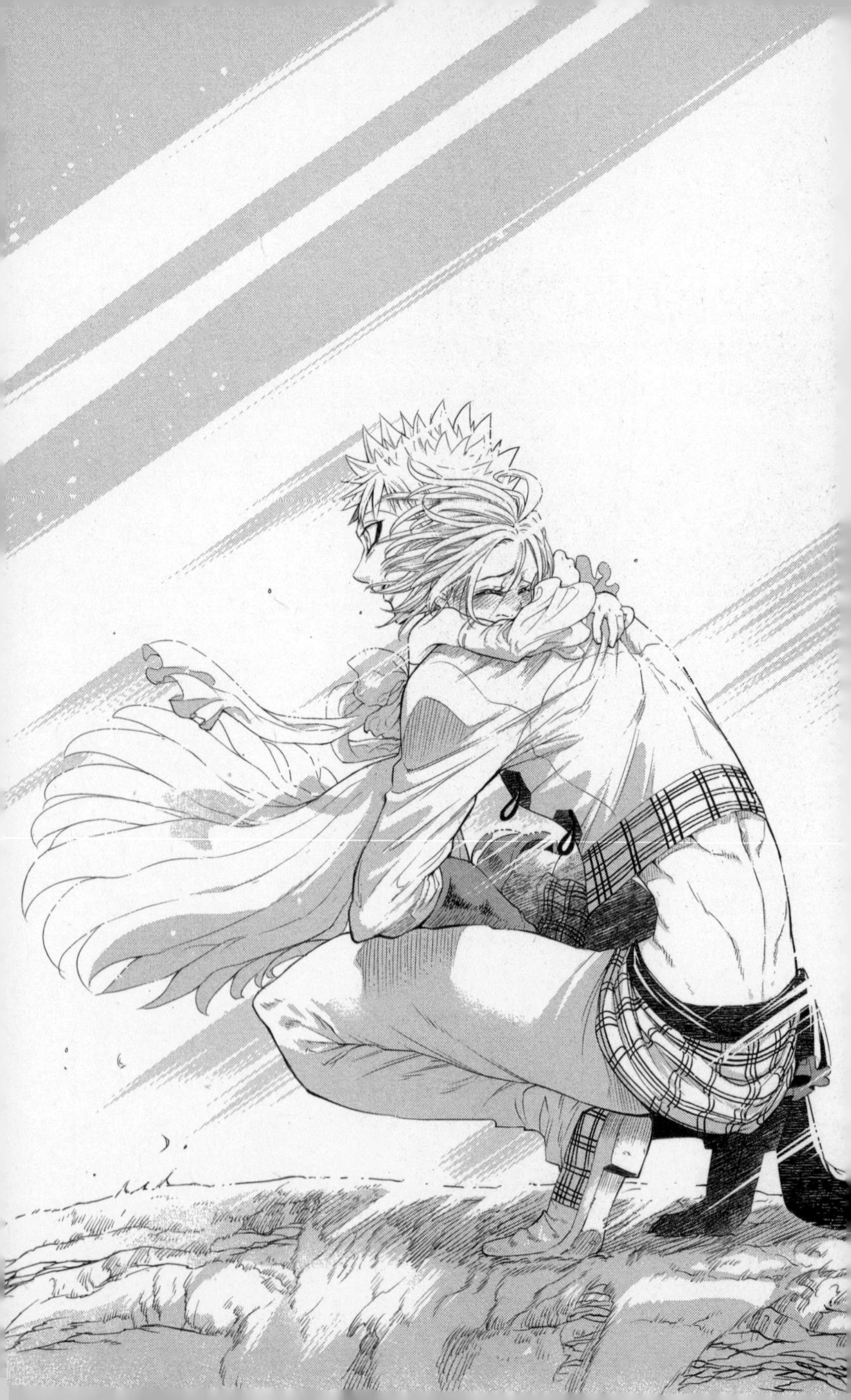

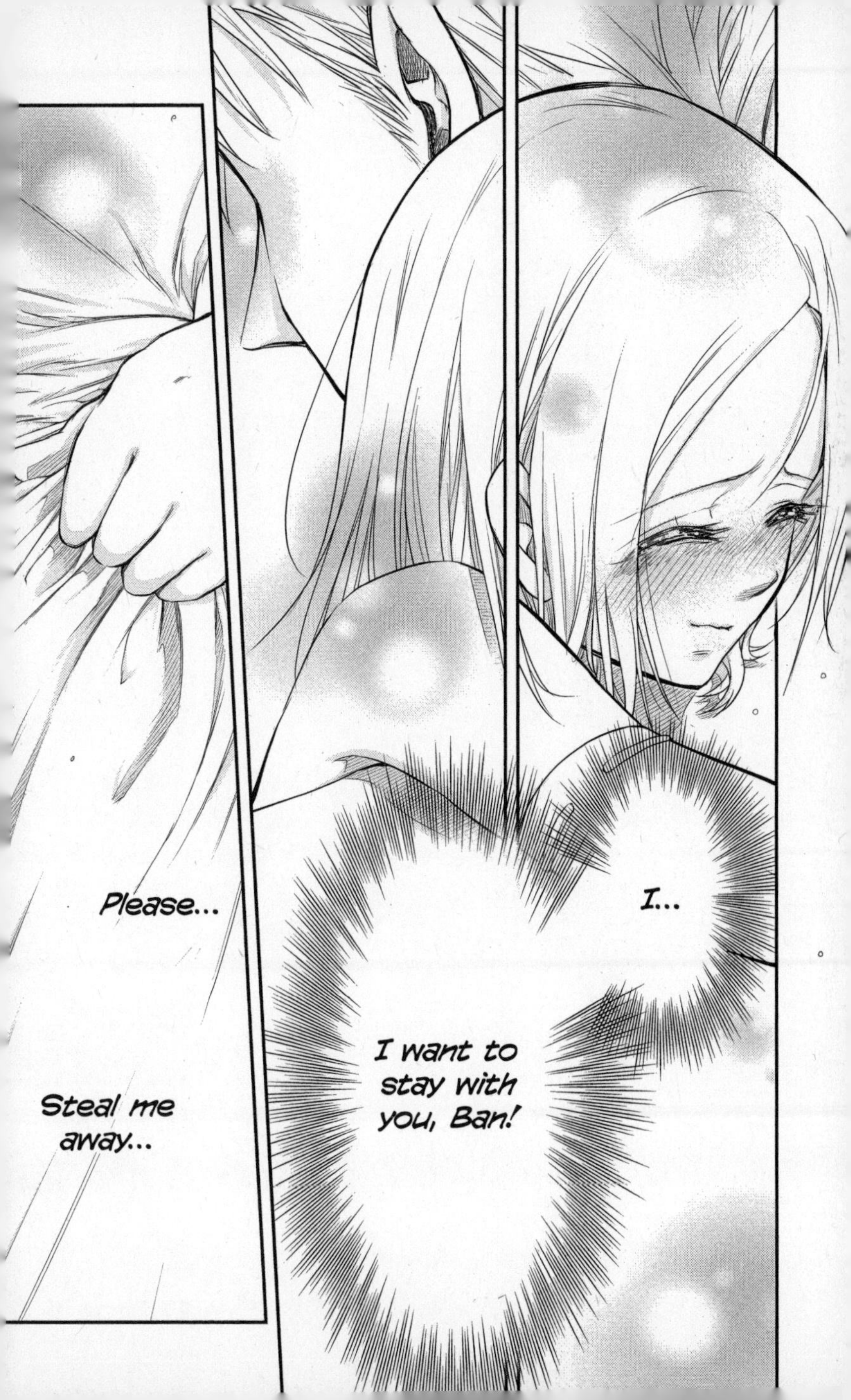
I...
I want to stay with you, Ban!
Please...
Steal me away...

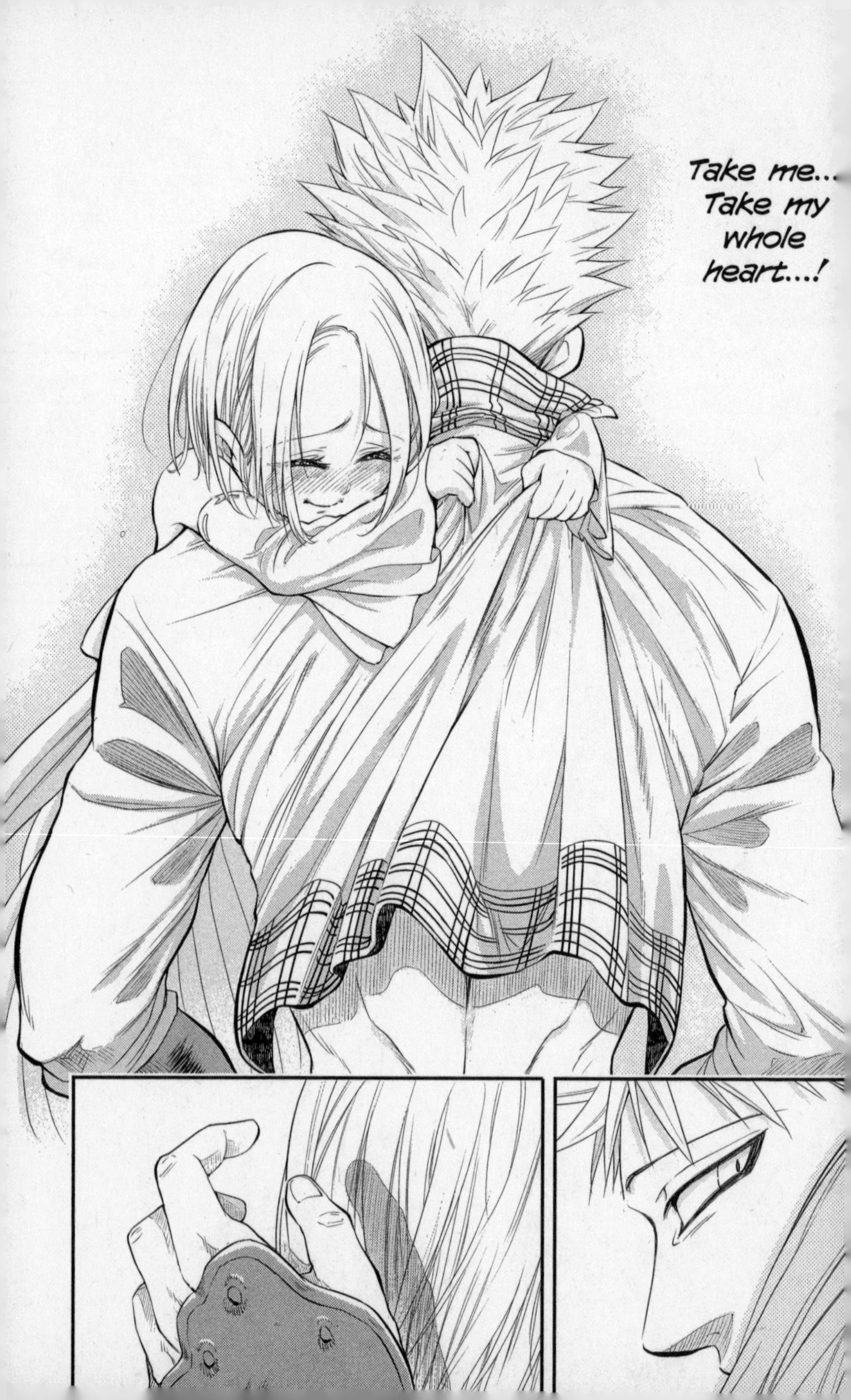
Take me... Take my whole heart...!

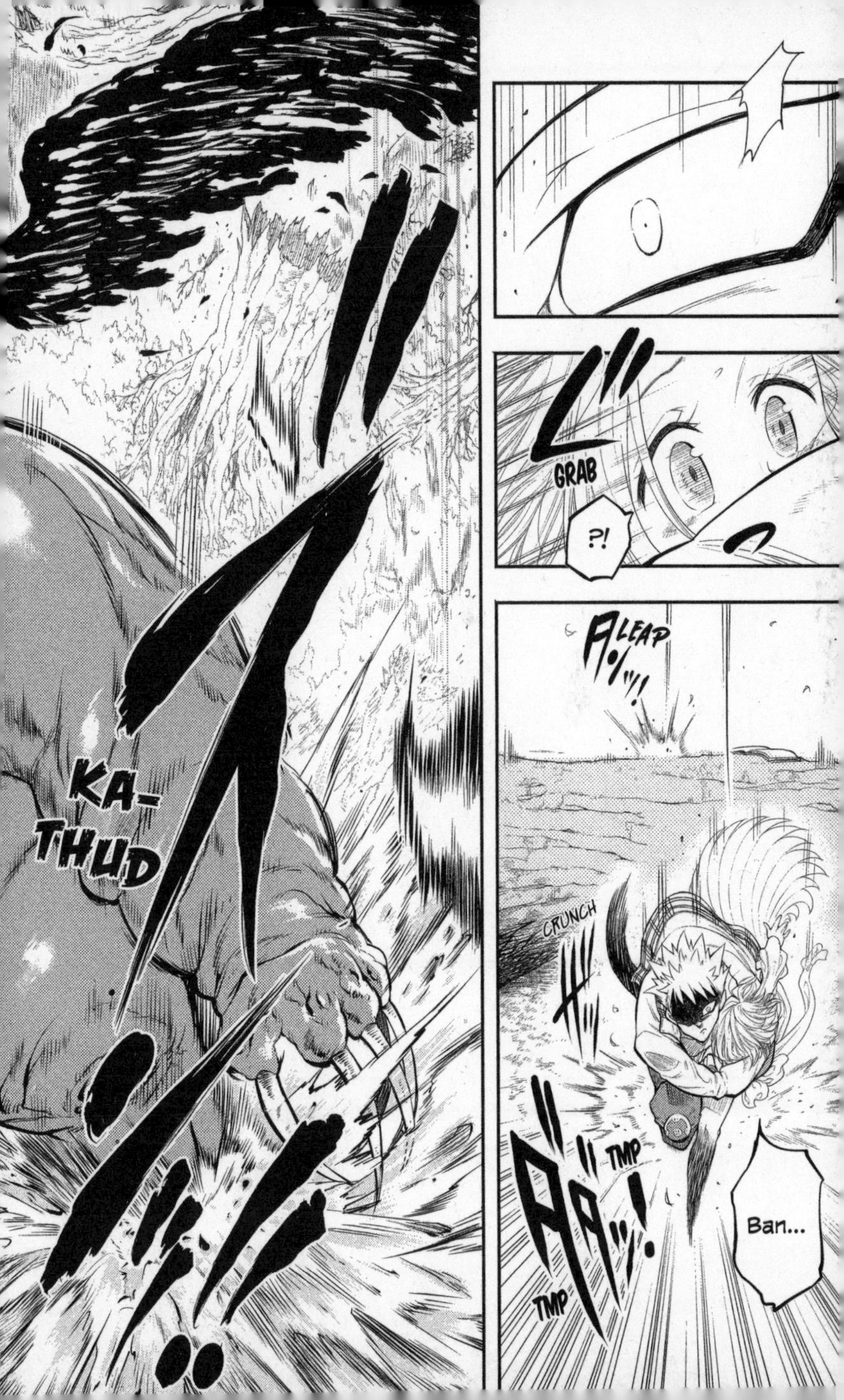
GRAB
?!
LEAP
CRUNCH
TMP
TMP
Ban...
KA-THUD

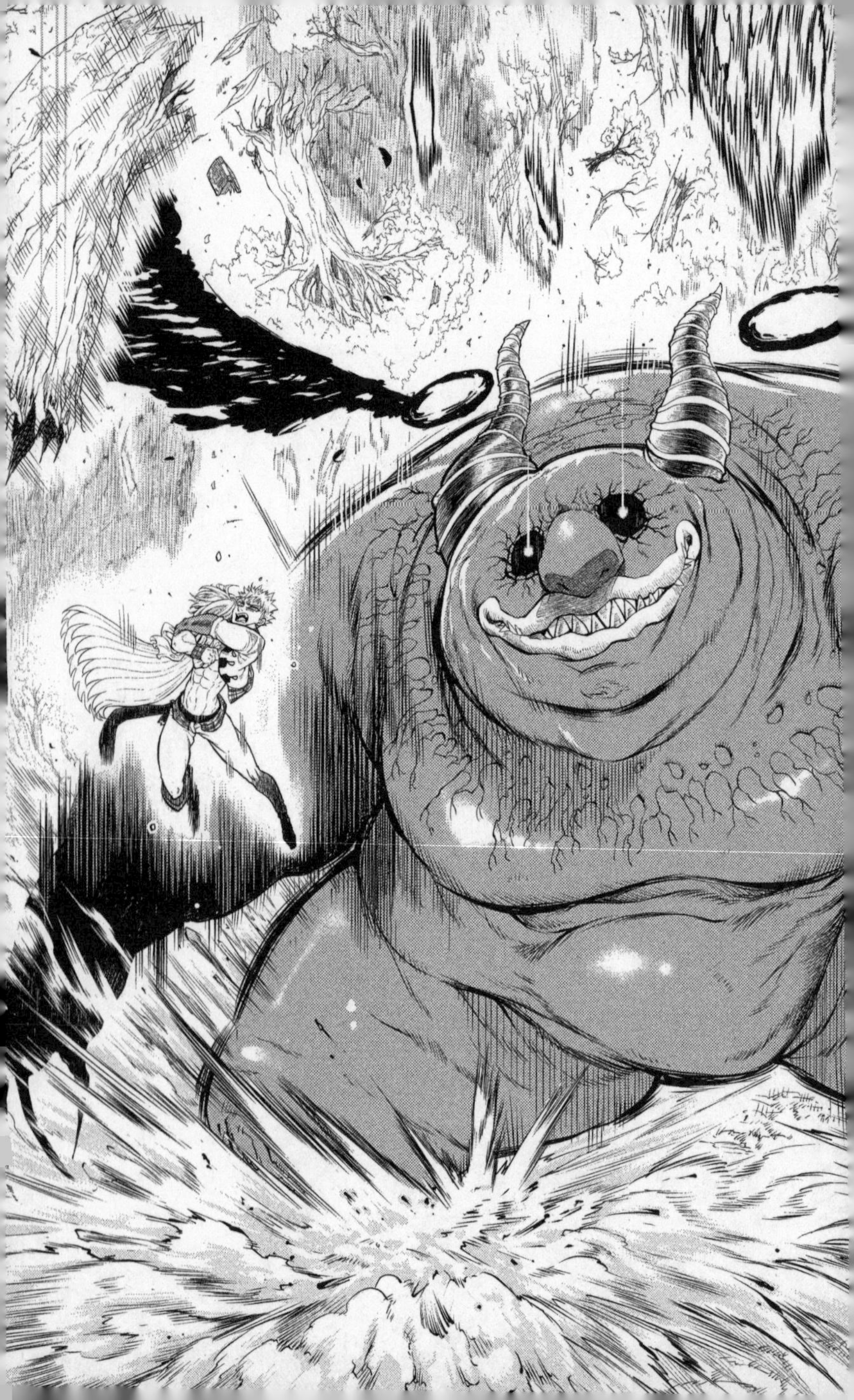

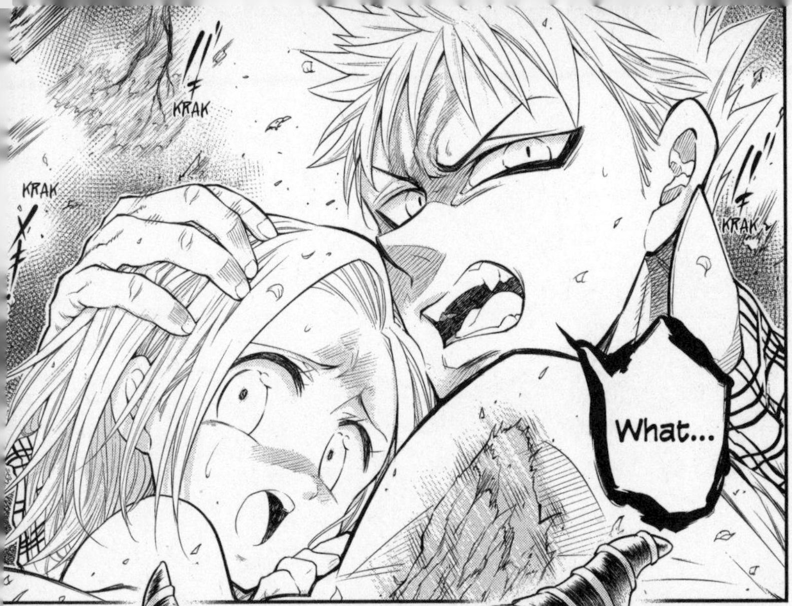
KRAK
KRAK
KRAK
What...
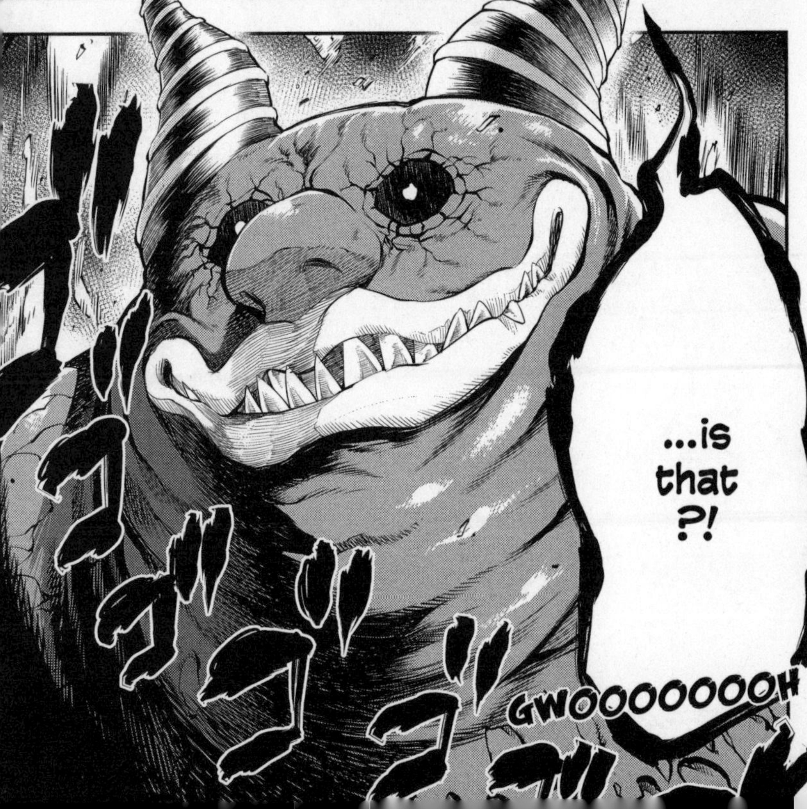
...is that?!
GWOOOOOOOH

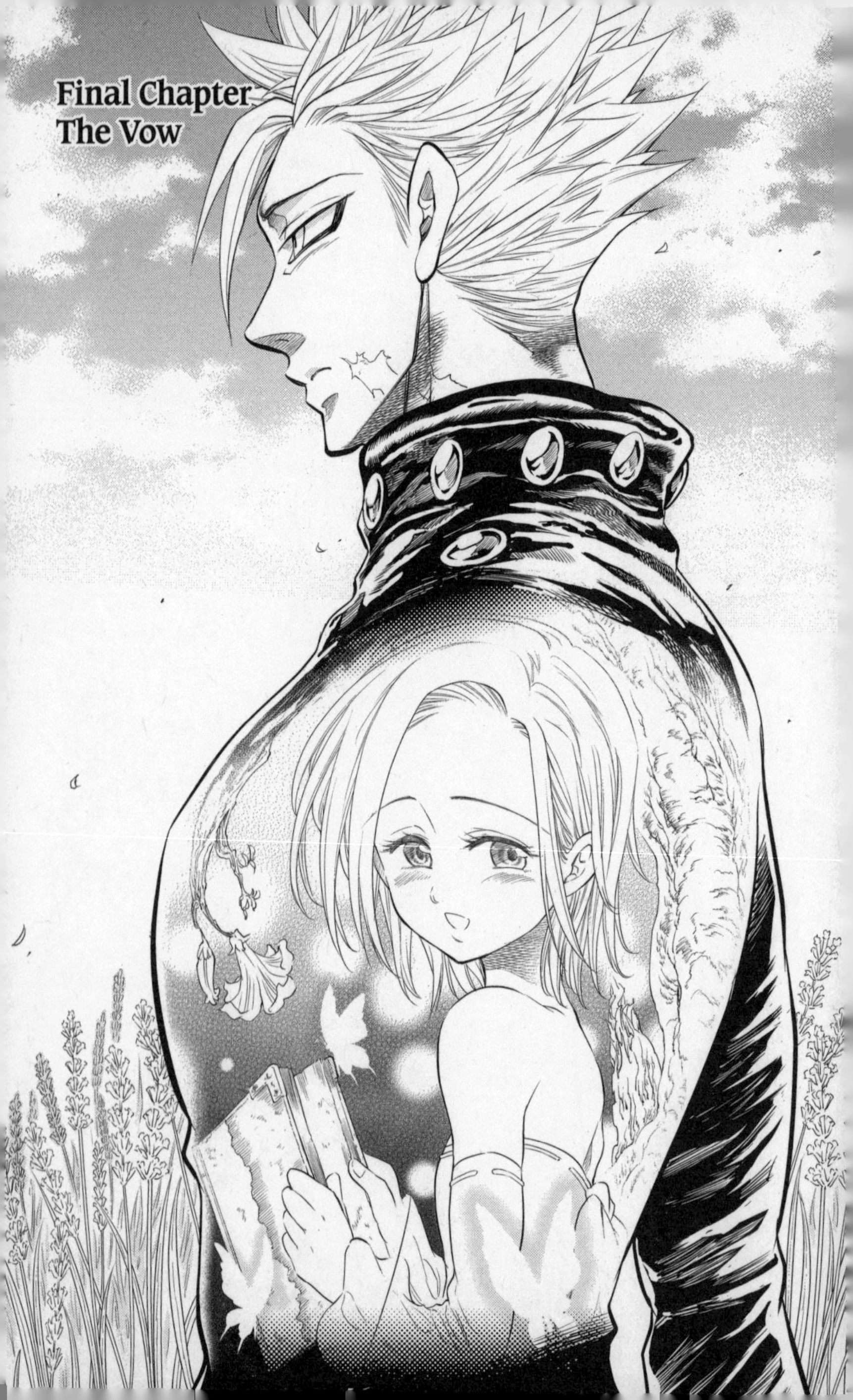
Final Chapter
The Vow

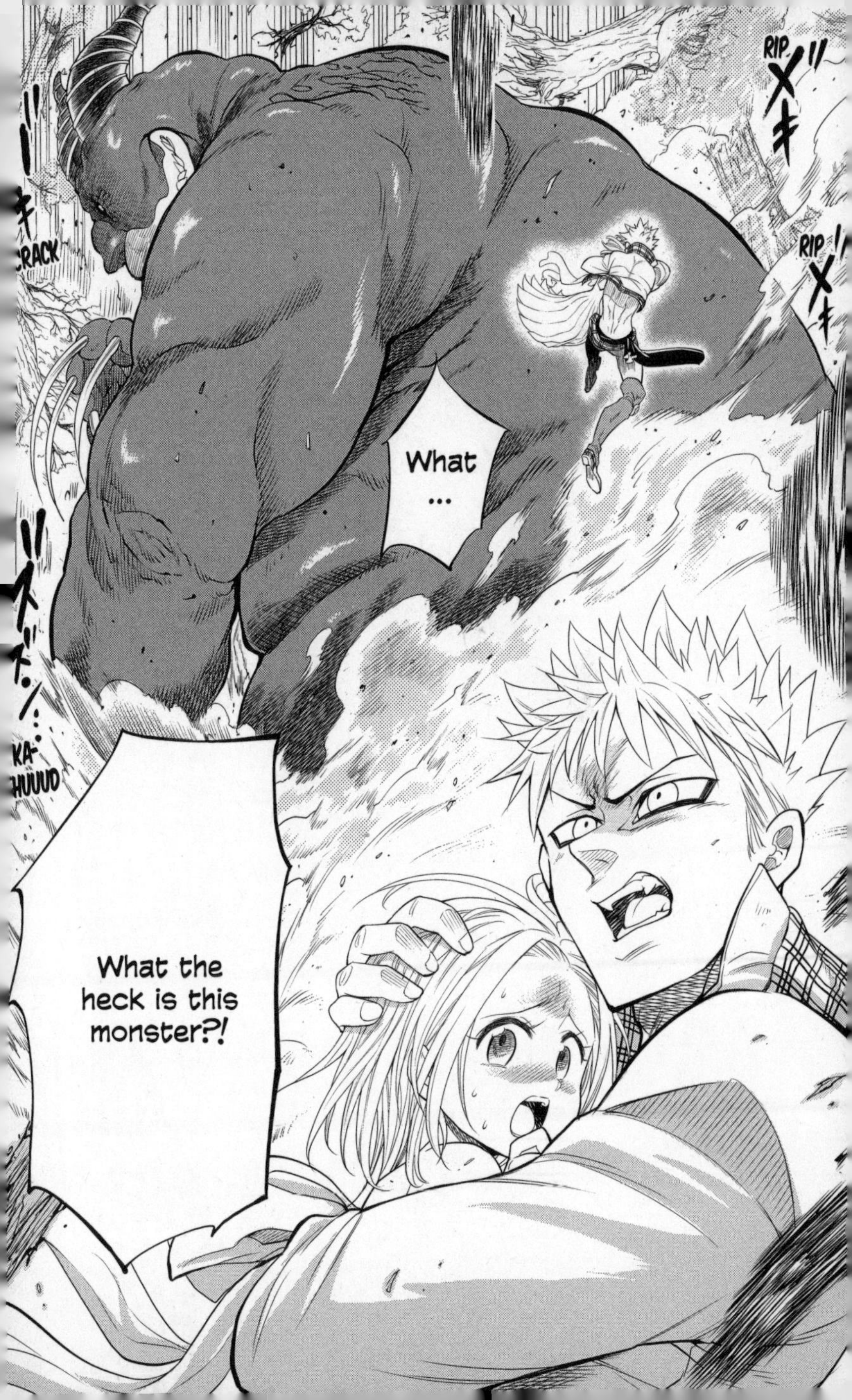
RIP
RIP
CRACK
What ...
KA-CHUUUD
What the heck is this monster?!

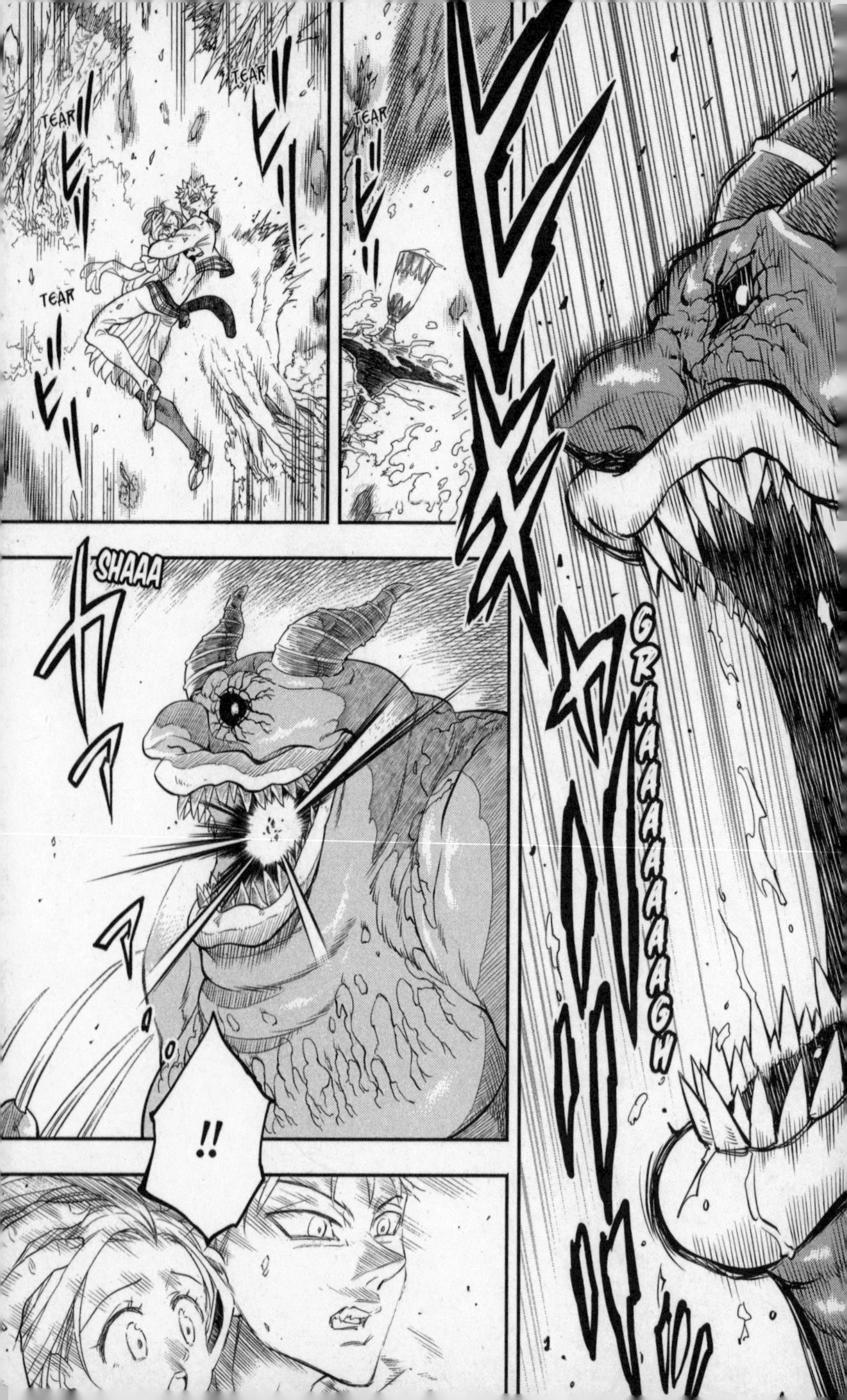
GRAAAAAAAAAGH
TEAR
TEAR
TEAR
TEAR
SHAAA
!!

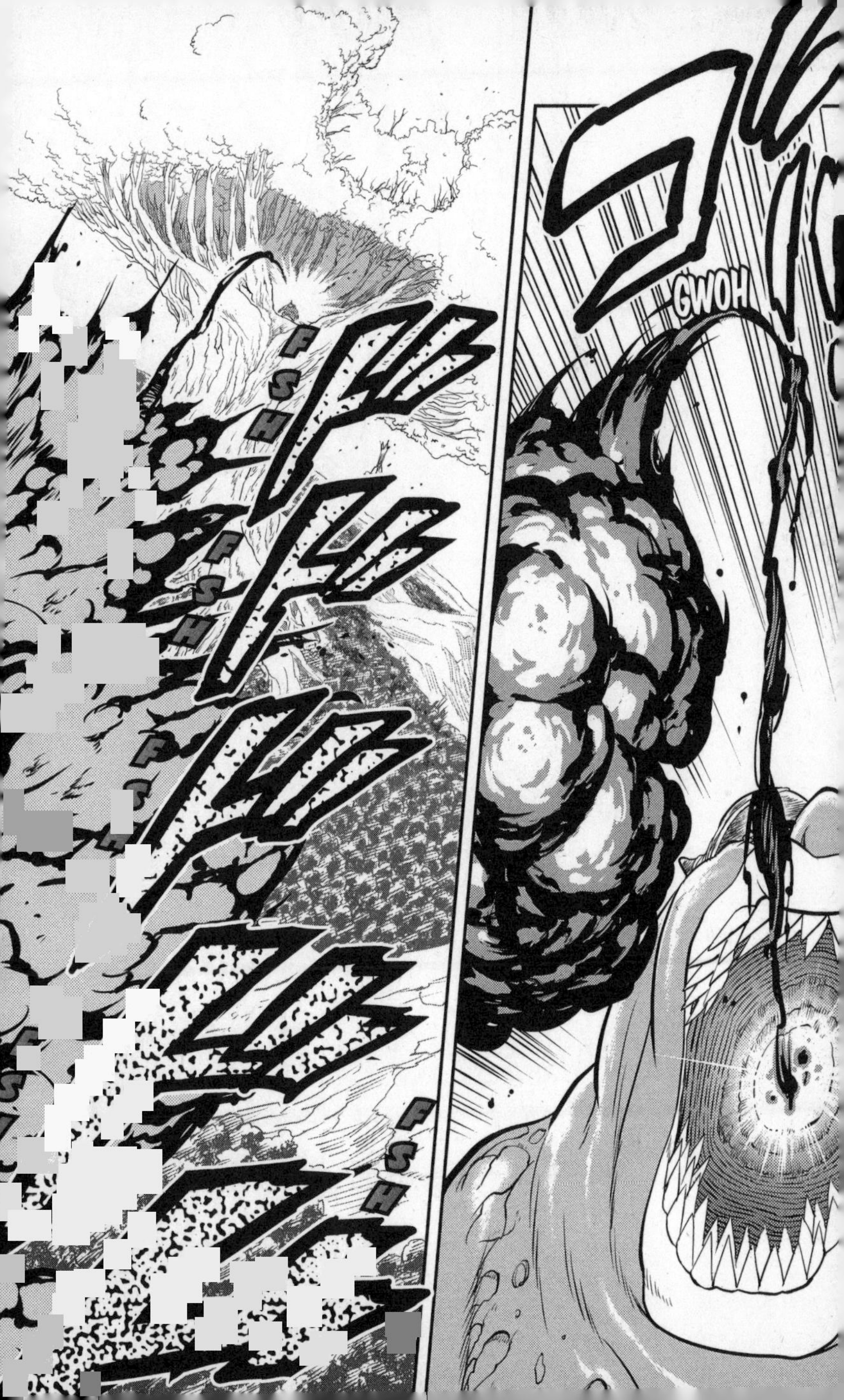
GWOH
FSH
FSH
FSH

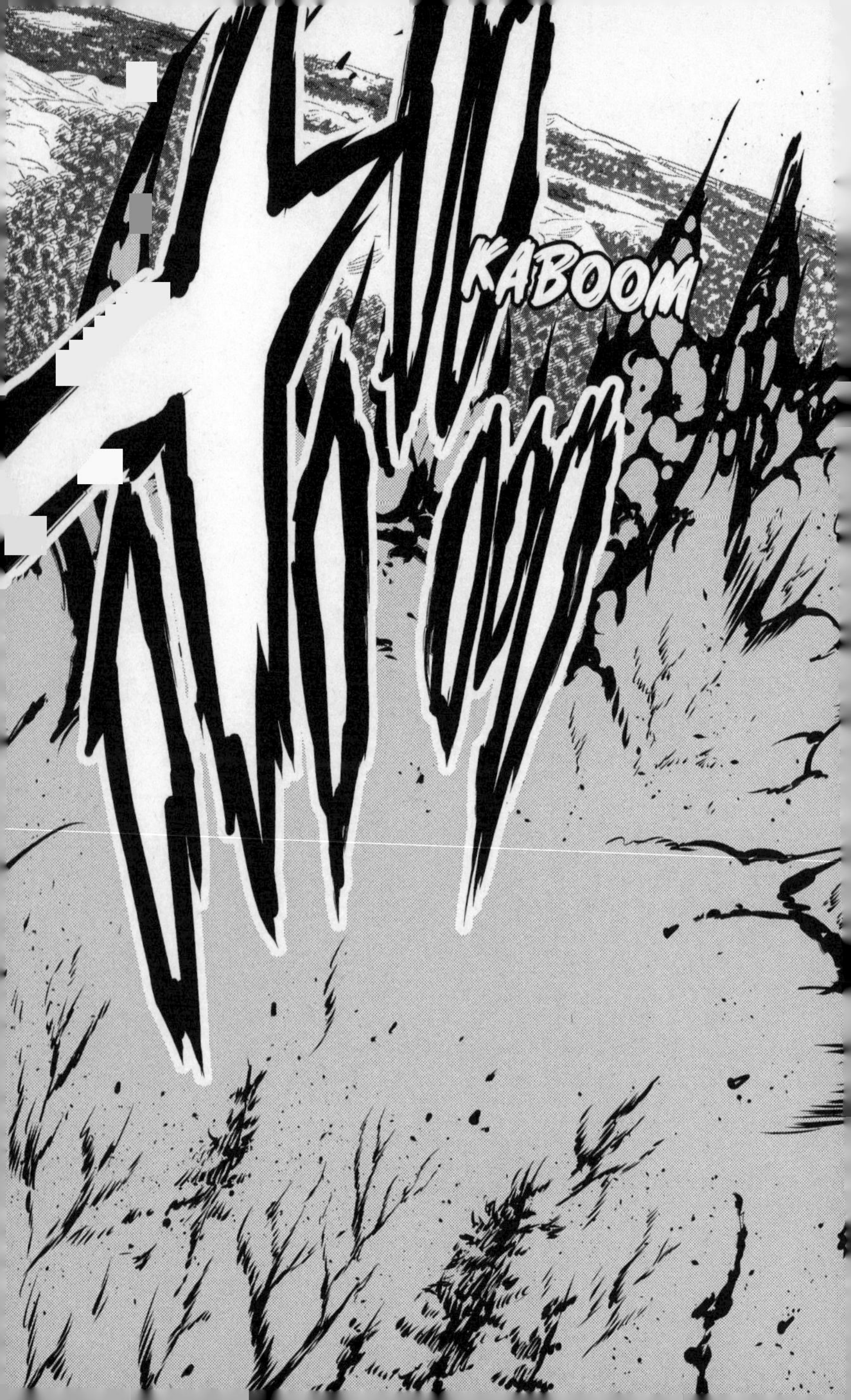
KABOOM

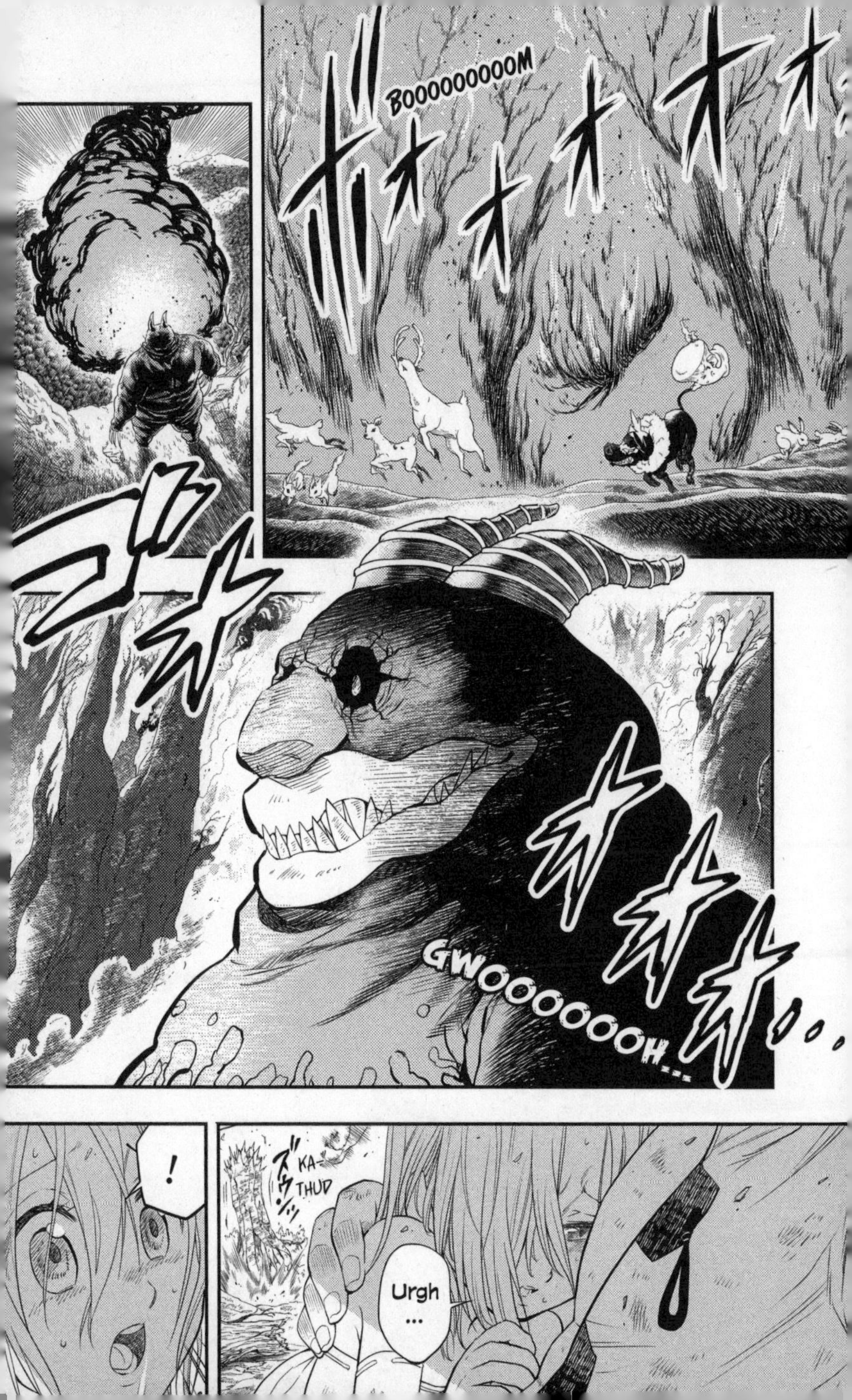
ゴォォォォォォ
BOOOOOOOOOM
ゴォォォ
GWOOOOOOOH...
ズゥン
KA-THUD
Urgh
...
!

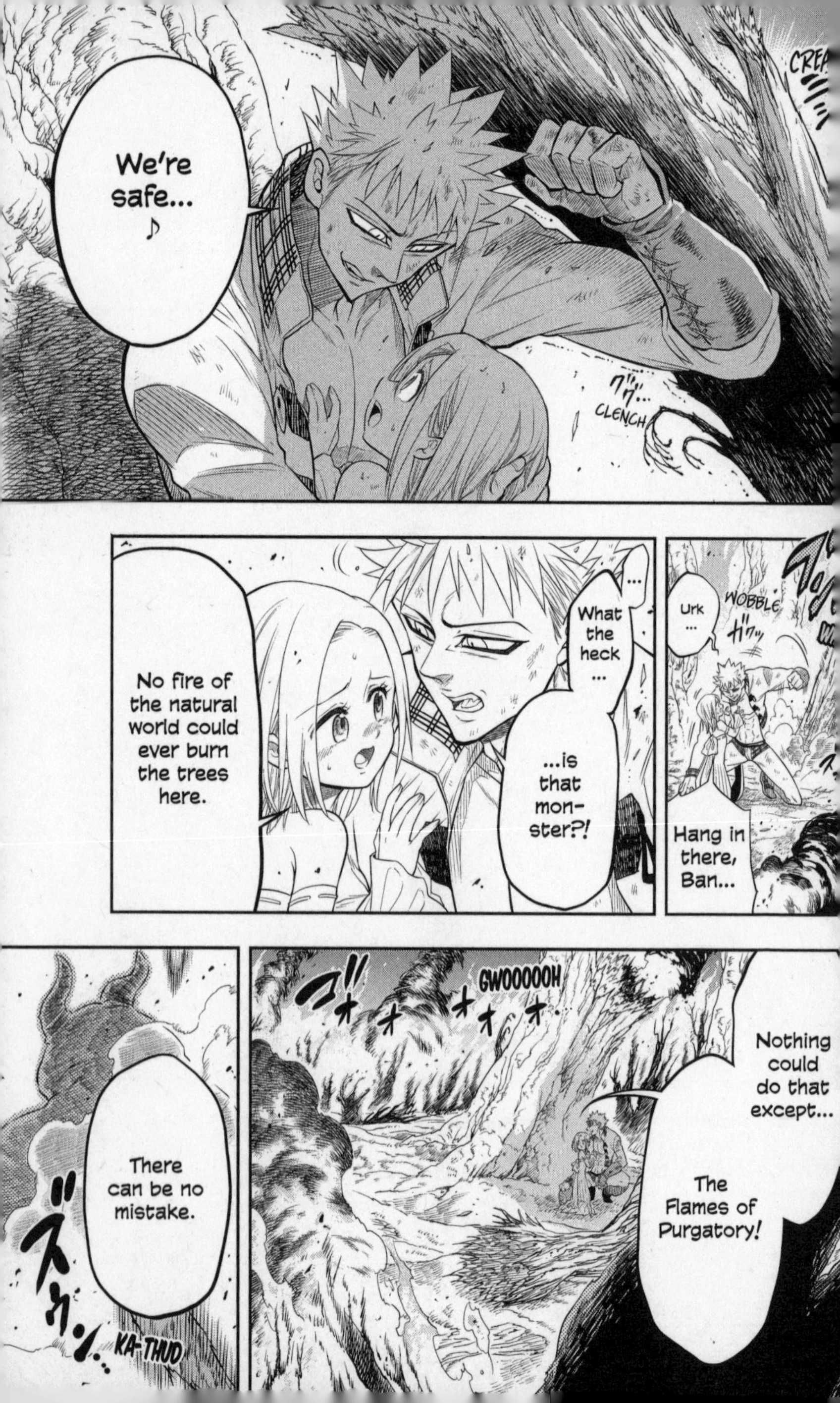

We're safe... ♪
CLENCH
Urk ...
WOBBLE
Hang in there, Ban...
...
What the heck ...
...is that monster?!
No fire of the natural world could ever burn the trees here.
GWOOOOOH
Nothing could do that except...
The Flames of Purgatory!
There can be no mistake.
KA-THUD

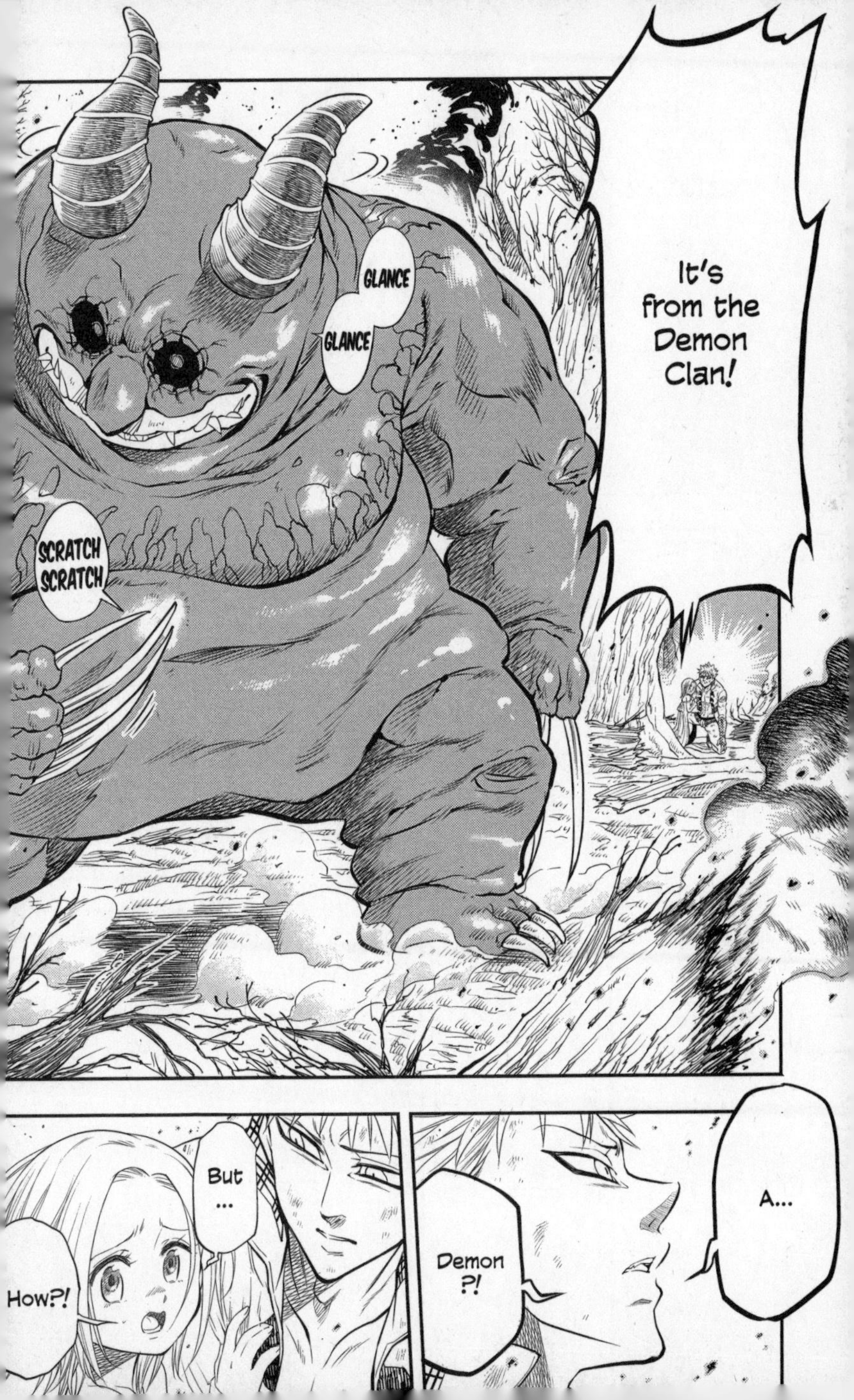
It's from the Demon Clan!
GLANCE
GLANCE
SCRATCH SCRATCH
A...
Demon ?!
But ...
How?!

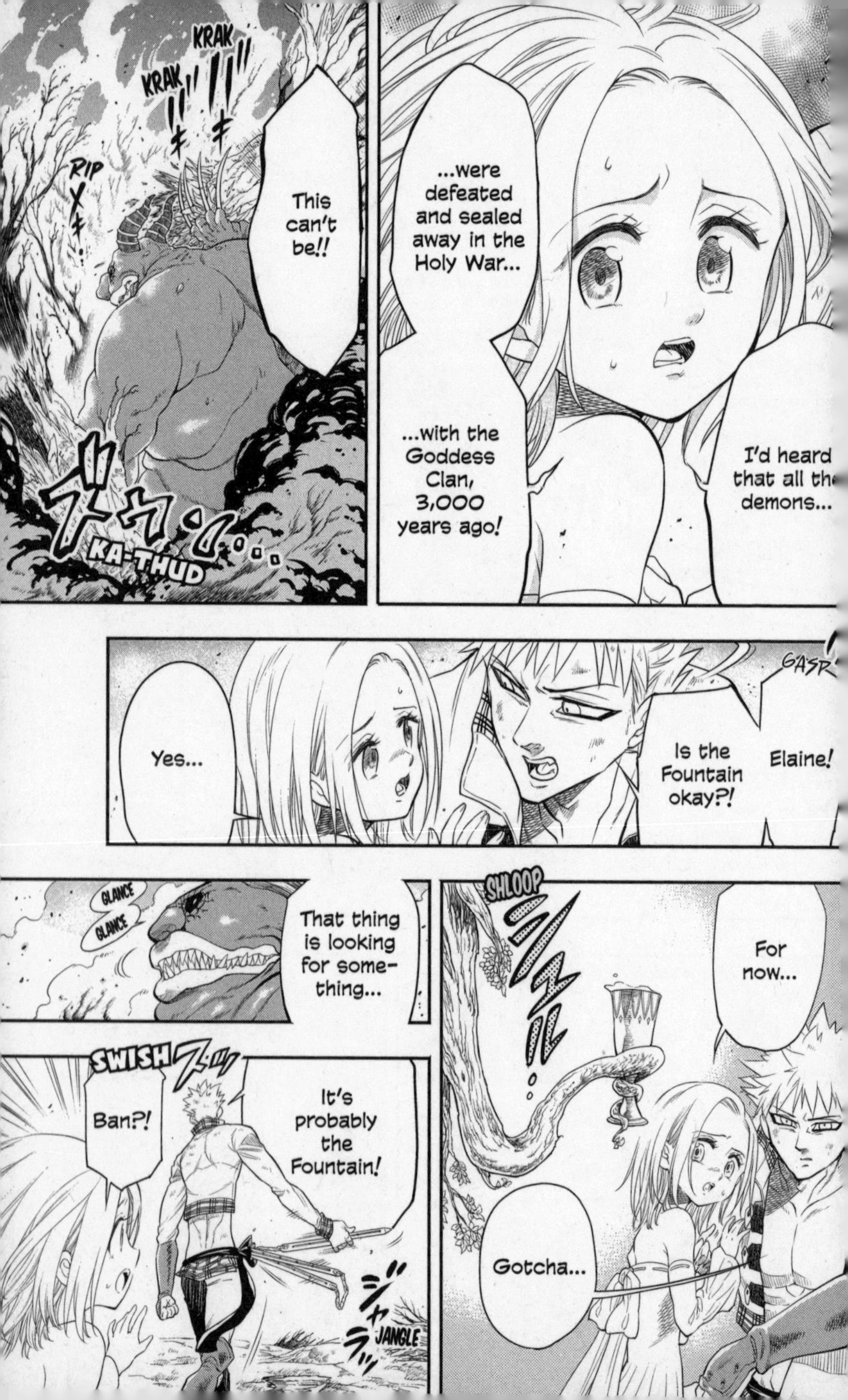
I'd heard that all the demons...
...were defeated and sealed away in the Holy War...
...with the Goddess Clan, 3,000 years ago!
KRAK
KRAK
RIP
This can't be!!
KA-THUD
GASP
Elaine!
Is the Fountain okay?!
Yes...
For now...
SHLOOP
Gotcha...
That thing is looking for some-thing...
GLANCE
GLANCE
It's probably the Fountain!
SWISH
Ban?!
JANGLE

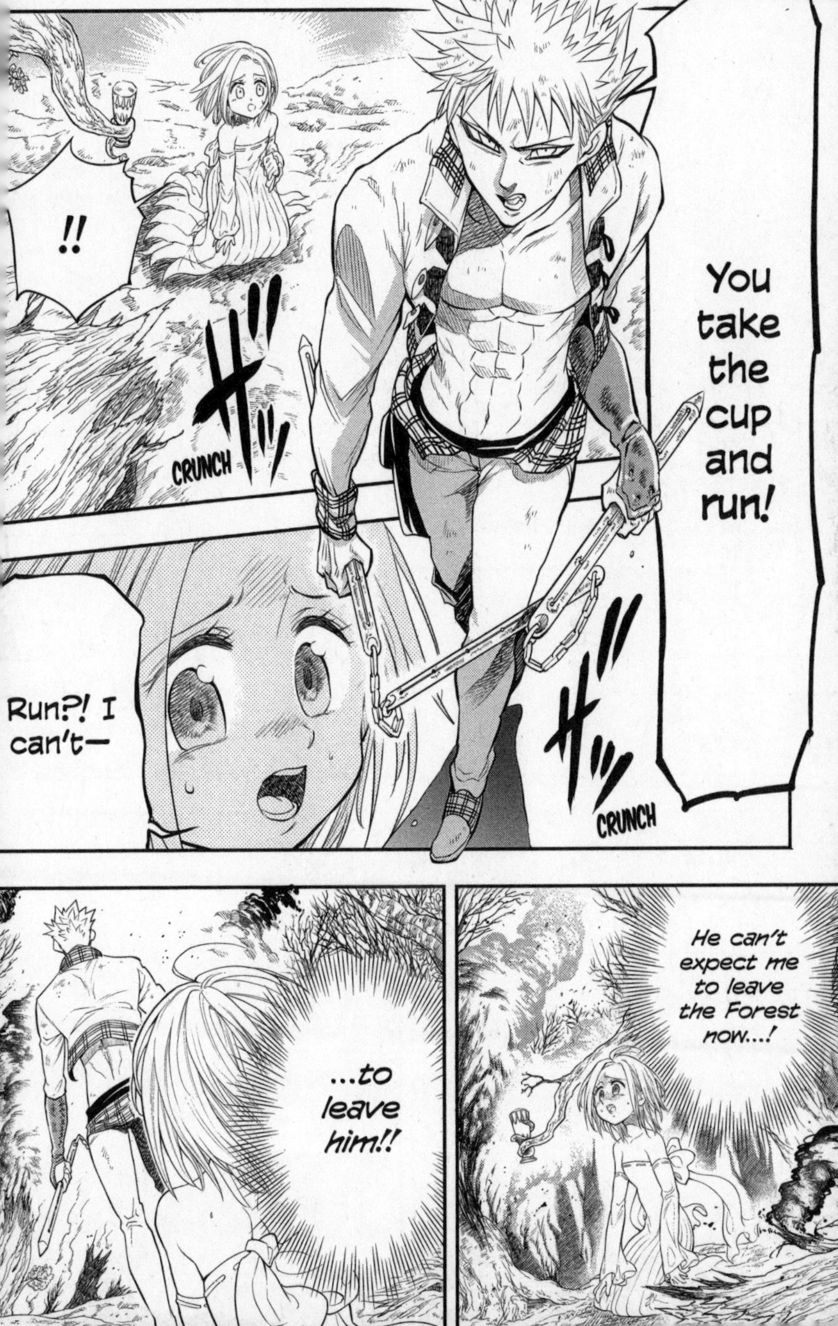

You take the cup and run!
!!
CRUNCH
CRUNCH
Run?! I can't—
He can't expect me to leave the Forest now...!
...to leave him!!

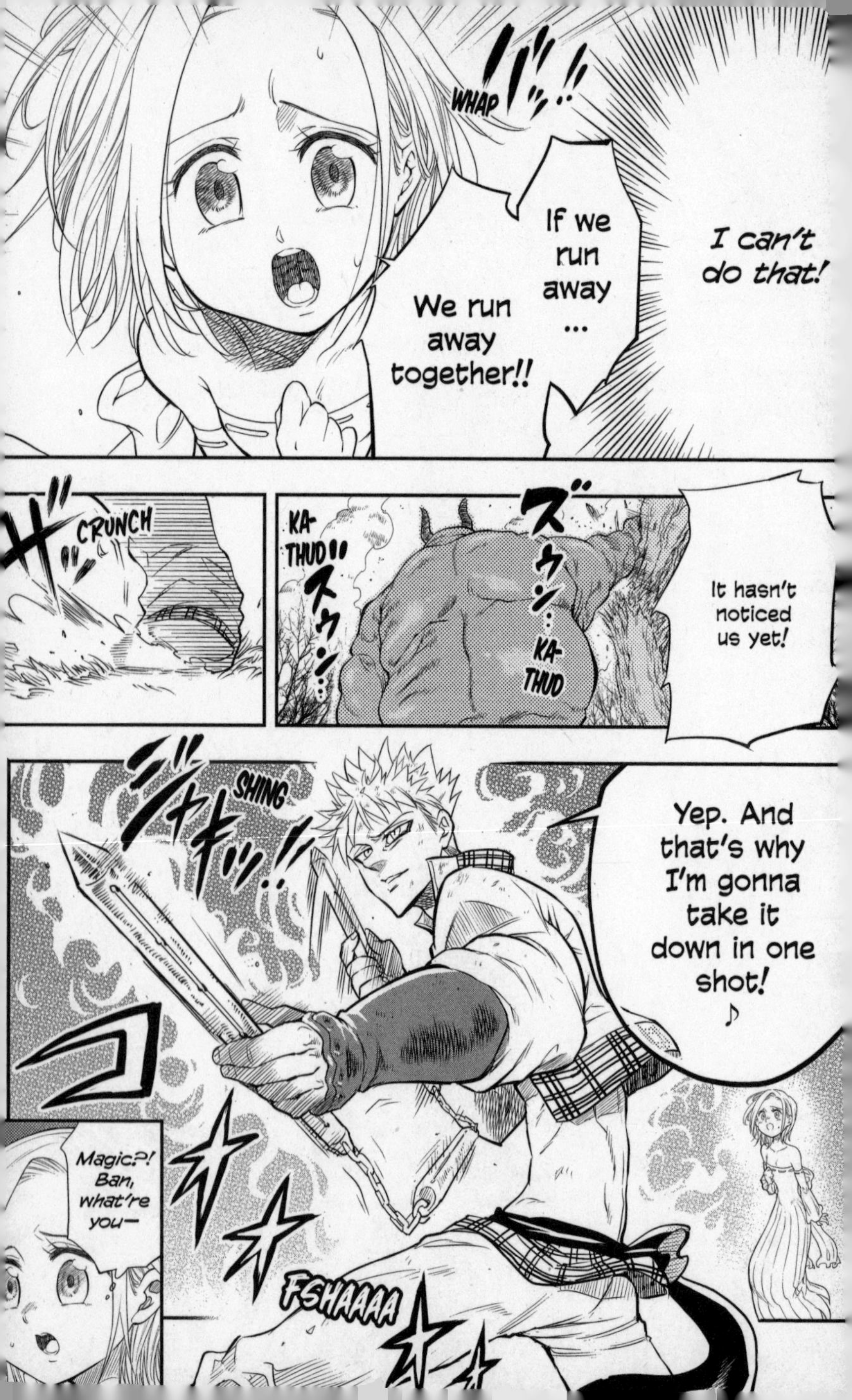
WHAP
I can't do that!
If we run away...
We run away together!!
It hasn't noticed us yet!
KA-THUD
KA-THUD
CRUNCH
Yep. And that's why I'm gonna take it down in one shot! ♪
SHING
Magic?! Ban, what're you—
FSHAAAA

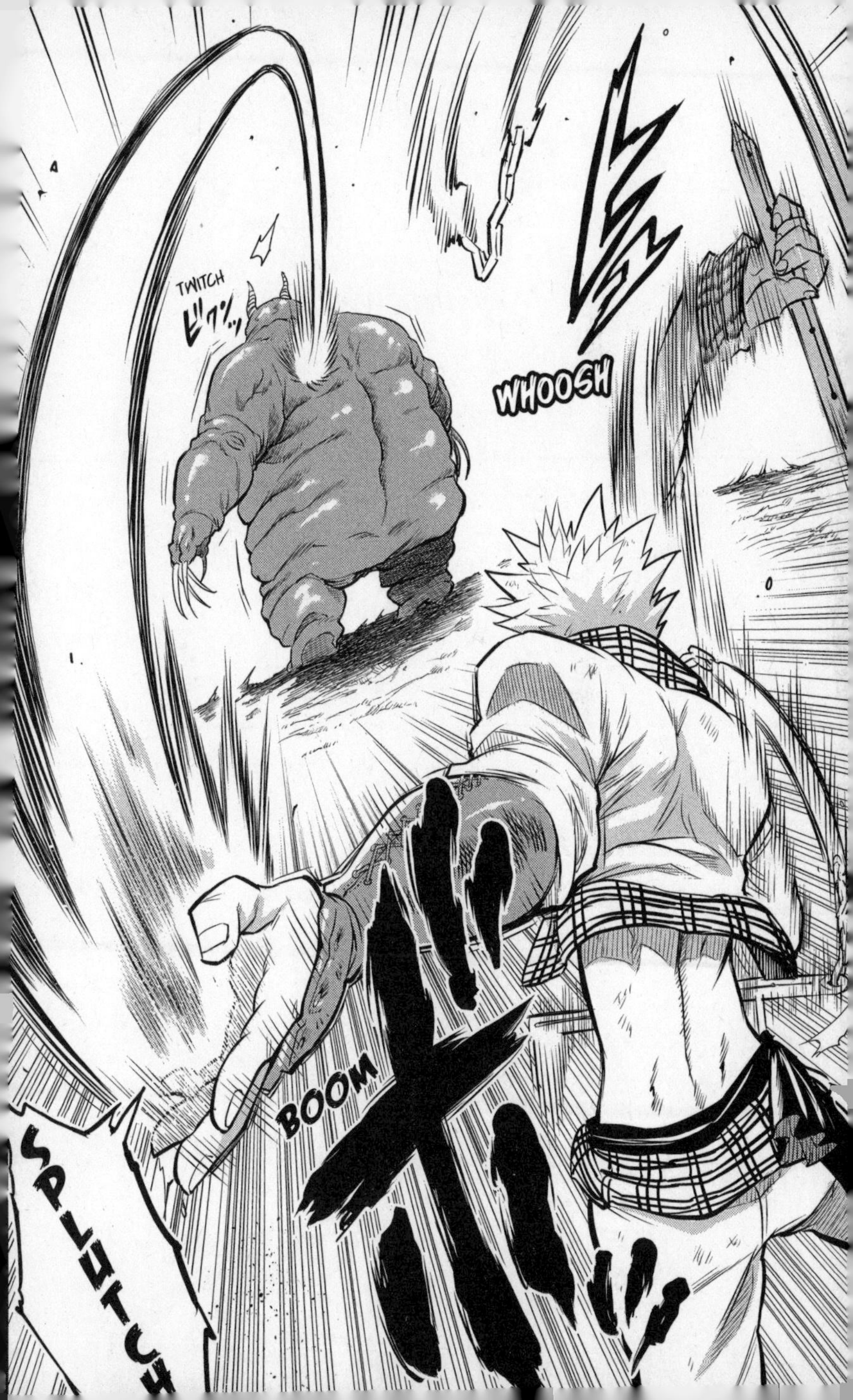
WHOOSH
TWITCH
ビクッ
BOOM
SPLUTCH

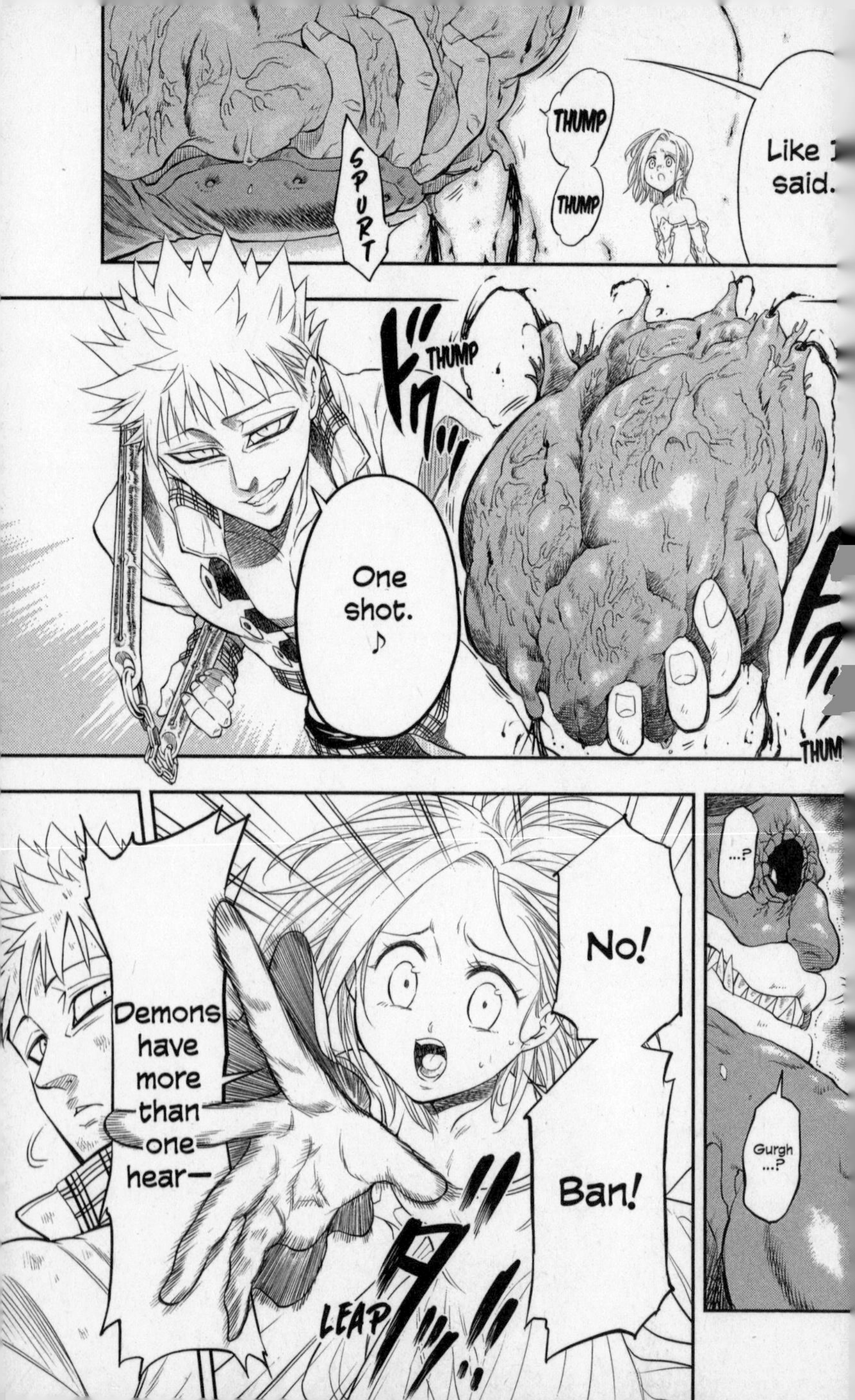
Like I said.
THUMP
THUMP
SPURT
THUMP
One shot. ♪
THUM
...?
Gurgh ...?
No!
Ban!
LEAP
Demons have more than one hear—

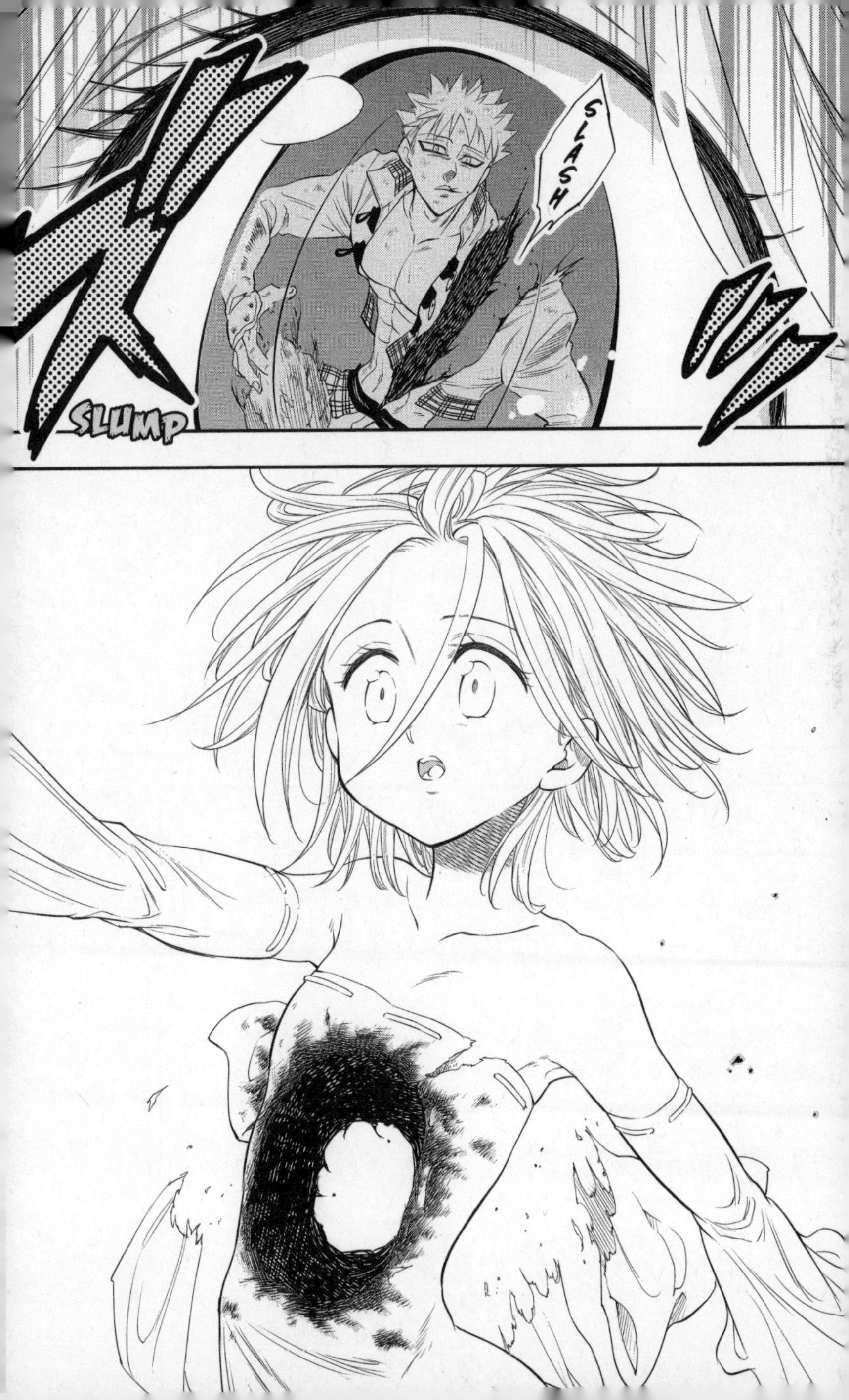
SLASH
SLUMP

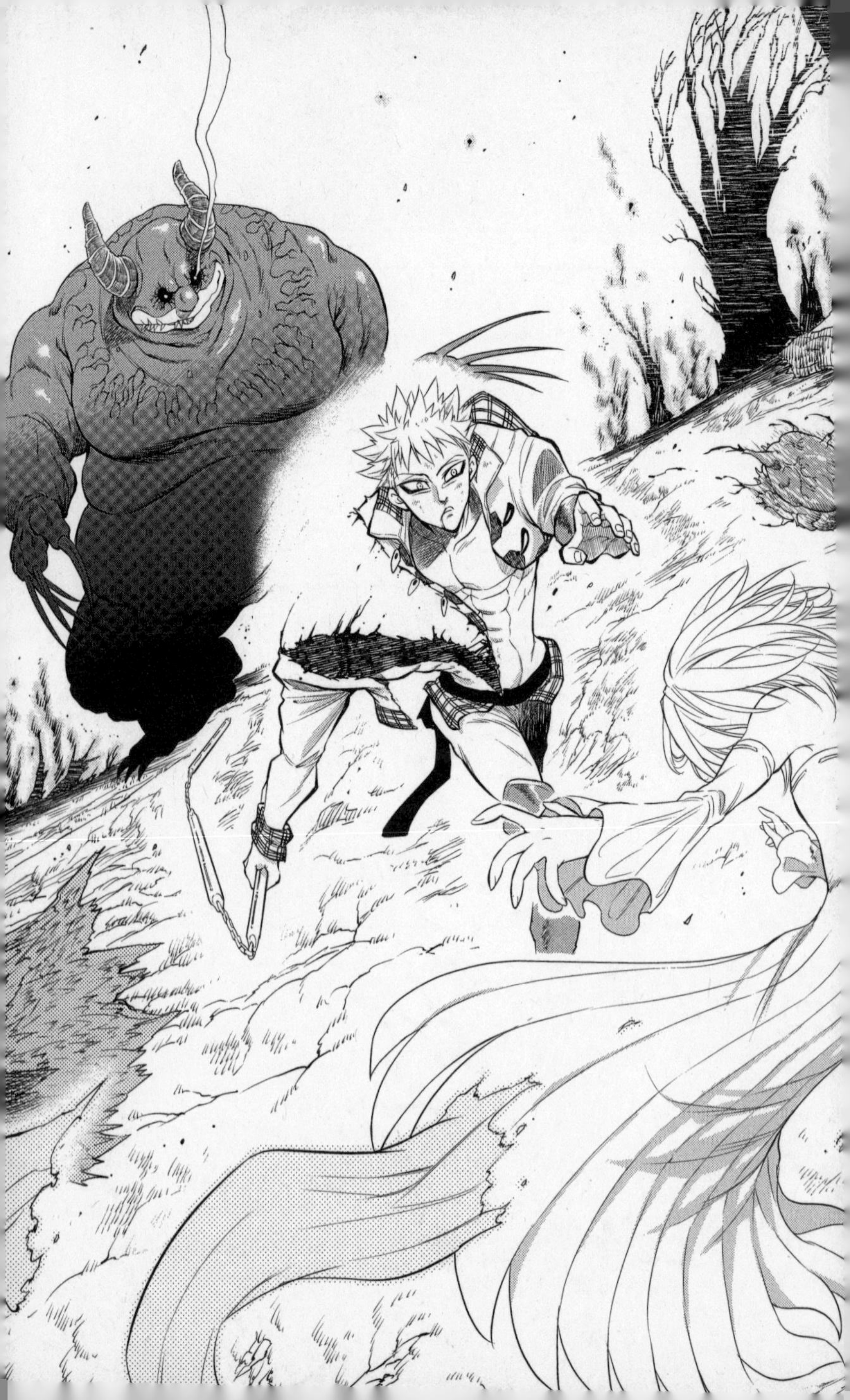

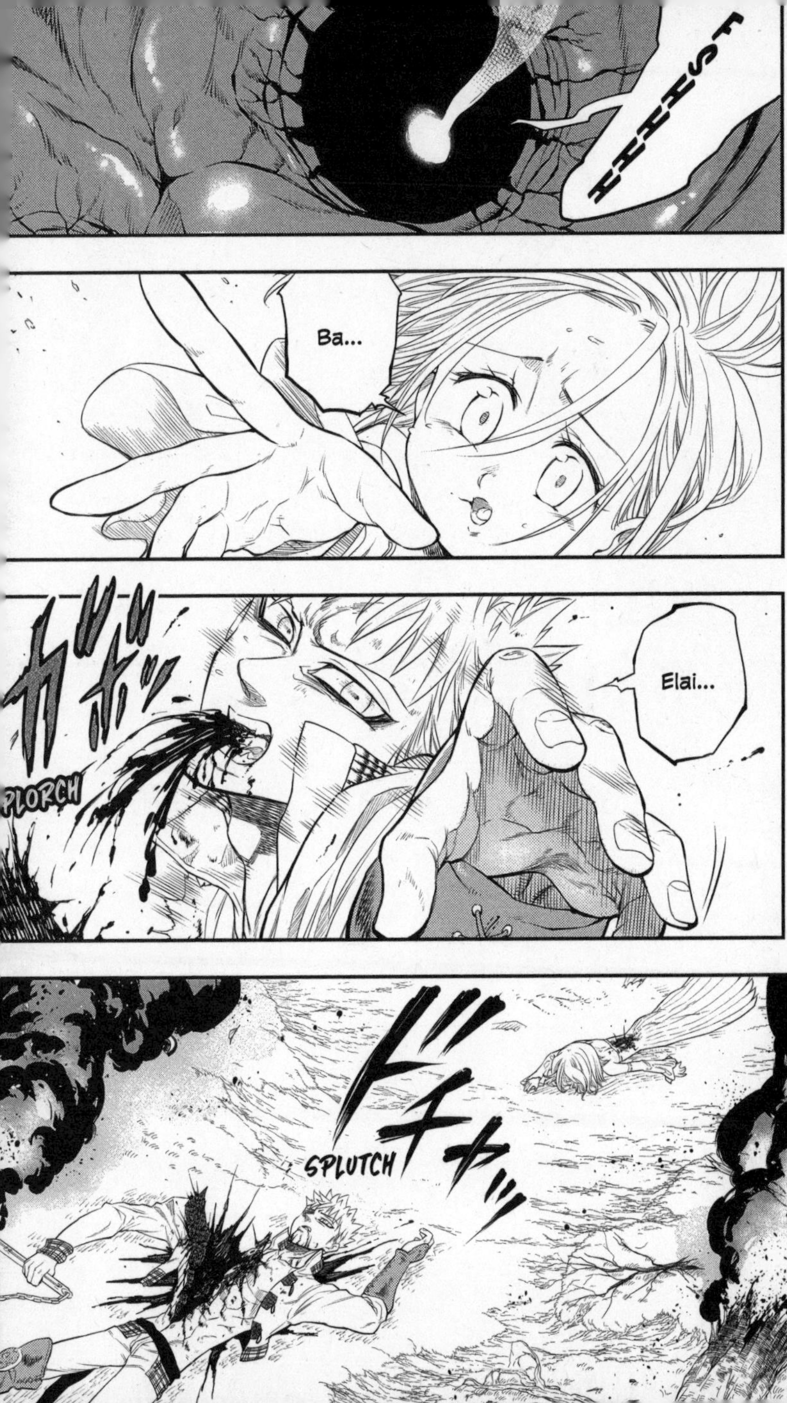
FSHHHHHH
Ba...
Elai...
SPLORCH
SPLUTCH

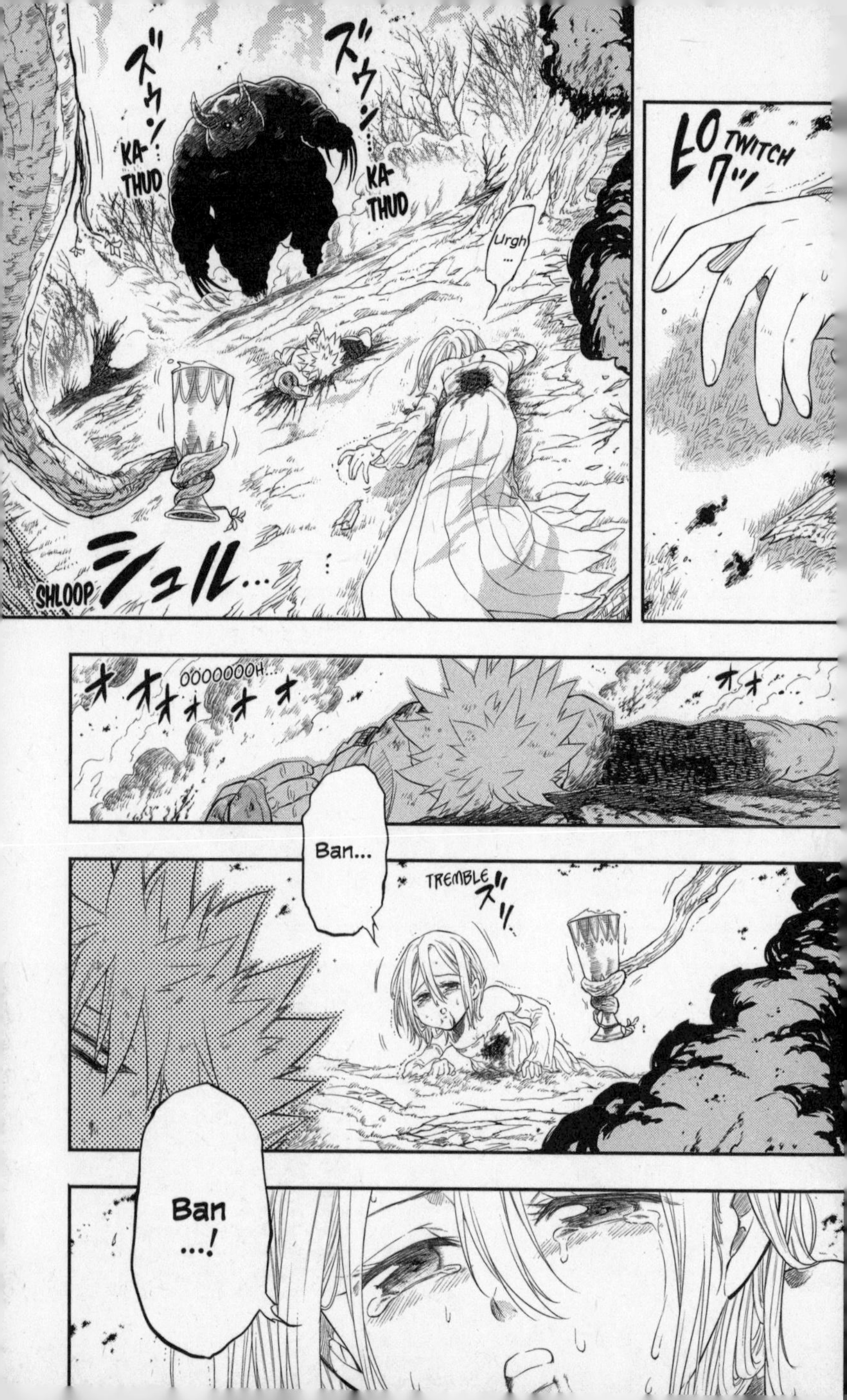
ピクッ
TWITCH
ズゥン…
KA THUD
ズゥン…
KA THUD
Urgh…
シュル…
SHLOOP
オオオオオオ
OOOOOOOH…
オオ
Ban…
ズリ
TREMBLE
Ban…!

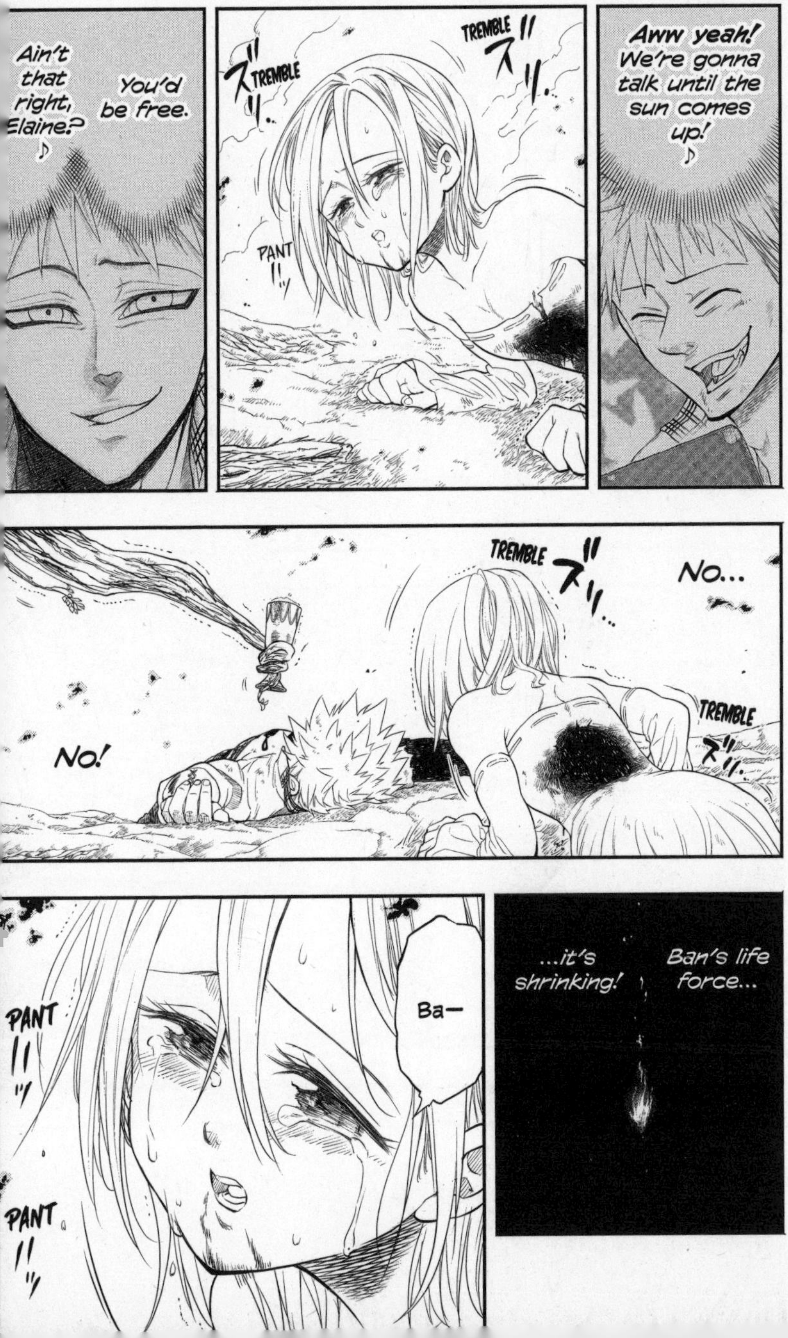
Aww yeah! We're gonna talk until the sun comes up! ♪
TREMBLE ズ…
TREMBLE ズ…
PANT
You'd be free.
Ain't that right, Elaine? ♪
TREMBLE ズ…
No…
TREMBLE ズ…
No!
Ban's life force…
…it's shrinking!
Ba—
PANT
PANT

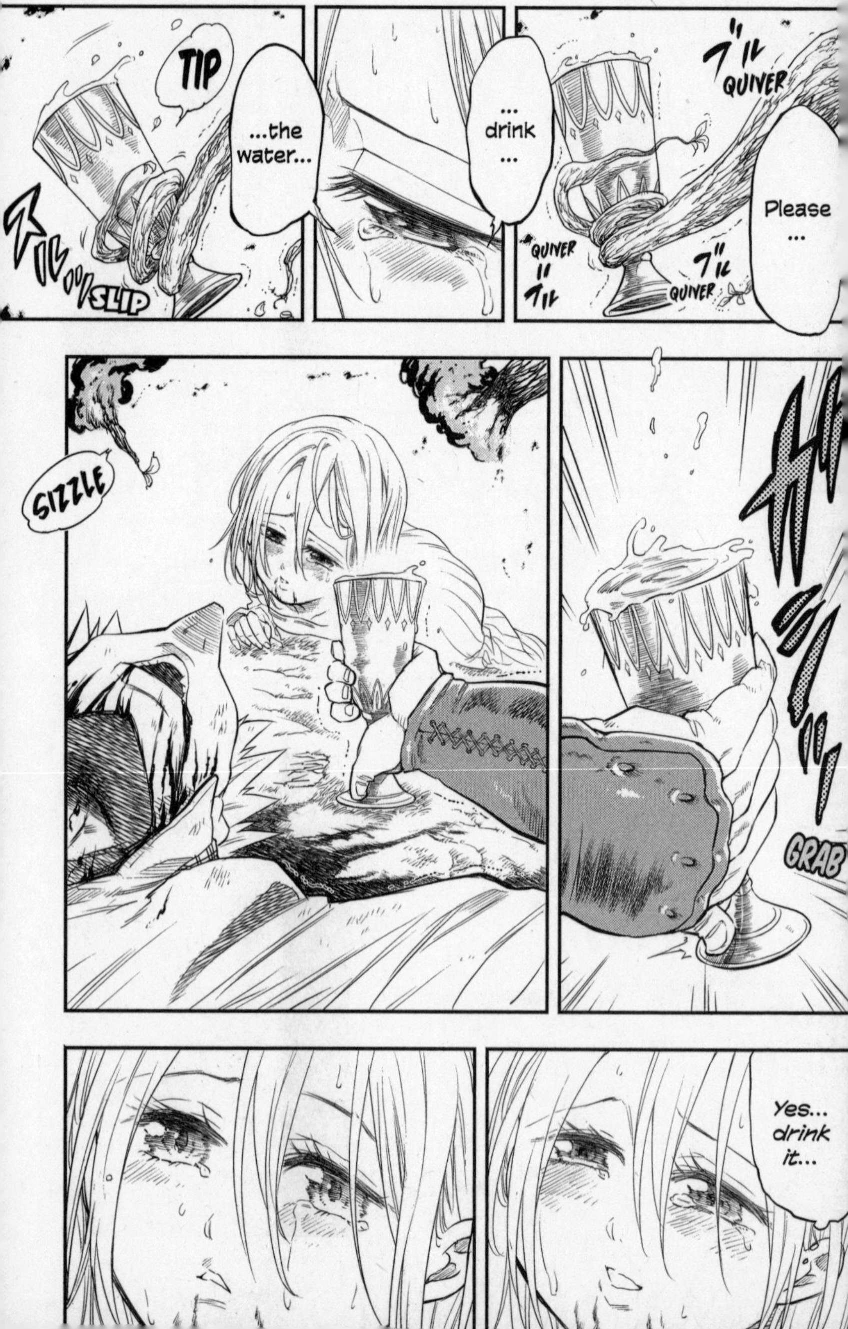
QUIVER
Please...
QUIVER
QUIVER
...drink...
TIP
...the water...
SLIP
GRAB
SIZZLE
Yes... drink it...

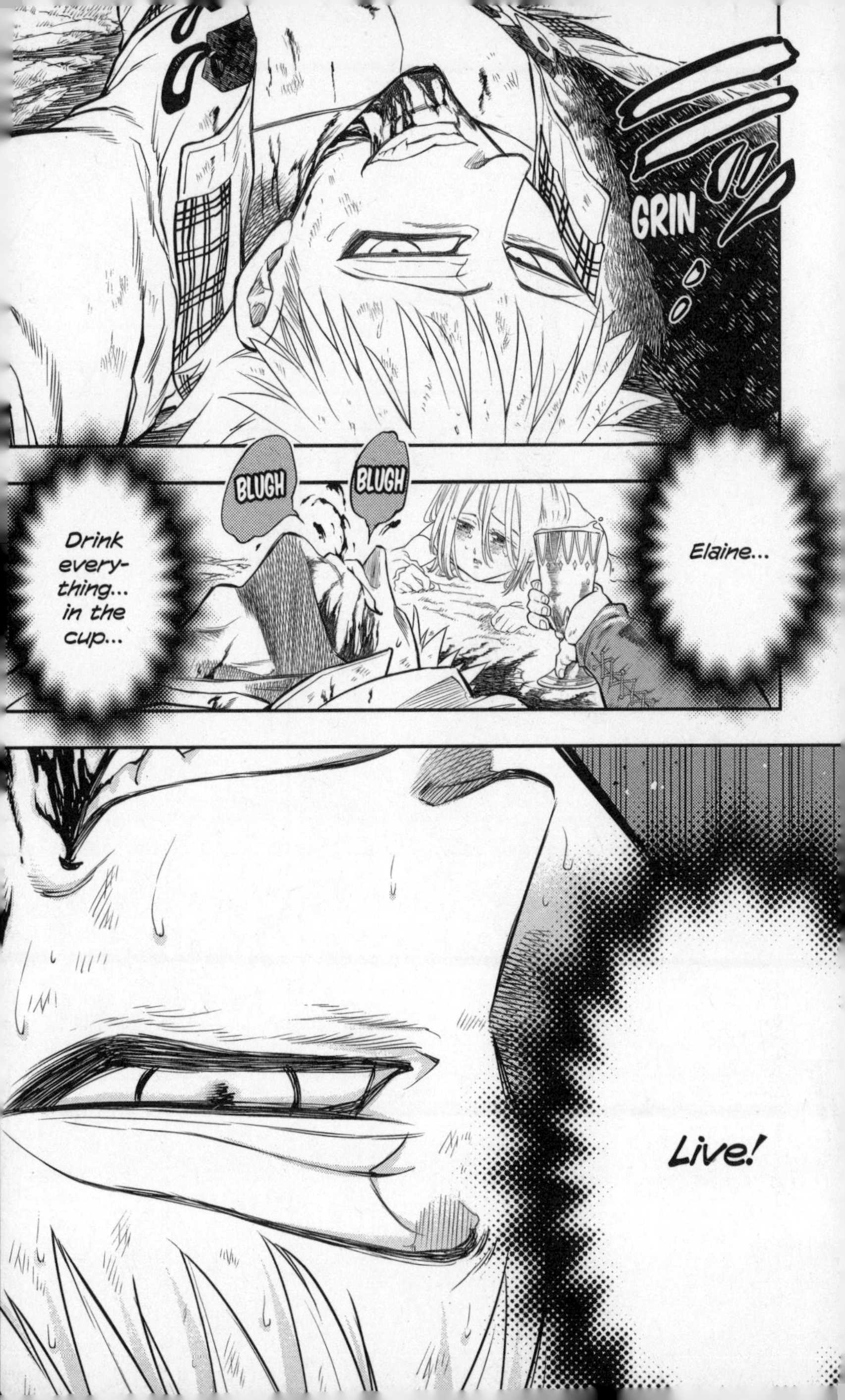
GRIN
Elaine...
BLUGH
BLUGH
Drink everything... in the cup...
Live!

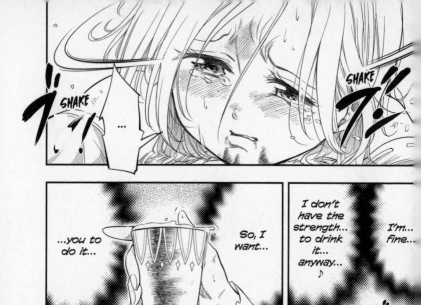

SHAKE ...

SHAKE

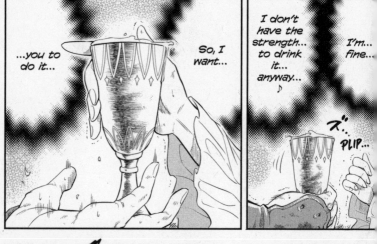

...you to do it...

So, I want...

I don't have the strength... to drink it... anyway... ♪

I'm... fine...

PLIP...

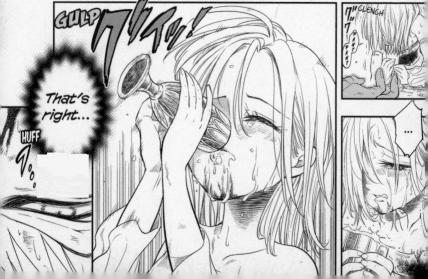

GULP

That's right...

HUFF

CLENCH

...

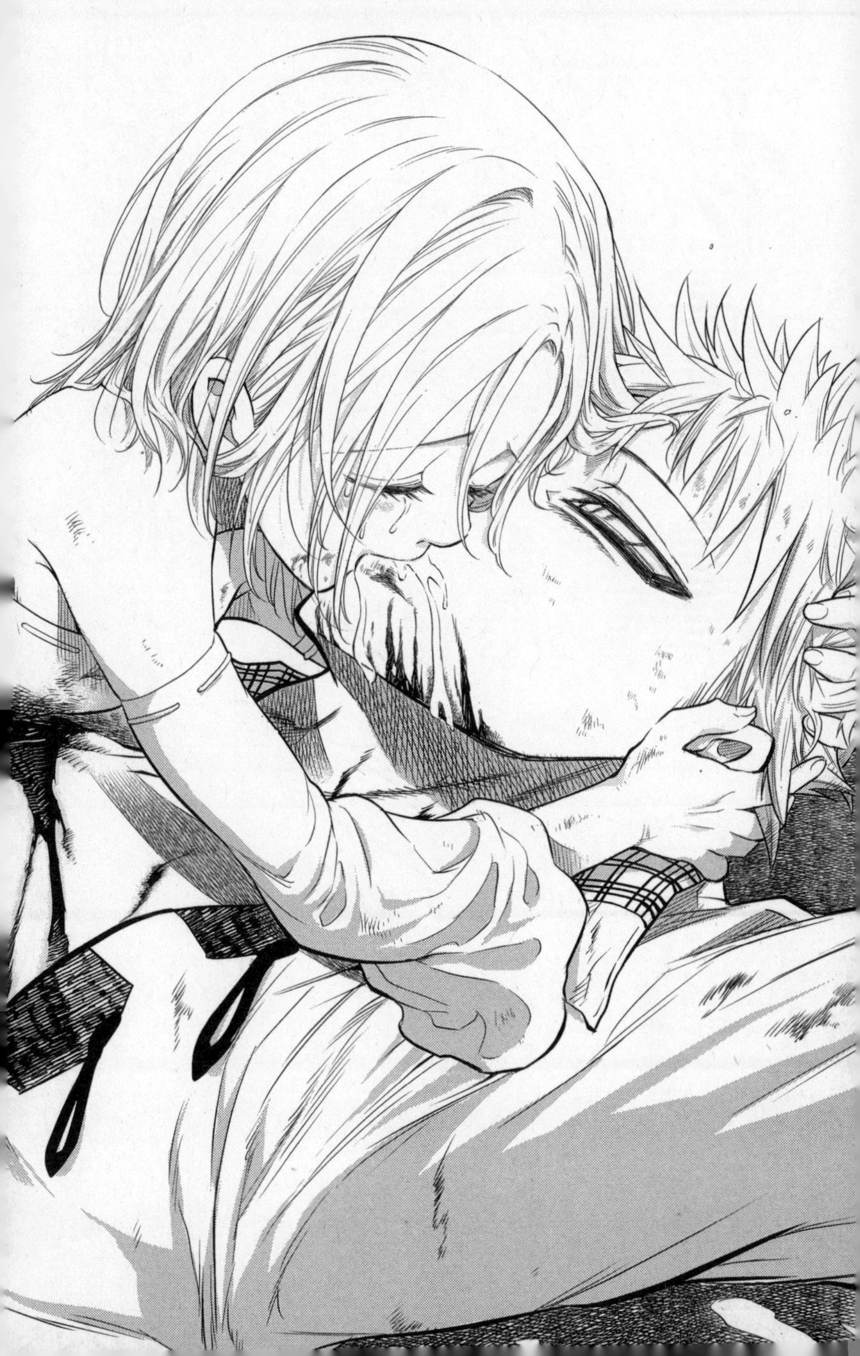

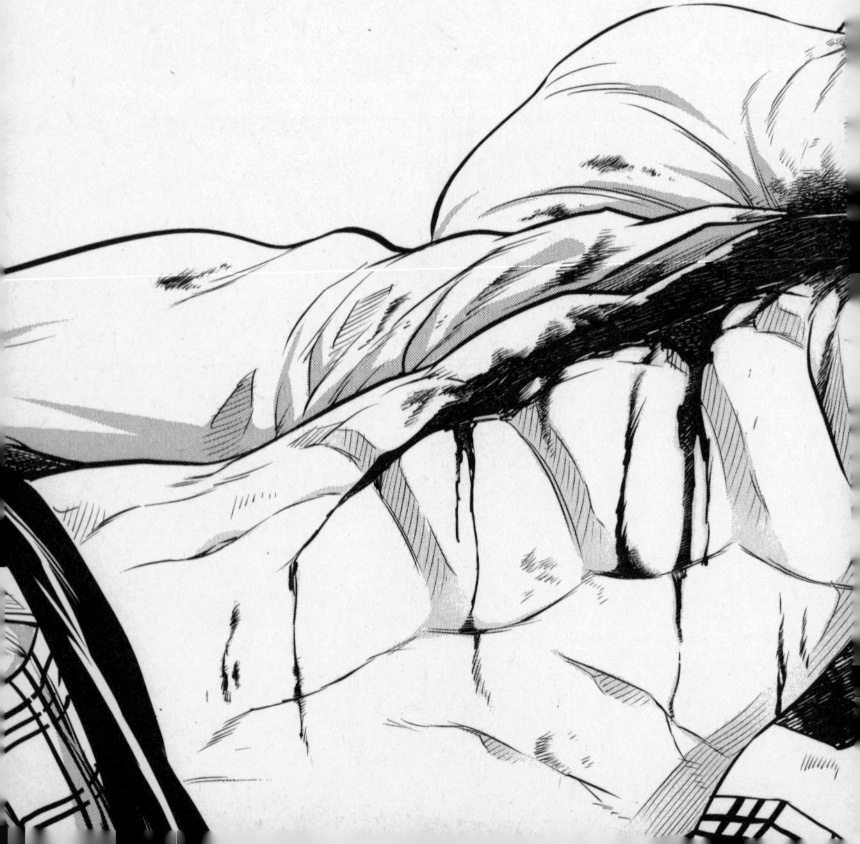

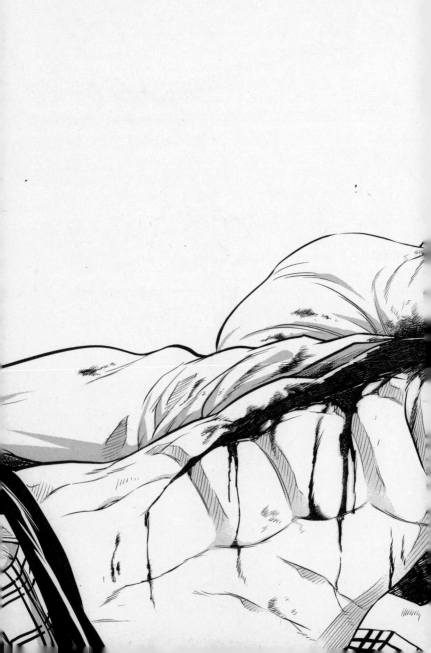

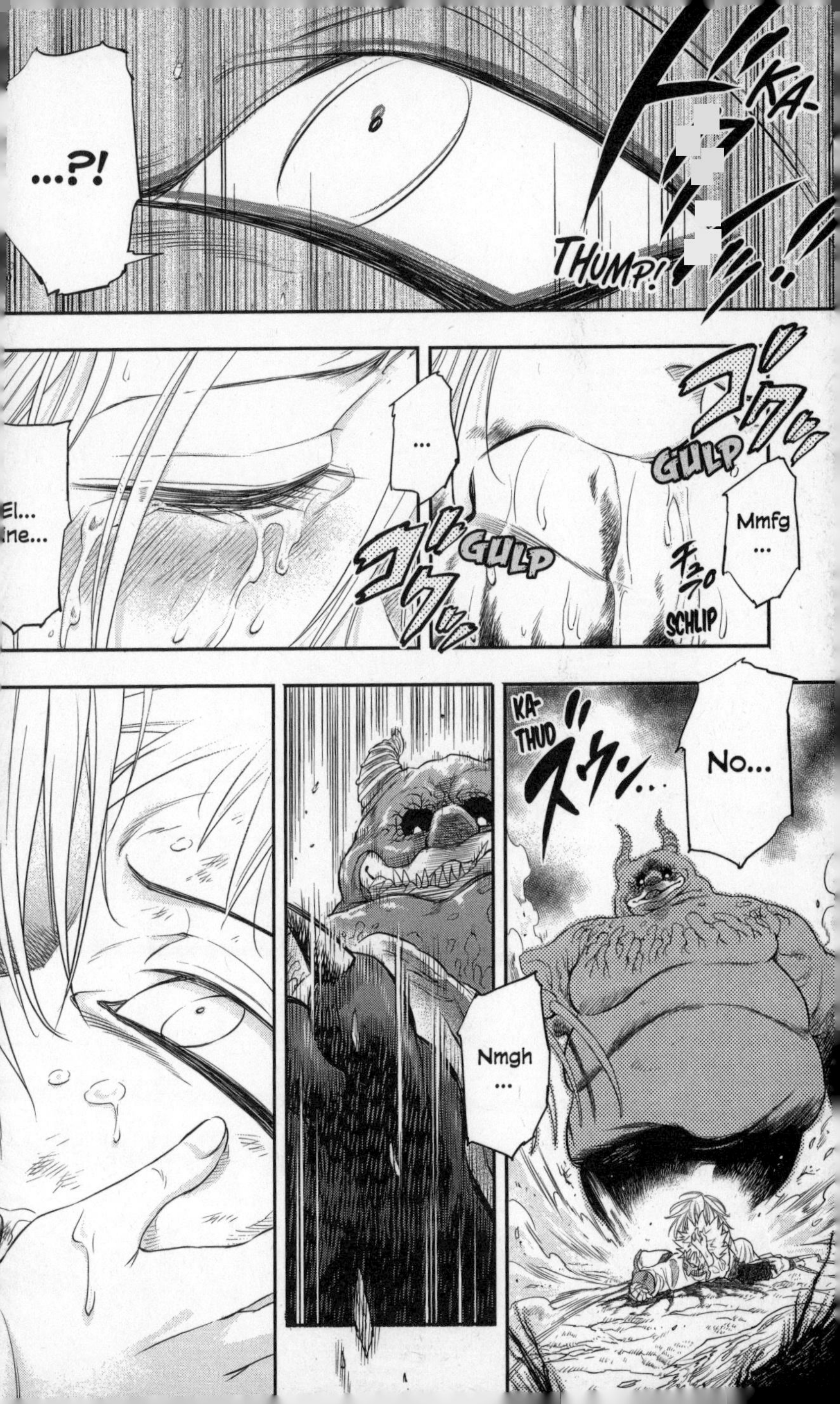

KA-THUMP!
...?!
GULP
Mmfg ...
SCHLIP
GULP
...
El...
ine...
KA-THUD
No...
Nmgh ...

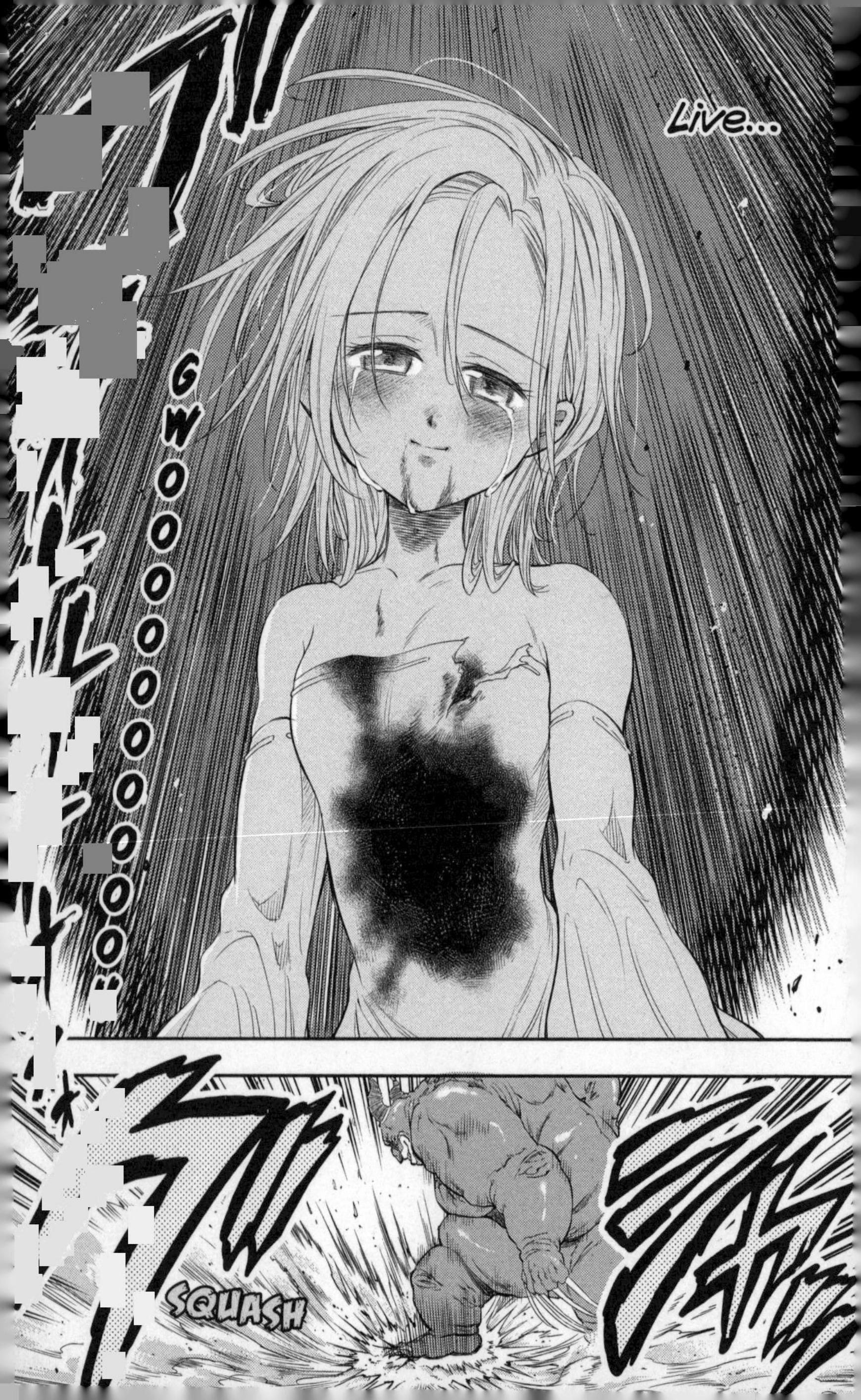
Live...
GWOOOOOOOOOOOOOO...
SQUASH

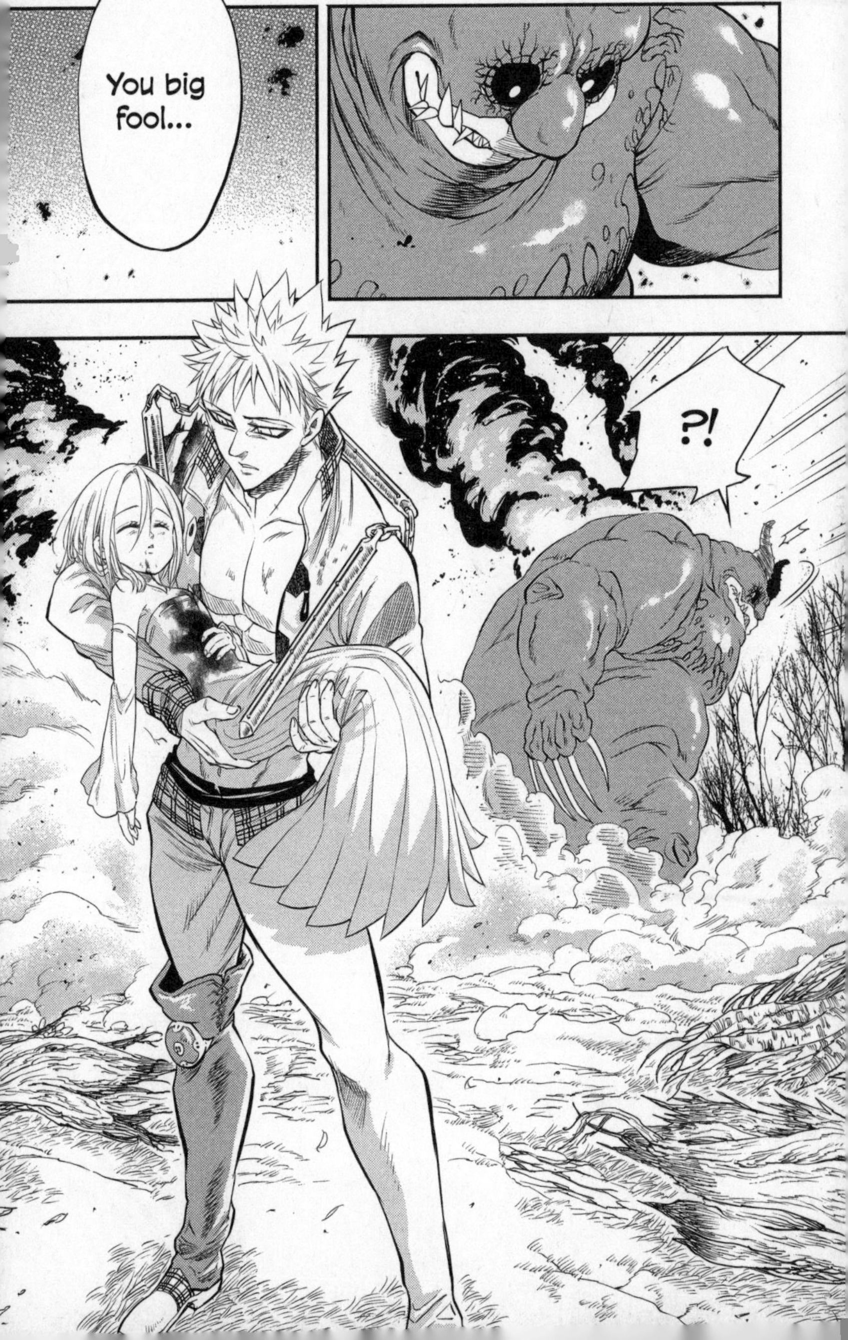
You big fool...
?!

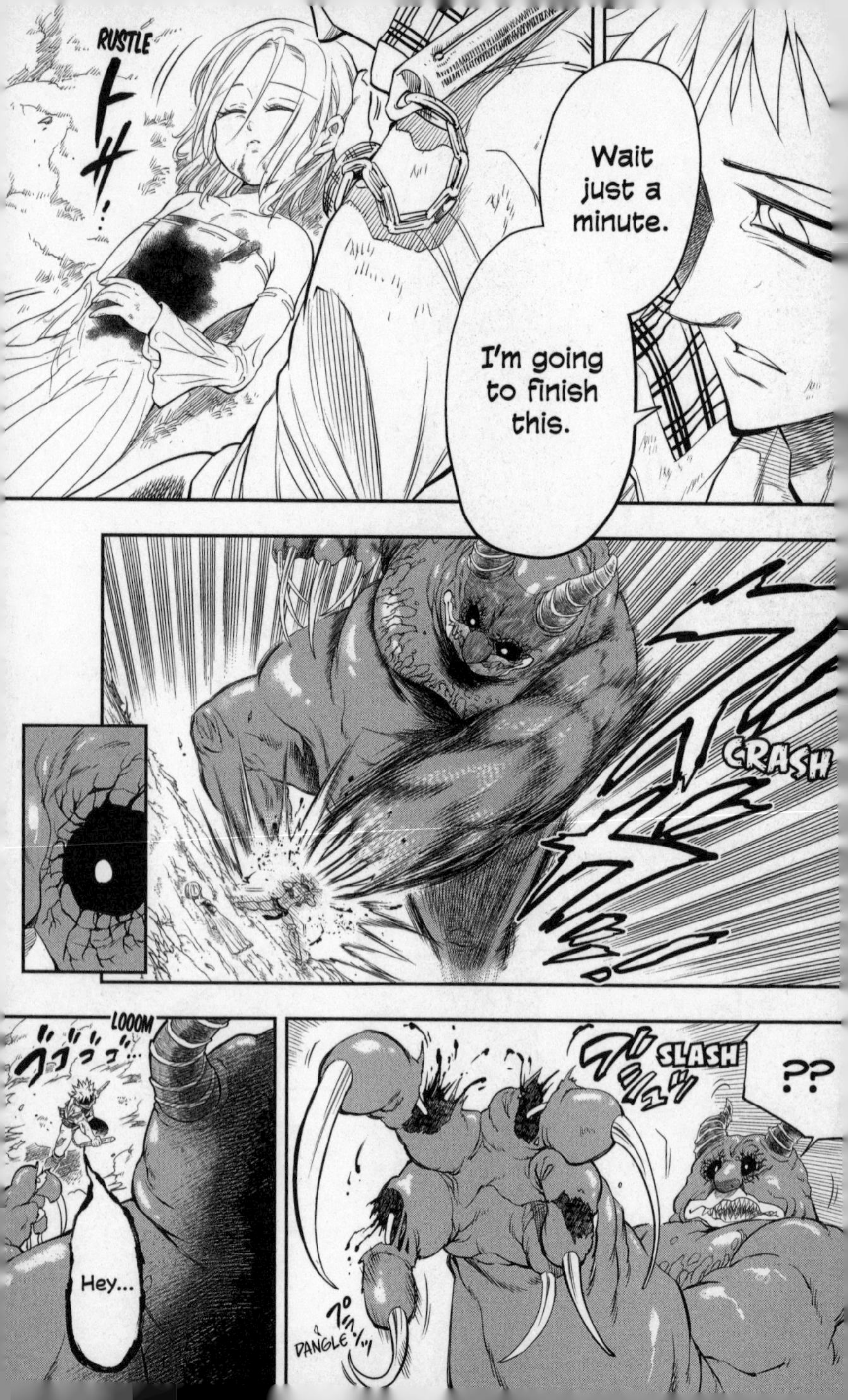
Wait just a minute.
I'm going to finish this.
RUSTLE
CRASH
SLASH
??
DANGLE
LOOOM
Hey...

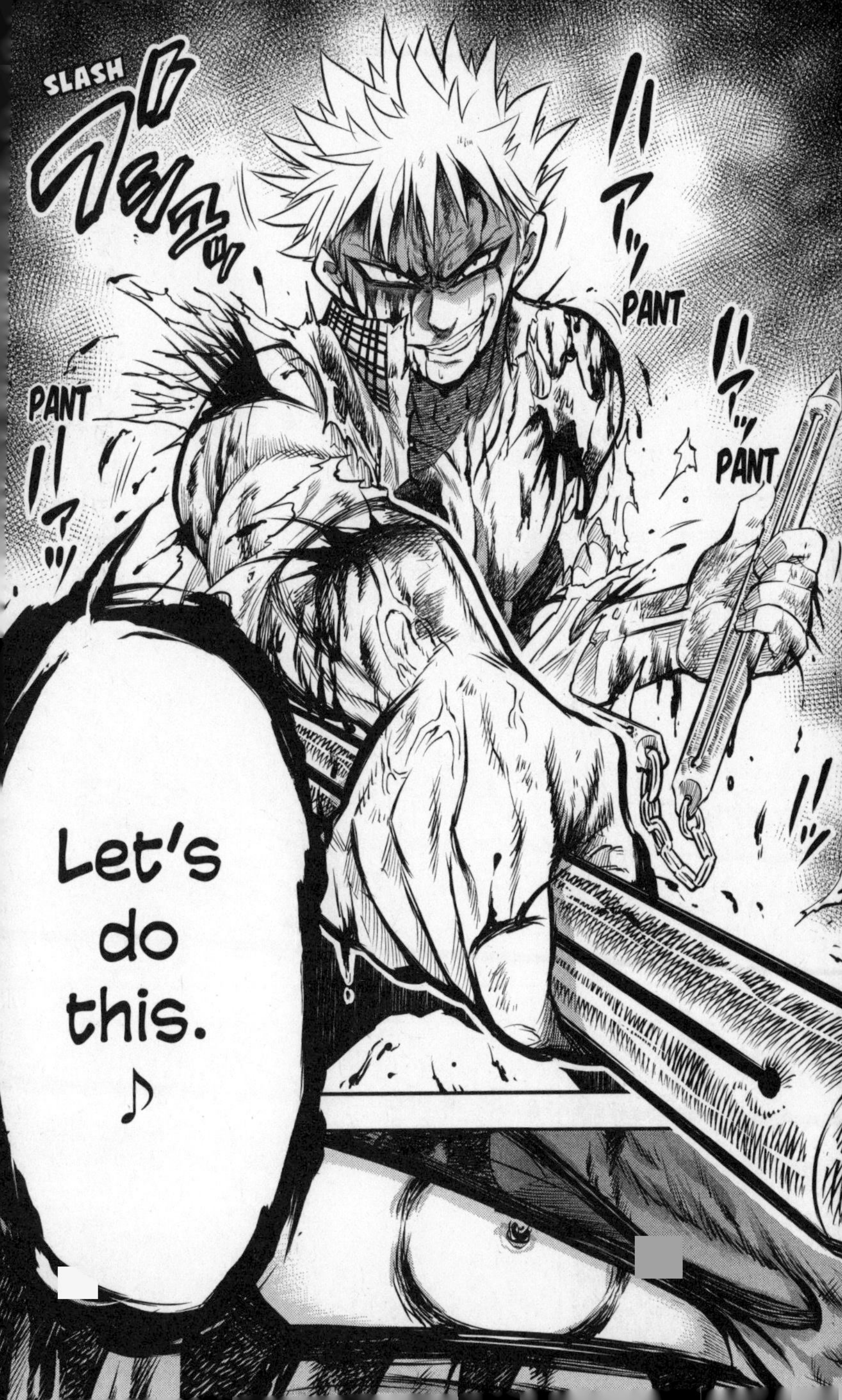
PANT
PANT
SLASH
PANT
Let's do this. ♪

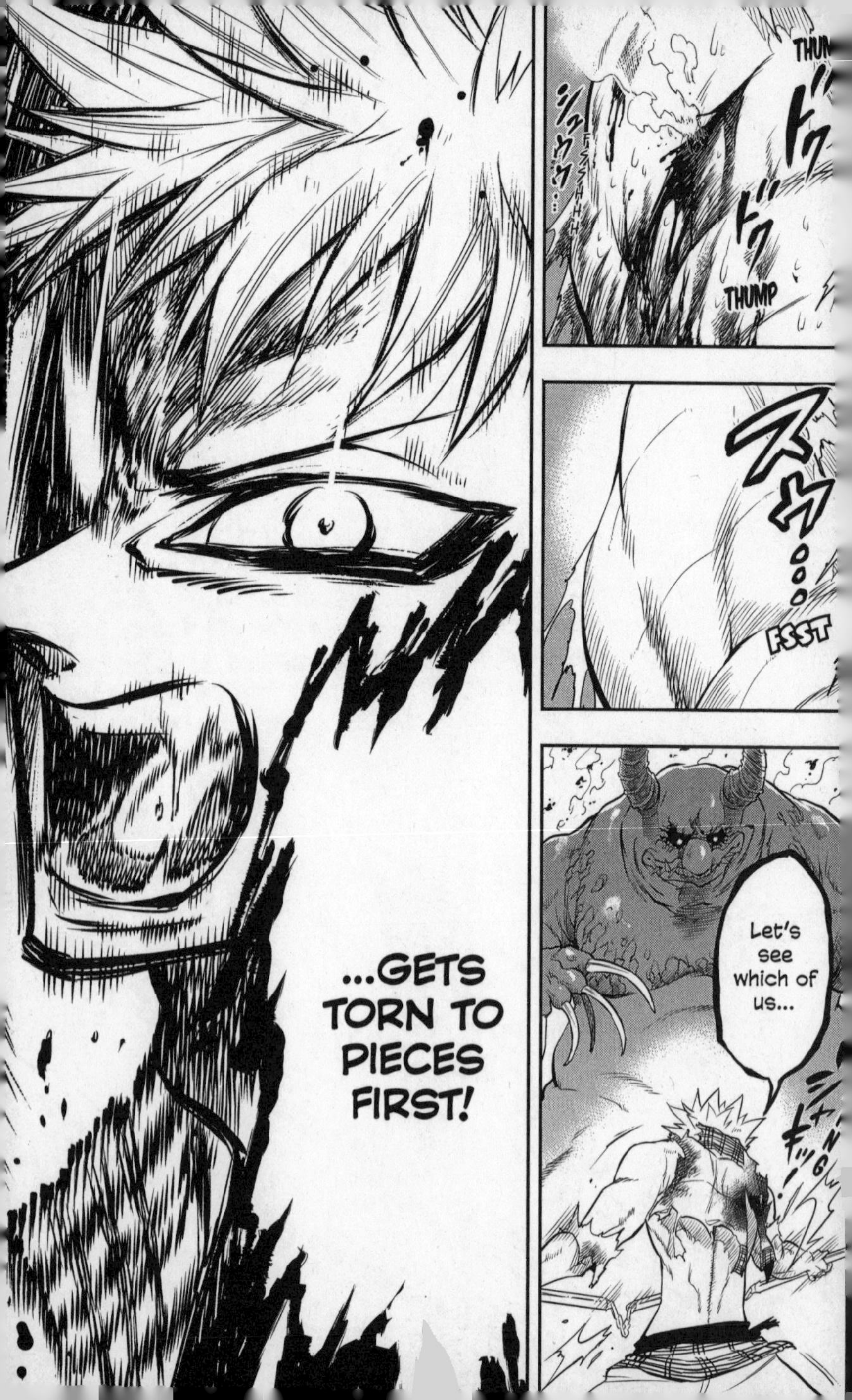
THUM
FSSHHH
THUMP
FSST
Let's see which of us...
NG
...GETS TORN TO PIECES FIRST!

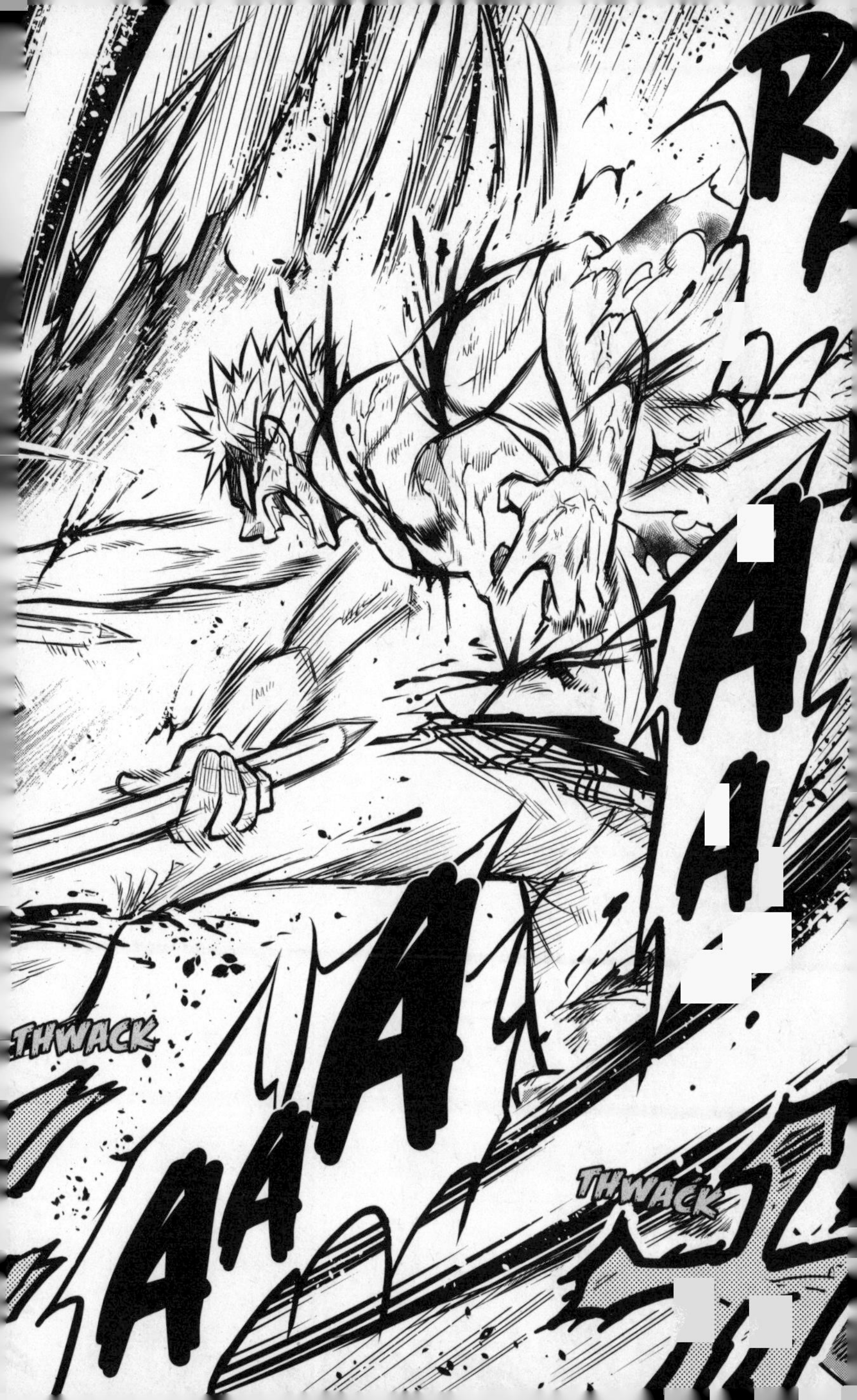
THWACK
THWACK

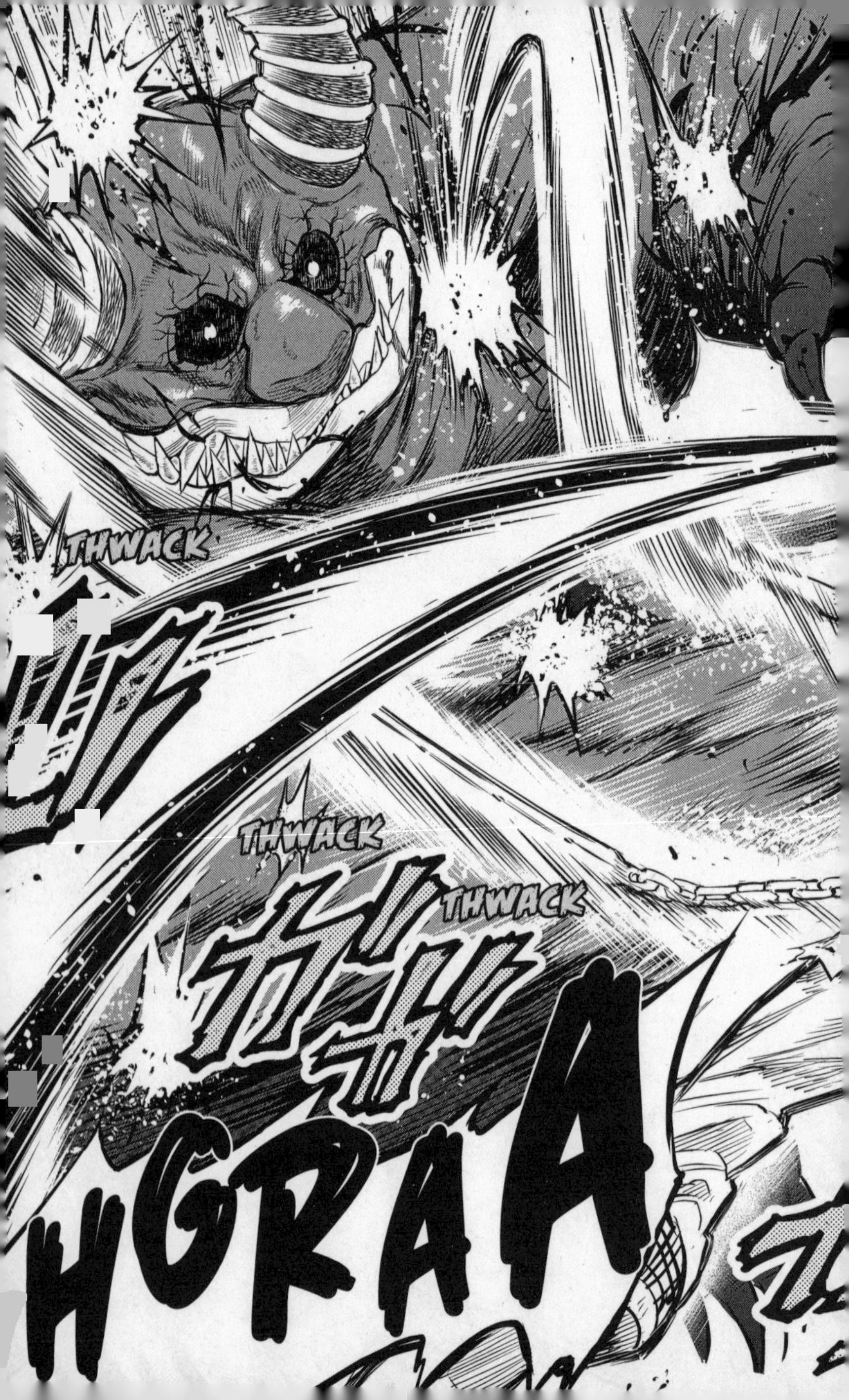
THWACK
THWACK
THWACK
HGRAA

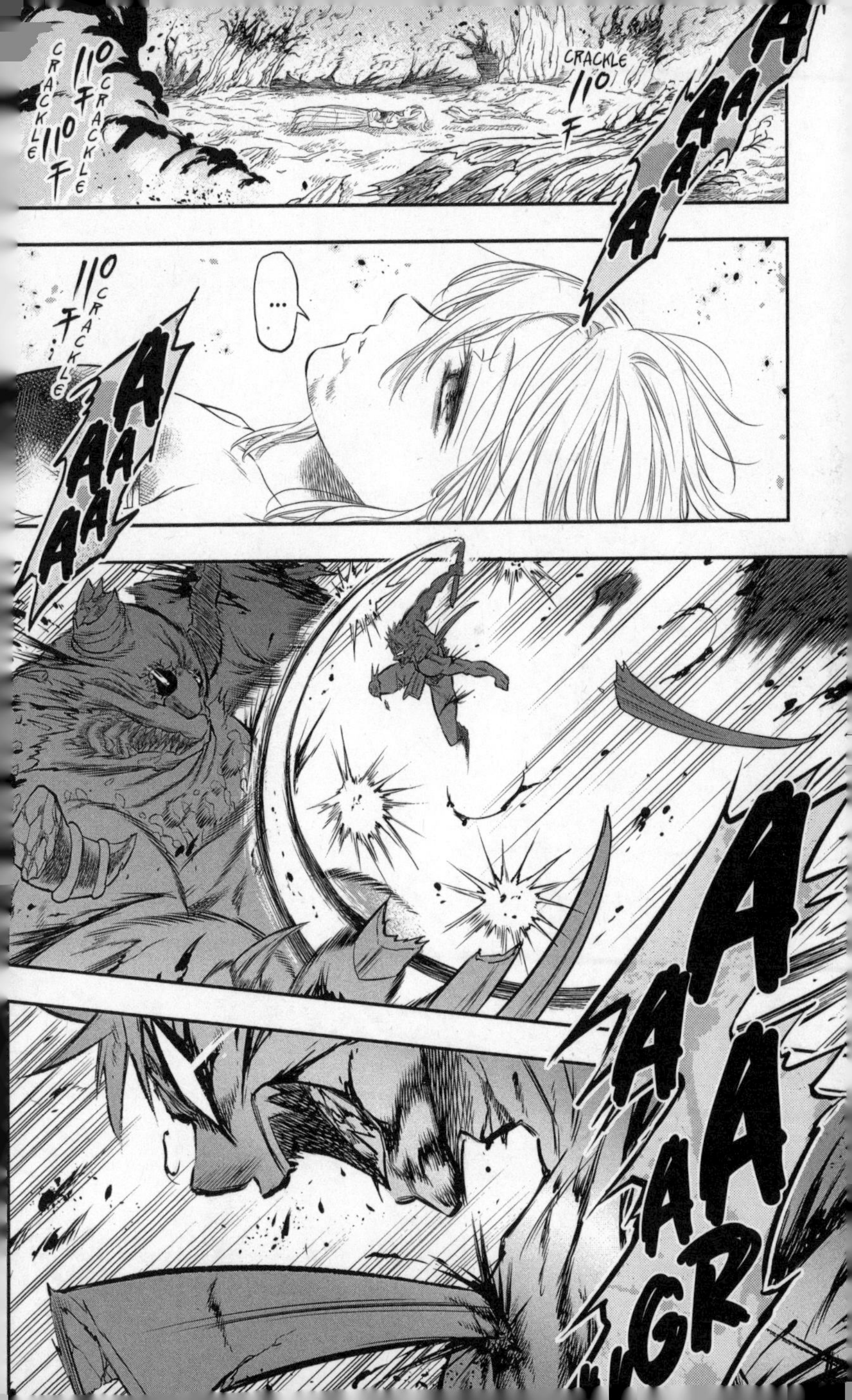
CRACKLE
AAAAAA
CRACKLE CRACKLE
...
CRACKLE
AAAAAA
GRAAAAA

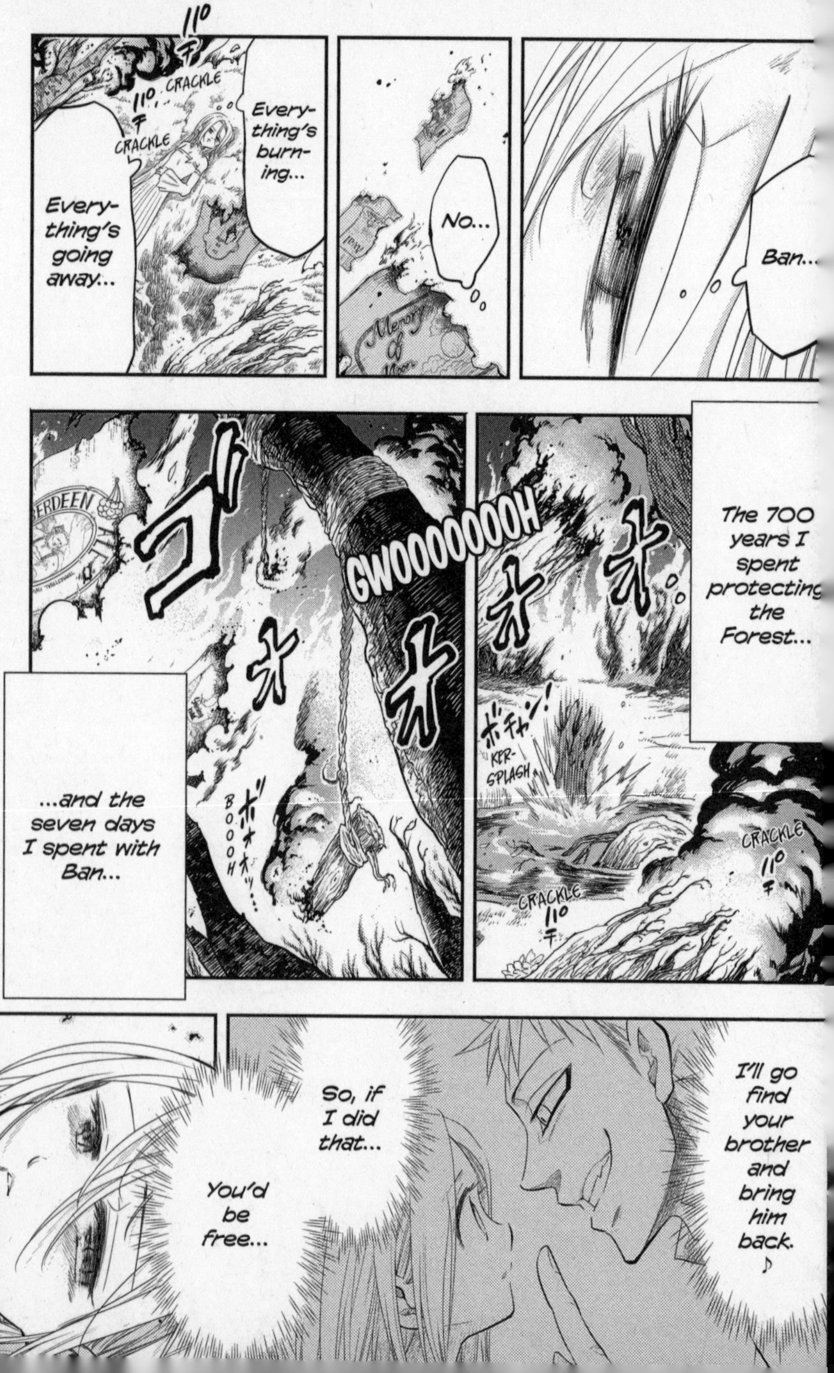

Ban...
No...
Everything's burning...
CRACKLE
CRACKLE
Everything's going away...
The 700 years I spent protecting the Forest...
GWOOOOOOOH
KER-SPLASH
CRACKLE
CRACKLE
BOOOH
...and the seven days I spent with Ban...
I'll go find your brother and bring him back. ♪
So, if I did that...
You'd be free...

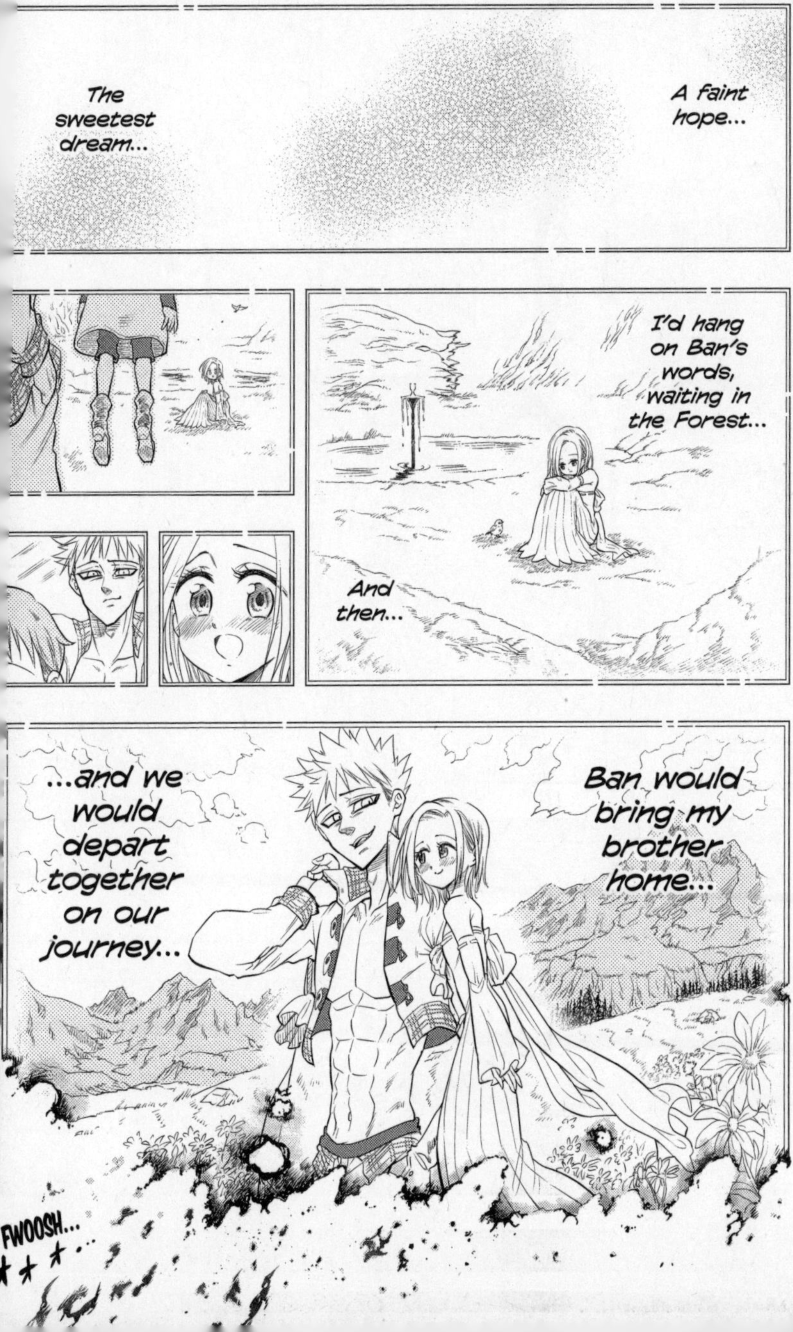
A faint hope...
The sweetest dream...
I'd hang on Ban's words, waiting in the Forest...
And then...
Ban would bring my brother home...
...and we would depart together on our journey...
FWOOSH...

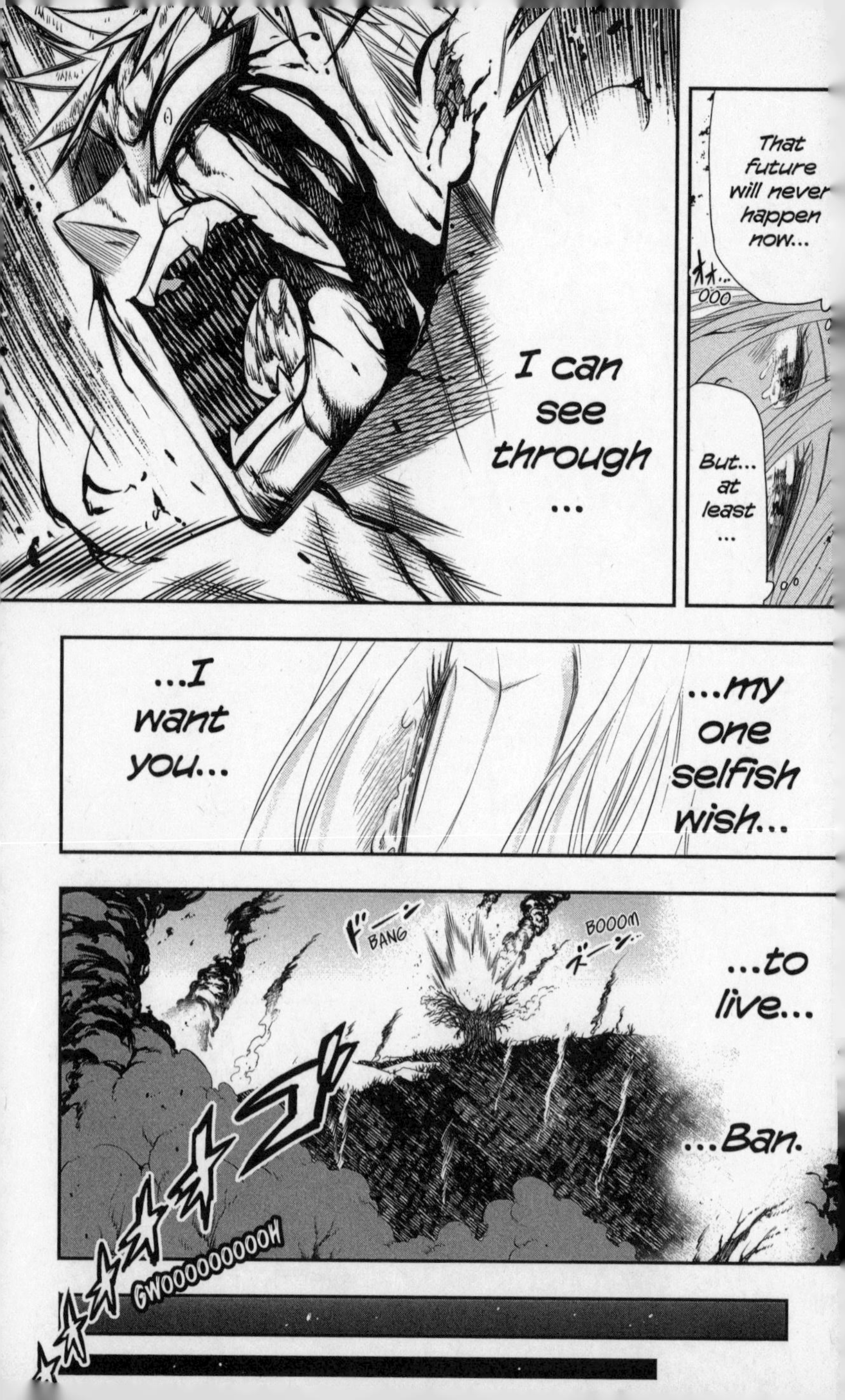
That future will never happen now...
OOO
But... at least ...
I can see through ...
...I want you...
...my one selfish wish...
BANG
BOOOM
...to live...
...Ban.
GWOOOOOOOOOH

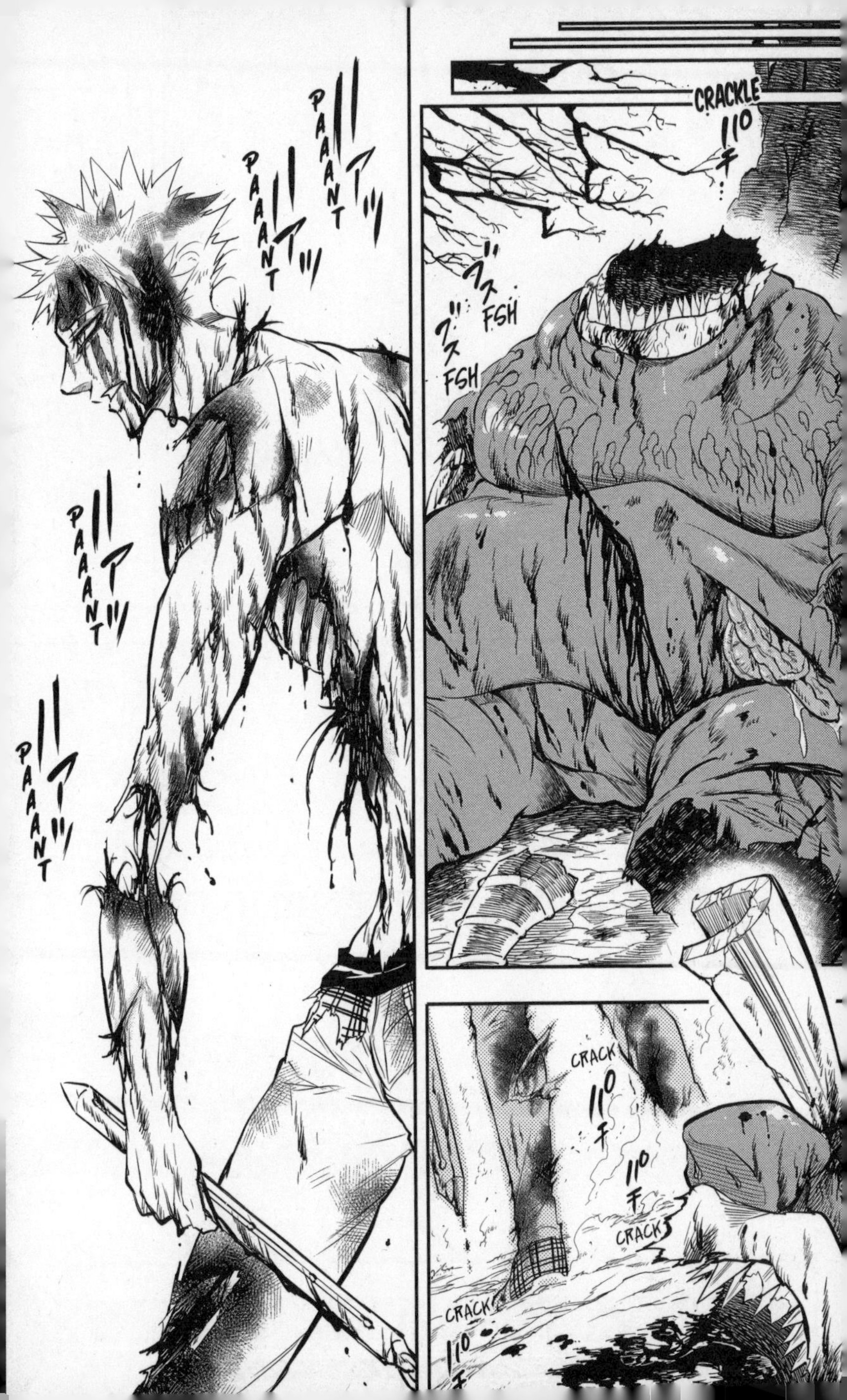
CRACKLE
FSH
FSH
CRACK
CRACK
CRACK
PAAAANT
PAAAANT
PAAAANT
PAAAANT

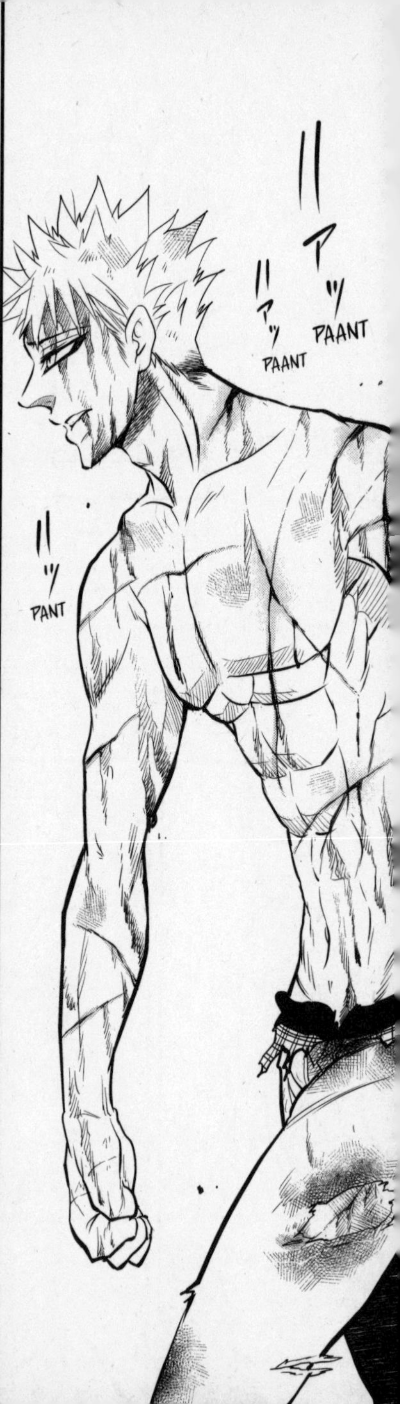
ハァッ
PAANT
ハァッ
PAANT
ハッ
PANT
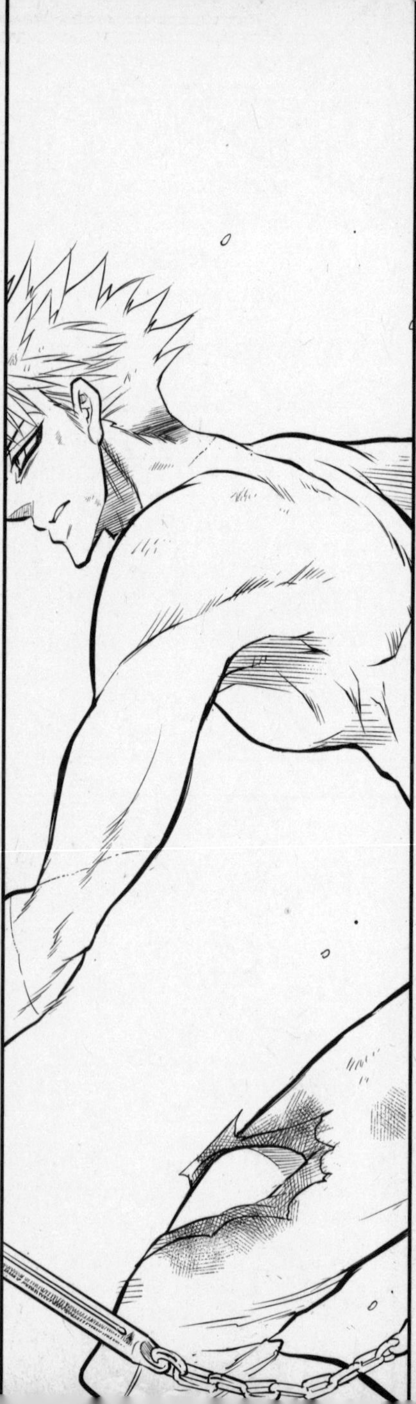

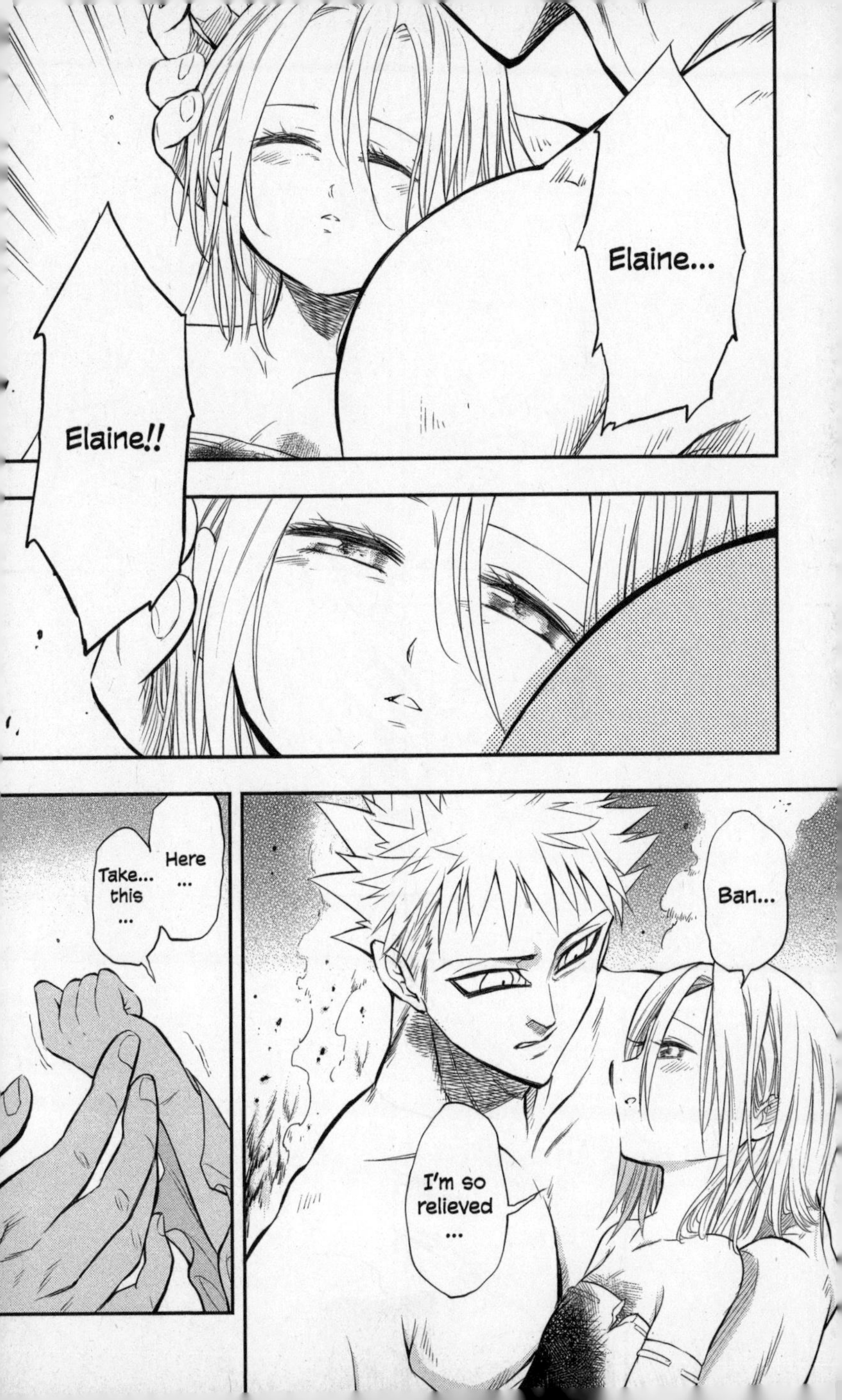
Elaine...
Elaine!!
Ban...
I'm so relieved ...
Here ...
Take... this ...

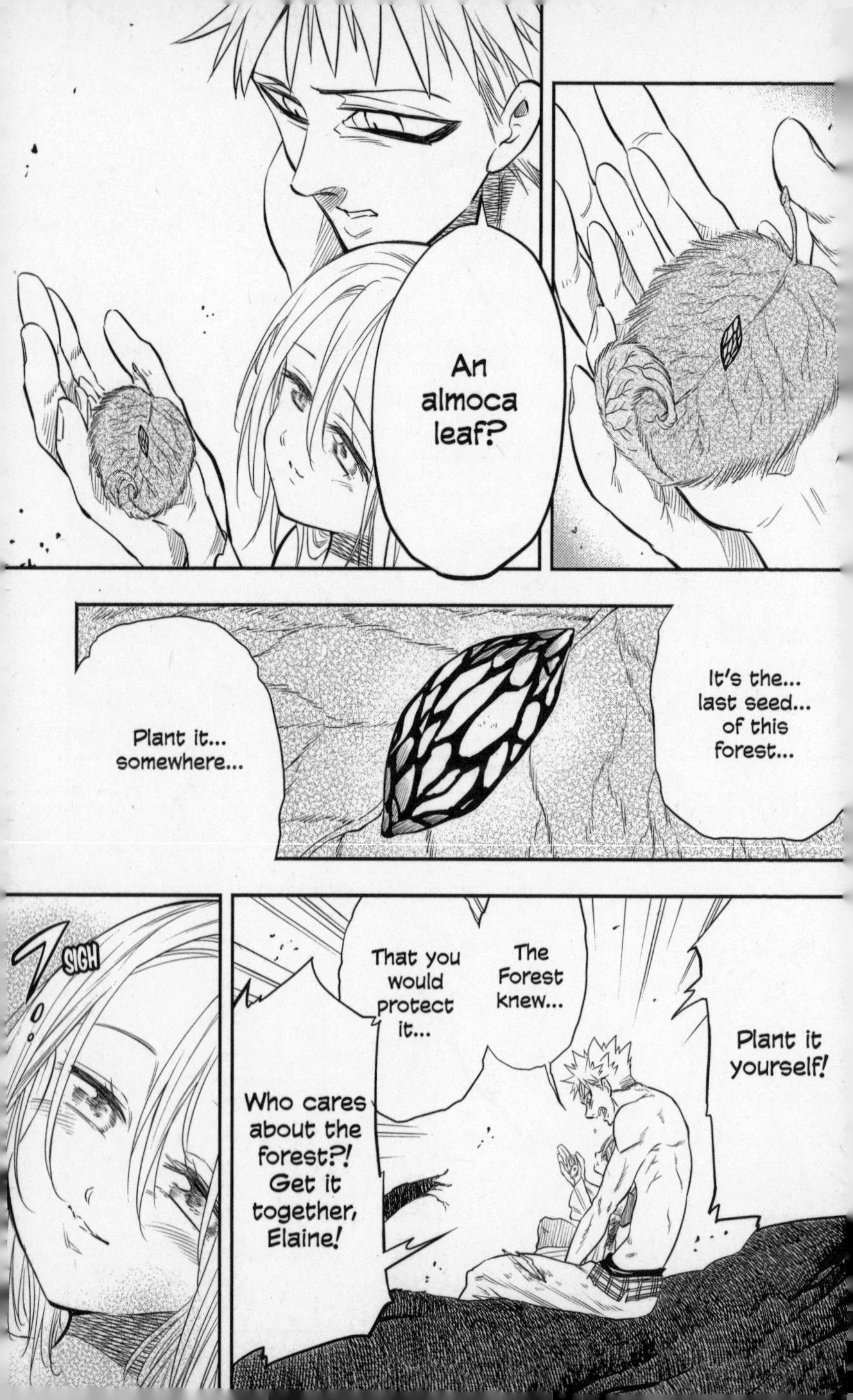
An almoca leaf?
It's the... last seed... of this forest...
Plant it... somewhere...
Plant it yourself!
The Forest knew...
That you would protect it...
Who cares about the forest?! Get it together, Elaine!
SIGH

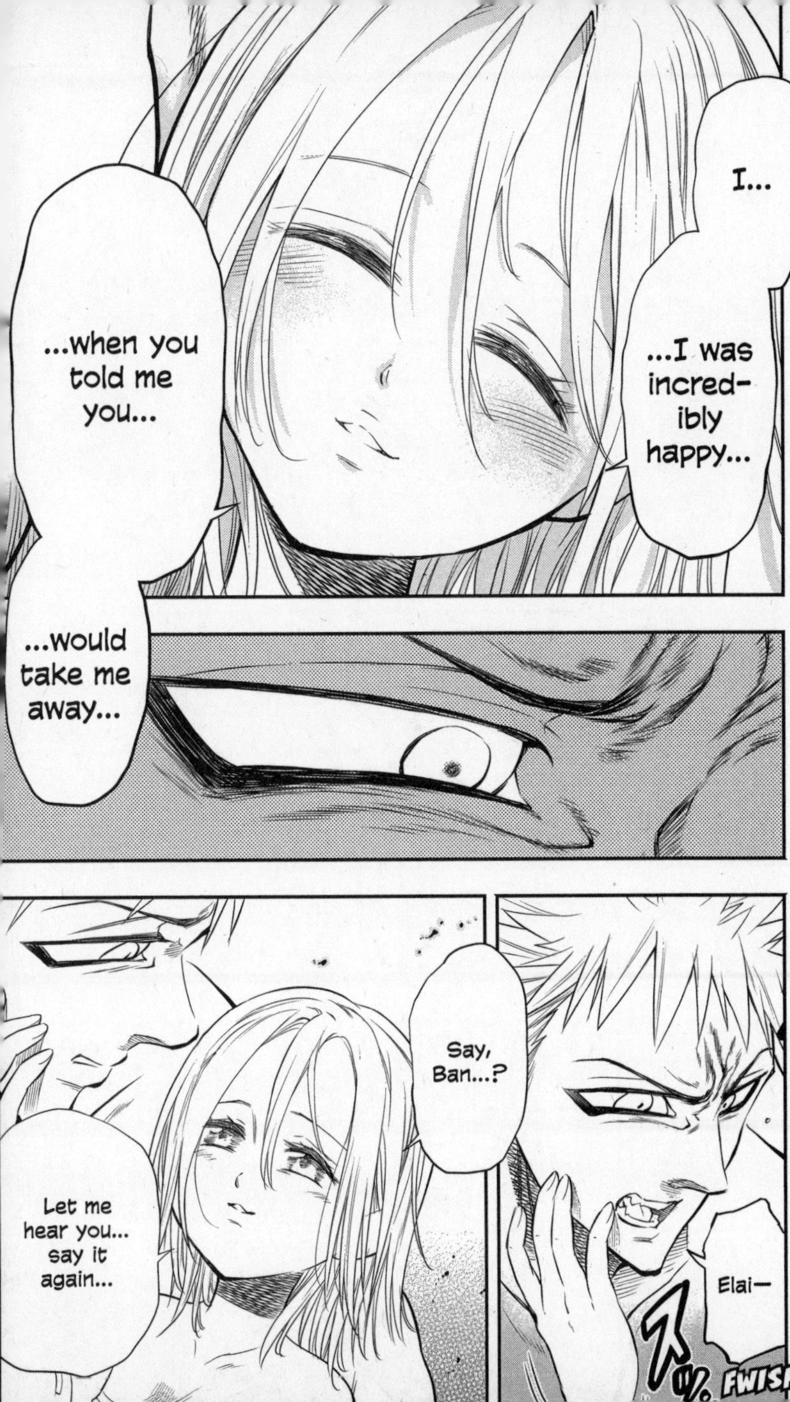
I...
...I was incred-ibly happy...
...when you told me you...
...would take me away...
Elai—
FWISH
Say, Ban...?
Let me hear you... say it again...

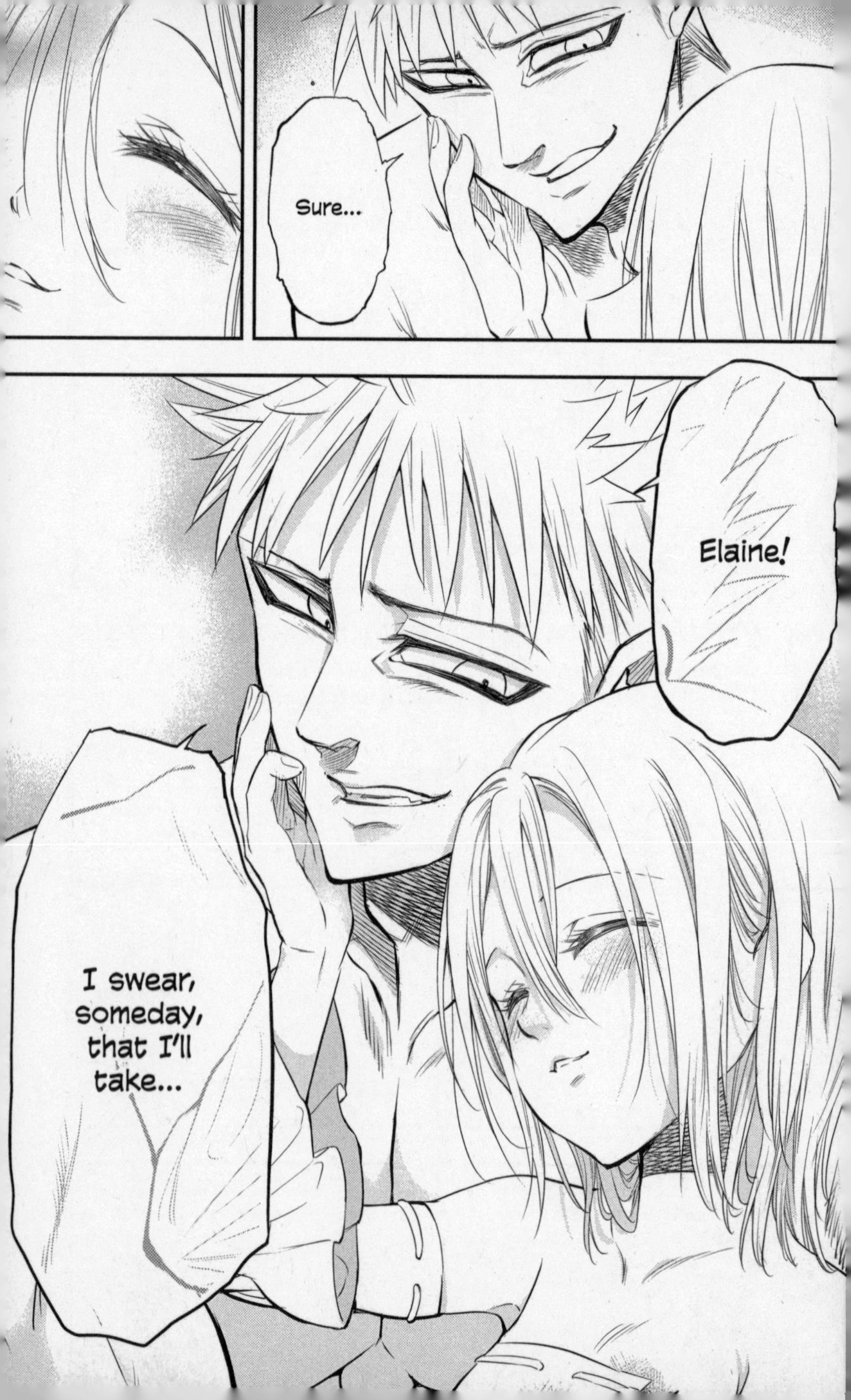
Sure...
Elaine!
I swear, someday, that I'll take...

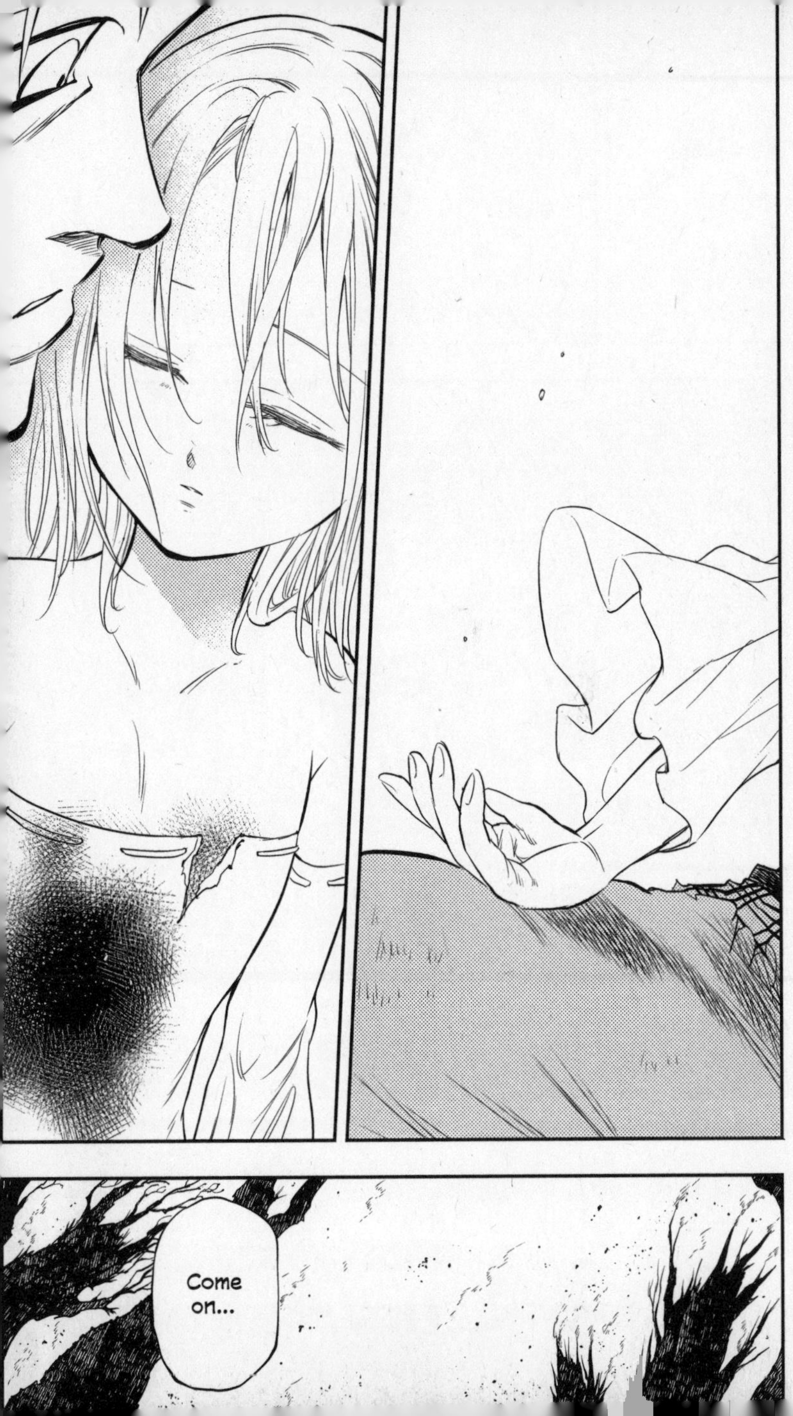
Come on...

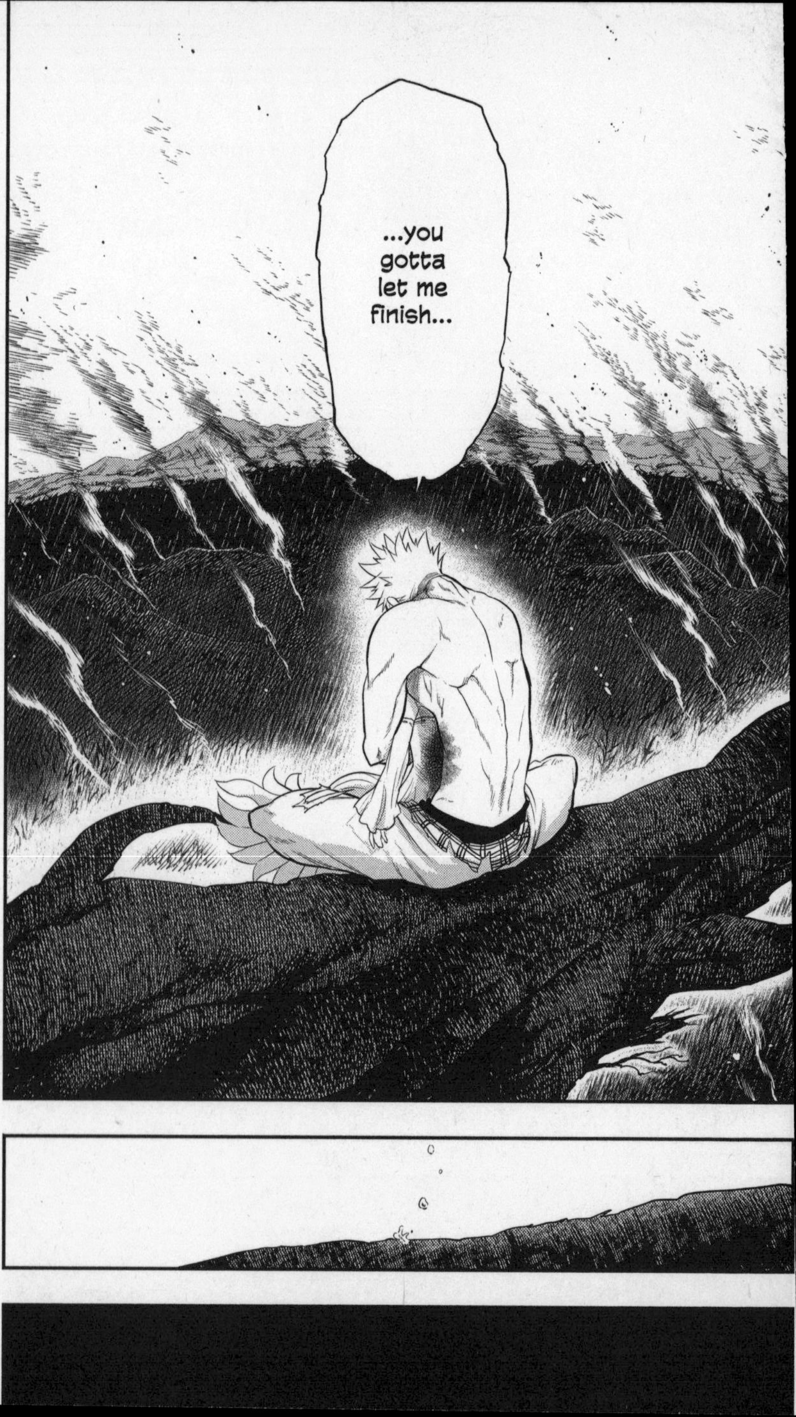
...you gotta let me finish...

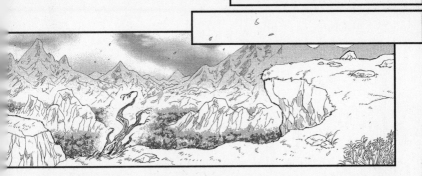

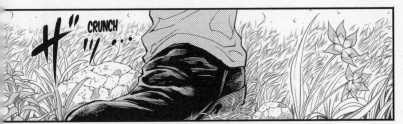

CRUNCH

Oh!

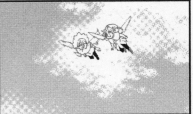

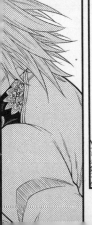

The Fairy King's back!

Every-one!

It's him!

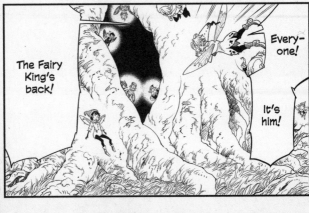

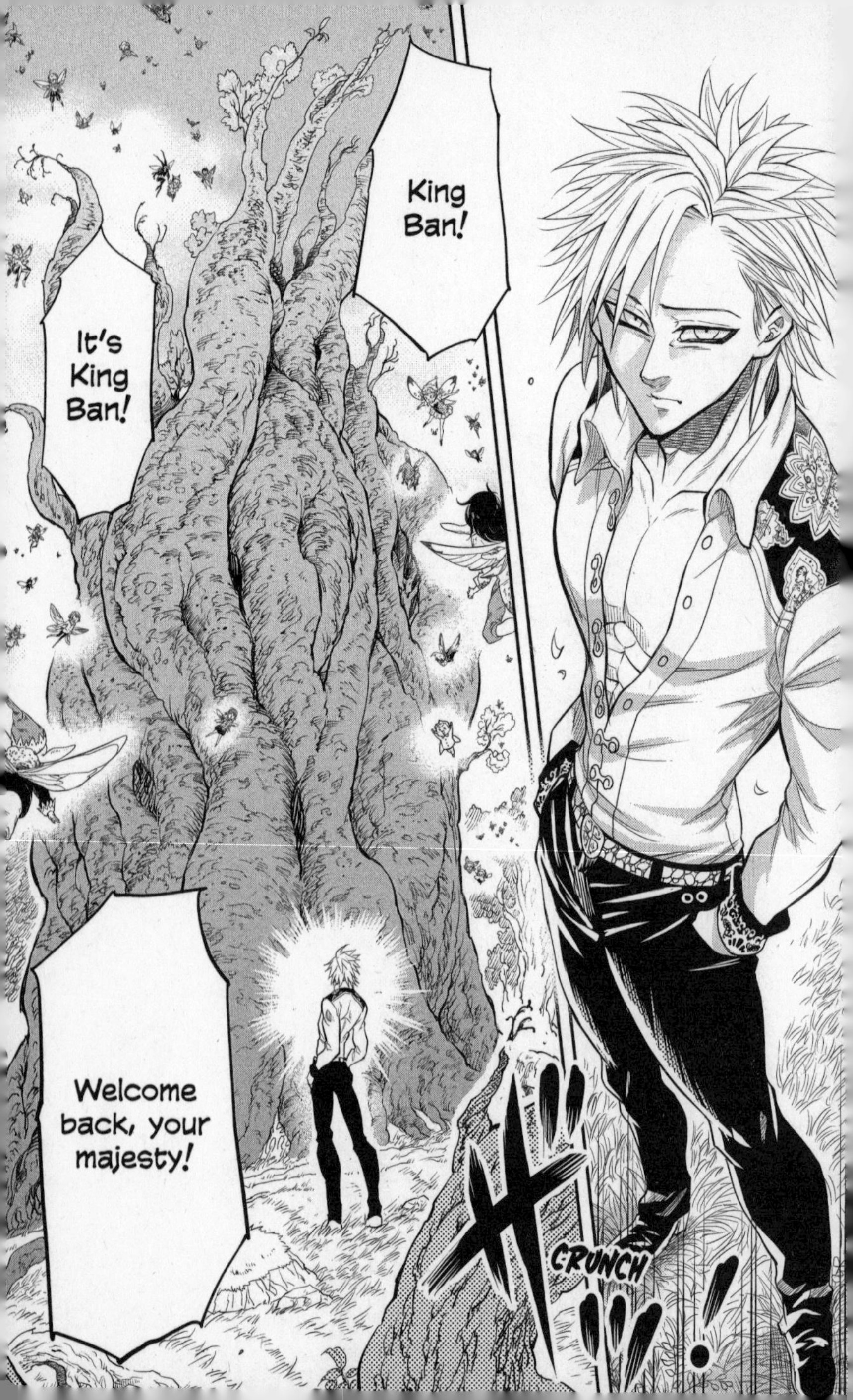
CRUNCH
King Ban!
It's King Ban!
Welcome back, your majesty!

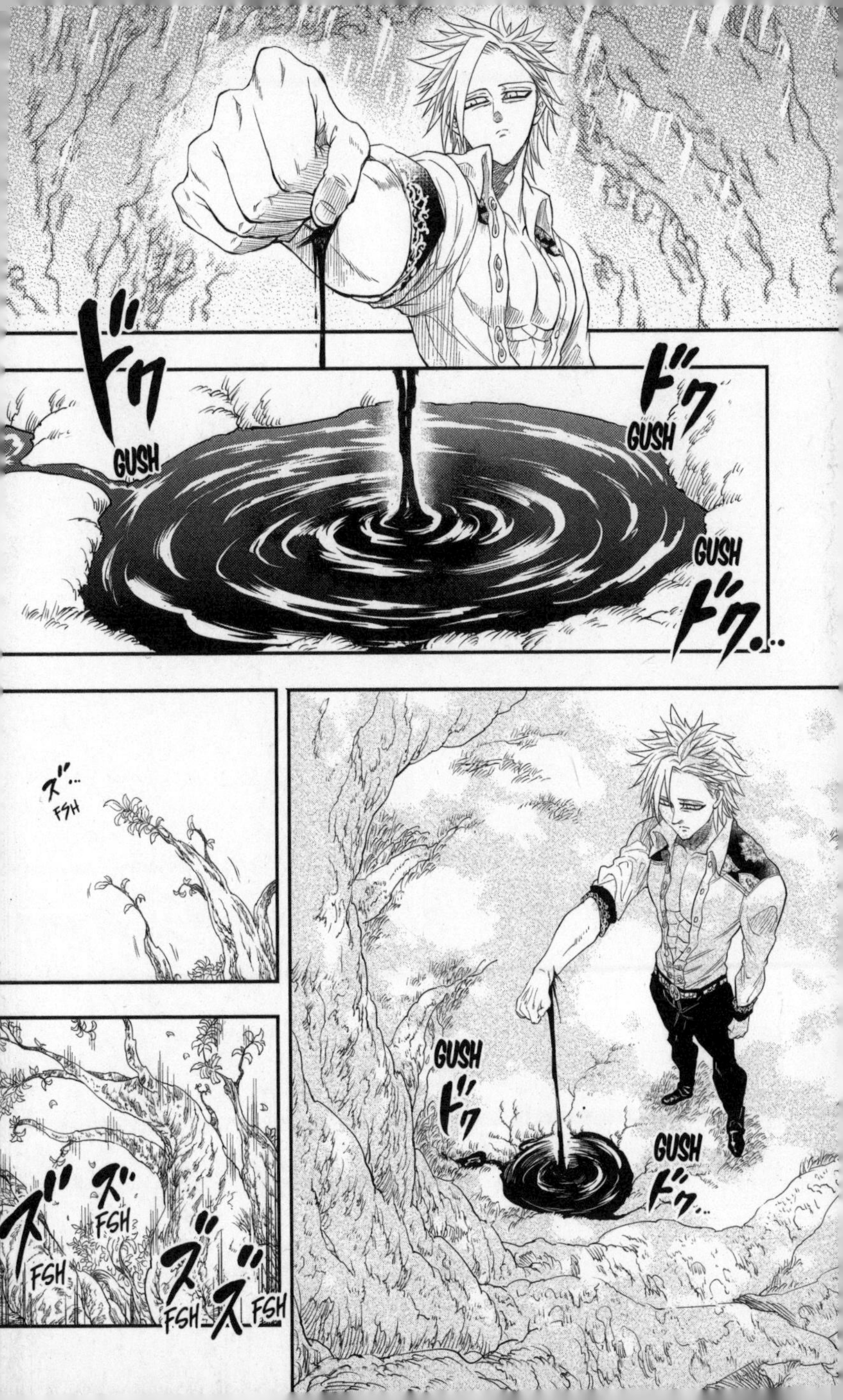
ドク
GUSH
ドク
GUSH
GUSH
ドク...
GUSH
ドク
GUSH
ドク...
ズ...
FSH
ズ
FSH
ズ
FSH
ズ
FSH
ズ
FSH

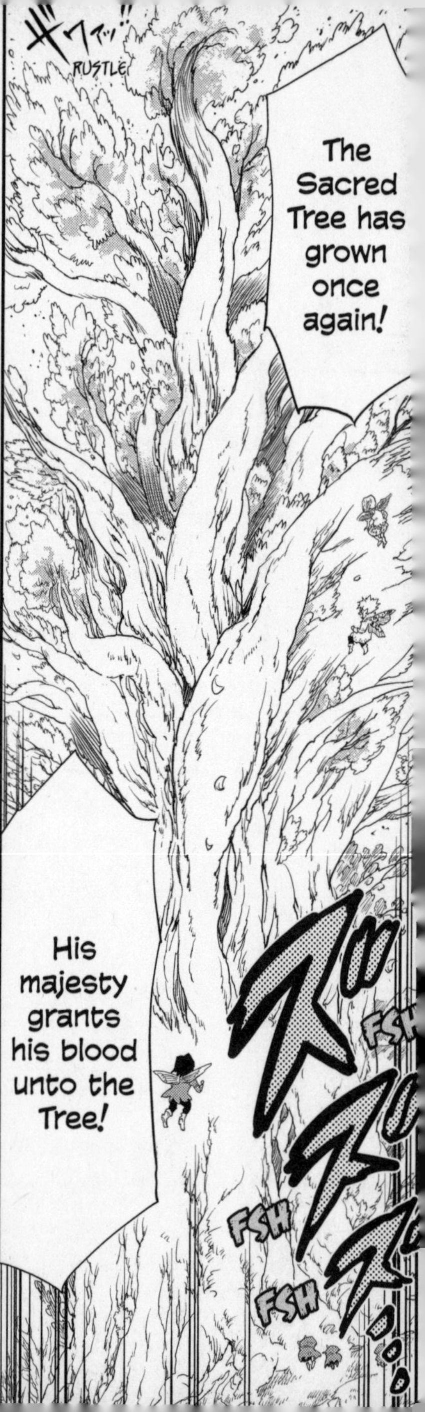
RUSTLE
The Sacred Tree has grown once again!
His majesty grants his blood unto the Tree!
FSH
FSH
FSH
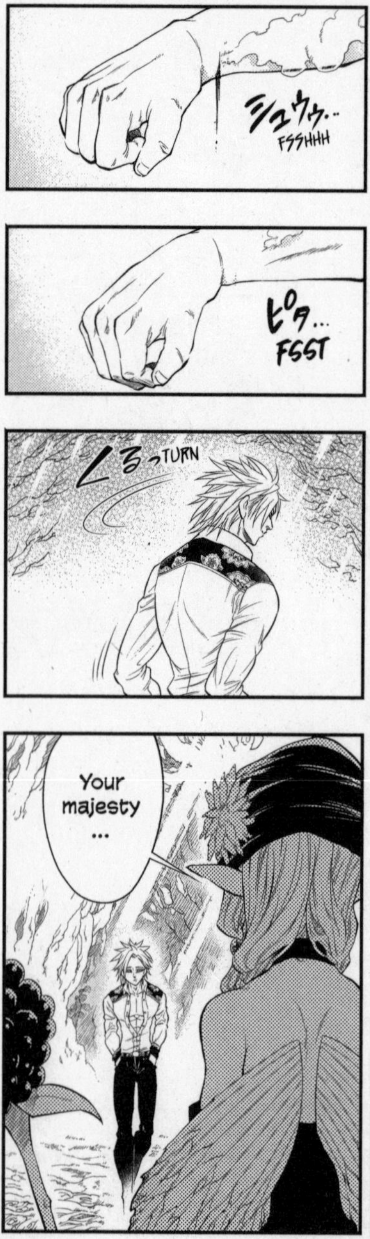
シュウゥ...
FSSHHH
ピタ...
FSST
くるっ TURN
Your majesty ...

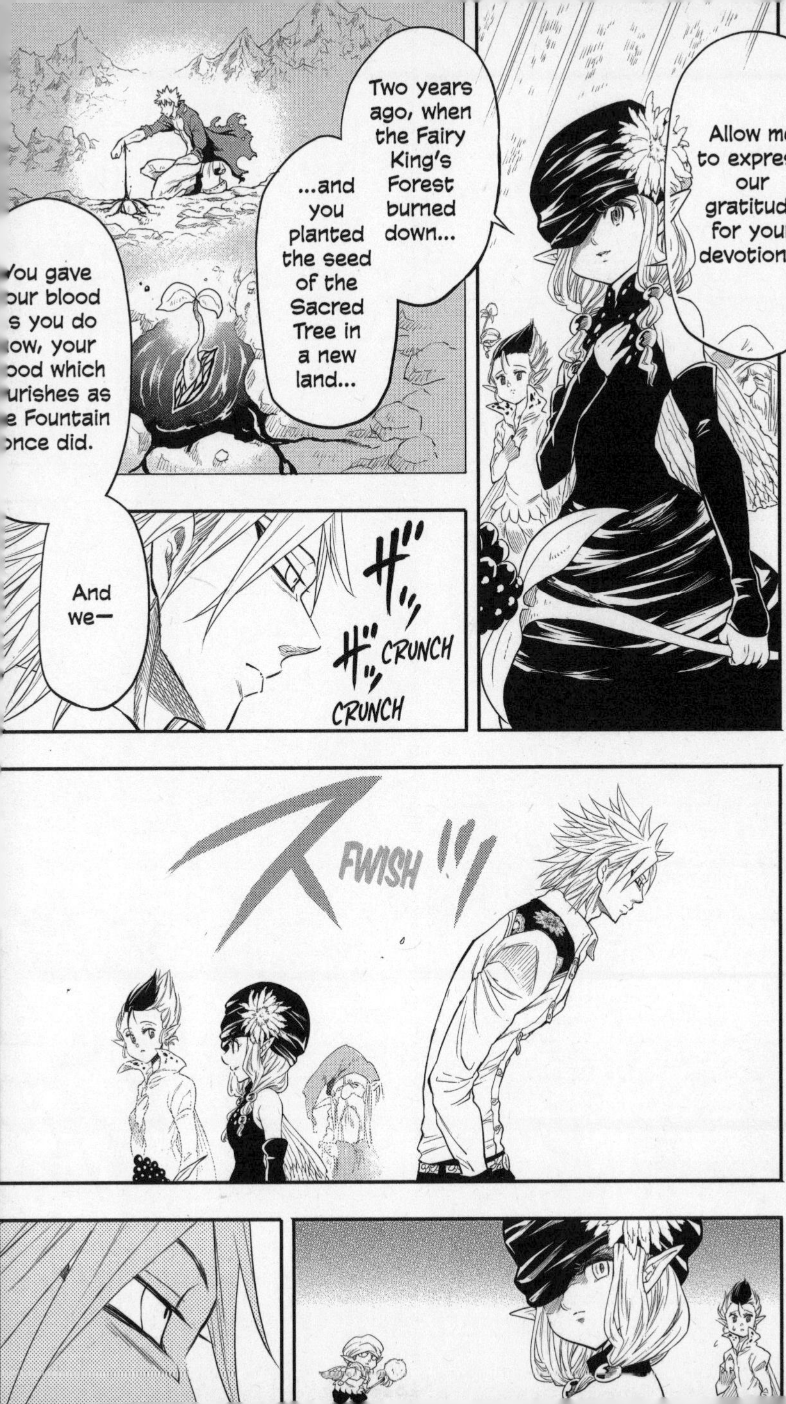

Allow me to express our gratitude for your devotions.
Two years ago, when the Fairy King's Forest burned down...
...and you planted the seed of the Sacred Tree in a new land...
You gave our blood s you do ıow, your ood which urishes as e Fountain once did.
And we—
CRUNCH
CRUNCH
FWISH

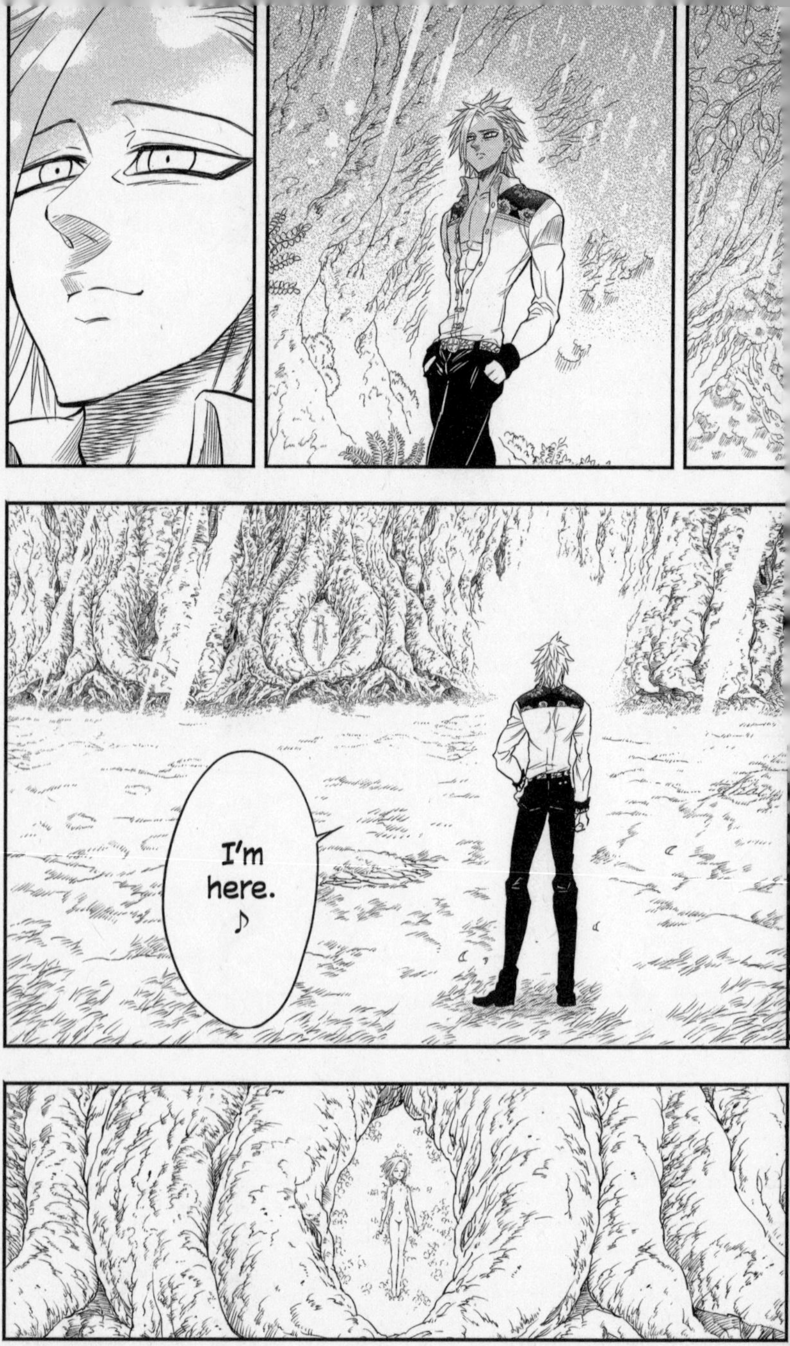
I'm here. ♪

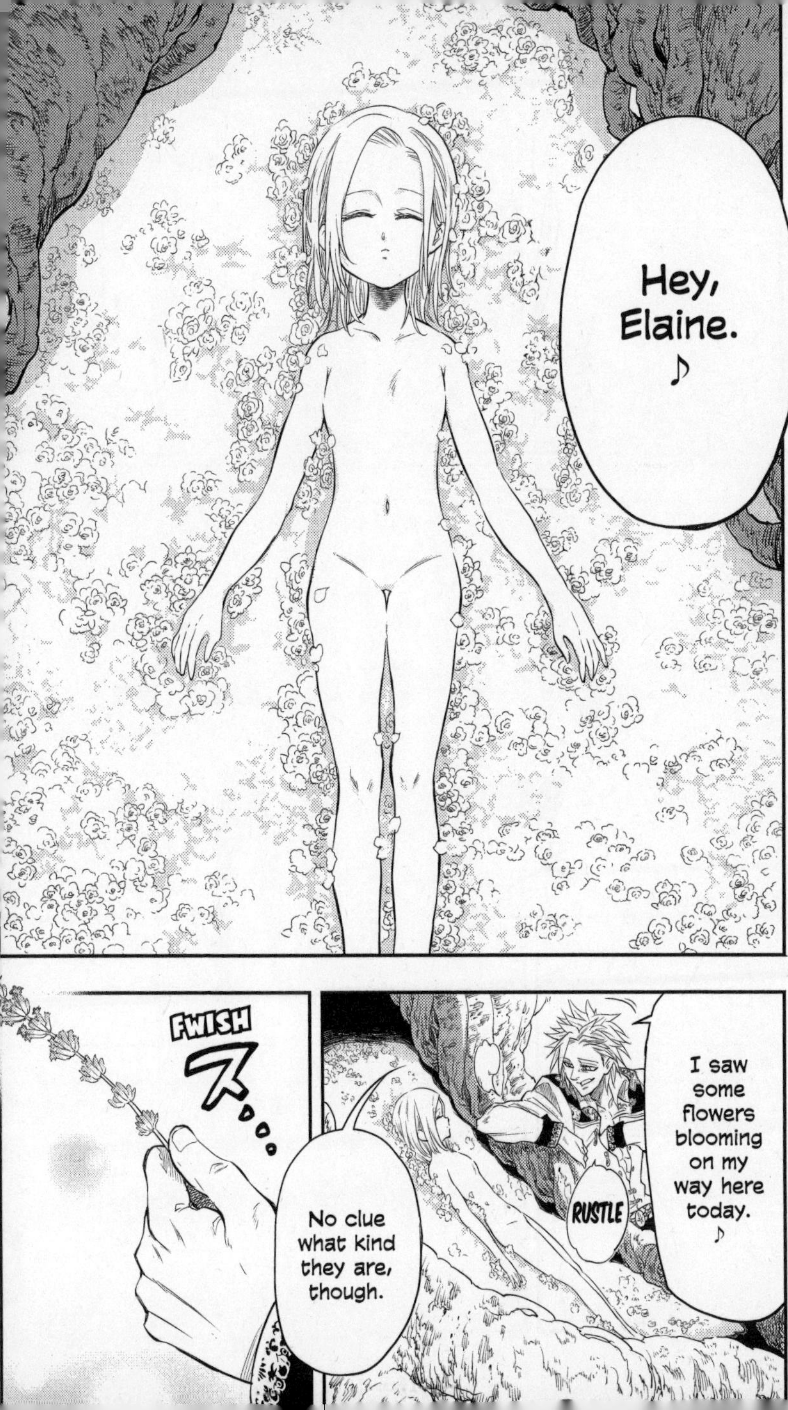
Hey, Elaine. ♪
I saw some flowers blooming on my way here today. ♪
RUSTLE
FWISH
No clue what kind they are, though.

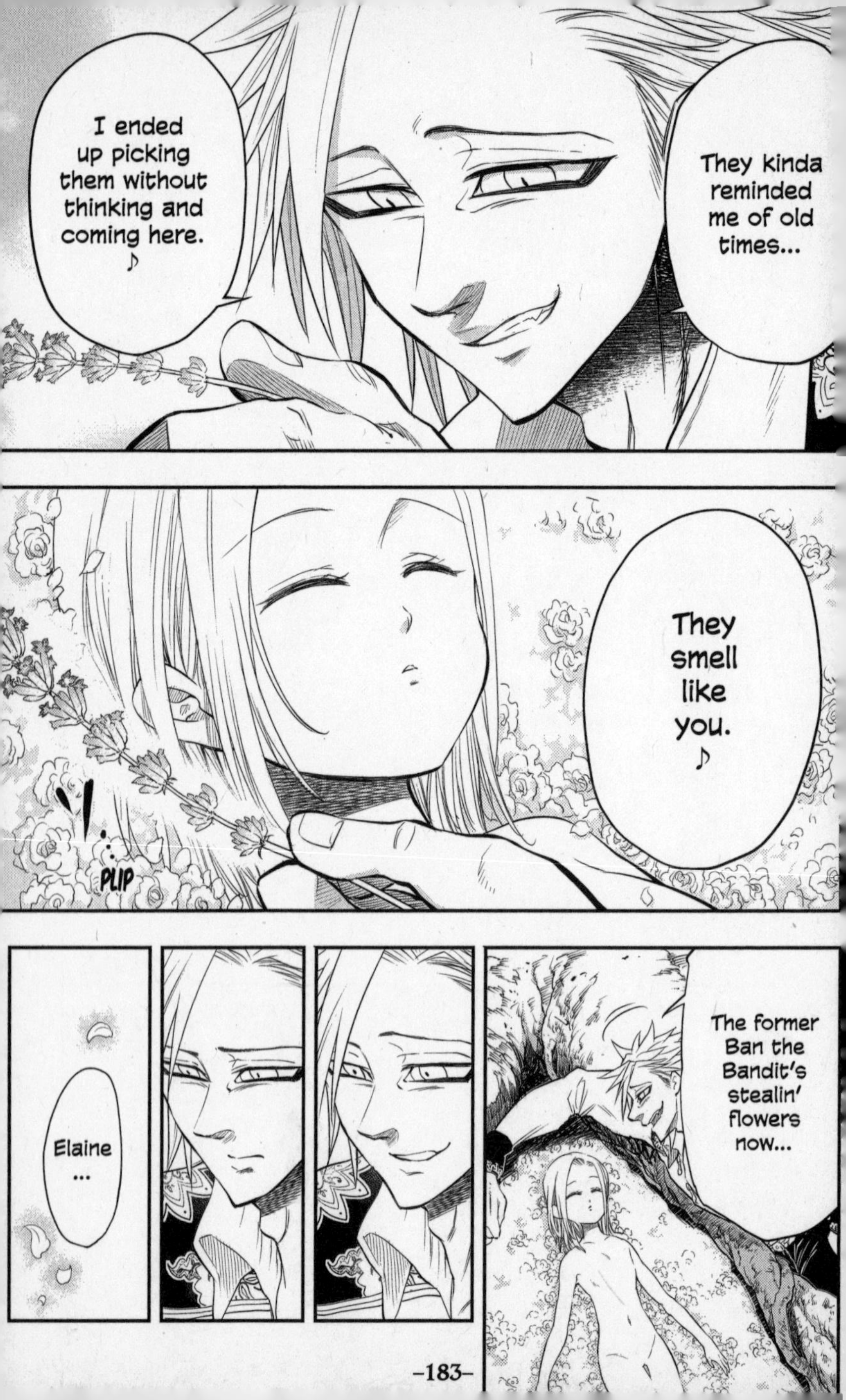
They kinda reminded me of old times...
I ended up picking them without thinking and coming here. ♪
They smell like you. ♪
PLIP
The former Ban the Bandit's stealin' flowers now...
Elaine ...

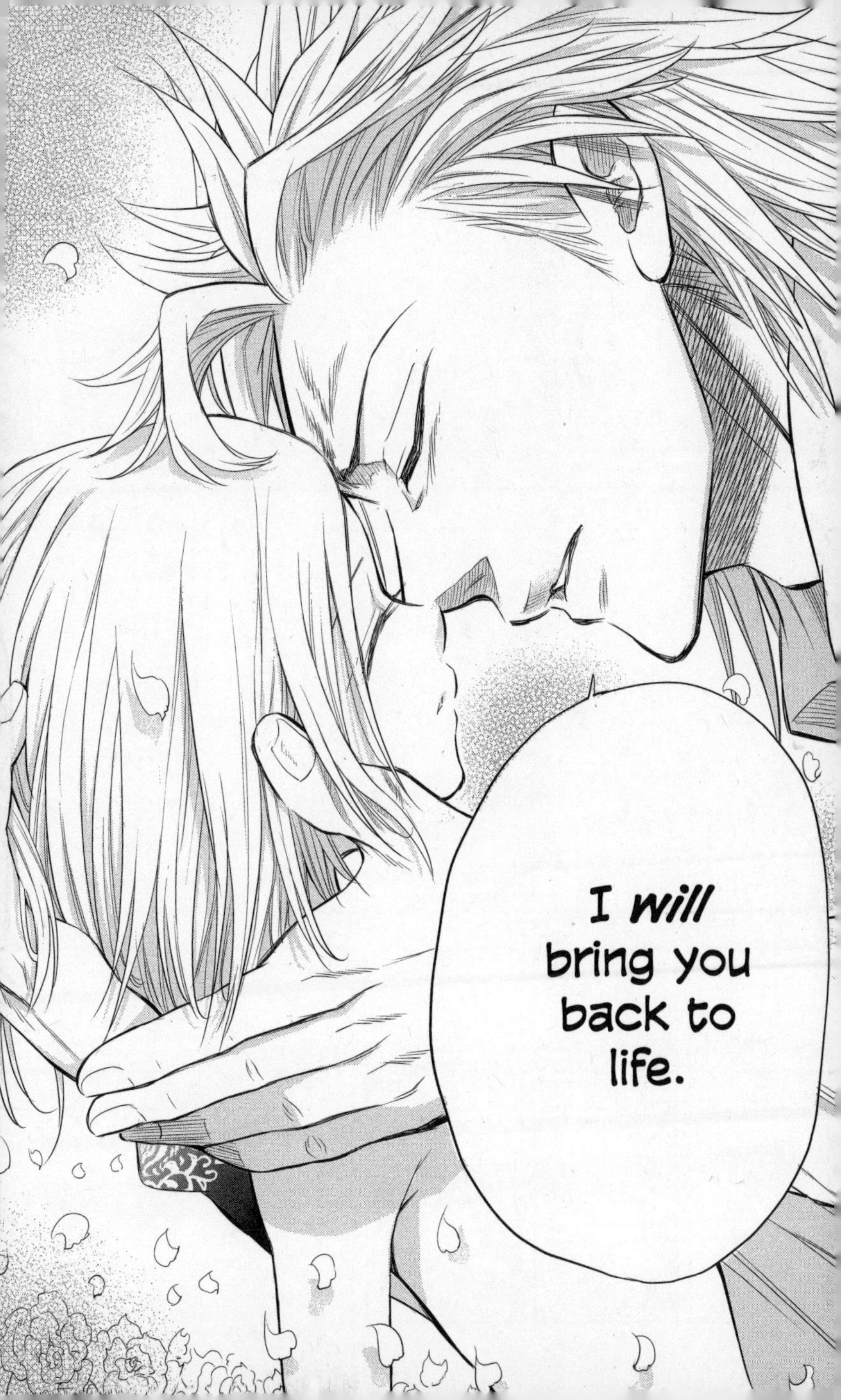
I *will* bring you back to life.

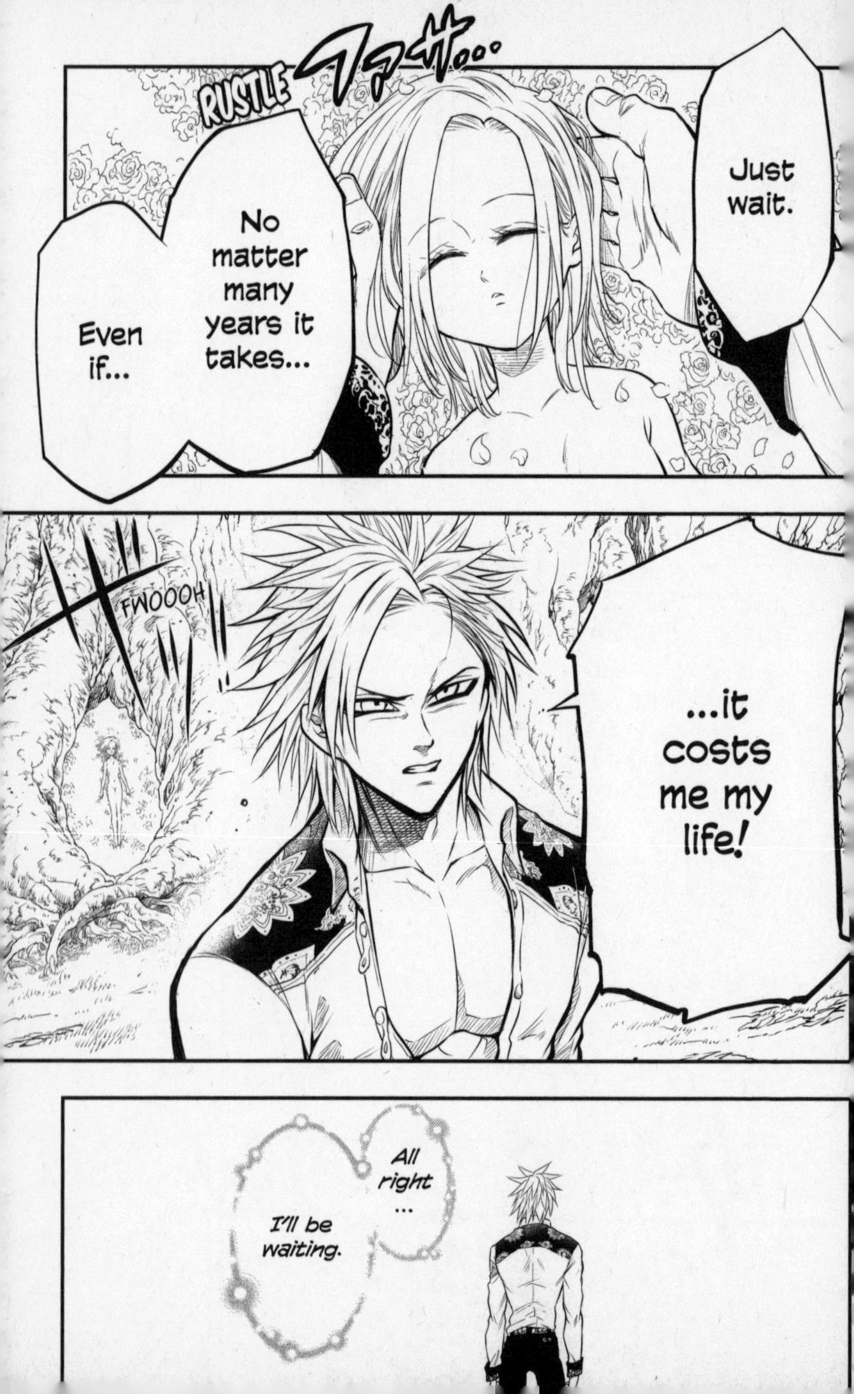
RUSTLE
Just wait.
No matter many years it takes...
Even if...
...it costs me my life!
FWOOOH
All right...
I'll be waiting.

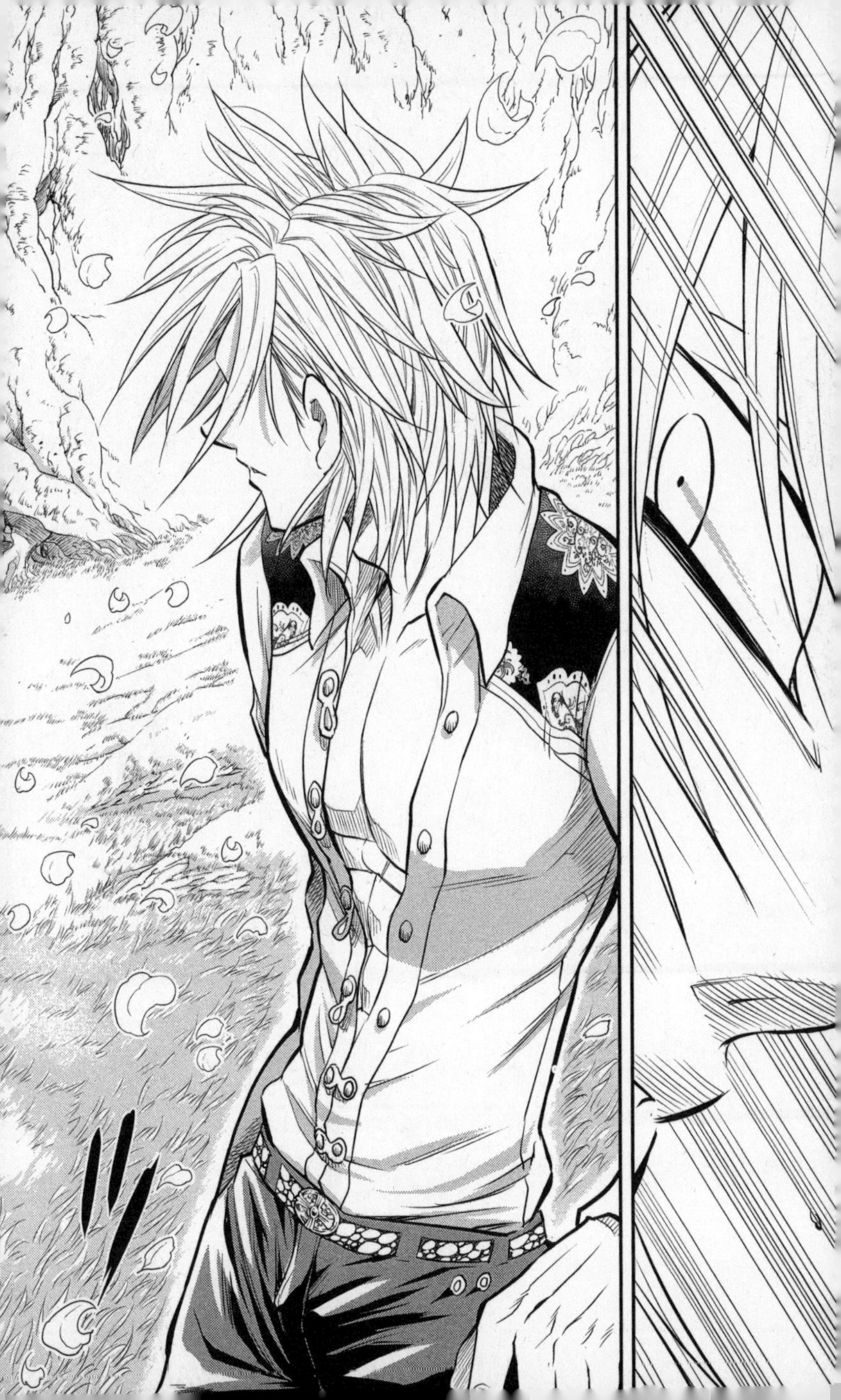

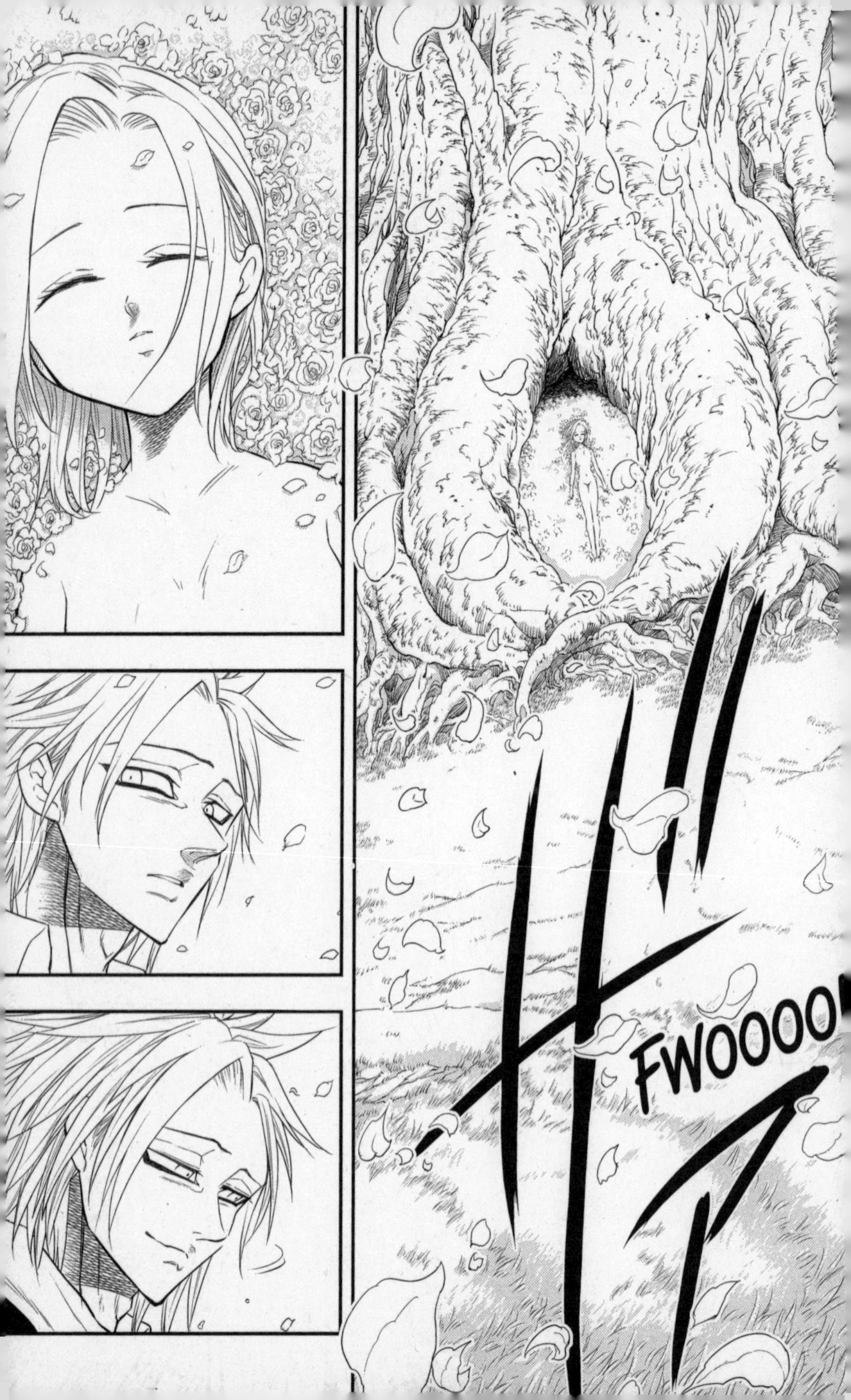
FWOOOOO

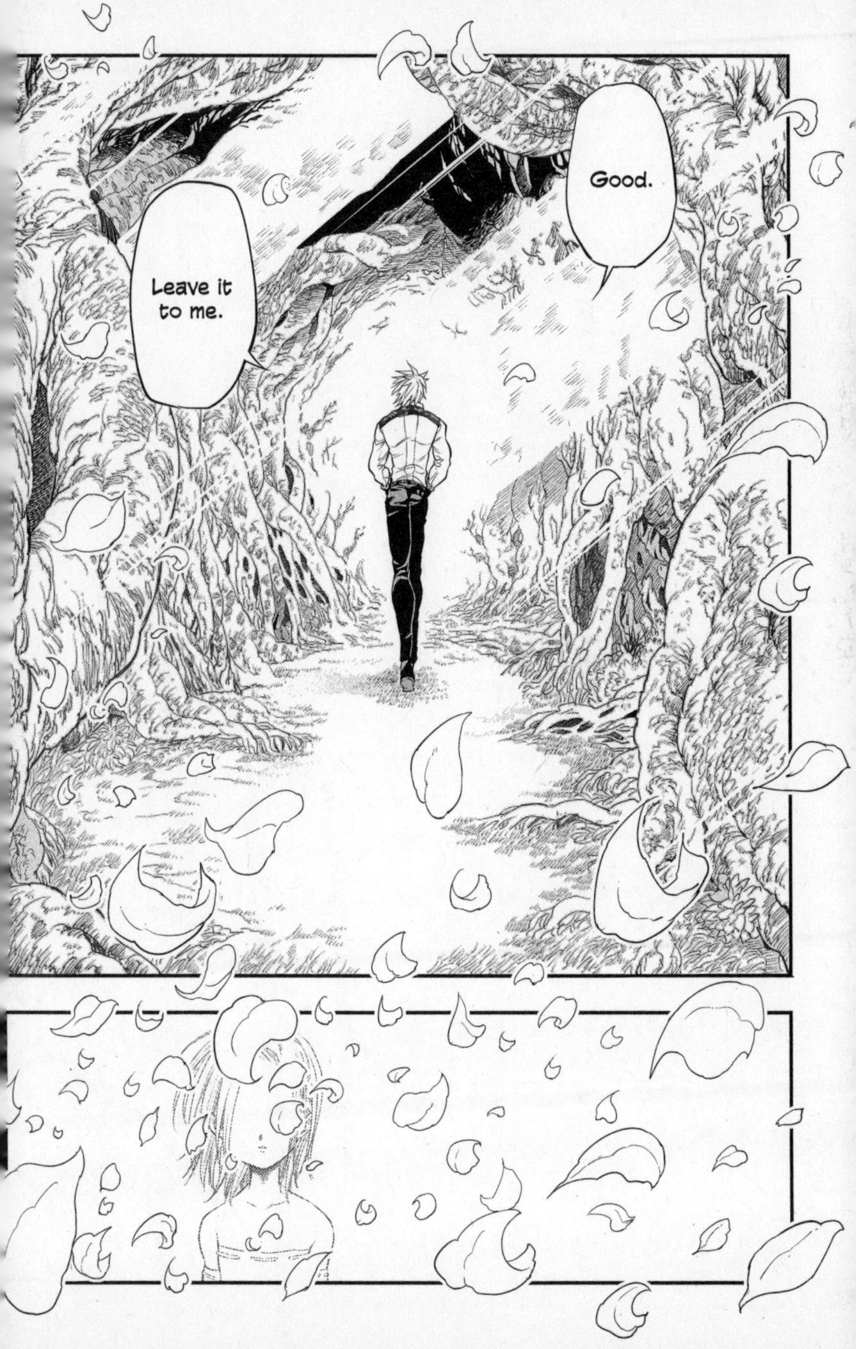
Good.
Leave it to me.

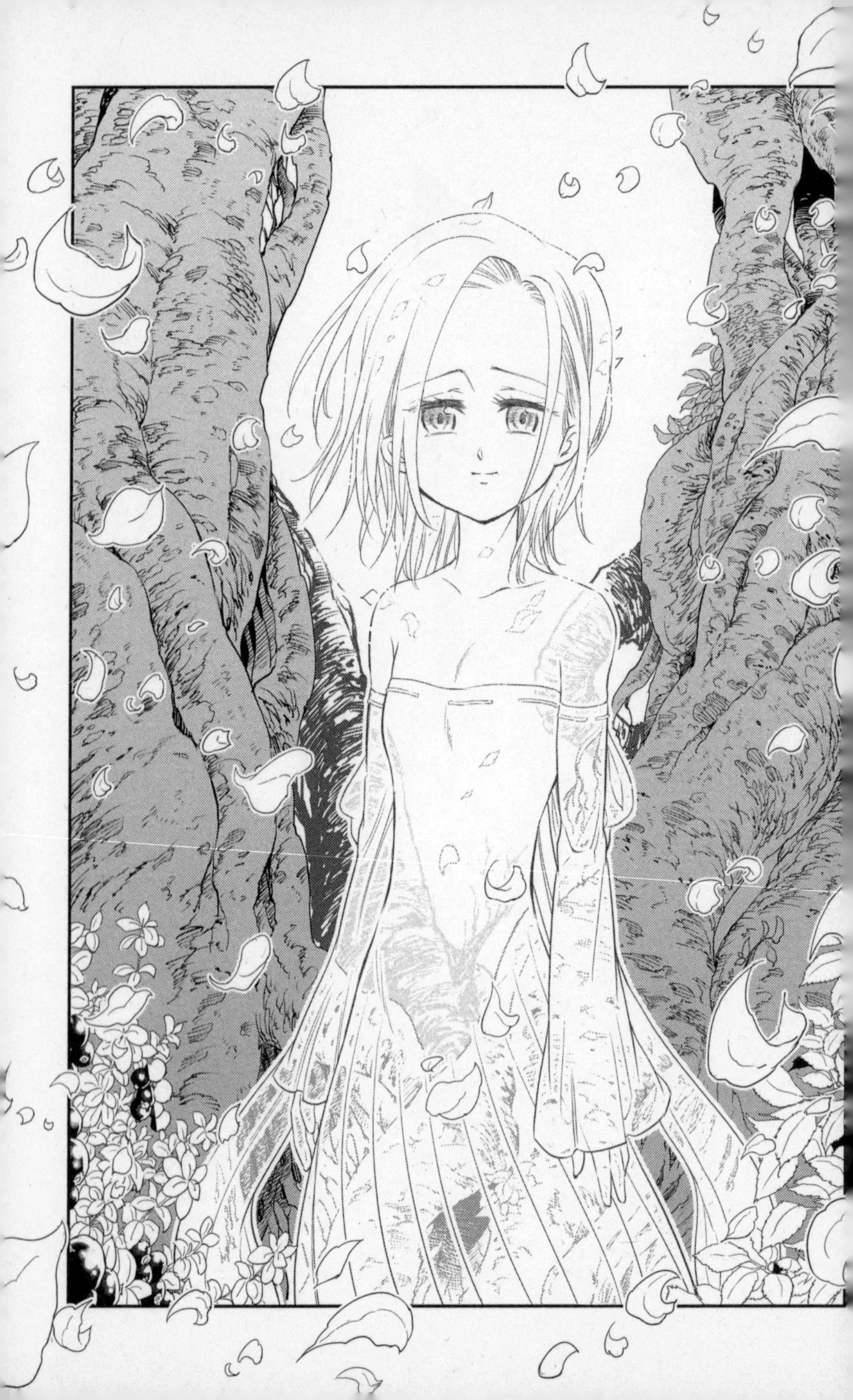

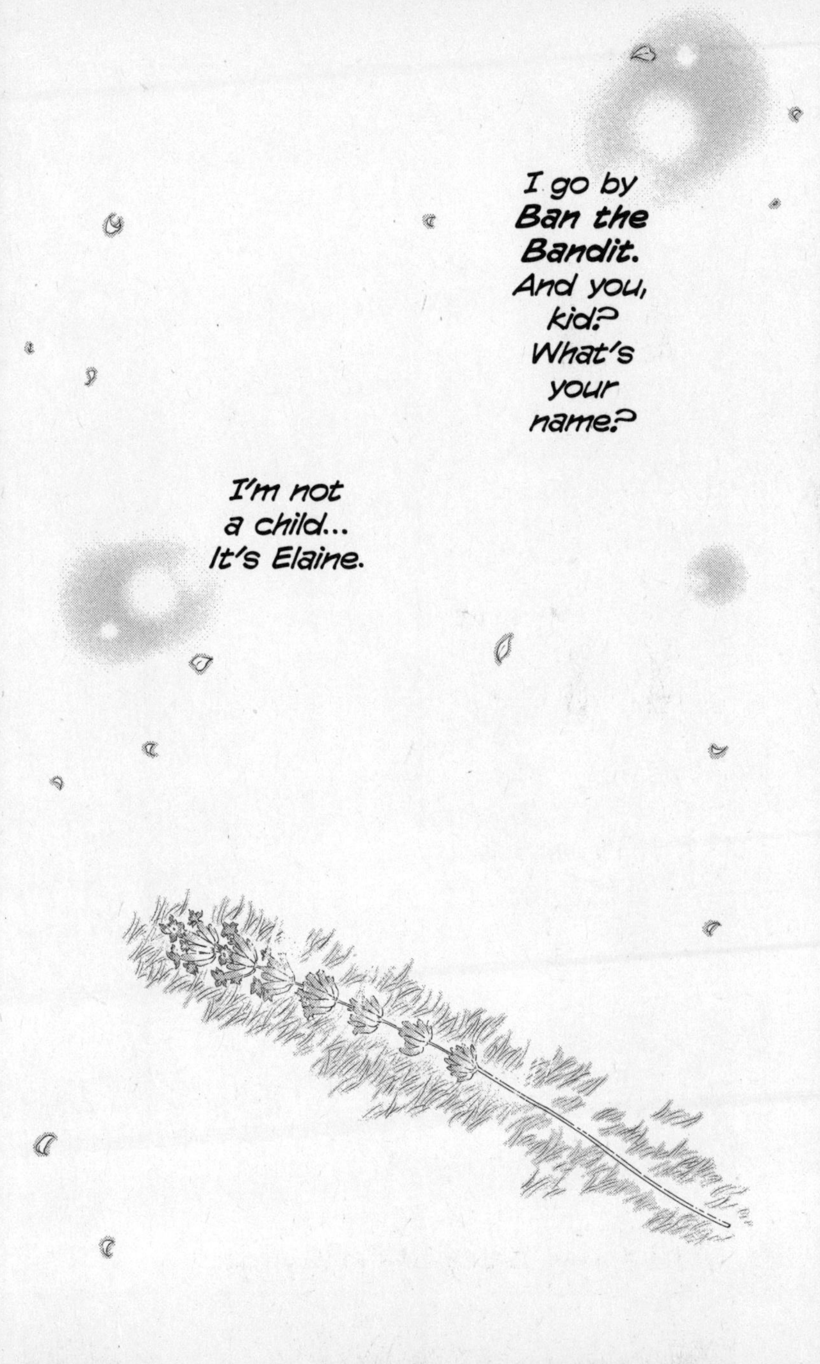
I go by Ban the Bandit. And you, kid? What's your name?
I'm not a child... It's Elaine.

the original
Nakaba Suzuki

novel
Mamoru Iwasa

comic
You Kokikuji

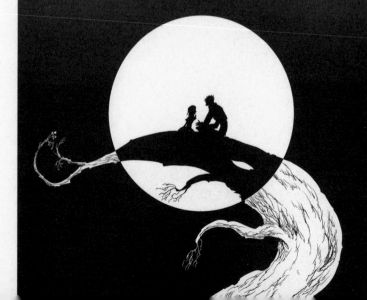

The Seven Deadly Sins: Seven Days volume 2 is a wor
Names, characters, places, and incidents are the pro
author's imagination or are used fictitiously. Any resemblance to actual events, locales, or persons, living or dead, is entirely coincidental.

A Kodansha Comics Trade Paperback Original.

Published in the United States by Kodansha Comics, an imprint of Kodansha USA Publishing, LLC, New York.

Publication rights for this English edition arranged through Kodansha Ltd., Tokyo.

First published in Japan in 2017 by Kodansha Ltd., Tokyo.

ISBN 978-1-63236-762-4

Printed in the United States of America.

www.kodanshacomics.com

9 8 7 6 5 4 3 2 1

Translation: Stephen Meyerink
Lettering: AndWorld Design
Editing: Lauren Scanlan
Kodansha Comics edition cover design: Phil Balsman